BARRED: WOMEN, WRITING, AND POLITICAL DETENTION

Barbara Harlow

 WOMEN,
WRITING, AND
POLITICAL
DETENTION

Wesleyan University Press

Published by University Press of New England

Hanover and London

For the Prisoners and Those

Who Struggle with Them

WESLEYAN UNIVERSITY PRESS

Published by University Press of New England,

Hanover, NH 03755

© 1992 by Barbara Harlow

All rights reserved

Printed in the United States of America 5 4 3 2 1

CIP data appear at the end of the book

The portion of "In the Place of Facts" by Jose
Roberto Cea, which appears on pages 165 and
166, is quoted from *El Salvador at War: A Collage
Epic*, edited by Marc Zimmerman. Reprinted
with permission of MEP Publications, University
of Minnesota, 116 Church St. S. E., Minneapolis,
MN 55455.

Contents

Preface

February 1992. On 5 February 1992 an officer of the RUC (Royal Ulster Constabulary, Northern Ireland's police force), later represented by government spokespersons and the media as suffering the effects of work-related "stress," posed as a journalist with an appointment in order to enter the Sinn Fein offices on the Falls Road in Belfast. There he opened fire, killing five people and wounding two others. Commenting on the massacre, Sinn Fein president Gerry Adams maintained that the shooting was implicitly condoned, if not actually endorsed, by the policy of "demonization" practiced by the British and Dublin governments alike against Sinn Fein, a legal political party in both the Six and the Twenty Six counties.

Less than a week later, the attorney general of the Republic of Ireland, citing a 1983 constitutional amendment, declared an injunction preventing a fourteen-year-old girl, pregnant as the result of a rape, from seeking an abortion in England. As the attorney general's unequivocal decision became a matter of popular controversy, street demonstrations, and Dail debate, the venue of Sinn Fein's annual Ard Fheis (or annual general meeting) was at the same time being contested by the Dublin government. Denied its traditional premises in the Mansion House in Dublin, and obstructed by official and unofficial pressure from meeting in a local hotel, the political party announced that the meeting scheduled for 22 and 23 February, would take place in the Ballyfermot community hall in working class north Dublin.

That same month saw as well the furor in the French government that resulted in the resignation and dismissal of several ministers over the permission granted to George Habash, leader of the Popular Front for the Liberation of Palestine (PFLP), to enter the country for medical treatment. And on 19 February, Joseph Doherty, IRA prison escapee detained without charge for more than eight years in the United States, was deported to England following a Supreme Court decision that he had no legal right to apply for political asylum in the United States.

Then as Israel, in bombing raids over southern Lebanon, killed numbers of civilians in Palestinian refugee camps, assassinated Hizballah leader Sheikh Mussawi, and announced further plans to "settle" the Occupied Territories, the Palestinian representatives to the "peace talks" continued to argue for full status as a delegation in their own right at the conference table.

All of these apparently disassociated—to some readers perhaps obscure or even esoteric—"faits divers" were culled as I consider my prefatory remarks here in Galway from a single month of available journalism and reportage. At stake in each set of events are the issues of "political status," self-determination, and self-representation—for women, for dissent, and, as I will argue, for "literature" as well. *Barred: Women, Writing, and Political Detention* proposes a reading, partisan and polemical perhaps, but no less crucial for that, of some of the preludes, precedents, preliminaries to certain persistently contemporary debates, debates that are at once academic and activist, and that, despite the bars placed around them, continue to engage multiple geographical spaces even in a historically altering global configuration.

As "negotiation" would seem, even if controversially, to be displacing "armed struggle" (in South Africa, in El Salvador, in Palestine, in Northern Ireland, for examples) as another means to resolve long-standing conflicts from the continuing history of colonialism, decolonization, and "post-colonialism," the issue of political status and its due recognition is critical to the full participation and self-representation at the conference table of all parties from the past on into the future of those conflicts. The discursive logic and structures of power that have long governed "interrogation" must be made to give way to the kind of redistribution of authority and realignment of locutionary positions that distinguish instead a "negotiation" process.

"Barred," then, refers to the policies—official and unofficial—that deny political status to women, to organized dissent, and to the literary. The post-colon side of this book's title, on the other hand, commands attention to the practices and practitioners that have been circumscribed, the writers and the works that have been banned, and the strategies, inside and outside of prison, within and without those bars, that contest such denial in their demand for recognition and political status.

Women

In an interview in the first issue of *Women in Struggle*, published by Sinn Fein's Women's Department, Bernadette (Devlin) McAliskey responds to a comment from her interlocutor in such a way as to suggest the complex intersections that reciprocally inform these discrepant issues. The interviewer had observed that "Some people would say that women are jealous of one another, particularly in regard to political success." McAliskey, in turn, responds at length:

That is an interesting statement. When men disagree about something, the basis for their disagreement is assumed to be one based on political difference, practical difference, or whatever.

If women disagree, it's all too often seen as personal, individual and emotional rather than the obvious that the women concerned are arguing about something politically.

The claim that women are jealous of one another is a perception rather than a reality and is based on the position of women in society rather than the reality of the ways that women conduct themselves.

Similar arguments include that women are slow to come forward to accept positions of authority and responsibility. Yet, when women do come forward all too often they are seen as belligerent, harsh, strident, or whatever.

Have a look at male dignitaries—for a man with a high profile, he can often be excused everything short of anything because that's just how a man is.

See a woman . . . no . . . that wouldn't do at all . . . she would be described as having an attitude problem, her social manners would put people off, she would be seen as belligerent and oppressive.

All too often the male perception is that power is somehow unattractive in a woman (McAliskey, 1992).

If the political role of women in resistance organizations, like the political status of the struggles themselves, demands to be recognized, then it is no less incumbent on those organizations to "socialize" their political agendas accordingly, to recognize that the seizure of state power is meaningless without a project of social transformation as well. Such a project has been carried out in significant ways in situations of political detention, and the resulting transformation has had enormous consequences—at once intimate and historic—in the lives of those women and men affected by it, from the prisoners themselves to their families, and including no less their comrades in their respective organizations. The question of gender, therefore, is not merely the purview of one gender alone, but integral to the shared work of the many parties partaking of its history. *Barred*, even as it subscribes in significant part to a broad feminist agenda, attempts also to re-examine some of the conventions of feminism and its critiques by locating these within the specific contemporary context of "political detention."

Writing

In terms of discipline, this project derives from the traditions of literary criticism and from current schools of cultural theory. Political detention, however, engages a redefinition of the scholarly practices implied in the term "discipline," and it is such a redefinition, waged through the different but linked institutional imperatives of the academy and the prison, that I have attempted to encounter here. The essays that follow move by way of example. This procedure is a calculated and not disinterested one. The major figures in the book, its cast of characters as it were, are the prisoners, male and female, their associates, and the specific organizations, struggles, and movements in which they have participated and for which they have been detained. Their writing, the subject of this book, is not just "raw material," but is itself an articulation of a critical perspective, one that I have attempted both to deploy and to demonstrate. Beyond that, what I have tried to do is to locate the prisoners in their own social, cultural, institutional, and historical contexts and, eventually, to argue the relationality of those contexts with that of the academy. These localities may not all be familiar to readers in our own academic milieu and I have therefore attempted to make the circumstantial necessity of reportage structurally, as well as theoretically, integral to the project. Such a contextualizing or localizing methodology necessarily implies, to paraphrase Stuart Hall, a certain time- and context-boundedness. Rather than a grand theoretical summation, then, what this study of "women, writing, and political detention" proposes is a collocation of material, admittedly selective (to be exhaustive, more examples from more and other geopolitical contexts would be needed), that will, even by its very selectivity, enjoin a realigning of current academic practices against the presently contested background of curricular change.

And yet this study, "literary-critical" as it is, deals with texts written and published by and about political prisoners. Their citation is crucial to the project's strategy. In its own way, it *is* that strategy. The very names are important. In this, my project does differ from parallel studies in other disciplines such as anthropology and political science. Allen Feldman, for example, in *Formations of Violence*, an inquiry into the "narrative of the body and political terror in Northern Ireland," acknowledges the "concern with anonymity [that] reflects the intense levels of surveillance and the fact that many of the people [he] talked with had been or were currently engaged in some form of clandestine political practice" (11). In working with published texts, the issue of "naming names" takes on a different range of disciplinary or canonical necessities. Similarly, the "divergence between . . . public transcript and the hidden transcripts" (x) of subordinate groups that importantly informs James C. Scott's *Domination and the Arts of Resistance: Hidden Transcripts*, is often itself made the core issue of prison writing.

In contrast and complement to such studies as these, I see my own project as a kind of heteroclite and experimental amalgam of history, criticism, and journalism, albeit without totally subscribing to any of these genres or their methodological conventions and professional rules. It is the texts themselves, writing from political detention, that mark here that crucial decision of "when to talk and when not to talk." In this sense the examples and citations function in ways that I consider to be critical to the project: to contribute material and historical specificity; to map, through that specificity, grounds and terrains for critical redefinitions of the "literary" and the "political" and their conflicted intersection; and finally to **xi** join ranks with a "cast of characters" who have been, explicitly and precisely for their intellectual and political work, removed from the premises. Rather than theoretical unities, it is the specific historical similarities and dissimilarities, conjunctures and "linkages" (a word once banned by the rhetoricians of Gulf War) that I have wanted to emphasize.

Political Detention

Political detention and the denial of human rights are not the prerogative of any one part of the world, and are certainly not peculiar to the "third world," or even the erstwhile "second world," as the representatives, spokespersons, and officials of "western democracy" often choose to argue. In 1992 the member nations of the European community will complete the process of opening their borders to one another. At the same time, the island of Ireland will remain partitioned and, in what has been described as "fortress Europe," the external frontiers of "Europe" will be reinforced by controls over the ingress and freedom of movement of refugees, applicants for political asylum, and other "illegal aliens." England's Prevention of Terrorism Act (PTA), originally passed in 1975 against Irish "terrorism" from across the channel, continues to legitimize detention without trial against other peoples as well and was invoked to justify the internment of Iraqi and other Arab nationals during the Gulf War in 1991. The act was renewed by Westminster again in February 1992. In the United States, whose own borders are ever more intensively patrolled, recent Supreme Court decisions ratifying the use of confessions extracted under duress as evidence in the courtroom and denying the right of prisoners to redress against unsatisfactory prison conditions suggest further restrictions on its internally incarcerated population—today the largest percentage of a citizenry of any country in the world.

The United States, like Great Britain, while a signatory to the United Nations Covenants on Human Rights, nearly half a century later has yet to ratify these treaties. Indeed, the actual implementation of the rhetoric of democracy and human rights that has underwritten much U.S. international and domestic policy seems still subject to the injunctions offered in 1951 by Senator John Bricker when he sponsored his amendment to the proposed conventions: "My purpose in offering this resolution is to bury the so-called covenant on human rights so deep that no one holding high public office will ever dare to attempt its resurrection" (cited in Kaufman, 1).

Against such denials and refusals—bars to political status—the writing of political detention militates on behalf of the human and political rights of the dispossessed and disenfranchized, proposing new models and genres for a politically critical literature. At this turn of the century/ millennium, it has become as necessary for those of us who "profess literature" to be able to read human rights reports and legal briefs as it has previously been to consult bibliographies and card catalogues.

Barred was written over a period of years, from 1988 through 1991. The individual chapters bear the traces of the pressure of events at the time of their writing. That dating, the mark of contemporary historical narrative, is also reconstrued across the chapters' trajectory and within the broader arguments concerning the cultural imperatives occasioned by "women, writing, and political detention."

The book is divided into five sections. Part I, "Against Discipline and Domestication," and Part III, "My Home, My Prison," together with the last section, *Nunca Mas*, seek to describe and locate the struggle against political detention as a contribution to what might become an emancipatory literary agenda; moreover, these sections argue for a relocation of academic inquiry into the global arena of national and international politics. These essays are the more literary-critical in design, reading the stories of women, men, and prison against generic distinctions and across geopolitical divides. They focus not only on women in prison, but on the larger effects that political detention has had on lived lives, both inside and outside of detention. The readings here are concerned with both the representation of *prison in writing*—in memoir, novel, poetry, documentary—and the places of *writing in prison*. By contrast, Part II, "The Resistance in Prison," is divided into six sub-sections, with separate chapters on Northern Ireland, Palestine, Egypt, South Africa, El Salvador and the United States, in an effort to present not only generic relations but historical specificities. Bibliographies are presented according to essay, in order to facilitate use by readers looking to pursue those specificities.

In tentative conclusion to these remarks, I might mention that I have often been asked, in the course of presenting this material in various lectures and seminars, if it is not "depressing" to read prison writing. On the contrary, it seems to me, discouragement comes not from the study of struggles against political detention and for recognition of political status, but from the ruthless persistence of the bars to that work. For example, Galway poet Rita Ann Higgins has, in her poem "Reading," described the poetry readings that she once gave for prisoners in the H Blocks:

> I read,
> they listened
> the one in the cage yawned
> an uninterested-in-poetry yawn.

The warder, that is, the one keeping guard from the cage:

> 'Slouched warder hears poetry
> in horizontal position.'

The poem continues:

> With the jingle of keys
> I was free to go,
> handshakes, smiles
> much left unsaid,
> the distance between us
> several poems shorter.

But, as she writes in the last line to the poem, "I feared the man in the cage" (10). Rita Ann Higgins is no longer invited to read poetry in the prisons. Prison authorities do recognize, if only by their denials, the political status of "women, writing and political detention."

Between the extremes, then, of interrogation and negotiation, academic discourse needs to reconstrue its own place within the practices of discursive exchange—perhaps by reading the writings on and across the walls of political detention.

Galway, Ireland   B. H.
June 1992

Acknowledgments

This book has been long in the making, perhaps too long given the urgency relayed by the struggles waged in and against political detention and the imperative to put an end to torture, disappearances, and the systemic and systematic denial of human and civil rights to peoples in nations around the globe. But perhaps it has not been long enough, in that those political and historical processes that have long underwritten political detention continue to hold their sway. To "end" the book—to end even a chapter or a case study—with no end in sight to political detention, without the release of the prisoners, seems to disengage from their struggle. The demands, however, of historical circumstance and the demands for political change continue meanwhile to be raised in narratives of contention that ensure continued resistance to exploitations managed on grounds of race, gender, and class. Those resistant stories and their makers have done much to develop this project on "women, writing and political detention." Delivering it now is in some significant part due to their demands and the pressures that they exert, and represents an attempt to recognize the necessity—even when untimely—of academic answerability, if not as yet a more fully transitive and interventionary intellectual practice.

While this book has been long in the making, many are the people who have contributed to it by reading sections, listening to portions, providing materials, opening doors, and setting an example. First and foremost to be thanked are prisoners, former prisoners, their friends, families, and supporters, and their movements, who shared their stories with me and taught me other ways of reading, as well as conveying the real and urgent need to read the kinds of texts that form the basis of this project. Parts of the book have been presented to academic audiences who have responded both critically and constructively, at universities such as Wesleyan, the University of Chicago, Southern Methodist University, the University of Miami, Occidental College, the University of Oregon, Oregon State University, Cornell, Rice, Brown, Carnegie Mellon, Ohio State University, Johns Hopkins, Columbia, Michigan State University, the University of

California at San Diego, and the Yeats Summer School in Sligo, as well as at meetings of professional organizations such as the South Central Modern Language Association, the Modern Language Association, the Middle East Studies Association, and the National Lawyers Guild. The Political Asylum Project of Austin (PAPA) taught me too well that some of us in the humanities still need to learn how to do research—and what research can really mean. Travis County of the State of Texas at one point intervened for a few days by summoning—and selecting—me for jury

xvi   duty. But I have to thank those responsible, and the other jurors with whom I served, for giving me that opportunity for further "fieldwork." In that case at least, the "good guys" won. The undergraduate students at the University of Texas in my humanities course on prison writing in fall 1988 and the graduate students in our seminar on writing and political detention in spring 1991 have read further into and out of this body of contested literature than I could ever have done on my own. I am also grateful to the Troops Out Movement (UK), the Winchester Three Campaign (UK), Sinn Fein (Dublin and Belfast), Palestine Human Rights Information Center (Jerusalem and Chicago), Al-Haq (West Bank), Women for Women Political Prisoners (Israel), the Union of Palestinian Women's Associations (USA), Dar al-Fata al-Arabi (Beirut and Cairo), friends in Egypt, participants in Austin's Central America Peace Initiative delegation to El Salvador and Nicaragua in 1987, El Rescate (Los Angeles), and Freedom Now (Chicago), for various combinations of materials and encouragement, as well as to all the prisoner support groups whose fliers, petitions, and printed hand-outs give a new meaning to "literature."

Friends, colleagues, and comrades provided much in the way of support, example, and solidarity (I resort here to alphabetical order): Raphael Allen, Shari Benstock, Tim Brennan, Elizabeth Butler-Cullingford, Rita Copeland, Ann Cvetkovich, Ioan Davies, Lisa Frank, Aklilu Gebrewold, Ferial Ghazoul, Craig Gilmore, Ruth Wilson Gilmore, Annie Goldson, Avery Gordon, Sarah Graham-Brown, Ibrahim al-Hariri, Ann Harlow, Joost Hiltermann, Nels Johnson, Neil Lazarus, Wahneema Lubiano, Charley MacMartin, Anne McClintock, Chris Maziar, Hatem Natsheh, Nimr, Rob Nixon, Lora Romero, Ellen Rooney, Edward Said, Ramon Saldivar, Raul Salinas, Paul Smith, Gayatri Chakravorty Spivak, Khachig Tololyan, and Abdul-Salaam Yousif. I also want to acknowledge the other co-workers of our "multicultural writing collective," persisting against all odds at the University of Texas: Brian Bremen, Ted Gordon, Michael Hanchard, Anne Norton, and Gretchen Ritter. Serving on the editorial committee of *Middle East Report* has given me many times over to rethink the "linkages" between culture and politics, as have my exchanges with the friends at the Institute of Race Relations in London. Joan Bothell has provided trans-Atlantic editorial assistance. The LBJ School at the University of Texas provided a small grant to enable me to do research in London in summer 1989. Otherwise the University of Texas paid my salary while I taught and committeed and tried in between to write this book, and "at the end of the day" did approve a leave of absence to allow the faculty exchange between UT Austin and University College Galway to take place. All through spring 1992, UCG has provided me with intellectual camaraderie and material assistance for doing the last bit. Special thanks to Donna Monroe here. M. Mac Craith in Irish Studies helped with some translation. And Bill Rolston in Belfast checked some references. Meanwhile, back in Austin, Laura Lyons (with assistance from Hosam Aboul Ela, Purnima Bose, Fran Buntman, Pedro Bustos-Aguilar, Luis Marentes, Louis Mendoza, Supriya Nair, and S. Shankar) brilliantly saw to the last details. xvii

In one of his letters from Turi prison to his mother, Antonio Gramsci wrote, "People don't write to a man in prison for one of two reasons. Either they are unfeeling, or else they are lacking in imagination" (24 August 1931). I have tried not to betray the political detainees whose stories form the basis for this book in either of those ways. But then again, as Gramsci wrote to his sister-in-law Tatiana from the same prison, "My not being able to write to you, and to forestall in time some catastrophic gesture . . . filled me with real fury, I assure you. I felt myself a prisoner twice over, because you too seemed to have decided not to fall in with any wish of mine. You seemed resolved to order my life just as ideas came into your head, and to pay no heed to my opinion—although I'm the one that's in prison! I know what it is to be in gaol! I've got the marks of it on my skin" (19 November 1928).

To the graduate students in English and Comparative Literature at the University of Texas at Austin: we are counting on you and your dissertations to do much of the rest.

PART I

AGAINST DISCIPLINE AND DOMESTICATION

Chapter One

Political Detention: Countering the University

British colonial officials have understood nothing about the development of colonial peoples. They have stood in the way of their forward movement from colonial status to freedom. The people who understand this had to go to jail. Gandhi and Nehru went to jail for any number of years. Nkrumah went to jail. Dr. Hastings Banda went to jail. Nyerere went to jail. All of them, and that priest from Cyprus, he went to jail also. So you notice that they didn't learn about democracy in British schools, they learnt it in the jails into which the British had put them; and from those jails they taught the population and taught the Colonial Office what were the realities of independence.

C. L. R. JAMES, *Spheres of Influence*

The most widespread error of method seems to me that of having looked for this criterion of distinction in the intrinsic nature of intellectual activities, rather than in the ensemble of the system of relations in which these activities (and therefore the intellectual groups who personify them) have their place within the general complex of social relations.
ANTONIO GRAMSCI, *Prison Notebooks*

We must prevent this brain from functioning for 20 years.

Prosecutor at Antonio Gramsci's trial

Aprendere a luchar desde esta celda. Esta sera mi trinchera. [I will learn to struggle from this cell. This will be my trench.] NIDIA DIAZ, *Nunca Estuve Sola*

Walid al-Fahum is a Palestinian lawyer in Israel and the Occupied Territories and an advocate for Palestinian political detainees. He began his legal work in the offices of the Israeli woman lawyer and activist Felicia Langer. In *These Chains That We Must Break* (n.d.),[1] a collection of writings on the prison situation under Israeli occupation, originally published in newspapers between 1974 and 1977, al-Fahum recounts an exchange that he had with one of his clients. The lawyer and the prisoner are discussing the unsatisfactory conditions of the prison, and the lawyer comments on the excessive crowding inside the cells. The crowding is so extreme, he says, that it is as if the detainees were "packed in like sardines in a can." The prisoner, however, responds, "No, my friend," and when al-Fahum expresses surprise at his disagreement, the prisoner adds, "We are like matches in a book of matches." Asked to explain, he replies, "Sardines are arranged next to each other in the can with the head of one next to the tail of the other. With a book of matches, the heads of all the matches are facing in the same direction" (163).

The prison writings of political detainees, of men and women, in Israel no less than in other countries throughout the world—whether "liberal democracies," "socialist states," or "military dictatorships"—offer a critique not only of the ruling systems that have incarcerated dissidents but of the very institution of literature as an autonomous arena of activity. Literature, that is, when abstracted from the historical and institutional conditions that inform its production—and its distribution—can serve in the end to underwrite the same repressive bureaucratic structures designed to maintain national borders and to police dissent within those borders. The literature of prison, composed in prison and from out of the prison experience, is by contrast necessarily partisan, polemical, written as it is against those very structures of a dominant arbitration and a literary historical tradition that have served to legislate the political neutrality of the litterateur and the literary critic alike. Reading prison writing must in turn demand a correspondingly activist counterapproach to that of passivity, aesthetic gratification, and the pleasures of consumption that are traditionally sanctioned by the academic disciplining of literature.

Such an imperative is enjoined by al-Fahum in "Pages from a Student's Notebook in the Occupied Land," the exemplary first article in *These Chains That We Must Break*. In this anecdotal lesson, the lawyer describes models for two counterstrategies of reading, strategies determined not by the traditions of literary distance or even poetic license, but rather by the material and political conditions of military occupation and economic and political disenfranchisement. According to the first of these examples, "in the long street, under the light of the street lamps, several Tulkarm students are escaping the [noise of the] song of Abd al-Halim [a popular Egyptian film star and recording artist]—'Lamplight.' . . . Their families have many children and the suffocating atmosphere is not conducive to study, either at night or in daytime. The children have developed a serious habit of studying while out walking by day and standing under the public street lights at night" (7). In the second example, al-Fahum describes the innovative practice of reading "upside down" (*bi-l-maqlub*) necessitated by restricted economic circumstances. Because there is not enough money to provide books for each child, two children must learn from one book. Sitting facing each other at the table, the two read the same page from opposite sides (7).

The economic and political conditions, occupation and dispossession, that have disrupted the ideal of the splendid solitude of scholarly pursuits and have made of learning a collective street activity, have inspired as well, in the course of decades of repression, the emergence of an organized Palestinian resistance movement demanding liberation of the land and autonomy and self-determination for the people living under occupation. The response of the Israeli military occupation to this challenge to its oppressive authority has been the consistent and massive detention, often without trial, of its opponents. In prison, however, and within the   5
collective framework of political opposition, the counterstrategies of reading and writing, a circumstantial necessity outside, are further exercised and developed as critical weapons in the struggle itself. The theoretical and practical reconstruction of the site of political prison as a "university" for the resistance, a training ground for its cadres, is more than a literary topos or metaphoric embellishment in the writings of political detainees, whether from occupied Palestine, South Africa, El Salvador, Northern Ireland or the United States.

For example, Paul Gilroy, (1987) has examined the relationship between the policing system in Britain, with its various definitions of criminality, and the recent history of legal and cultural constructions of English national identity through and against the immigration laws. In *There Ain't No Black in the Union Jack* he has argued that "new kinds of struggle can be solidified by the very institutions which are deployed to answer their demands and to channel them into fragmented individual solutions: into separate cases and claims" (34). Similarly, in "Marxist Theory and the Specificity of Afro-American Oppression," Cornel West (1988) has described the processes whereby what are presented as "structural constraints" are reconstrued through the analytical practices of political engagement as "conjunctural opportunities" (24). The institutional and physical restrictions of political detention, that is, like the material and economic limitations on the daily lives of particular disenfranchised ethnic, gender, class, or political constituencies outside the prison, are thus forcing the outlines of the dichotomizing definitions of the separatist relationship between literary and political practices and establishing as well the discursive grounds to challenge a dominant history of the state-sponsored suppression of internal and external dissent.

In his novel *Requiem for a Woman's Soul*, the Argentinian novelist-in-exile Omar Rivabella (1986) narrativizes the radical exigencies of a critical reading of the literature of political detention, incarceration, and torture. The story opens in a local church, at the 7 A.M. Mass, when Father Antonio sees among the congregation a woman "alone in the last row of pews,

hugging a large cardboard box, that partially hid her face, on her lap" (3). That box, left with Father Antonio by the unknown woman after the Mass is over, contains, underneath "an intense odor as of a mixture of urine and human excrement," a collection of "abundant wads of paper" (5). At once repelled and intrigued by the box and its confused contents, the priest struggles with his political consciousness, his moral conscience, and his human curiosity until, eventually, his daily pastoral routine is transformed into the painful deciphering of the words on the many partly
6 decomposed pieces of paper—matchbooks, toilet paper, newspaper margins, the foil from cigarette packages—into a chronological story and the reconstruction of the "diary of an unknown woman" (7), that other story of the arrest, torture, and presumed death of "Susana."

Requiem for a Woman's Soul is made up out of the counterpoint of the dated, recomposed fragments of Susana's writings and Father Antonio's italicized account of his paradigmatic experience with textual editing, his encounter with the contents of the woman's box. He finds himself mentioned by name, as is one Nestor, on one of the pieces of paper, and realizes his own recondite role in the history he is piecing back together: "I had been Susana's family priest in my previous parish." He recalls that Susana had once introduced him to her friend Nestor as "the priest who will marry us" (17). His involvement with the reconstruction of the diary leads first to Father Antonio's neglect of his official priestly duties toward his parishioners and chastening reminders from his bishop, and then to the denunciations in his sermons of the growing corruption throughout the bureaucracy of the country, followed by visits from the police commissioner and an army captain. The searing task of editing the tortured woman's diary, her daily notations challenging his daily routine, progressively leads Father Antonio back into the community and to Rosa, one of the "mothers of the disappeared" in his local congregation, and the other "mothers of the children lost to the forces of repression" (56).

Written into the body of Susana's dismembered and dislocated story, as Father Antonio learns, is the further account of its own production, of how, together with two other detainees, Alicia and Luisa, whom she meets in the prison yard, the woman prisoner agrees to write of her detention and commission it for "publication" by Father Antonio. The other women provide Susana with the few scraps of paper they are able to retrieve here and there from the prison refuse, and it is these scraps, covered with Susana's writing, that are eventually delivered to Father Antonio.

By the time he has completed his demanding editorial work, although the diary is still truncated, incomplete, Father Antonio has been voluntarily relieved of his pastoral responsibilities. He evades the supervision of his companions assigned to look after his health and mental stability in order to seek out Susana's parents. He finds them, old and decrepit with worry and care, in a run-down house in a well-to-do neighborhood. Susana's father, once a physician, now sits mesmerized by the vision of a large jar in his small laboratory: "Inside were two hands, severed at the wrists. One of them bore a ring on the middle finger. Together they floated in the bloody liquid, in a macabre ballet. There was Susana's engagement ring" (114). The clandestine practicum of strategies of writing from inside the prison here enjoins a new political responsibility on the reader-critic outside, a responsibility that, even as it is carried out, mobilizes still larger 7 popular and literary constituencies in the reworking of narrative.

Requiem for a Woman's Soul ends with an epilogue, a copy of a letter sent by Rosa to the novelist Omar Rivabella in New York City, with what might have been the final words of the priest, now hospitalized in the National Institute of Mental Health: "He took my hands, just the way he used to when he comforted my sorrows, and pronounced some unintelligible words. Then he pulled from his shirt pocket a piece of paper he seemed to have prepared for this last interview. He gave it to me and said in an enthusiastic tone, 'To him, send it to him.' On the piece of paper was your name and address" (116).

This "piece of paper," no less than the carton with the "abundant wads of paper" that Susana had left to Father Antonio, is not the natural transmission to posterity of a lettered corpus. It calls for more than a traditional response to an author's literary legacy left to a posthumous readership or a university archive. Rather, it demands a political critique of the institutionalized complicity—political and economic, and crossing national borders as well as geopolitical divides such as that between First and Third worlds—of Argentinian (for example) prisons and detention camps, the Catholic Church, even the family, and the metropolitan publishing industry. As if combining two of the "languages of pain," Amnesty International letters and "poems and naratives of individual artists," that Elaine Scarry has described in *The Body in Pain* (1985) breaking through the resistance of physical pain to "objectification" in language (5), Father Antonio's own slip of paper within the contrivances of Omar Rivabella's novel proposes a rethinking by way of reading and writing of the contestatory possibilities that these several institutional sites contain.[2]

Rivabella's novel *Requiem for a Woman's Soul* is itself finally participant, if for no other reason than its publication by Penguin, the traditional guardian of the classics in paperback and a major arbiter in the selection and dissemination to a mass but choice public of contemporary works and writers. The novel participates, that is, in the institutional network at once decried by the mutilated screams of the tortured political prisoners and challenged by their counterstrategies of writing. That participation is a critical one, whereby, perhaps, the complicity in the structures of institutional domination can be remade as an act of collaboration in a larger collective resistance. Thus, though Rivabella the novelist radically rewrote the makeshift pieces of Susana's prison diary into his contrapuntal narrative, another novelist, Hernan Valdes, found his novel-in-progress subjected to a literary critique different from that generally provided and therefore anticipated by members of the academic establishment.

8   Valdes, a Chilean writer, was arrested on 12 February 1974 in the months of oppression immediately following the overthrow, assisted by the U.S. Central Intelligence Agency, of Salvador Allende's Popular Unity government and held in Tejas Verdes, one of Chile's concentration camps, or what Valdes refers to as a "political detergency apparatus" (6), until his release on 15 March 1974. His prison memoir, *Diary of a Chilean Concentration Camp* (1975),[3] was, as he writes in the Foreword, "reconstructed after the event (it would be inconceivable for anyone under such conditions to find the means of producing a written text, quite apart from the impossibility of achieving a state of mind that would allow one to attempt such a thing in the first place)" (5). At the time of his arrest, Valdes was in the middle of writing what he had, outside the prison, thought was a political novel. That novel, at one point during his detention, became the focus of his interrogation, and questions of its form and content abrasively posed to him by his interrogators-cum-literary critics forced him to reexamine not only his own role and critical responsibility as author but also the very generic criteria by which literary works are constituted, appreciated, and judged.

"What's your novel about?" the interrogators ask.

This question throws me more than anything else. My memory goes a complete blank. Whenever anyone's asked me that kind of question in the past I've always felt incapable of replying, but in previous instances it was different. This time I have to say something, I can feel their breath on my face, their fists are at the ready. There's no plot, it's a novel of situations. I reduce what I thought was an existential drama to a romance for shorthand typists. Maybe that's all it was. I feel wretched. (38)

The author here, brutally interrogated by the servants of the state, can neither escape his pressing critics through a retreat behind his work nor claim judicial impunity on the "new critical grounds" that the work "speaks for itself." Indeed the academically sanctioned question, "What's your novel about?," when asked in the context of torture, disappearance, and political detention, exposes the coercive machinery of political containment that is complicitously prescribed by certain established literary critical practices. The writer then chooses for himself a not uncompromised alternative: "I reduce what I thought was an existential drama to a romance for shorthand typists."

Such a "reduction," with the feeling of "wretchedness" that it produces for the writer's sense of professional excellence, raises still another question, that of the relation between "high art" and "mass culture." The critical inquiries posed by the state apparatus, "fists at the ready," force Valdes the writer-prisoner to replot his narrative and thereby to rearticulate, if only temporarily and in the most provisory way, his social and political relations to his readership, even to rethink implicitly who that 9 readership might be. Is he, that is, writing existential dramas for a lettered elite or romances for shorthand typists? And what would be the difference between the two projects?

The apparent critical apologias that preface much prison writing, such as Hernan Valdes's statement that his diary was not written *in situ* but was "reconstructed after the event" or others that purport to excuse the limitations of style and literary technique, represent not so much the disarming disclaimers of a false modesty, or even the tacit acknowledgment of "literary standards," as the coercive pressures of traditional abstract ideals of "art" and "culture" and the antisystemic possibilities for submitting those same ideals to the political and material demands of historical conditions and priorities.

Rene Cruz, in the prologue to Ana Guadalupe Martinez's narrative of incarceration and torture, *Las carceles clandestinas de El Salvador* (1980), locates Guadalupe Martinez's memoir as necessarily integral to the larger revolutionary struggle. The woman commander had been arrested in 1976 as a guerrilla and member of the Ejercito Revolucionario del Pueblo (ERP) and held in El Salvador's secret prisons.

[The book] is an initial effort to write the history of our revolution from the trenches of combat themselves and not from the comfortable desks of inconsequential bystanders. In this sense we are not going to find here in the text any literary pretentions of a recherché style. It is time now that the revolutionaries transmit in an effective way their experience to our people in their own language, with a sensibility that the people understand and have lived. Much concrete experience has been lost for not having been processed and transmitted. Still another part has been essentially deformed for having been elaborated by leftizing [*izquierdantes*] intellectual intermediaries who adjust it not to the necessities of the revolution but to a bourgeois fictionalization and theorization of the revolution. (12)

Nearly ten years later, in April 1985, when Nidia Diaz, herself a *commandante* in the Farabundo Marti National Liberation Front–Democratic Revolutionary Front (FMLN-FDR), the combined resistance organizations of El Salvador, was arrested in a raid on guerrilla bases in the mountains of San Vicente, the prison record of Guadalupe Martinez served as an example of detainees' oppositional strategies. She in turn wrote these strategies into her own prison memoir, *Nunca Estuve Sola* (1988). With regard to the putative literary critics who would prefer to see Commandante Nidia as an autobiographer or diarist rather than acknowledge her as a revolutionary leader, Diaz has said, "I am told that I have put more of my revolutionary ideology into my book than of my personal emotions. But in prison, if you don't hold fast to your convictions, your ideology, you are lost. You can display nothing personal to your captors and interrogators. Nor did I want to. And afterwards this same thing came out as I set down to write. I lived prison minute by minute, guarded and resistant" (8). For Maria Lopez Vigil, in her foreward to the volume, *Nunca Estuve Sola* stands as an example of "how books are and how they are made in times of war. With urgency and without much polish, in hatchet strokes [*a hachachos de esfuerzos*], keeping problems of style 'in the schoolbag' [*a mochila*], and with the clear objective of assisting in the reconstruction and interpretation of an immediate history. With the dream of contributing something to the transformation of the history of war into a history of peace" (8).

Penal institutions, despite, if not because of, their function as part of the state's coercive apparatus of physical detention and ideological containment, provide the critical space within which, indeed from out of which, alternative social and political practices of counterhegemonic resistance movements are schooled. Crucial to such practices, at once cultural and political, are not only the narrative means whereby prison is re-presented in literature, but also the multiple contestatory roles played by literature in the prison itself. According to H. Bruce Franklin, in *Prison Literature in America* (1982), his study of the "victim as criminal and artist," prisons in the United States have contradictorily served to reeducate their inmates in radical self-constructions in writings that challenge the state's authority to contain their lived biographies within the boundaries demarcated by the penitentiary walls. "My subject," writes Franklin, "is literature created by those members of the oppressed classes who have become artists with words through their experience of being defined by the state as criminals. . . . The authors' 'crimes' are mostly those peculiar to the condition of poverty and forced labor: refusal to work; desertion and escape; mutiny and revolt; revolution. Their art expresses the experience of being legally kidnapped, plundered, raped, beaten, chained, and caged—and the understanding that results" (xxix–xxx). Unlike the political detainee, however, Franklin's "criminal narrator is sharply marked off from the readers. He or she speaks as a lone 'I'—an outlaw, a desperado, a deviant, or a member of an alien underworld—to society in general, or, more usually, a respectable reading public, incarnate in the reader" (126).

The intimate and ideological relationship, then, articulated and managed differently by various governments and judicial systems, between criminal (or social) and political prisoners is of no less critical consequence to the practical and theoretical organization of resistance movements, both inside and outside the prison. For criminals, female as well as male, whether convicted of petty theft, prostitution, murder, or simply social deviance, the experience of prison can, at given times and in particular circumstances, provide the historically necessary conjunctural premises for reframing the stories of their individual "crimes" as constituted by a sociopolitical system of economic exploitation and political disenfranchisement. Political prisoners in turn, when confined together with "criminals," must often reformulate their preconceived ideological constructs of "the people" and the entailed interaction between a vanguard party and its claimed popular constituencies.   11

The urgent complexities of this relationship between criminal and political prisoners, disputed by both the state and its organized opposition, is dramatized in Michel Foucault's account (1974) of Jean Genet's prison experience of being transferred for sentencing, during World War II, from detention at the Santé to the Palais de Justice:

at that time the custom was to handcuff the prisoners two by two to lead them to the Palais de Justice; just as Genet was about to be handcuffed to another prisoner, the latter asked the guard, "Who is this guy you're handcuffing me to?" and the guard replied, "It's a thief." The other prisoner stiffened at that point and said, "No, I'm a political prisoner. I'm a Communist, and I won't be handcuffed to a thief." And Genet said to me that from that day on, with regard to all forms of political movements and actions that we have known in France, he has not had merely a distrust but a certain contempt. (159)

Prison, then, as an always already immediate political fact both for the payrolled and self-appointed guardians of the state no less than for the organized opposition, continues to insist on the necessity once and again of rethinking critical strategy. According to the lawyer and activist, Bettina Aptheker (1971),

If we begin to grapple with some of these developments; if we begin to see the relationship between the prison system and fascist ideology and program; if we begin to see that we must develop our concept of the political prisoner; and if we begin to see the relationship between confinement at home and counterinsurgency and aggression abroad—then, we will have opened up whole new avenues for legal and political defense involving many thousands of people. (48)

The "criminals" imprisoned over the last two centuries by the United States penal system, whose writings inform Franklin's proposal for reconstructing the "victim as criminal and artist," insistently remind the critic that "whereas the literary criteria dominant on campus exalt what is extraordinary or even unique, most current autobiographical writing from prison intends to show the readers that the author's individual experience is not unique or even extraordinary, but typical and representative" (250). Franklin's preliminary conclusion, however, that "the prison and the university provide the contradictory poles defining the field of aesthetics, as well as some other areas, for in our society the two main competing intellectual centers may be the universities and the prisons" (235), might **12** be further adumbrated by the writings produced out of the experience of "political prison" in particular, in such a way that the prison and the university, while representing "contradictory poles," are also seen to function as complicit parts of the same operational system of dominant state control of dissent and the containment of antisystemic challenge.

"The Kerchief That Resists," written in 1981 by the former Palestinian prisoner Muhammad Abu Nasr[4] and included in his collection of short stories Men . . . and Bars (n.d.), tells of a composition class in a school and the teacher's amazement at the writing of his pupil Nasrin. "Where had she gotten a vocabulary like that?" the teacher asks himself, and then asks her, "Nasrin, has anyone in your family ever been arrested?" (12). Nasrin, as the teacher learns, came home from school one day to find her father, an employee of the Jerusalem Electric Company, in the process of being deported. The employment of Nasrin's father is significant here, for the Jerusalem Electric Company, which provides electricity to a large area around Jerusalem that includes a number of Israeli settlements, was one of the few such services still remaining in Palestinian control. As a result, it was forced to contend continually with Israeli attempts, abetted by the Jordanian government, to wrest that control from their hands. No less significant to the story, though, is the kerchief that her father gives Nasrin as he bids her goodbye and leaves across the bridge to Jordan. The scarf is in the forbidden colors of the Palestinian flag.

Like Ghassan Kanafani's much earlier story "The Slope" (1984), set in a United Nations Relief and Works Agency (UNRWA) school in exile in the first decade of Palestinian dispossession, "The Kerchief That Resists" uses the classroom setting to narrativize a challenge on the part of a child, a student, a new generation, to the conventional learning that underwrites the teacher's authority. Within each of the stories, it is the telling of a story that is at stake in the struggle to alter critically the unequal balance in the relationships of power. For the child in "The Slope," written in 1961, seven years before the establishment of an independent organized Palestinian resistance movement, the issue was to mobilize a collective participation in the construction of the narrative. Nasrin, in Abu Nasr's tale two decades later, draws on her related experience of prison and deportation to enlist her teacher in the cultural production of a new vocabulary, a new narrative of resistance, one compiled out of the experience of political detention. "Resistance literature" (*adab al-muqawamah*) is being historically rewritten as "prison literature" (*adab al-sujun*).

When Fadl Yunis arrived in Gaza Central prison's cell number 7 with his compatriots from Asqalan prison, only to confront the apparent failure of the resistance to establish itself on these premises, the men began together to consolidate their own internal strategies of solidarity and oppositional stances (Yunis 1983). On the one hand, in the public space **13** of the prison, they had recourse to passive resistance and refused, for example, to leave the wash area until they had completed their tasks there: rinsing off the soap, cleaning their plates, and so on. On the other hand, inside their cell, the men organized their program of study:

"Well, it looks as if we're settled here. Let's organize our program for the future. We'll use this time for study."
"Good," I said. "I want to begin to learn Hebrew, and for my part I'm ready to give English lessons starting today."
Everyone agreed to this and we established a Hebrew lessons program led by Abdallah as teacher and an English lessons program with myself as teacher. Hasan asked, "Shall we try to get some more books from the prison library?" (23)

The literacy program in Gaza Central prison's cell number 7 was not an isolated phenomenon. As "revolutionary academies" and "training schools for the resistance," the walls of Israeli prisons bear witness not just to hunger strikes and work boycotts, but to an enormous cultural production and a clandestine educational program as well.

Musa Abu Bakr, who had been Yunis's partner in shackles in the transfer from Asqalan to Gaza Central prison, collaborated with him in these projects. Released in the 1983 prisoner exchange, Abu Bakr recounted in an interview, published in Munira Samara and Muhammad al-Dhaher's *Scenario of Zionist Prisons* (1985), the critical role played by literacy and literature in structuring the prisoner movement and emphasized Yunis's contribution to it.

Fadl Yunis was one of the leaders of the literary movement in the prison, the first to devise the "prison magazine" in the prisons of the occupied land. He had no paper and pens, but Fadl Yunis made use of the wrappers from the milk containers, washed and stuck them on the wall to use as a simple magazine. This magazine, however simple, was, by its form and content, a kind of reminder and awakening. It broke through the stagnation and daily routine in the lives of the prisoners and opened their eyes to the cultural dimension which had been neglected inside them. (81)

In Jenin prison too, according to former prisoners, in the late 1970s a magazine was published monthly, sometimes including forty to sixty pages of prisoners' writing, as well as a biweekly newsletter that served to keep the prisoners in different cells and sections of the prison and in other prisons in touch with one another and with the world outside through the pieces and fragments of news that succeeded in penetrating the prison barriers. The poet Adil Wazwaz (n.d.) likewise describes the crucial importance of the literature movement in developing and sustaining the prisoners' organization and resistance: "In the midst of this repressive atmosphere a number of young literati and writers were born who defied the shackles and seized in their struggles and the struggles of their comrades the opportune moment to begin their attempts at writing. This was the beginning" (11). The magazine *Nafha al-Thawra* (Nafha Revolution) started to appear regularly in Nafha prison.

Paper and pencils are as subversive in the hands of political detainees as weapons, guns, and knives might be, and the retrieval and use of any scrap of paper from the sparse prison furnishings, like the "wads" in Susana's box, on which to compose words to break the ideological chains incarcerating the prisoners is an important motif in all prison literature. In his prison diary, *Detained*, the Kenyan writer and political prisoner Ngugi wa Thiong'o (1981) called this writing, the culture of prison, "toilet paper culture" (5–6), for often toilet paper is the only medium available inside the cell. Fadl Yunis used the wrappers of milk containers for his "magazine," and in Ansar in southern Lebanon Dr. Ahmad Subara (1984) saved the instruction sheets from medicine packages so that the cell leaders could keep track of the identification numbers of those prisoners who had been taken away for interrogation. Muhammad Abu Nasr's short story "Janin" in *Men . . . and Bars* describes the paintings done by prisoners on tiny bits of tattered rag that had to be concealed each time the cell was searched. Later they would be smuggled out, piece by piece, by visitors, to be reassembled for the 17 April commemoration of Palestinian Prisoners Day. Nizam Aboulhejleh (n.d.) and his comrades made use of cigarette packages: "We used the tiny paper inside the package of cigarettes for writing to teach the less fortunate ones among us. We collected several clippings and formed an inside newspaper that had a political article, a historical topic and one dealing with the experiences of other peoples" (n.p.).

One dilemma, however, to which Aboulhejleh refers, faced by many Third World writers and intellectuals is that of audience, particularly in those contexts where, under the repressive conditions of colonialism and the exploitation of neocolonial regimes, enforced illiteracy has been the norm for a large portion of the population. As John Beverley (1984–85) has pointed out in his study of El Salvador and prerevolutionary Nicaragua, "while the achievement of Cardenal, Dalton and their colleagues is to have created in their poetry a revolutionary sense of the *national-popular*, to use the Gramscian term, they are only heuristically genuinely national or popular poets, given among other things that illiteracy or partial literacy are problems the revolution can solve at the level of the whole society only after taking power" (52). Like Nicaraguan Minister of Culture Ernesto Cardenal's *poesia de taller*, the poetry workshops designed to teach working people how to write poetry in the new Nicaragua, however, the Palestinian prisoners' literacy programs inside Israeli prisons have begun to transform, as part of the revolution itself, the hierarchical **15** relationship between poet and audience into one of collective production and the elaboration of a new set of literary and cultural criteria.

"Where had she gotten a vocabulary like that?" Nasrin's teacher had asked himself in "The Kerchief That Resists." Abu Hassan, a Palestinian from Gaza, gives a partial answer in an interview given to Paul Cossali and Clive Robson in *Stateless in Gaza* (1986). He describes the contradictions implicit in the confrontation between the prisoners' resistance and the state's oppression:

I was jailed in 1970 and because I was a teacher I was told to help invigilate the Tawjihi exams [the Jordanian high school leaving exams administered to Palestinian students living in the Occupied West Bank and Gaza Strip]. Some UNESCO invigilators came too and we all gathered on the roof of the prison; us and rows of teenage students sitting in the sun trying to answer the questions. There was a small room near the roof, separated from us by a door and a heavy piece of cloth. Suddenly we heard this terrible screaming coming from inside. It was so high pitched and terrifying that we couldn't tell if it was a man or a woman. The students just carried on with their exams as if nothing was happening. A UNESCO man came over and asked me if I knew what was going on in the room. I just stared at the ground but when I looked up I saw that he was crying. He had no idea that these things happened here. (64–65)

While the Israeli military police sought to obstruct Palestinian education by detaining students at just that time when they should be sitting for the Tawjihi, the prison experience was countering by creating new forms of resistance and new forms of expression for that resistance. According to Nizam Aboulhejleh (n.d.), describing the cultural formation within the prison, "one person in each room gave cultural seminars according to his specialty. . . . We succeeded in turning the prisons of torture and oppression into schools that radiated knowledge and culture for the freedom fighter" (n.p.). In Neve Tertza, the women's section of Ramla prison, the older women, long-term prisoners, provided education and instruction, from primary and secondary school levels, to the younger detainees.

This effort to educate, however, must contend with the different designs of the prison system itself. Walid al-Fahum, the Palestinian lawyer,

describes in his account of Palestinian women prisoners, *Birds of Neve Tertza* (1984), the retribution exacted by the prison authority from Rawda for her instruction of her fellow prisoners. "Rawda said, 'One day I was punished in the isolation cell when I used as an example in the teaching the sentence "I am a Palestinian woman (*Ana filastiniya*)!" I was at the moment teaching my comrades the grammar of the English language . . . and translated it into resistance" (34). As the researchers who developed the Nicaraguan Literacy Crusade in the first year of Nicaragua's new gov-
16 ernment discovered,

> Literacy is a basic right, not a privilege, but it is meaningless without the right, also, to use the skills for one's own benefit and for one's family and community. Unless there is the intention to open more than the printed page to literacy learners, the skills are the route to a dead end. A literacy campaign must create new options and build hope. It must be both a symbol and a foretaste of a future that calls forth and rewards the best that each can contribute to the common good. (St. John 1985, xiv).

The Israeli occupation prisons, while they have brutally scarred the Palestinian social body, function also as historical sites for the radical transformation of Palestinian social and political structures. As elsewhere, the prison regime of interrogation, punishment, and deprivation that seeks to isolate the individual and undermine her or his personal identity and social integrity is effectively challenged by the countering strategies of collective resistance from within the prison no less than across the prison walls. The most ordinary of daily encounters between victim and victimizer managed by the prison apparatus and its routines are remodulated into a historical struggle. The confrontations might be momentary, such as that described by Argentine Alicia Partnoy in *The Little School* (1986): "'Slap his face. He's got bad manners. Make him pay for his bad manners,' said Loro, placing my still untied hand on the other prisoner's cheek. I caressed his face" (131). Or they might be momentous, such as the confrontation that forms the basis for Muhammad Abu Nasr's "The Two Comrades Meet" (1984). Abu Alaa is in Nafha prison commemorating the fourteenth anniversary of his arrest when he hears on the radio that a Palestinian commando from Syria has been captured inside Israel. The cell learns too that the prisoner is being brought to Nafha prison, and Abu Alaa hopes perhaps to receive news of the family he himself had left behind in Syria when he joined the resistance so long ago. "*Baba, khudni ma'ak*," his young son had pleaded. "Take me with you, Papa." And Abu Alaa had promised, "I'll take you with me when you've grown to be a man" (46). Abu Nasr's story ends with father and son, two comrades, meeting again inside the prison. "Family reunion in the Israeli fashion," as Salah Ta'mari (1984) referred to it.

The prison as a meeting place, as a historical conjuncture and site for remaking the social relationships based on gender, race, and class, or reforming political alliances, is examined again, critically, in Hasan Abu Libdeh's story "Wound in the Bad Time" (1982). Hasan Abu Libdeh was arrested in 1975 and sentenced to eighteenth months in prison for "membership in an illegal organization." His story is set in Beersheba prison and tells of the meeting of two prisoners, Samir and Sami. Samir, wealthy and well-traveled, entertains Sami, whose life has been spent in refugee camps, with stories of his adventures abroad. Sami is reticent, at **17** times even suspicious of the class differences that separate the two prisoners, but eventually he is drawn into Samir's plan that he, Sami, should marry Samir's sister Fatima when he is released from prison. Sami and Fatima begin a correspondence and exchange notes on literature, Kafka, Fanon, Lorca, and Ghassan Kanafani. As it happens, Samir is transferred to another cell and Sami is released to return to his home in the refugee camp. Fatima's parents, however, disapprove of a marriage begotten in prison between wealth and refugee poverty, and Fatima is obliged to return Sami's present of a book by Ghassan Kanafani. At stake are more than political issues drawn along lines of antagonistic nationalisms, for in the prisons social stereotypes, class barriers, and societal strictures are being reworked. The resistance movement from within the prisons is enlisting the larger society not only in a struggle against Israeli occupation but in a reexamination of its own received traditions, conventions, and priorities.

In *Women, Resistance and Revolution* (1974), Sheila Rowbotham tells the prison story of the French feminist socialist and trade union activist Jeanne Deroin. In the 1840s in France Deroin had "worked out with a group of male trade unionists the idea of a federation of all existing workers' associations," but the idea was temporarily frustrated when she and her coworkers were arrested on conspiracy charges. In prison, just before the trial, Deroin's lawyer, on behalf of her male colleagues, asked her not to "disclose her part in the idea of a federation," lest the suspicion of a woman's responsibility in the project undermine its eventual "chances of success." According to Rowbotham, "Jeanne Deroin was caught in a strange irony. She was being asked to step back, to confirm the passivity of women's role, her inability to initiate and participate in a movement designed to benefit women as well as men workers. She spent a troubled night but finally decided to pretend ignorance of the plan for federation. Though she compromised on this occasion she continued to argue socialist feminist ideas" (110).

The political role of women, often marginalized and rendered secondary if not at times altogether denied, even into the twentieth century, by masculinist or male-oriented opposition movements to oppressive state power and control, is submitted to a new scrutiny and revision by the extreme conditions of political detention. The incident described by Alicia Partnoy in *The Little School*, in which the woman prisoner counters the guard's order to "slap the face" of her fellow prisoner by caressing it instead, suggests, even in the very minimalism of its narration, not only the active potential for resistance on the part of women to hierarchical orders of power and subordination but their reorganizing and consolidating capacity as well. An alternative set of relationships to that of brutalized submission is sketched in the Argentine woman prisoner's abbreviated gesture. And while Hasan Abu Libdeh's story, "Wound in the Bad Time," leaves temporarily intact the patriarchal structures, such as arranged marriages, that characterize traditional Arab society, its critique of class privilege and sectarian bias locates, albeit implicitly, the issue of gender as central to these distorted internal relationships of power. Fatima alone, at this point, is in a position to challenge the interdictions of her parents' authority.

It is indeed Palestinian women prisoners who are exemplarily contesting the traditionally enshrined concept of "honor," or *sharaf*, manipulated by the men in Arab society no less than by their Israeli interrogators in order to contain the women's resistance. According to Nada Muzaffar (1987), the psychological torture tactics of Israeli prison officials include "first, the creation of a situation of terror in the ranks of the women fighters through recourse to social concepts," and "second, the exploitation of social factors to prevent the woman from participating in the struggle under the pressure of the concept of the woman's honor (*sharaf*) belonging to her husband, father, or brother." But, Muzaffar goes on, "the women prisoners respond in the face of their interrogators, 'our honor is in removing you from our land, honor is when the nation has become free, honor is the end of occupation'" (6).

In August 1989 Raymonda Tawil, a journalist who spent a year under house arrest in 1976–77 and whose Jerusalem publishing house and monthly news magazine *al-Awdah* were closed indefinitely in May 1988 by Israeli occupation authorities, wrote an open letter to al-Mutawakkil Taha, a Palestinian writer, journalist, and executive of the West Bank Writers Union who was imprisoned in Ansar 3 during the second year of the *intifada*. In the letter, printed in *The Return*, an English-language magazine published in the U.S. in the early period of the intifada, she instructs her male counterpart in the lessons to be learned from political prison: "In harsh human conditions, Palestinian political leaders, the elite, the clergy (both Christian and Muslim), professors, students, lawyers, laborers are all there in prison with you. This is the best school for cadres and disciples noted an Israeli official. 'It is amazing how experienced the detainees have become in self-control, regardless of how much their opinions may differ.' " But Tawil also remonstrates with Taha over what she sees to have been a dangerous tactical error—in terms of both public opinion and the internal integrity of the uprising—committed by one part of the resistance and Taha's own imminent implication, even while in prison, in this deviation: "Last month's kidnapping of Christopher George, the American co-director of Save the Children in Gaza and the West Bank, a friend to the Palestinian people, might be the beginning of a dangerous phenomenon. Mutawakel, your name was listed as one of the detainees the kidnapper(s) asked for in exchange for Christopher George. It was wrong to kidnap, even out of desperation. It was worse to kill, as the Israelis did, when they gunned down Mohammed Abu Nasr, the alleged kidnapper" (5). Raymonda Tawil's letter to al-Mutawakkil Taha, sent from a woman cultural combatant to her writer-activist colleague in prison, exemplifies in significant part the effective consequences of both long- and short-term political detention generally for members of the resistance organization and the political party; more specifically, it reveals the ways in which the social and political functions of women and gender are constructed and contested (or not contested) by the resistance movement itself.

19

If one of the manifest purposes for the state and its apparatus of control through political detention is the isolation of the opposition leadership from its base of popular support in the larger community, it is that very purpose that is being disarticulated and turned to other ends through the differently reconstituted social and political relations across the prison walls between the militants incarcerated and the population outside. In 1928, when Antonio Gramsci was sentenced to twenty years, four months, and five days imprisonment, the prosecutor at his trial had argued on behalf of the state: "We must prevent this brain from functioning for 20 years." In prison, Gramsci's self-proposed "adjustment" to an extended period of confinement and physical and worldly isolation that would claim the middle years of his manhood and paternity—indeed, all the rest of his life—that "adjustment" involved the organization of a major plan of study. The mind that the prosecutor wanted to prevent from functioning for twenty years produced instead a critical written corpus of political thinking and theorizing, Gramsci's prison notebooks.

In that corpus, too, were the letters that for ten years Gramsci wrote from prison. In an early letter from Milan prison, written prior to his sentencing in March 1927 to his sister-in-law Tatiana, Gramsci wrote, "You see, I'm haunted—and this, I think, is a phenomenon quite familiar among prisoners—by an idea, that it is necessary to do something *fur ewig.* . . . In short, I want, according to a prearranged plan, to occupy myself intensively and systematically with some subject which will absorb me and provide a central channel for my inner life" (1988, 45). To Giuseppe Berti, a fellow communist, however, Gramsci a few months later reproached himself, "I'm not doing any work; you can't call reading work when it's purely and simply reading for pleasure. I read a great deal, but unsystematically. I receive a few books from outside, and I read the books from the prison library week after week, taking whatever I get from the farthing dip" (1988, 63). Two years later, again to Tania, the now veteran political prisoner was giving informed advice on how a prisoner could use his time "to advantage." First of all, Gramsci insisted one must "rid oneself of the mental overcoat of academicism, and not cherish the vain illusion that one can pursue regular and intensive courses of study; that sort of course is out of the question, even for people in less difficult circumstances." Gramsci then added, "Nevertheless it's my opinion that a political prisoner must find ways and means of squeezing blood from a stone. The main thing is to do one's reading with a certain end in view, and to take notes (if one is allowed to write)" (92–93).

One of Gramsci's main correspondents, and an important visitor who provided him with reading and study materials as well as news of world events and party comrades, was Tania, sister of his wife, Giulia. To Giulia, or Julca (as he often addressed her in his letters), however, Gramsci wrote from Turi prison in 1931: "You intend, you say, to study . . . wouldn't it be a good idea to study certain things which interest me too and so start a correspondence with me about material which is of interest to the two of us because it is a reflection of the present intellectual life of [our sons] Delio and Giuliano?" (184). The student of political theory and imprisoned party militant was finding that in detention his own sons were inevitably estranged from him, living now in Russia, where they had gone with their mother. Giulia, furthermore, like Gramsci's own mother before her, was concealing from their children the fact of their father's detention (243n). The tormented need to rethink radically their affective bonds and marital loyalties haunts Gramsci's letters to his wife: "We must hurl all that's past into the flames and build new lives from the ground up. Why should we let ourselves be crushed by the lives we've led up to now? There's no sense in preserving anything at all but what was constructive and what was beautiful. We must get out of the ditch, and throw off that silly toad sitting on our hearts" (225–26).

The prison notebooks alone, all thirty-three of the extant exercise books, testify to the continued if reconstructed importance of writing and the written to Gramsci in prison. No less significant, however, as evidence of the discursive effectiveness of the scriptural are Gramsci's prison letters written variously to his wife, his children, his sister-in-law, and his political associates and party comrades. The notebooks, the record of Gramsci's prison scholarship and political intellection written from behind the walls, were eventually "saved" by Tatiana and are still in the process of being edited, published, and translated posthumously for audiences that were intended perhaps, but still unforeseen to their author. Gramsci considered this question of readership and the radical constraints inflicted on reading and research alike by the multifarious circumstances of political detention in a letter to Tania concerning his critical work on Dante:

I have read Professor Cosmo's observations on the Tenth Canto of Dante's *Inferno*. 21
I would like to thank him for his suggestions, and the list of books I might consult. However, I don't think it's worthwhile getting hold of the copies of the reviews which he mentions: what would be the point of it? If my intention were to write an essay for publication, this material wouldn't be sufficient (or at least, in my present state of mind which is a compound of gloom and dissatisfaction, it would not seem sufficient to me); and if all I wanted to write was something just to please myself and to pass away the time, it would not be worth while disturbing such solemn monuments as the *Studies On Dante* of Michele Barbi. (1988, 220–21)

The letters, by contrast, had immediate reading receivers: their addressees, to be sure, but the prison censor as well, who, following prison regulations, rigorously reviewed all prisoner correspondence. Indeed, the very conditions of prison and the specific restrictions that they impose— from the prison censorship, to the limits in length and frequency of letters, to the designation of approved recipients—present a dramatic example of the necessary connections between the formal criteria of genre and historical and institutional circumstances.

Gramsci's prison letters, then, the *lettere dal carcere*, recount an immediate narrative of maintaining and reconstituting erstwhile personal and political relationships across prison barriers:[5] his critical concern over directions and tendencies assumed by the Italian Communist party as well as developments in the Soviet Union, but his anxiety too over his wife's physical and mental health and his suspended relationship to his two sons, whose education he still, even incarcerated, wished to supervise. The man—intellectual, party leader, husband, father, son—both reveals and transgresses his masculinity through these letters. As he wrote to his mother but a few days before his trial on 10 May 1928, "For the sake of my own peace of mind I would like you not to be too frightened or upset, whatever the sentence they mean to hand out. I would like you to understand, and to feel, that I am a political prisoner and that I have nothing to be ashamed of, and never will have anything to be ashamed of. . . . Life is like this, very hard; and sons must sometimes cause great grief to their mothers if they wish to preserve their honour and their dignity as men" (cited in Fiori, 1990, 290–91). Gramsci, seriously ailing, was transferred from Turi prison to Civitavecchia in 1933. He died four years later, on 27 April 1937, never having seen his two young sons again.

The political reconstructions of organized opposition and party structures, the theoretical work of the prison notebooks, are shown then in Gramsci's prison letters to reverberate on the most intimate level of personal relationships as well, and new modes of articulating those relationships demand, passionately and painfully, study and new elaborations. As Rosa Luxemburg (1981) wrote from prison in Zwickau to her "comrade and lover" Leo Jogiches, addressing him in the feminine appelative of Leonie to avoid prison censorship, "When I left, you promised you'd read one book a day. Do you? You *must*, I beg you! Now I appreciate again the value of making serious books a part of daily life. It saves the mind and the *nervous* system. But Marx, you know, ends up by making me angry. I still *can't get the better of him*. I keep getting swamped and can't catch my breath" (137).

The experience of prison—from state apparatus to prison counterculture, and its impact on the larger society—proposes new priorities and agendas for political organizing and cultural mobilization, with critical implications for altering the curricula of other public institutions as well. "Prison," for Molefe Pheto (1983), "political prison, is a university" (195). Pheto, a South African writer, and organizer of MDALI (Music, Drama, Arts and Literature Institute) in Soweto, spent a year in South African prisons just prior to the Soweto uprisings in June 1976. His prison memoir, *And Night Fell*, narrates his de-education, his reappraisal from inside the cement-block walls of the prison compound of the ivy-covered walls of university quadrangles. His prison experience, which included interrogation, the attempt to establish communication with fellow prisoners from other organizations, and the effort to enlist the aid of sympathetic guards, provides the foundation for his radical critique of his academic credentials, granted by Western or Western-sponsored institutions and for his reeducation as a partisan in the local struggle against apartheid.

Pheto, at the time of his arrest, was a member of the Pan Africanist Congress (PAC), which had broken away from the African National Congress (ANC) in the late 1950s. The PAC emphasized black African resistance to the structures of apartheid, whereas the ANC promoted multiracialism. Pheto remained a PAC partisan, but his political reeducation in the prison was assisted by various of the groups represented there: the torturers and interrogators whose "language" he had to learn if he was to succeed in not communicating any information to them; imprisoned members of the ANC whose political tactics and ideological analyses differed from his own; and the children of the townships who understood as well as

Pheto the meaning of the word "politics." On more than one occasion, Pheto was asked, across the barriers of enforced isolation, by supposed "criminals," why he was being held in solitary confinement. His efforts to define political detention usually revealed to him instead the heightened degree of political consciousness that characterized these "criminals." Indeed, it was the most common criminals, the women, the prostitutes, and shebeen queens who, by making available to him the new rhythms and songs to which people were dancing in Soweto, were most effective in reintegrating the party militant into the politics of popular resistance. **23**

Prison education, unlike much university instruction as professed in the Western academy, functions to undermine the very walls and premises that contain it. It raises the question of the extent to which an academic discourse functions to perpetuate disciplinary structures erected to maintain order and punish transgressions; it asks why scholarship so often "bantustanizes" the sociopolitical realities of the areas whose cultural production it appropriates. Programs in various ethnic and area studies and women's studies, for example, which appeared in United States universities following the campus activism and political agitation in the 1960s, were established by these universities, as Rosaura Sanchez (1987) points out, "not out of a state interest in a body of knowledge but out of interest in ensuring campus order and security" (86). The work of political prisoners, men and women, and even children, on a discursive level no less than in the political arena, presents a powerful challenge to such disciplining.

Area studies programs and departments of national literatures have extracurricular analogues in the state bureaucracy that closes its internal borders as readily as it allows for a calculated permeability of external boundaries. On 29 October 1986, for example, the United States Bureau of Prisons opened a multimillion dollar maximum security prison for women in Lexington, Kentucky. Designed to house sixteen inmates, for over a year the facility contained only two detainees, Alejandrina Torres, a Puerto Rican nationalist, and Susan Rosenberg, a revolutionary political activist from New York City, both confined under extremely brutal conditions criticized publicly by Amnesty International as constituting "cruel and unusual punishment." Less than a year later, death squads from El Salvador extended their sphere of activity into the United States, when three Central American women were abducted from the streets of Los Angeles, tortured, and then returned to the streets badly beaten, as a "message" to their supporters. The Lexington "high security unit" has since been closed by court order, in part in response to pressures such as Amnesty's protest. The closure has been appealed by the United States government. Torres, convicted of seditious conspiracy, was transferred to the Metropolitan Correctional Center in San Diego. In the meantime, Susan Rosenberg with five codefendants is awaiting trial in Washington, D.C., on charges of conspiracy associated with a series of bombings in the capital in 1983 following the United States invasion of Grenada. The "resistance conspiracy trial" and its attempt to criminalize political activism in the United States will, according to Susie Day, "probably unearth in the Left profound questions about the nature of justice and criminality in our society" (88). The ultimate intended effect of such "messages," however, whether from the United States government or from Salvadoran death squads, is to disenfranchize the political for the sake of the national patriotic, and reassert the dominant boundaries.

Most analyses of the modern prison system, even those that are critical, such as Michel Foucault's *Discipline and Punish* (1979) and Dario Melossi and Massimo Pavarini's *The Prison and the Factory* (1981), remain outside the walls of the prison and thus in some way on the side, so to speak, of the prison and its officials. Foucault, for example, following his historical narrative of the transformation of the public spectacle of punishment into coercive and secretive model of the "power to punish," discerns two images of discipline in the modern penal system:

> At one extreme, the discipline blockade, the enclosed institution, established on the edges of society, turned inwards towards negative functions: arresting evil, breaking communications, suspending time. At the other extreme, with panopticism, is the discipline mechanism: a functional mechanism that must improve the exercise of power by making it lighter, more rapid, more effective, a design of subtle coercion for a society to come (209).

Massimo and Pavarini, in turn, locate the practices associated with such "images" in the rise of the bourgeois industrial state and thus assimilate the architecture, both political and ideological, of the modern prison to that of the factory. According to the two Italian researchers, the "penitentiary invention" is that of the

> "prison as a machine" capable of transforming, after close observation of the deviant phenomenon, . . . the violent, troublesome and impulsive criminal (real subject) into an inmate (ideal subject), into a disciplined subject, into a mechanical subject . . . [and assisting the] production of subjects for an industrial society . . . [the] production of proletarians by the enforced training of prisoners in factory discipline (144).

Even such critiques of the prison system, however, too often can be subjected to the consent of that same prison system and its apparent insistence on a language of authority and objective responsibility that requires a complicit compromise from the would-be researcher and attempts to usurp his/her own project. Thus, R. Theodore Davidson (1974), who investigated social formations and networks among Chicano prisoners in San Quentin in the 1960s, introduced his study with an explanation of his own situation within the system: "Prison administrators realized the delicate nature of the information I would probably encounter if I were to accomplish my task, so it was agreed that I would not have to reveal any confidential information to the staff. The only exception would have been if I had learned that someone was going to be physically harmed or that the prisoners were going to destroy the prison in some manner" (1). This "only exception," however, is twofold, and the requirements of the prison administration and the unitary language serve only to conceal concern for the stability of the prison itself ("destroy the prison in some manner") under an ostensibly humanitarian sensitivity for the safety and well-being of the anonymous prisoners ("someone was going to be physically harmed"). The testimonies of prisoners betray another analysis, that of an engaged and partisan counterhegemonic cultural production. 25

Addressing themselves in particular to the "Troubles" in Northern Ireland and the concerted British judicial and technological response to the organized republican and nationalist resistance to British military occupation of the Six Counties, Carol Ackroyd et al. (1977), in *The Technology of Political Control*, raise more generally the current issues of a "new type of weaponry. It is the product of the application of science and technology to the problem of neutralizing the state's enemies" (11). The authors consider the battle of the Bogside, fought in Derry in 1969 between Northern Irish Catholic residents of the area and Protestant militia and constabulary with the eventual assistance of the British Army. The battle of the Bogside, which followed upon a series of civil rights marches in Northern Ireland, marked the first and a very extensive use by British troops of CS gas against a civilian population in the United Kingdom.[6] It announced as well the arrival of the British army forces in Northern Ireland and the beginning of an occupation that has lasted more than two decades. This escalation of the "technology of political control" was followed, in the summer of 1971, by the introduction of rubber bullets, which were to be used, it was claimed, in the nonlethal dispersal of riotous crowds, and by the use of sensory-deprivation torture, known as "depth interrogation," in the questioning of interned Irish Republican Army (IRA) suspects.

Writing in 1977, the four British scientists, all members of the British Society for Social Responsibility in Science (BSSRS), note that their approach "may seem a curious amalgam of technological expose and political analysis. It is not a particularly familiar or apparently natural one. But it is an approach which is being used more and more by scientists who are becoming aware of the political implications of their work" (11). Defining "technology" as "any device or method which exploits knowledge from any of the sciences from physics to psychology" (19n), they argue throughout their study that the "motives behind the technology of political control are not humanitarian. These technologies are used by states to achieve specific political goals" (21). Such motives are in particular associated with what are called "strong states," the liberal democracies in which power relationships are largely veiled and the continual increments in political control of internal dissent are made in small, often imperceptible, steps such as greater funding of the security apparatus or expansion of the state bureaucracy. Equally significant for these governments, however, are the uses of legal innovations and sanctions to ratify for public consumption and acquiescence the alterations in the government's modus operandi. Much of the "technology of political control" used by Britain in Northern Ireland—not only computerized intelligence networks but also gas and plastic bullets—was first developed, the authors indicate, in the United States. As Ackroyd and her colleagues point out, these technologies are designed to "maximize repression, subject to a constraint that any political backlash must be kept to manageable proportions. Backlash depends not on how harmless the technologies are, but on how harmless they *seem*. 'Humanitarianism,' then, is not an objective, but a propaganda claim" (41). After all, they say, "It is easy enough to kill people. It is harder *not* to kill them, but to stop them all the same. 'Non-lethal' riot-control technology provides governments with sophisticated methods for controlling unruly populations. At the same time, it avoids the public outcry which results from outright massacres such as Bloody Sunday" (197).

Torture in the twentieth century has its own material and ideological specificity. Despite its long history, dating back further even than classical Greece, when it was designed to elicit a confession that would suffice to convict and condemn the accused, torture today has acquired new ends and a radical technologization of its means (see Peters 1985). The attack on the personal identity and the body of the victim is calculated now to undermine the social body as well. Nor is it, for the most part, only information that the system of power is concerned to extract. Torture in political detention is calculated rather to produce propaganda and to intimidate, if not destroy, the human and political constitution that continues to resist. The witnessing of torture by the tortured yields, however, another kind of information, that is, the testimony, often clandestine, of the political prisoner who survives. The danger inherent in such testimony is precisely that represented by the political prisoners themselves, the danger that caused their detention in the first place. Ackroyd et al. conclude that the danger is threefold: "Firstly, there is the damaging effect of publicity surrounding their trial and imprisonment. Secondly, there is the danger of increasing the political commitment of both political prisoners and 'criminal' prisoners who are exposed to their influence, and of others not in gaol. . . . Thirdly, there is the danger that political prisoners will provide a focus for the organization of political movements within the prisons" (255).

Historically, in Europe in the Middle Ages, and in Latin America, and even in the United States as recently as the 1960s, the university, or the academy, has at times served as a recognized site of sanctuary, a coun-tenanced alternative space or critical counter to the institutions of sov- **27** ereign or state power. That once acknowledged space is now being ever more systematically occupied by the various apparatuses of state domina-tion, both repressive and ideological. In Chile, for example, in September 1973, with the overthrow of the Allende government, Chilean troops in-vaded the National University to arrest those Popular Unity supporters or even "neutral" observers who had taken refuge there. Between 1980 and 1984, the University of El Salvador was occupied by the Salvadoran army, and professors, staff, administrators, and students continue to be regular victims of the paramilitary death squads. Through the 1980s uni-versity administrations in the United States called in city, rather than campus, police, to disperse—and arrest—demonstrating students. Pales-tinian universities and schools in the Occupied Territories are militarily closed more often than they are open. Indeed, in order to accommodate the large numbers of detained protesters since the beginning of the *inti-fada*, the Israeli authorities have sometimes used the closed schools as makeshift prison centers.

The threat that prisons and universities pose to the state if not prop-erly policed or effectively disciplined is told in a short story by the Israeli writer Matt Nesvisky (1989). "The Game's Up" relates a Navy frogman attack on a boat moored in international waters off the coast of Israel. None of the commandos involved in the operation know what they will find there: "Military intelligence hasn't determined if it's drug-smuggling, gun-running, white-slavery or terrorism. But we do know the gambling is a front for something big, and our job is to find it. Any more questions? Okay, men, after me—and good luck." The attack is carried through suc-cessfully and the ship's gamblers are "herded into the central lounge." But there is still a locked door belowdecks, which must be opened with plas-tic explosives. There the Israeli frogmen confront forty West Bank pupils and their teacher. " 'I suspected as much!' Bar-Barian snorted. 'A clandes-tine matriculation class! In the name of the Civil Administration, I hereby arrest you for illegal education!' "

"Illegal education," the kind practiced clandestinely offshore or in underground prison cells, proposes a counter to the university and can also make for, if not its effective dismantling, at least individual or even collective escapes from prison. *Escape from Pretoria* is Tim Jenkin's account (1987) of how he and two other prisoners, Stephen Lee and Alex Moumbaris, accomplished their escape from Pretoria Prison, "New European Section," on 11 December 1978. Although, as Jenkin claims, "For us an escape was a political act, not an individual flight for freedom" (95), the escape plans themselves caused a considerable controversy among the ten detainees held in their section of the facility.

28   Arrested in 1978 and charged under Section Six of the Terrorism Act, Jenkin had been sentenced to twelve years' imprisonment. Lee, his co-worker in the distribution of "illegal pamphlets" for the ANC, received an eight-year sentence. Their fellow prisoners included Denis Goldberg, one of the Rivonia trialists from 1964 serving three life sentences. Other of the detainees were in various stages of sentences ranging from seven to twelve years. Lee and Jenkin had been extremely frustrated at their trial because they had submitted, despite their own political convictions, to their lawyers' decision to appeal to the mercy of the court. Jenkin describes the two prisoners' reaction to the sentence when the proceedings were concluded: "In the cells below, the two of us felt sick. Not because of the sentences imposed on us, but because we'd failed to raise our fists and shout *Amandla!*—"Power!" as is fitting and proper for political prisoners to do when sentenced. Why had we succumbed to the appeals of our lawyers?" (65). The decision to escape then was construed as a challenge, at once personal and political, to the South African court and its penal institutions.

The debate among their fellow prisoners, however, concerning the nature of that challenge engaged still larger and more complex issues of political organization, personal alliances, and strategies of resistance:

> While our unity and comradeship was our greatest source of strength it was also the source of the controversies that arose over the planning of the escape. A failed attempt, everyone knew, would lead to severe disruption and threaten the unity which gave us our strength. The differences arose out of this: some felt that the preservation of unity was paramount; those bent on getting out found it difficult to accept that others did not display the same drive to get out. (96)

For those who agreed, at various stages of the planning, to participate in the escape attempt, other, more detailed questions were raised: Was it necessary to "theorize" the escape before attending to its practical exigencies? Should the resistance organization outside be involved? If so, in what ways? And so on.

In the end, and in part for circumstantial reasons, these questions were answered negatively. The key to the escape was to be in making keys, keys to the ten doors that stood between the prisoners and freedom. Jenkin became, during his months in prison, a master locksmith, as well as a skilled tailor, in order to remake used prisoner garb into unidentifiable streetwear. When the time came, only one door, the tenth and the last, refused the designated key, and it was necessary to force it open. The escape was successful—for the individuals involved—but it was not without its consequences for others, both inside and outside the prison walls.

The escape had profound consequences for many people: for our comrades who stayed behind it meant three years of unhappy confinement in the "condemned" **29** section of Pretoria Central where prisoners awaiting execution are held; for political prisoners in other jails around South Africa it served as an inspiration and a boost to morale; for a prominent member of the ANC it meant an international kidnapping; for Sergeant Vermeulen it meant a five-month-long trial to prove his innocence; for several comrades in South Africa and my brother it meant detention, torture and jail; for our enemy, the apartheid rulers, it meant a terrible embarrassment and defeat; for Alex, Steve and me it meant freedom and the chance to throw ourselves back into the struggle against apartheid. (231)

Many were the political lessons of theory and practice still to be learned.

Different lessons would figure in the partially successful mass escape in September 1983 of thirty-eight IRA prisoners from "The Maze, Her Majesty's Prison"—popularly known as the "H Blocks"—in Northern Ireland. Recognized as the largest jailbreak in Europe since World War II, the escape, which followed upon the blanket protests, the no-wash protests, the dirty protest, and a series of hunger strikes during the preceding years, was constructed by the strictly disciplined internal organization of the political prisoners within the prison itself. *Out of the Maze*, Derek Dunne's account (1988) of the escape based on interviews with escapees— some recaptured, others still on the run—and prison officials and police alike, narrates the development of that organization and the radical challenge it posed to Britain's "technology of political control." The escape plans involved such extensive strategies as "getting the blocks solid" and establishing connections with the IRA outside which was to see to the eventual transport and security of the escapees, as well as the details of smuggling in the needed weapons, setting up a communications network, and memorizing the minutiae of the layout of the entire prison. The preparations also involved the difficult decision of who would go and who would stay behind. On the day set for the escape,

the Provos would carry out the largest operation in their history. The escape would be a morale booster, a propaganda exercise and would put some of their most capable men back into circulation. And that was the last question that needed to be answered. Who was going out? The lorry couldn't take any more than forty men. In H7 there were 125 men in the Block. There was going to be some bad feeling on the day when the takeover took place, when some men would realise that they had no part in the escape, that they were going to be left behind. (59)

In the end, an unanticipated delay in the rounds of the food truck to be used in the escape produced a confrontation at the prison's outer gate, and the truck was unable to go through. Only twenty-one of its thirty-eight passengers managed to get out on foot, and many of them were sooner or later recaptured. For those who did elude prison, however, even escape did not necessarily mean untrammeled freedom: "The men from Belfast and Derry could not go home. They would be recognized immediately if they went back to visit their families and friends. They underwent a period of adjustment, which in some cases took years. There were, of course, furtive meetings with families and loved ones south of the border. But they had to break completely with their past" (130).

Prison escapes, like Tim Jenkin's key, even as they materially and symbolically challenge the state's apparatus of control and containment, and effectively assist the resistance and its political and military struggle outside, leave the state institution of detention intact. The escapes do serve, however, as blueprints, drafts, for the project of its dismantling. Like "statements from the dock" by political prisoners, the last public words before being condemned to the silence of a prison sentence, the discursive contestations of the judicial system, the escapes enact an emergent alternative history lesson, a collective counter, to the history of dispossession, exploitation, and systemic injustices waged by the state's prisons and universities alike. In 1964, prior to his sentencing to life imprisonment, Nelson Mandela addressed the court assembled in Pretoria's Palace of Justice: "I am the First Accused" (Benson, 1976, 111), he said; he proceeded to instruct those present in the history of South African resistance, from the formation of the ANC in 1912, through the Defiance Campaign in the early 1950s and the Sharpeville massacre in 1960, to the establishment of Umkhonto wa Sizwe, the armed wing of the ANC, in 1961. Bram Fischer, who had been a defense lawyer in the trial of Mandela and others detained at Rivonia, addressed the same court from the dock in 1966: "I cannot address any argument to this court. What I can do is to give the court certain facts regarding the manner in which the criminal law has come to be administered in political cases in this country. It presents a picture which is horrifying to those brought up with traditional ideas about justice" (46).

In 1975, four young people, three men from Northern Ireland and an Englishwoman, now known as the "Guildford Four," were convicted of the 1974 pub bombings in the English towns of Guildford and Woolwich and were sentenced to some of the longest prison terms ever imposed in Britain. In *Time Bomb*, Grant McKee and Ros Franey (1988) tell the personal histories of these four individuals and describe the crime, its investigation, the trial—and the subsequent confessions to the same crime by four members of a Provisional IRA Active Service Unit in London who were arrested a year later. Tried and convicted for numerous other bombings, IRA member Joe O'Connell, against IRA policy which refuses to recognize the legitimacy of the British system of justice, rose to address the court from the dock following the proceedings:

31

We have recognized this court to the extent that we have instructed our lawyers to draw the attention of the court to the fact that four totally innocent people— Carole Richardson, Gerard Conlon, Paul Hill and Patrick Armstrong—are serving massive sentences for three bombings, two in Guildford and one in Woolwich. . . . Time and again in Irish political trials in this country innocent people have been convicted on the flimsiest of evidence, often no more than statements and even "verbals" from the police. Despite the oft-repeated claim that there is no such thing as a political prisoner in England . . . (McKee and Franey 1988: 384–86)

In October 1989, the conviction of the Guildford Four was finally reversed, and Richardson, Conlon, Hill, and Armstrong were released after fourteen years spent in British prisons. Hill issued a statement on his emergence into freedom in which he asked, "We hope that we have breached the wall. . . . At the moment, it's damage control—it's everybody's duty to insure that they don't shore up the hole in the wall, so we can ensure that the Birmingham Six [held on similar charges and on equally dubious evidence] will eventually emerge. Then, perhaps, we can finally smash the wall—once and for all" (*Guardian*, 15 November 1989, 15).[7]

In the United States, in El Salvador, in Israel, in South Africa, and elsewhere throughout the world, the work of political prisoners, their "illegal education," is challenging the contemporary university structure and the institutions of state of which it is a part to rethink the social and cultural traditions—including patriarchy—that the university has inherited and is engaged in reproducing.

Chapter Two

Women and Resistance

██

She was also subject to another great delusion believing that women were protected from repression, and that the leaders considered political fights to be strictly between males. In fact, with women's greater access to certain powers, they began to watch them more closely, and perhaps with even greater hostility. Every feminine act, even charitable and seemingly unpolitical ones, were regarded as a rebellion in this world where women had always played servile roles. Marie Rose inspired scorn and hate long before the fateful day of her arrest.

However, fear of torture often crossed her mind. She had told her friends that if she refused to join certain clandestine political parties it was because of her fear of prison. But she supported the Resistance with a profound conviction, and because it seemed more a question of love than politics, a question of Life and Death for all Arabs. She believed that this cause must be sacred to all, and when she suspected hypocrisy, she silenced her mistrust.

Torture preoccupied her because she saw in it, or rather in the person who could resist it, the summit of human courage. She hated physical suffering, abhorred it, and considered it a fundamental injustice to Nature. She was persuaded that men could be cured of moral and physical ills if only, if only. . . . She sometimes managed to convince herself that torture did not exist, while she knew it was practiced in all the capitals of the world.   ETEL ADNAN, *Sitt Marie Rose*

██ When Yolla
Pollity Sharara became active in the political arenas of Beirut in the 1960s, she, like Marie Rose Boulos, confronted the traditional social barriers to women's entry into a historically male public space of meetings, demonstrations, and organizations. "I think," she wrote, "I experienced my relationship with politics as the transgression of a taboo." Sharara went on to say that for her, a Lebanese woman, even ten years after enfranchisement, when veils were no longer the norm and education was available, "the world of politics had the taste of forbidden fruit" (1983: 19–20). The participation of women in political activities has necessarily contended with the socially conditioned reluctance of male comrades to admit wives, sisters, even mothers, into the ranks of the resistance organizations, just

as that participation has been condemned, and at times persecuted, by the conservative or authoritarian governments whose repressive rule is challenged by the popular opposition movements. The apparent intersection of interests around gender roles on the part of governments and their opponents in maintaining the barriers, both formal and informal, to women's participation in the political struggle is itself challenged by the demands of women for access to the public modalities of confrontation and processual change. The particular strategies of resistance available to women, their need to circumlocute the cultural traditions and social mores that prescribe their positioning in the inherited arrangement of public and private space, are in turn forcing a radical rethinking of the mobilizational tactics and structures of contestation that historically have been articulated on masculinist grounds by protest movements and resistance organizations. The "structural constraints" of what has often been referred to as the "double colonization" of many Third World women,[1] colonized by a traditional patriarchy as well as by metropolitan imperialist interests, are being reconstituted, in Cornel West's formulation (1988), as "conjunctural opportunities" (24) as women coerce the multiple limitations of their traditionally ascribed domestic roles to raise their voices and assert their own priorities in the public forums of ideological debate and political struggle. For example, the isolation of the woman in the home and her economic marginality have allowed women in Mexican squatter towns to defend their family's land claims and to "fend off police, tax assessors and other state agents" while the male family members were at their daytime jobs (Eckstein 1989, 25).

If the "efforts of the politically and economically weak to resist conditions they consider unjust" are of necessity realized in large part "through noninstitutionalized channels" (Eckstein 1989, 9), then the specific challenge of women among these resisters not only is noninstitutional but defies traditional patterns of culture and behavior as well. The account of Bhuvaneswari Bhaduri with which Gayatri Spivak (1988) concludes her inquiry into the question "Can the subaltern speak?" exemplifies starkly the female revolutionary's refusal to reproduce culturally sanctioned practices and her radical transformation of those same practices into a taboo-breaking critique of traditions that have long served to subordinate women's lives to the life histories of men.

A young woman of sixteen or seventeen, Bhuvaneswari Bhaduri, hanged herself in her father's modest apartment in North Calcutta in 1926. The suicide was a puzzle since, as Bhuvaneswari was menstruating at the time, it was clearly not a case of illicit pregnancy. Nearly a decade later, it was discovered that she was a member of one of the many groups involved in the armed struggle for Indian independence. She had finally been entrusted with a political assassination. Unable to confront the task and yet aware of the practical need for trust, she killed herself. (307)

As Spivak makes clear, Bhuvaneswari Bhaduri's suicide is an "unemphatic, ad hoc subaltern rewriting of the social text of sati-suicide as much as the hegemonic account of the blazing, fighting, familial Durga" (308). Bhaduri's death both appropriates the social prescriptions of a wife's suicide on the death of her husband and publicly transgresses the traditional ordinances of private bodily cleanliness that have circumscribed the female identity. The story of the suicide, however, even as it challenges a given social text, leaves intact that other narrative of political opposition in which the female revolutionary Bhaduri has failed to carry out the political assassination "finally" assigned to her by the resistance movement. Does her death, then, in addition to its challenge to traditional authority, represent as well a double failure on the part of the revolutionary organization: "Unable to confront the task and yet aware of the practical need for trust, she killed herself." The politician targeted for assassination remains alive and the woman charged with carrying out his death has herself been sacrificed. What remains unexplained still is what may have impeded Bhaduri in her mission: her own "weakness," material circumstances, a breakdown in the organization's political coordination? Who failed whom? And what, further, is the character of the trust so needed that the woman must die at her own hands in order to preserve it? How has the construction of trust been gendered? How, that is, must Bhaduri, in her particular function as a female member of the resistance, be obliged to prove herself and maintain the confidence of her male comrades?

Some four decades later, in the Naxalite peasant rebellion in northern West Bengal, Mahasweta Devi's story "Draupadi" (1987) was construed. According to the story, Draupadi Mejhen, a tribal woman whose husband is deceased, has become an underground partisan in the resistance. In the introduction to her translation of Devi's story (which could be read almost as a sequel to the biography of Bhaduri), Gayatri Spivak emphasizes the coalition of peasant and intellectual that distinguished the rebellion. Problematizing the geopolitical ramifications of such a coalition, Spivak goes on to read the character of Senanayak, the army officer responsible for the capture and torture of Draupadi, as figuring both the "pluralist aesthete" and an "approximation to the First World scholar in search of the Third World" (179).

Pursued by Senanayak's army functionaries in the hope that her capture will yield the information he wants about her companions, Draupadi reflects on her imminent arrest and, like Marie Rose, is concerned about whether she will be able to withstand the brutality of interrogation and protect her comrades by withholding the coveted information. "Dopdi knows, has learned by hearing so often and so long, how one can come to terms with torture. If mind and body give way under torture she will bite off her tongue. That boy did it. They countered him. When they counter you, your hands are tied behind you. All your bones are crushed, your sex is a terrible wound. *Killed by police in an encounter . . . unknown male . . . age twenty-two*" (192). In anticipation of torture, countering, Draupadi invokes the exemplary conduct of a young male comrade, "that boy," and his self-mutilating defiance of his torturers, biting off his own tongue. When Draupadi's own turn at the hands of Senanayak's men does come, however, her confrontational response will be altogether different. The masculine example in which the young man silences himself is exchanged for a challenge that only Draupadi, the female revolutionary, has at her disposal. Raped and mutilated, she is summoned to appear before her captor, but the prisoner defiantly refuses to attire herself in her piece of cloth for the presentation and instead confronts the man, his military authority and his manhood, with her uncovered brutalized and battered body.

Draupadi wipes the blood on her palm and says in a voice that is as terrifying, sky splitting, and sharp as her ululation. What's the use of clothes? You can strip me, but how can you clothe me again? Are you a man?

She looks around and chooses the front of Senanayak's white bush shirt to spit a bloody gob at and says, There isn't a man here that I should be ashamed. I will not let you put my cloth on me. What more can you do? Come on, *counter* me— come on, *counter* me—?

Draupadi pushes Senanayak with her two mangled breasts, and for the first time Senanayak is afraid to stand before an unarmed *target*, terribly afraid. (196)

Here the story ends, and the consequences of Draupadi's defiance remain unnarrated. Nonetheless it is Draupadi's captors, the male, the army, and the state, who are here silenced and rendered impotent, as the woman's different repertoire of protest is deployed. Taking even further Bhaduri's resistance tactics, Draupadi must challenge too the masculine cultural hegemony in her own militant movement, its own shame at her violation, no less than the state's political domination. Draupadi's resistance allows thus for the beginnings of a theorization of the place of women in the revolution.

While the political resistance of women is intolerable to the state and its representatives in the repressive apparatuses of control, that same resistance can become exemplary, constitutive even, for male comrades in revising the social agenda of the struggle. Women political detainees especially, held behind bars with or without trial, captured like Draupadi by the Indian army or kidnapped like Marie Rose by a Christian Phalange militia during the Lebanese civil war, represent by their very presence in the prison—and more importantly still by their studied defiance of the system that has incarcerated them—an unparalleled position from which to articulate alternative forms of collective resistance. These forms necessarily rework the received gender roles of traditional and patriarchal authority. Women prisoners, together with the female relatives of male detainees, in turn figure critically in the construction and reconstruction by male comrades in detention of the experience of political prison and its place in the resistance narrative.

36

A crucial point, central to his personal narrative and decisive for the subsequent historical development of Fadl Yunis's Palestinian prison memoir, *Cell Number 7* (1983), is that moment when he is obliged, as part of his own interrogation ordeal, to witness the torture of a woman political detainee. Yunis has been transferred to Gaza Central prison from Asqalan prison, where he had reputedly been one of the organizers of a hunger strike by the Palestinian political prisoners. The transfer was intended by the Israeli prison authorities to defuse the strike by decapitating its leadership, and Yunis's memoir tells the story of the failed efforts of himself and his fellow prisoners from Asqalan to organize the detainees in Gaza Central prison.

The encounter with the woman prisoner comes precisely midway through his narrative, as part of a series of incidents in which the prisoner is removed at night from his cell, to be variously and on different occasions questioned, beaten, or simply left waiting, at times even made the object of "seduction" attempts by one of the Israeli women guards. Then he meets the Palestinian woman. "This was the first time in my life," Yunis writes, "that I ever saw a Palestinian woman commando. And where?! In prison. . . . Being interrogated." Yunis is kept at a distance from the scene, barely able to see and quite unable to hear the drama taking place. When the brutality that he had been witnessing has subsided for a moment, "it seemed like an ordinary discussion, an exchange of opinions, but then the features of the interrogator hardened, and he began to speak irritably, but the woman shook her head resolutely." Yunis can only imagine what might be about to happen. "What would he do with her? Electricity? Lashes? Hanging by the hands? A Coca-Cola bottle?" When they brought him before her, the woman was naked. "Tears came to my eyes," he writes, "but she said, addressing me in a collected voice: 'Don't worry, brother. It doesn't matter that you see me naked. After all, you're my brother . . . and I'm your sister'" (76–77).

The role of the woman in the Palestinian resistance, its literature and cultural iconography, has long been limited by social tradition and aesthetic convention to that of mother, sister, wife, symbol of the raped land, the wounded honor of Palestine which must be restored. As one Palestinian proverb formulates it, "Mothers build homes and sons build countries." The torture scene with the woman commando in Gaza Central prison is thus critical to Fadl Yunis and what will be his reexamination of the larger sociopolitical dimensions of the resistance struggle. A new meaning is given by the woman in the encounter—arranged for other purposes by the prison officials—to the word "sister," a meaning that no longer insists on masculine authority and the patriarchal family, but both contests the authority that would belong to commando and interrogator 37 alike as males, and realigns the partisans in the resistance according to another vision of solidarity and affiliative commitment.

The idea of political activism for women as the "transgression of a taboo," as "forbidden fruit," as Yolla Pollity Sharara described her own initial entrance into public events, reproduces, according to gender, the propagation of the hierarchical order of knowledge and access to power that has characterized the unequal relations, both economic and cultural, between the First and the Third worlds. Whether renarrated as "civilizing mission" or admitted as abusive exploitation of land, people, and natural resources, the practices of territorial colonialism in the nineteenth and early twentieth centuries, and their later variations in the postindependence period and in neocolonial contexts, have underwritten longstanding cultural paradigms of the colonized as either prelapsarian innocents or unschooled ignorants, the most "deserving" among whom still await tutoring by their more politically advanced, "developed" colonizers.

The struggle for national liberation, for political self-determination, on the part of Third World peoples is thus often construed by their metropolitan patrons as, at best, the "transgression of a taboo" and the entry into the international political arena as a kind of "fall," or else as, less beneficently, an unfortunate indication that political power has been acquired prematurely by persons whose education in the European Enlightenment values of reason and restraint has yet to be sufficiently developed to guarantee a judicious political practice. Margery Perham, for example, worried that J. M. Kariuki might well become the unwitting victim of his own all too rapid political advances. Perham, a liberal British sympathizer with Kenyan demands for independence throughout the 1950s, wrote the Foreword to Kariuki's prison memoir, "Mau Mau" Detainee (1963). Kariuki, as he recounts it, was "a Kikuyu who was detained in fourteen of Kenya's detention camps between 1953 and 1960" (1). His first-hand account of those camps, published in London and Nairobi in the same year that Kenya won national independence, raised difficult questions for its British audience, which had, for the full decade of the struggle of the Kenya Land and Freedom party (otherwise known as "Mau Mau"), refused to acknowledge the excesses and atrocities committed in Kenya by British settler and military colonialism. Perham, in introducing Kariuki's account, expresses her admiration for the former detainee but modifies that admiration with her concern for the consequences of the political experience that the man has acquired:

> But the time comes when the Africans lose their innocence: with western education and contact with the world they escape the simpler imperatives of tribal life and eat of the knowledge of political good and evil. In this story we can almost watch the young Kariuki partaking of this dangerous knowledge. (xviii)

38

Eric Rouleau, a Middle East correspondent for *Le Monde*, a decade and a half later expressed similar reservations about the political maturity and objectivity of his interlocutor in the Palestinian memoir *My Home, My Land* (Abou Iyad 1981). Abou Iyad, the nom de guerre of Salah Khalaf,[2] who was in the late 1950s one of the principal founders, together with Yasser Arafat, Faruq Qaddumi, and Khalil al-Wazir, of Fatah and chief of the Palestine Liberation Organization Special Services, agreed to work with Rouleau in the writing of his own life history and, by implication, that of the Palestinian resistance. In the Preface to the resulting text, the French journalist described his initial misgivings about the collaborative project:

> precisely because of [his] prominence, I was reluctant to take on the task of writing this book with Abou Iyad. I was afraid he would sidestep questions. I wondered if it would even be possible for him to go beyond the natural restrictions imposed on him by his responsibilities. It seemed unlikely that he would be ready to speak with the necessary frankness: It would be all too easy to end up with a political pamphlet or, at best, a hagiography, instead of the desired historical work. (vii)

The critical difference, suggested by Rouleau, between a "political pamphlet" and a "historical work" is a paradigmatic distinction of genre written into the hegemonic narrative of development and underdevelopment, a narrative that represents Third World political struggle against First World domination as in some way intellectually and systemically regressive, evidence of a not-yet-having-come-of-age on the part of the resistance organizations and their partisans. Only, it would seem, when the political pamphlet has been recuperated and contextualized within a Western historiography and literary history can it be elevated from its ephemerality to the status of a "work."

That same paradigm, then, which articulates as historically necessary the unequal relation of dependency between metropolis and periphery, can be reiterated within the programs of the resistance organizations in the description (internalized as it has been by Sharara) of women's participation in the public arenas of political struggle as the "transgression of a taboo," the partaking of the delights of a "forbidden fruit." This quasi-biblical explanation of women's political consciousness, their insurgency (ultimately refuted nonetheless by Sharara in her larger accounting of Lebanese women's public activism), denies that consciousness its historicity and its agency. Like the "prose of counter-insurgency" described by Ranajit Guha (1988) in reference to British imperialist accounts of peasant resistance in colonial India, "it distributes the paradigmatic relata along an axis of historical continuity between a 'before' and an 'after,' fore-lengthening it with a context and extending it into a perspective. The representation of insurgency ends up by having its moment intercalated between its past and future so that the particular values of one and the other are rubbed into the event to give it the meaning specific to it" (66).

The historical questions, then, of uneven development and unsynchronic chronologies that are raised in terms of global capitalism by the dependent relations of the Third World to the First find a persistent analogy in the positioning of women within the sociopolitical programs of many resistance organizations. The counternarratives, however, generated by the emergent participation of women within these organizations as well as in extraorganizational domains and spheres of activity are challenging the ascendancy of these paradigms, both economic and gendered, of dependency. Their defining impact can be traced in the often tense but reciprocal counterpoint of men's and women's accounts of opposition and struggle against local dictatorial regimes and on the staging grounds of national liberation. In Che Guevara's manual (1961) of guerrilla warfare, for example, which drew in particular on the experience of organized armed struggle with Fidel Castro in Cuba, leading to liberation of that country in 1959, a particular role is assigned to women in the necessary gathering of information about the enemy. Information, according to Che, is crucial to the successful functioning of the guerrilla movement: "Nothing gives more help to combatant forces than correct information" (147). And while much of this information can come spontaneously from sympathetic local inhabitants, its gathering, Che insists, must be "completely systemized." To this end Che enlists the female membership of the movement: "An intelligence service also should be in direct contact with enemy fronts. Men and women, especially women, should infiltrate; they should be in permanent contact with soldiers and gradually discover what there is to be discovered. The system must be coordinated in such a way that crossing the enemy lines into the guerrilla camp be carried out without mishap" (147). The special perils to which women might be subjected through these reconnaissance missions and their insinuation into compromising situations with enemy soldiers in order to elicit information are, of course, manifold. Senanayak's "countering" of Draupadi in order to extract information to be used against her comrades and Bhuvaneswari Bhaduri's suicide are only two examples of the physical consequences women are exposed to as a result of even the subsidiary functions designated for them by the guerrilla organization. Che's emphatic choice of women, "especially women," to assist in intelligence operations at once exploits the traditional construction of the "seductive woman" and at the same time leaves her open, her mission accomplished—or failed—to the revenge or the rejection of a tradition-bound society that prizes the un-

40 stained honor of its women.

Che's manual of guerrilla warfare, with its brief instructions for women cadres, was largely compiled in 1960. In 1979, at the International Conference on Exile and Solidarity in Latin America held in Venezuela, Gladys Diaz, a Chilean woman and a member of Chile's Central Committee of the Movement of the Revolutionary Left (MIR) who now lives in exile, proposed that the position elaborated by Che stood in need of revision: "Today no one would dream of saying that the tasks of liaison should be done only by women" (Diaz 1983, 33). Earlier, the sexism characteristic of the military had permitted women a certain easy mobility that facilitated their intelligence-gathering and liaison tasks. With time, however, and the eventual inevitable capture, detention, and disappearance of significant numbers of these women, the declared gender specificity of liaison work urgently needed rethinking. Diaz, in the meantime, prefaced her remarks at the international conference by situating them firmly within a framework of political solidarity between women and men in the resistance: "We see the women's struggle, our struggle, in the context of the class struggle and, therefore, we consider the struggle of our people to be a priority; that is why we conceive of exploited men and women as a group, as one single class" (30).

The growth and consolidation of women's participation in the struggle is mapped by Diaz in three major stages, each with its own material specificity and each constituting particular ideological rechartings of the sociopolitical positioning of women in the organizational structure.

Today, thinking Chilean women, committed to their class, are present on three battle fronts which the Resistance has set: underground, prison and exile. On all these fronts women are writing an important page, seeking to win a protagonist's role, to be a part of the fighting army which will one day free our people. With the firmness of a conscientious artisan, with a deep sense of responsibility, of discipline, of creativity, the women in this struggle have been learning and teaching their *compañeros* and organizations that they are capable of doing all types of jobs, that they ask for an opportunity to demonstrate this, that they hope for understanding so as not to be denied the right to be party members or active members of the Resistance, without abandoning their integral development as women, in relation to their mates, their families, their children. (Diaz 1983, 33)

Underground, according to Diaz, women not only did liaison work, but formed revolutionary committees, worked in factories, and founded a clandestine newspaper. The *compañeras'* work soon succeeded not only in earning them new stature within the movement but in attracting the less-than-solicitous attention of the military. In prison, in Tres Alamos, for example, where Diaz was detained, these women were subjected to interrogation and tortures no less brutal than those faced by male prisoners. But the military and the torturers also devised psychological and physical stratagems designed to manipulate the particular vulnerabilities of women: threats against their children, sexual abuse, rape, and bodily mutilation. In addition, some women "were forced to confront their bleeding, dying *compañeros;* the torturers hoped that this would demoralize the men, that the women would beg their men to confess. Thus they were forced to weight their love for their *compañeros* against their love for the people and the cause of freedom." What Diaz insists on, however, in her account of Chilean women's experiences of prison, is "the sense of pride [that] came from having been able to reject our traditional role at a critical moment" (35).

Diaz goes on to describe the emergence of a women's community within the prison, enabled by, yet defiant of, those same adverse conditions of detention formulated and implemented precisely to undermine bonds of political solidarity and interpersonal commitments. In the absence of their male *compañeros*, the women prisoners creatively combined their resources, each contributing her own skill or particular ability. According to Diaz, "we converted the prison into a school for well-trained cadres" (35–36). There were wall newspapers, poems, and theatrical works. Children born in prison were collectively provided for. These children, "Miguelito, along with Amanda, Alejandrito, and so many others, lived a new conception of the family" (36). This new conception of the family, elaborated by the women in the prison setting and conditioned by prison's political exigencies, and thus too by the altered ideal of the traditionally valorized women's role in a domestic space, posed new and still unresolved problems for male-female relationships, both during detention and more acutely after the women were released and, most often, sent into exile. At that point,

the debate, which often became collective, began. In the light of the growth achieved, the whole concept of the couple was reformulated. In exile, the topic has been brought up more energetically, sometimes advancing the discussion, at

41

other times hampering it, and at still others leading to the break-up of the couple, because women and men emerged from a rich but difficult experience and because both had grown, but not always in parallel ways. Exile has tended to create an inhospitable framework for discussion. (37)

The liaison work to which female cadres were initially assigned in the early period of the resistance culminated then, in the Chilean case, in constructing the possibilities for new, sometimes unprepared-for, structures of affiliation and relationship based on immanent transformations of gender identification within the larger social order.

42

Both men and women have grown in the resistance organization and in prison, as Gladys Diaz wrote, "but not always in parallel ways." In a 1984 letter written from exile in Holland to her husband, who is about to be released after twelve years of incarceration in a Uruguayan prison, Clara Piriz (1988) describes still a different version of the "unequal development" produced by the radicalizing experience of political detention. The lives of women, both inside and beyond the walls, are being changed by the experience of prison. In this case, it is the man who has been absented from the sociopolitical development of his wife and the responsibilities, both personal and public, that she has had to assume in his place and for herself. Can the changes in the different lives any longer be communicated, especially given that the very channels and modes of communication, which have so long been distorted or even closed by prison censorship, are now submitted to the altered circumstances of the woman's life without her husband? "Dear Kiddo," Clara Piriz writes,

I'm writing this letter with no margins, without counting lines, or pages, without measuring my words a damn bit. Our first communication uncensored and uncut.

The big question is if I will manage to write without self-censorship . . . internalized censorship. Fear. My fear of causing you pain, of showing myself as I am, of confusing you in my confusion. . . . My fear of losing what I've gained and gaining what I've lost. (242)

Piriz goes on to narrate the difficulties and cultural pitfalls of political exile, so different, albeit perhaps less extreme, from the brutality of prison. Nor is it clear whether her husband's joining her in Holland upon his release will actually effect a mutual intersection, a reintegration, of their separated lives. The prison experience behind him, the husband will have now to catch up with his wife's development in exile.

Besides, as a couple we're going to face a very strange situation. I have matured in this country, I have carried out a whole process of learning, of critical integration, of getting situated here, which you, one way or another, will have to carry out. This puts you in a position of dependence on me, which does not contribute to a healthy adult emotional relationship. (244)

Clara Piriz goes on further, refusing to promise what may be impossible, unrelenting in her critique of the danger inherent in a perpetuation of models of dependency, even if such a perpetuation does involve a role reversal. She describes the elements, the stages of the development she has undergone, a classic one for many women in both First and Third worlds, but dramatic nonetheless for the urgent questions it poses for the very real and material consequences of political commitment and organization. She has raised their daughters alone, has struggled with government repression in her own country and a strange and alien culture in exile. She no longer likes "to be ordered around, or told what to do" (245). And her husband's dreams of domestic serenity, nurtured in prison and solitary confinement, are no longer dreams she cares to help realize. Piriz will partake of homemade ravioli and wine with her husband, but she will not prepare them for him. And, in answer to his question, she writes that she has a male companion. "Why do I want to see you?" she concludes. "Because I do. . . . Because I want a second chance. Because only you and I can decide if it'll work or not. That decision is not for time, or distance, much less for the military to take. It's ours. . . . We'll have to see if my way and yours will meet—and grow" (246). Exile, however, as Gladys Diaz's experience taught her, "has tended to create an inhospitable framework for discussion."

    The critical and historical discussion over women's participation in organized resistance movements and in public activity, as well as the status of that participation and the degree to which the organization must evolve and restructure itself around the issues generated by gender, is being waged in the writings of the women themselves, in interviews, *testimonios,* and the manifestos drafted by the women's committees. This public female voice, raised as it has been in conflicted international forums—such as the three meetings held in Mexico City, Copenhagen, and Nairobi to commemorate the beginning (1975), the middle (1980), and the end (1985) of the United Nations Decade of Women—as well as inside prison cells and among party cadres, constitutes new structures of collective opposition to state repression and traditional restrictions alike. At the same time, however, this challenge elicits opposition of a different sort from the self-appointed guardians of the value system that it threatens to displace and dismantle.

    That the confrontation should now be located significantly around the instantiation of women as a critical part of the national liberation struggle is, of course, not without historical precedent in metropolitan settings. As Peter Stallybrass (1989) has pointed out in his study of European iconography, the "woman with her mouth open" has long imaged for the hegemonic state the very essence of social and political transgression: "In

Delacroix's painting [of Liberty leading the people at the barricades], as so often in enclosure riots in early modern England, the tearing down of boundaries, the overthrow of political and legal enclosure, is figured by the transformation of the female body from private and passive enclosure to public and active transgressor.

The typing has been persistent even pervasive. In 1979, just two years before Zimbabwe's independence, Jane Ngwenya of Zimbabwe African People's Union (ZAPU) was asked in an interview by the *Anti-Apartheid News*, "What particular problems do women in Zimbabwe face in getting involved in the liberation struggle and in political activity?" She replied, "Traditionally a woman cannot be involved in things that are done by men" (1983, 78). Conditions evolved in the process of Zimbabwe's independence struggle, and even those women who had joined the tradition-bound males in censuring women political activists for the "abnormal" behavior were enlisted in the resistance by events themselves:

> No, things have changed radically indeed. More women are arrested than men, not because men are not there, but because they are more vulnerable to shooting. Before martial law, before the war came to what it is today, women became more active because many men were arrested and no man could speak openly, because he would just be arrested and tortured. So they became a bit afraid and those who spoke out tended to be women. (80–81)

It is difficult, even controversial, for historiographers, analysts of popular revolt, and the opposition leadership itself to determine the precise moment of the outbreak of a given rebellion, as well as the triggering events. So too the emergence of women into radicalized political consciousness, public activism, and organized resistance struggle is embedded in manifold historical circumstances and material conditions, informed by the individual women's life histories as well as the geopolitical context within which they contest exploitative power and authority. In *The Wretched of the Earth*, (1982) Frantz Fanon described the moment in which anticolonial armed struggle could and did break out: "it is in these circumstances that the guns go off by themselves, for nerves are jangled, fear reigns and everyone is trigger-happy. A single commonplace incident is enough to start the machine-gunning" (56). Women partisans provide different and various explanations for their politicization. Whereas Marie Rose Boulos in 1975 was reluctant to join any of the Lebanese underground organizations for "fear of torture," it was her activism on behalf of women, trade unions, and Palestinian refugees that led to her execution by Christian militias. Rose and Nyasha, two young Zimbabwean women, participated in the war for independence. Rose remained in Zimbabwe itself, as a *chimbwido*, or female supporter of the freedom fighters. As she said in an interview, "I tried my level best to get to Mozambique but I couldn't find anyone to give me advice about how to get there. I was still young, I didn't know anything" (Nyasha and Rose 1983, 106). Nyasha, by contrast, at seventeen joined the armed struggle in Mozambique, crossing the border when she realized that only the organized resistance and national liberation would alter the conditions of blacks in white Rhodesia: "It was easy for white girls to go for nursing or even for a degree. Then I heard it said that if the armed struggle was successful we would have the same education as the whites. So I really couldn't wait for a moment to complete that Form IV and join the armed struggle" (99). **45**

Whereas women's narrations of their politicization emphasize the need to transform tyrannical and exploitative constructions of gender certainly, but also of race and class, just as often, and contrary to the popular representations of women's romances with guerrilla fighters, the "little drummer girl syndrome," it is the very values of *machismo* and the self-styled commando that underwrite the conscription of young men into the resistance organization. Omar Cabezas, for example, a former Sandinista National Liberation Front (FSLN) combatant and subsequently head of the Nicaraguan Ministry of the Interior's Political Section, described his own enlistment in his autobiography *Fire from the Mountain* (1985). Approached by a friend in 1968 and asked to join the resistance, the student Omar felt considerable ambivalence.

But you'd better believe I was perfectly composed in front of Juan Jose. I couldn't let him think I was a coward. Still, though I thought of all those things, I also thought of my barrio. Remember, I didn't have any firm political convictions. I wasn't a theoretician, not even a theoretician! Worse, I had serious doubts about whether Marxism was a good thing or a bad thing. Finally, more out of confidence in Juan Jose than out of any personal conviction, "Sure, hombre," I said, "certainly." It was more or less a question of manhood. What I mean is, I knew what I wanted. I wanted to fight the dictatorship. But I wasn't very sure, and not only that, I had a sort of fear or doubt, or who knows what I felt, about seeing that commitment through to its final consequences. (10)

Che Guevara himself, in his *Reminiscences of the Cuban Revolution* (1968), articulated a similar infatuation, despite certain political reservations, with the romance of armed struggle that first led him to join Fidel Castro in Mexico in the guerrilla movement to liberate Cuba: "My almost immediate impression, on hearing the first lessons [in military tactics], was of the possibility for victory, which I had seen as very doubtful when I joined the rebel commander. I had been linked to him, from the outset, by a tie of romantic adventurous sympathy, and by the conviction that it would be worth dying on a foreign beach for such a pure ideal" (38). Political prison, then, as part of the narrative of resistance becomes a site in which these gendered values, the cultural traditions of patriarchy and women's passivity, her honor as national symbol belonging to her male guardians, hierarchical structures of domination and the exploitation of categories of race and class, all are submitted to the systemic brutality of torture and interrogation—and transformed.

46

Political prison is critical to the life histories and personal itineraries of partisans in organized resistance movements. The prison experience, as necessitated by circumstance, figures in crucially structural ways in the written autobiographical or testimonial narrations of those lives. The determining impact of detention on the political vision of the detainee is integrated into the plotted construction of the guerrilla's textual account of her/his struggle. In many prison memoirs, the prison space itself provides not only setting and plot but also a cast of characters, protagonists and antagonists, aligned according to their position within the relations of power defined by the penal institution: political detainees, criminals, collaborators, torturers and interrogators, wardens, guards, and prison administrators. In other narratives, prison might provide the frame story within which a larger history, of the prisoner and the resistance movement, is told. In still other constructions, prison articulates a critical and decisive juncture, a turning point within the larger narrative, that forces a reworking of previous sociocultural paradigms and conduces to new coalitional possibilities.

Each of these narrative formats, with its particular positioning of prison and determination of the significance of prison, partakes to some degree in certain features of the *testimonio*, a genre that developed out of the recent history of Latin American military dictatorships.[3] The *testimonio* stands at once as a personal statement of struggle, a political indictment of oppression and exploitation, and a documentary of systemic abuses of human rights. A decisively twentieth-century genre, the *testimonio* nonetheless contradicts another focus peculiar to twentieth-century literary developments from modernism to postmodernism in the Western academy, and that is the self-absorbed, self-reflective obsession with the "undecidability," the unreliability, of language. According to Doris Sommer (1989), *testimonios* "never put the referentiality of language in question. . . . In testimonials, too much hangs on the reality to which words refer for meaning to be indefinitely delayed. Inadequacy of words to their referents reflects on an imperfect and necessarily evolving language rather than on some notion of necessarily unstable or unreachable referents" (119–20).

A major difficulty posed by J. M. Kariuki's *"Mau Mau" Detainee* (1963) for its English readers was precisely the referentiality of its language, the relentlessness of its personal account and first-hand documentation of the widespread existence of prison camps and their horrific conditions, a system maintained by the British army for the Kenyan people who opposed British occupation. That referentiality needed to be confronted, however, as Margery Perham wrote in her Foreword to the book: "For us British, whether in Britain or in Kenya, who were shocked by the character of the Mau Mau outbreak, to know all may not be to forgive all but it is still important to *know*, and few who read this book are likely to close it with quite the same views of Mau Mau, or, perhaps, of Africa in general, as those with which they opened it" (xi). For Kariuki, however, his story was   **47** "written not in any spirit of bitterness or spite but because [prison experiences] have become an important part of the history of my country" (1). That history, the history of the Kenya Land and Freedom Army's struggle for independence, has been largely suppressed. Secrecy has been maintained by the British government, which in 1955 confiscated the KLFA's underground archive, and by the successive neocolonial Kenyan governments of Jomo Kenyatta and Daniel arap Moi, which have supported the British decision not to release the documents until the year 2013. Suppression has been continued by the Kenyan government's detention of popular (as opposed to official) historians of Mau Mau, such as Maina wa Kinyatti. Kariuki himself was assassinated in 1975.

"Mau Mau" Detainee assigns to women an incidental but critical place in prison and in the narrative itself. In various of the camps in which Kariuki was held, detainees' committees were formed in order to maintain, to the extent possible, conditions of sanitation and hygiene and the orderly distribution of food, and to settle disputes that might arise among prisoners. In the Camp of the Three Dry Hills, the committee was obliged to take on another responsibility, the protection of Wanjiku, the only female detainee in the camp:

She was in a difficult position, especially as many of those desiring her falsely promised they would marry her when released. The committee were remarkably successful in protecting her although a man called Thuo who went too far had to pay a ram. We arranged ourselves to partition off a separate place for her in the biggest tent so that she should not have to sleep in the same place as the men (47).

When other women prisoners later joined Wanjiku in the camp, the task, according to Kariuki, became more difficult as many of the male detainees were devising clever stratagems to avoid the committee's regulations and to arrange "nocturnal assignments in the bathroom" (53). Eventually a deputation from the prisoners committee had to intervene with the camp's commandant to construct separate quarters for the women until they were all finally transferred to Kamiti Prison outside Nairobi.

This organizational need, expressed by Kariuki, to protect women in the detention camps from the predations of the male prisoners, is instructive for Kariuki himself. His own prison experience is framed by his family relationships, first with his mother, and then, on release, with his new wife. When he was a child at school, Kariuki relates in the opening pages of his memoir, his mother served two years in prison on drug charges, drugs that she had been making and selling to pay for her son's education. The mother's "crime," the result of poverty and denial under British colonialism, is transformed, by her son's own participation in the independence struggle, into a political charge, a critique of the system that had criminalized his mother. Kariuki's mother, separated from her son for seven years, died just prior to his release. Instead of celebrating a family reunion, the freed prisoner was to strive to organize forms of collective action other than those provided exclusively by family, such as a letter-writing campaign to protest forced "communal labor" and the formation of a political party.

Kariuki was arrested a second time for these activities. Released again, he was dining with his family when his aunt, he explains, "reminded me that it was time I married. For several months my political activities prevented any serious consideration of this problem but I had to admit that she was right. I was 31 and all my sisters were now married" (172). *"Mau Mau" Detainee* thus can be read not only as a narration of the Kenyan struggle against British colonialism, or as the memoir of a Kenyan prisoner in British prison camps, but just as well as a contributing history of evolving male-female relationships as these are affected by political struggle.

The incidental but constitutive position of women in Kariuki's prison memoir and that text's representation of the Kenyan liberation struggle from 1952 and the British declaration of the State of Emergency to independence in 1963 are more fully developed in Muthoni Likimani's collection of narratives entitled *Passbook Number F.47927* (1985). The passbook was an identification document that Likimani, like all members of the Kikuyu, Embu, and Maru tribes, was required by the British to carry in order to move about her country, and especially the capital city. The particular difficulty for women, who needed either an employer's letter or a husband's signature to obtain such a document, created the phenomenon of "passbook wives" described in several of the stories. Women who were unemployed and unmarried, and thus denied even the minimal privileges attached to the passbook, would often arrange for men living in Nairobi to endorse their applications. The story "Komerere—Lie Low" relates the enforced dependency of women legislated by this system: Nyakio, "as tough as she was, as strong-minded as she was, this was emergency time and she had to lie down, and become one of the famous passbook wives" (112).

Not a continuous, uninterrupted narrative, recounting a single individual's life history, *Passbook Number F.47927* is instead a collective work composed of nine stories. These stories all tell of women who, from their different, admittedly socially restricted situations, contributed in critical ways to the freedom fight: for example, women who concealed the forest fighters in their homes even at the risk of collective punishment for their entire villages; women who, as nurses and health workers, crossed class and tribal barriers and kept political detainees under their supervision in touch with the outside; and women who urged their sons to take the Mau Mau oath. Other women struggled against forced communal labor or fled the work site to seek their husbands in Nairobi. Their journey, traversing the land, became a kind of radicalizing rite of passage, a miniature of the long trajectory of women from domestic servitude to active political consciousness.

In the story entitled "Forced Communal labor," Wambui sees her son Kaman arrested when he joins a protest against the market-day roundup of townspeople in order to make up an audience for the district officer's public address. At that point, helpless to rescue her son, "[p]oor Wambui wished that she was a forest fighter. This would satisfy her, even if she got killed, at least she would not die like a sheep, not like a woman, but like a man fighting for the land" (69). Wambui follows her son to the detention center, where she bangs on his cell door, screaming louder and louder, "Lock me in! What is there left for me? Lock me in now!" (70). Her son Kaman begins pounding on the door in return, and the unwonted vociferous communication of mother and son across the "prison walls" soon attracts the attention of the guards, who attempt by use of force to stop the mother's appeals. Wambui, who had earlier regretted that she was not a forest fighter, now, like Draupadi in Mahasweta Devi's story, resorts to her own women's arsenal of protest:

One homeguard slapped her face again and the chief ordered another slap. Flushed with pain and anger, Wambui slipped off her top *shuka* and threw it on the ground. But by the time she was untying her skirt, all the *askaris* had run away. They disappeared, for an old woman stripping herself naked is the nastiest abuse one can expect from a Kikuyu woman. It is the worst curse one can expect. (71)

Women's resistance in Kenya has a long history. Among its most prominent and much-sung representatives must be counted Me Kitilili, who in 1913 led the Giriama people against the British occupation of Kenya, and Mary Nyanjiru Muthoni, leader of a group of workers massacred in 1922 by the British army while demonstrating against the arrest of Harry Thuku. The history of political detention in Kenya is equally long and has continued just as egregiously under the neocolonial governments of Kenyatta and Moi. Indeed, according to *Struggle for Democracy in Kenya* (1988), a document compiled and distributed by the London-based United Movement for Democracy in Kenya (UMOJA), what distinguishes Kenya from other neocolonies is the "sheer unbroken continuity between the form of the colony of yesterday, and the neo-colony of today" (3).[4]

In 1977 the distinguished novelist, critic, and university professor Ngugi wa Thiong'o was detained without charge and held for a year, although it was widely believed that his work with the popular village-based Kamiriithu Community Education and Cultural Centre was decisive in his arrest. The diary of Ngugi's detention, *Detained* (1981), tells the combined stories of his imprisonment in Kamiti Maximum Security Prison, of the colonial and anticolonial history of Kenya, of the village theater project, and of the writing of his Gikuyu novel *Devil on the Cross* (1982). Like Kariuki's memoir, however, *Detained* narrates as well the understated but dramatic alterations in the prisoner's relationship with his wife. Even to be allowed a visit from Nyambura, Ngugi refuses to accept the requisite shackles (112). The couple's visit is thus long delayed, but the state's attempt to manipulate family traditions in order to subvert the political struggle is also thwarted. In the meantime, though, Nyambura herself has devised alternative means of communication and ascertaining the well-being of her husband. Ngugi tells of his emergent understanding of his wife's political strategy:

> And now I am studying a few lawyer's words asking me to sign a few cheques to enable Nyambura to withdraw money for my children's school fees. When I am released I will learn that the cheque book sent for by Njugi at the request of Nyambura was their first assurance that I had not been sent to Ngong Hills.
>
> Then I did not know. But at the very time I was studying Njugi's and Nyambura's signatures to convince myself of their authenticity, they were studying my signature at home to convince themselves of its authenticity.
>
> Words? It depends on the reality they reflect. (122–23)

Implicit, but no less important, in the transaction between husband and wife is not only the defeat of the prison administration's effort to sabotage communication both among prisoners and between prisoners and the outside, but also the economic empowerment, even if only temporary, of Ngugi's wife. In this scene the signed checks, an overdetermined symbol of the capitalist system, of exchange value, are revalued and used as weapons in the resistance struggle against both capitalism and patriarchy.

Indeed, as Ngugi recounts in his intellectual autobiography, *Decolonizing the Mind* (1986), it was a peasant woman from Kamiriithu who first involved him in the collective theater project that ultimately lead to his detention.

> Early one morning in 1976, a woman from Kamiriithu village came to my house and she went straight to the point: "We hear you have a lot of education and that

you write books. Why don't you and others of your kind give some of that education to the village? We don't want the whole amount; just a little of it, and a little of your time." There was a youth centre in the village, she went on, and it was falling apart. It needed group effort to bring it back to life. Would I be willing to help? I said I would think about it. In those days, I was the chairman of the Literature Department at the University of Nairobi . . . Sunday was the best day to catch me at home. She came the second, the third and the fourth consecutive Sundays with the same request couched in virtually the same words. That was how I came to join others in what later was to be called Kamiriithu Community Education and Cultural Centre. (34)   **51**

Ngugi describes this involvement as decisive, as decisive as prison, in his political and intellectual life, as an "epistemological break" with his past (44) and an experience of "continuous learning" (45). That particular learning process, furthermore, transformed for Ngugi the traditional hierarchies of intellectual and peasant, male and female, in his narration.

Ngugi was released from prison in 1978, following Kenyatta's death. The announcement on that occasion by Daniel arap Moi, who succeeded Kenyatta as president, of the release of all political prisoners was quickly followed, however, by the passage of a new act, the Public Security (Detained and Restricted Persons) Regulations, which gave Moi the right to bypass parliament and suspend the constitution at his own discretion. A new reign of terror was unleashed. The Kamiriithu Centre was destroyed in 1982. Massacres and mass detentions, together with unexplained deaths in detention, became commonplace and were documented by international organizations. In the summer of 1985, while the final international conference of the UN Decade of Women was meeting in Nairobi, twelve air force men accused of involvement in a 1982 coup attempt were executed in that same city.

Finally, in 1988, in order to consolidate his one-man rule over Kenya, Moi called for general elections—but abolished the secret ballot and instituted instead a queuing system, whereby voters were counted as they lined up by the picture of their candidate of choice. According to a poll in the *Weekly Review* cited in the UMOJA document, some officials supported this system, claiming that queuing was "more honest, less expensive and it will eliminate election petitions if adopted." Others, however, including women, protested. For Agnes Ndetei, member of Parliament for Kibwezi, the queuing system "would lead to a situation like this year, where some women were forced by their husbands not to vote for me." With a secret ballot, Ndetei said, "The weak, and especially women, can vote freely without the pressure of coercion" (49–50). Popular disenfranchisement through state repression, that is, served again to reinforce the traditional discrimination against women; the sociopolitical advances achieved by women through their participation in the public arena and the resistance organizations, advances that are anathema to the Kenyan state, are in turn dismantled by the self-interests of the unpopular regime.

The placement of women in the narratives of resistance, the significance given to that placement, and the role assigned to women by the authors of the narratives, are critically informed, if not determined, by the strategic position of women within the resistance organization. The written or textual evidence provided by the memoirs and autobiographies, as well as by pamphlets, manifestos, and position papers produced by the organization, thus contributes to the still-incomplete theorization of women and political struggle. For Che Guevara, women were vital to the intelligence gathering of the guerrilla group. In other contexts, for other organizations, women are variously constructed as the background support of family, as idealized wives, mothers, and sisters, who represent actually and symbolically the possession that must be protected and safeguarded, or redeemed through struggle. Or, as lovers, women are often imagined by the male commandos isolated in conditions of extreme physical rigor to solace their loneliness or bolster their self-confidence. The physical and active presence of women in the organization, however, can raise acute political and ideological problems for its very structure and mobilizational tactics, problems that require either containment within the preexisting structures or alteration of those structures to allow the integration of women.

Abou Iyad's autobiography, *My Home, My Land,* (1981), which also narrates the history of the PLO over three decades, from the 1948 establishment of the state of Israel to Anwar Sadat's trip to Jerusalem in November 1977, exemplifies this dilemma. Abou Iyad's historical narrative of Palestinian resistance contains but a single paragraph on the role played by women. This brief paragraph, however, condenses several other plots, the truncated stories, prescient of the *intifada,* of the individual maturation and political development of Palestinian women, from the participation of schoolgirls in violent street demonstrations to the rape of women political prisoners:

Many women joined the Resistance. Their daring and self-sacrifice won the admiration of everyone, even those who generally looked down on them. Schoolgirls were the first to join violent demonstrations, the first to fight back when the police attacked. Many women were charged with delicate missions, such as carrying secret messages and transporting arms. Those who were arrested behaved with a courage which surprised even their jailers. One of them, who gave birth in prison, stoically endured separation from her child. Another, who refused to confess, was raped by her captors in a Gaza prison. Many Palestinian men offered to marry her. This unprecedented occurrence, virtually unheard-of given the prevailing mentality in a conservative society such as ours, was repeated several times in similar cases. One of the side effects of the Resistance was to promote the emancipation of women, and as a corollary, men's liberation from fossilized traditions (60).

The conclusion narrated by Abou Iyad to these multiple plots, the marriage offers made by Palestinian men to dishonored or violated women, betrays on one level the traditional need for a romantic ending according to convention. On another level, however, the paradigmatic ending here is a radical violation of the very traditions that it would seem to uphold: a dishonored woman is the family's shame, and that disgrace must be avenged by the woman's brother in the murder of his sister and her defiler. Abou Iyad thus terminates his synoptic history of women and resistance in a twofold gesture, a move that both challenges received tradition and reconstitutes the raped woman as marriageable. The radical ambivalence of the conclusion is, however, obviated finally by the relegation of "women's emancipation" to the status of a "side effect of the Resistance," and of the attendant liberation of men from "fossilized tradition" to a mere "corollary" of that "side effect" of the national liberation struggle.

53

The politicization of women, summarized and contained in a single, albeit crucial, paragraph in this resistance narrative is amplified in the fictions and novels of Palestinian and Lebanese women writers. These works, whose common plot is the conflicted political development of women, provide alternative explanations and competing conclusions to the contested narrative of women and resistance. Etel Adnan's *Sitt Marie Rose* (1982), Hanan al-Shaykh's *Story of Zahra* (1986), and Hala Deeb Jabbour's *Woman of Nazareth* (1988)[5] all refuse the convention of marriage as a conclusion or resolution to their stories. Rather, marriage itself is shown as a site of intense conflict, whether ethnic, religious, or sexual, and is ultimately rejected by the novels as a solution to their heroines' struggles. For example, Marie Rose's political work led first to the dissolution of her marriage and then, as she was condemned for her transgressions of family, racial, and class taboos, to her execution.

In *The Story of Zahra*, Zahra herself becomes an emblem of the psychological breakdown of a young Arab woman for whom marriage offers only humiliation and self-hatred. Dishonored by an illicit affair in Lebanon, she visits her emigrant uncle in Nigeria, where she marries his best friend, Majed. Her stained secret is exposed but her husband agrees to keep her anyway, even against her own inchoate wishes. Finally Zahra divorces the man and returns to self-imposed withdrawal in her parents' home in a Beirut ravaged now by civil war. Zahra's interest in the war, however, is revived by the presence of a mysterious sniper on the roof of a neighborhood building. Her infatuation with Sami and the regular afternoon clandestine visits to the rooftop leave her pregnant. Sami agrees to marry her but is violently angered when Zahra accuses him of being the sniper, an accusation that he insistently and aggressively denies. At dusk Zahra goes down from the roof in anticipation of Sami's ritual visit along with his family to her family on the following day. For Zahra, "It seems as if the war has suddenly come to a stop with his promise that we will marry. Everything seems normal" (181). In the street, on the way home, however, Zahra collapses and dies in a pool of blood, shot by the unknown sniper.

Hanan al-Shaykh's novel implicitly proposes at once a condemnation of the Arab tradition of patriarchy and a no less powerful indictment of Zahra's own political naivete, which allows her to avoid an ideological analysis of the relation between her personal predicament and the social structures with which she is herself complicit. Her complicity comes by way of a romantic illusionism and a deluded belief in the idolized stereotype of the guerrilla fighter, a stereotype that is perpetuated at times as much by the resistance itself as by the bourgeois culture of fabricated happy endings. Although both novels end with the assassination of their female protagonists, *The Story of Zahra* consigns Zahra's political fate to an unreconstructed despair, whereas *Sitt Marie Rose* charts a trajectory by way of which women's access to the public arena of political activism can transform the structures of sectarianism that have killed the two women.

With the Lebanese civil war also as its central moment, *A Woman of Nazareth* presents a different but complementary perspective on contemporary Arab history. On one level, Jabbour's story of Amal is constructed out of the same conventions of romance and seduction that govern Zahra's story. Amal flees Palestine with her family in 1948, to grow up in the refugee camps of Lebanon. She breaks free, violating tradition to become an airline hostess for Middle East Airlines, where she meets a Saudi prince with whom she falls in love. After marriage and divorce, she joins the Palestinian resistance and in turn falls in love with one of her comrades. In the 1976 siege of the Tell al-Zaatar refugee camp, Amal's entire family is massacred, a massacre that her younger sister Sumaya had cautioned her was imminent. Sumaya had criticized Amal's stubborn refusal to heed her warning: "You people on the outside don't know" (176). The death of Amal's family in Tell al-Zaatar is a crucial moment in the novel in that it raises the many historical contradictions both of Amal's personal choices and of the political trajectories of the Palestinian movement, which must come to terms with a people living and enduring both in exile and under occupation. *A Woman of Nazareth*, which ends with the departure of the PLO and its fighting forces from Beirut in September 1982 following the summer-long Israeli siege of the city, rewrites the paradigmatic conventions of Amal's personal itinerary into the documentary narrative of post-1948 Palestinian history.

Palestinians, according to Fawaz Turki in *Soul in Exile* (1988), have a special relationship to airports: "Where have Palestinians been more wounded at the core than at airports, refused entry, detained, expelled, questioned, humiliated, and so on, because of their travel documents, their national identity, and their revolutionary reputation?" (10) As an airline hostess, then later as a messenger for the PLO, and finally as a refugee again en route to Tunis in 1982, Amal came to know the capital cities and airports of the Arab world and of Europe.

Airports are central, too, to Leila Khaled's Palestinian autobiography, *My People Shall Live* (1973), where they are associated with prisons as well. On 29 August 1969, Leila Khaled hijacked Trans World Airlines flight 840 en route from Rome to Cairo. Together with Salim Issawi, a Palestinian from Haifa, and using the nom de guerre of Shadiah Abu Ghazalah, after a Palestinian woman from Nazareth who died in an explosion in her home while manufacturing hand grenades for the resistance, Leila Khaled diverted the plane from its scheduled route to fly over Palestine and finally to land in Damascus. Issawi and Khaled identified themselves to the plane's passengers as the Che Guevara Commando Group of the Popular Front for the Liberation of Palestine (PFLP) and asked their co-operation. Finally, after the passengers and flight crew were all released unharmed, the plane was blown up and the two Palestinians were taken into custody by the Syrian authorities, who detained them for forty-five days. A year later, following three plastic surgery operations to change her by now well-publicized appearance, Leila Khaled, this time in the company of Patrick Arguello from Nicaragua, hijacked an El Al plane that had taken off from Amsterdam airport. This September 1970 operation, unlike the previous one, ended in tragedy when Israeli security forces on board the plane opened fire on the commandos, killing Arguello and slightly wounding Khaled, who was then held and interrogated in British prisons. She was eventually exchanged for hostages taken in still another coordinated plane hijacking.

Leila Khaled and Dalal Moughrabi, who was killed in a 1978 bus-hijacking operation in Israel, are perhaps the best known of the Palestinian women *fedayin*. Khaled's reputation, as a result of her role in the two hijackings, has acquired the status of legend among Palestinians in and outside the organized resistance movement, living under occupation and in exile. The story of her emergence as a political fighter in the ranks of the PFLP, founded in 1966 and one of the several subgroups that make up the PLO, is told in Khaled's autobiography, written in collaboration with George Hajjar after the two hijacking episodes and after Khaled had

55

gone underground. Leila Khaled's story, sensational as it may seem, resembles that of many Palestinians. Like Abou Iyad's personal memoir and Jabbour's novel, *My People Shall Live* opens with the Palestinian family's departure from the land of Palestine in the midst of the fighting that surrounded the creation of the state of Israel in 1948. The chronological narrative of her subsequent life, in the refugee camps of Lebanon and later as a schoolteacher in Kuwait, is punctuated by a series of critical moments of consciousness: of the "historic roots" of her people (22), of class **56** differences (35), of the "loss of a comrade in battle" (47), and of the influential power of public speaking (54). These crises of awareness culminate in 1968 in Khaled's enlistment in the PFLP. "I felt I was on the road to Haifa. I was coming out of the abyss" (112).

The narration of that personal itinerary is, however, significantly articulated with the larger history of the trials of dispossession and occupation of the Palestinian people in the decades since 1948, an articulation that is designed to give political and historical consequence to the popular but reductive stereotype propagated by the West and its media apparatus of the guerrilla as a ruthless, reckless adventurer. According to Leila Khaled,

We do not embark haphazardly on adventurous and romantic individualistic projects to fulfil "individual needs" or "act out of frustrations and hostilities" as Western "scientific" psychologists hypothesize. We act collectively in a planned manner either to neutralise a prospective friend of the enemy or to expose a vital nerve of the enemy and, above all, to dramatise our own plight and to express our resolute determination to alter "the new realities" that Mr. Moshe Dayan's armies have created. (125–26)

No less decisive in the narrative of Leila Khaled's political development than the two plane hijackings in which she participated are the periods of political detention, first in Syria and then in England, which followed the incidents. In Syria, Khaled and her companion Issawi were first held at the police headquarters until, following a hunger strike protesting the conditions of their detention, they were removed to a hospital and then kept in a series of "guest quarters" and apartments. Hafez al-Assad, then Syrian minister of defense, insisted that the two Palestinians were simply the recipients of Syrian "hospitality," but for Khaled, the stay in Damascus was unequivocally one of "internment" (156). "It was hard," she writes, "to accept emotionally that I was in an 'Arab prison'" (155). Critical to this Syrian detention of the two Palestinian commandos is the struggle between Arab regimes to control the direction of the PLO and to appropriate its legitimacy and the Palestinian resistance struggle for self-determination and national independence. "The Syrians, I am certain, were not afraid of Salim or me. They feared the Front and its heroic exploits. They must have remembered vividly how Dr. Habash [George Habash, the founder of the PFLP], whom they imprisoned in 1968 was 'kidnapped' with his Syrian guards by the Front from the most guarded security prison in Syria" (154–55).

In Britain, at Ealing police station a year later, a different version of the effort to appropriate the Palestinian historical narrative was again challenged by the prisoner. Leila Khaled's first demand of her captors, before she submits to their interrogation, is that she, a Palestinian woman and plane hijacker, be recognized as a "commando" (193). She then takes their questions, aimed, like those of Senanayak in "Draupadi," at "information retrieval" in the service of the West's master narrative, and deflects them, responding instead with a history lesson of her own.

> "Who issued this passport to you?" "The PF," I said. "Where were you going to take the plane?" "Somewhere." "Where?" "Somewhere," I insisted. "Who is Abd Arheem Jaber?" Now I brightened up and decided to deliver my first brief speech and refuse to talk further if I were stopped. The officers sensed my determination and remained silent.
>
> "Jaber is a Palestinian hero in Zionist dungeons . . ." (194–95)

The discursive struggle throughout Khaled's confrontational interrogation by British security officials is waged not only as a punitive action for political offenses but over the control of the historical record as well. Critical to that record is the specificity of Leila Khaled's role in the resistance as a Palestinian woman commando.

Following her second hijacking, Khaled, because of her by then internationally publicized image, was obliged to withdraw from the public operations of the PFLP and go underground. Her story, which had begun with her expulsion from Palestine, concludes here with her removal from the world stage. According to George Hajjar, who writes the final words to her narrative,

> Since this book was completed Leila Khaled has been doing "mass political work", organising the guerrilla camps and contriving to recruit supporters. She and I work closely together in the Popular Front for the Liberation of Palestine. Now that Leila is known throughout the world, her picture having appeared in every western newspaper, we are not likely to permit her in the foreseeable future to participate in foreign, political or military missions. Her role is now to work inside the Arab world for the day when our people can once again return to their homeland. (223)

Hajjar's attempt here to explain Khaled's "disappearance" is nonetheless also an attempt to recontain the work of the woman revolutionary. As such, it threatens to reiterate around gender and from within the resistance organization the recuperative stratagems, earlier evident in Eric Rouleau's introduction to Abou Iyad's memoir, of First World mediators to

57

neutralize as underdeveloped the political and theoretical consequences of Third World liberation struggles.

Paradoxically perhaps, Sir John Glubb, a British officer who had served in Jordan with British Mandate forces, wrote the Foreword to *My People Shall Live*. Although Glubb is "charmed" by the woman commando's life, he dismisses her historical analysis as still inadequately developed:

> while her own experiences are narrated factually and simply, her political opinions largely reflect the oversimplified views of the extreme left wing Palestine parties. The Palestinians have been treated with so much cruelty and injustice that it is not surprising that they should develop a persecution complex. Yet this factor makes it difficult for their sympathisers to assist them, for all their attempts to help are denounced as treachery and deception. Like other young revolutionaries, Miss Khaled divides the world into good guys and bad guys. (8)

Except for her term as Secretary of the General Union of Palestinian Women at the UN Conference for the Decade of Women in Copenhagen in 1980, Leila Khaled has continued to work discreetly with women on women's issues within the Arab world, in the refugee camps in Lebanon or with the PFLP in Syria, where she appears occasionally at public forums and meetings. In late 1988 she was interviewed by Gulshan Dietl (1989), who asked her why she now allowed her photograph to be taken. Khaled's terse answer was deceptively simple: "the Intifidah." She went on to explain: "it is still dangerous—only more so. Abu Jihad was killed only a matter of months ago and yet there is no fear now but much more confidence. Besides, it is the duty of each one of us to speak out in support of the Intifidah and seek support for it" (60).

As a new recruit in the training camps of the PFLP, Leila Khaled had been an active participant in the theoretical and strategic debates concerning the Front's programs and priorities, with particular emphasis on the place of women in those priorities, but also with regard to the historical relevance of armed struggle both inside and outside occupied Palestine. These debates and arguments are given further elaboration in Hamida Nana's novel based on the Leila Khaled "legend." *My Homeland in My Eyes* (1979) is set in Paris and narrates the early days of Khaled's life underground. The structure of the novel is organized by a long letter written by Nadia, the story's protagonist and the Leila Khaled figure, to her French lover, Frank, in which she finally reveals her concealed identity and explains the reasons why she has decided to return to the resistance fighters in Beirut. Those reasons are embedded in the details of her life story as she relates it to her lover: the training camp, the death in an aborted operation inside Israel of her closest comrade, and the tense and often acrimonious arguments over the armed struggle, over whether it should be fought on the "outside" (*fi-l-kharaj*) or the "inside" (*fi-l-dakhil*), that is, internationally, or within the borders of Israel and the Occupied Territories. Most of all Nadia is critical of the way in which she, the former hijacker and now international celebrity, has been made a fetish by her own organization: "they have made me into an illusory heroine . . . they have made me into a commodity, a consumer item" (121).

Frank is a professor idolized by his students for his own past history as a partisan in Third World revolutionary struggles. What Nadia cannot understand is his subsequent decision to disassociate himself from those movements and settle down to live and work in France. Nana's novel, which concludes with Nadia's return to Beirut and Frank's pending decision to follow her, thus proposes a combined critique of the intersection of exploitation based on gender, on the one hand, and distorted global relations of power and dependency between the First and Third worlds, on the other. It suggests as well, from within the speculative and fictionalized narrative of Leila Khaled's underground experience in Paris, the imperative of reconstituting the theoretical and political bases of an internationally organized resistance to hegemony that would nonetheless account for the historical specificities of national culture and the critical differences of gender, race, and class.

The act of "going underground," not unlike Leila Khaled's "removal" from the stage of world vision, raises complex and controversial questions for the personal and political identity of the resistance partisan who is required to withdraw from the arena of public action. That disappearance can be variously motivated and accordingly take different forms. For example, the organization may consider that the individual will be more useful to the resistance agenda at a given moment by an apparent disassociation from the group that will allow her/him to carry out significant and necessary civilian functions foreclosed to cadres known as such to the military or the government's security forces. In the case of Leila Khaled, by contrast, it was her previous distinction as a militant and the media's dissemination of her image that later made it impossible for her to take on assignments that would her expose her to public recognition.

In either case, however, whether the partisan assumes a kind of double persona or disappears into the clandestine network of the resistance movement, the question of identity—and identification—looms urgent for the persons involved. The need *not* to be identified by the government and its agents makes ambivalent and problematic the recognition by comrades within the movement itself. Either these comrades themselves have been kept ignorant of the underground's adherents or, for security reasons, they are not allowed to recognize publicly, even to greet on the street, their *companeras* and *companeros* in the resistance. This inability to acknowledge and to be acknowledged, imposed by historical circumstance and the conditions of political opposition against a repressive government or in a police state, forces the members of a resistance organization to seek politically informed criteria for the construction of self-image, persona, and relationships other than the exclusively personal or ego-centered ones provided by bourgeois traditions of individualism. The interference of these socially constructed conventions of identity, however, like the patterns of patriarchy, if uncritically assimilated in certain contexts, threaten to establish structural affinities between a guerrilla movement and the bureaucratic apparatus that it opposes. That is, the "practical need for trust" from her movement that was written into Bhuvaneswari Bhaduri's suicide is systematically manipulated by the interrogators of political detainees when, for example, they taunt their resisting victims with the threat of exposing to their comrades that they have abdicated under pressure and revealed vital information.

The conventional expectations that govern the psychological peripeties of bourgeois-novel-type plots must just as often be dismantled, or at least suspended, and another set of relational premises, based on material circumstances and political exigencies and accounting for the possibilities of both treachery and trust, must be elaborated. Omar Cabezas, for example, describes in *Fire from the Mountains* (1985) his astonishment when he discovers who is the unidentified driver of the car taking him and his fellow recruits to the Sandinista training camp in the mountains: "After a while I noticed that Federico was talking to the driver, then— holy shit!—I recognized him—it was Cuqui Carrion" (50). Carrion, a well-to-do middle-class youth from Leon, had in the past lent his apartment to Cabezas and his girlfriend, Claudia, for afternoon trysts. Eventually, Cabezas noticed, Carrion and his friends began to develop politically. They stopped smoking dope and started attending committee meetings and activities. Then Cabezas was ordered by the Frente to cease visiting the apartment and, as he writes in retrospect: "I guessed the Frente was using [it] for meetings, among other things. And in fact they were. But actually Cuqui was already the underground driver for Pedro Arauz Palacios and couldn't afford to be compromised, so they yanked him out of CUUN [University of Nicaragua Student Council] activities, too. I thought: Cuqui's dropping out, he's lost interest, he's given up the fight, or who knows what. So when I saw him there, Cuqui so deeply committed, I was very happy" (51).

The political experience of clandestinity is described somewhat differently, however, by comrades of Commandante Eugenia in El Salvador's Farabundo Marti Popular Liberation Forces (FPL). At the end of 1976, when political circumstances required Eugenia to go into hiding, it was

Commander Isabel who had to explain to her what this meant and what it would require of her. Isabel recalls the conversation between the two women in the testimony she contributed to Claribel Alegria's biography of Commandante Eugenia, *They Won't Take Me Alive* (1987):

"You," I told her, "will leave your family, your friends, and it's inevitable that some of your loved ones will die. Perhaps they'll kidnap your relatives to test if this'll lead them to you. You won't be able to do anything about it. You'll even see people you know in the street, and your heart will be in your mouth with the desire simply to say hello, but you won't be able to. You'll have to pass by on the other side. Perhaps they'll think, 'How stuck up Eugenia's become' and you won't be able to turn and look at them and that'll hurt you." (72)

61

Eugenia and her husband, Javier, went underground just after they were married, and Javier in turn recalls the unwonted conditions to which their marriage was subjected by the political commitments that they shared: "The step into secrecy obliged us to opt for a path that we couldn't count on being able to tread together the whole time. We could foresee the risks and the possibility of one of us losing the other" (80).

Commandante Eugenia, born Ana Maria Castillo Rivas in San Salvador on 7 May 1950, was machine-gunned to death on 17 January 1981, when the truck she was driving with weapons for a major guerrilla offensive was ambushed by a Salvadoran paramilitary patrol. *They Won't Take Me Alive*, written by Alegria to "fulfil a promise" to Javier, who wished he could have been a writer and could tell Eugenia's story himself (32), reconstructs the Salvadoran woman militant's life history and describes through written and oral testimonials the radical intersection between the stages—of daughter, wife, and mother—of conventional female autobiography and the political development of a partisan in the resistance.

The title to the memoir also describes, in a refracted way, Commandante Eugenia's view of prison, an ordeal that she categorically refused, choosing death instead. According to another comrade, Ricardo, "Eugenia was not someone to let herself be taken prisoner. She was very clear and certain on this point. Her decision about the terms of combat proved final" (144). Eugenia's relationship to prison was instead mediated through Javier's detention, a mediation that simultaneously engaged her multiple roles, in what are otherwise divided between personal and public spaces, as wife, future mother, and militant. Javier recalls: "I remember the first little note to reach me in jail, after the fortnight spent at Santa Tecla prison under court orders. She told me that one of the greatest sufferings she had to undergo was that of not having become pregnant. That was the opening sentence of her letter" (86). The final exchanges between Eugenia and Javier, just prior to the launching of the offensive, were letters concerned with the care and health of their two-year-old daughter, Ana Patricia. For Eugenia, "it was through involving our people in the revolutionary struggle that women would liberate themselves, obtaining their true and fair place" (87).

Commandante Eugenia represents a long, if contested, history of women's participation in the Salvadoran resistance struggle, from the nineteenth-century Indian uprisings, led by Anastasio Aquino, against Spanish domination to the contemporary organization of COMADRES (Committee of Mothers and Relatives of Political Prisoners, Disappeared and Assassinated of El Salvador, Monsignor "Oscar Arnulfo Romero"), founded in 1977 by women seeking to locate their disappeared children and husbands. In the 1920s the Salvadoran leader Agustin Farabundo Marti had traveled to Nicaragua to fight with Sandino's forces against the occupation of that country by United States marines and, according to his biography, *Vivir significa luchar* (Martinez et al. 1987), had been impressed by the actively militant role played by women in the Sandinista popular army (33–45). Marti, who posthumously gave his name and reputation to the Farabundo Marti National Liberation Front (FMLN), was executed by a firing squad in January 1932 for his leadership role in an aborted popular uprising that culminated in the 1932 *matanza*, or massacre, of some thirty thousand people by the Salvadoran army.

Miguel Marmol was a member of El Salvador's Communist party and a trade union organizer, at the same time that Marti was in Nicaragua with Sandino. Unlike Marti, however, Marmol survived his own execution. Then, following a period on the run and underground, Marmol was arrested and came to know from the inside the jails of General Maximiliano Hernandez Martinez, then president of El Salvador (Martinez, who ordered the *matanza*, gave his name in the 1980s to one of the most notorious of El Salvador's death squads). On his release from prison, however, as Miguel Marmol told Roque Dalton, the Salvadoran poet and militant who transcribed Marmol's *testimonio* entitled *Miguel Marmol* (1987), the Communist militant had to deal not only with the mistrust of his comrades but also with what he saw as the perfidy of his wife: "Some freedom: the situation in my family was awful. . . . Nobody would give me a job. . . . My friends avoided me. . . . But what really got me angry was that the comrades in the Party were wondering why the government had set me free so fast. . . . My wife began to change. . . . We separated and I was left completely crushed" (383–85). Furthermore, according to Marmol, a number of critical changes had transpired within the party's organization during his prolonged absence, significant among which was the increased influence of intellectuals—and women—in the decision-making structures of the organization.

The political and ideological conflicts raised by questions of gender and the theorization of the struggle are constitutive issues for Marmol's recollection of his past history and that of the Communist party in El Salvador, polemically informing his reconstructive analysis of events as well as the relationship between himself, as the older party member, shoemaker, and union organizer, and Dalton, as the younger militant, poet, and theorist of the resistance. The issue of the role of women in the resistance organization or national liberation movement is a critical one, whether it is deemed, even temporarily, as secondary, with what are seen as women's 63 issues postponed for the sake of a nationalist agenda, or whether it constitutes a political priority, transforming the nationalist agenda in order to integrate women's concerns within its defining parameters.

In the most practical terms, the need to theorize the position of women within the resistance is unrelentingly stated by the Palestinian novelist and critic Ghassan Kanafani in the last article that he wrote before his death in 1972, assassinated by the Israeli secret service in a car-bomb explosion in Beirut. The first half of the posthumously published article, "The Case of Abu Hamidu and Cultural Cooperation with the Enemy" (1972), treats of an incident in southern Lebanon in 1971 in which Abu Hamidu, a Palestinian *fedai*, allegedly raped two village girls. The villagers responded angrily and the PLO tried and executed the commando. The sisters were killed by their brother to avenge the shame they had brought on their family. According to Kanafani, this incident demonstrated that the Palestinian resistance had doubly failed in its revolutionary practice. First, it had failed to develop a working and political relationship with the Lebanese and Palestinian populations in whose midst it had settled following the massacres of Black September and King Husayn's expulsion of the PLO from Jordan. Second, and just as important, because of its connection with the popular issue of relating to the region's inhabitants, the resistance had failed to educate its own commandos on the needs and priorities of a social revolution as well as a military and political victory.

The connection between a social agenda and the political struggle is argued again by Bernadette Devlin in her autobiography, *The Price of My Soul* (1970), written, as Devlin says, "in an attempt to explain how the complex of economic, social, and political problems of Northern Ireland threw up the phenomenon of Bernadette Devlin" (vii). Devlin (now Bernadette Devlin McAliskey), a Northern Irish militant who was elected to Parliament in 1969, at the age of twenty-one, describes the course of her politicization from her childhood in Cookstown in the 1950s to the violent battle of the Bogside in Derry in 1969. As a child, she recalls, her family was ostracized by their own Catholic townspeople because her mother had married "below her class." That the Presbyterians in the town were the only neighbors willing to associate with her Catholic parents did much, according to Devlin, to undermine early for her the "traditional Catholic ideal of sticking to one's own" (21) and much to inform the political and secular bases for her later participation in the civil rights movement in Ireland, in the organization Peoples Democracy, and eventually in the Irish Republican Socialist Party (IRSP).

As a student in 1965 at Queen's University in Belfast, Devlin was drawn into political circles, but at that time politics for her "meant debate, not **64** action" (70). The civil rights movement, popular protest against Britain, the Special Powers Act, and the policy of internment in Northern Ireland, and finally the march on Derry in October 1968, all provided Devlin a prominence that led to her standing in by-elections as an anti-Unionist coalition candidate for Parliament as the representative from Mid-Ulster. Two complicit and interrelated issues were debated around her candidacy. The first issue, that of participation in electoral politics, was of larger significance to the organization itself.

We didn't want to get into Parliament, but here was the chance we'd been waiting for to explain our policies to the people. The police were bound by law to protect a parliamentary candidate; we could send an election manifesto into every home in eight constituencies, with the Post Office paying for our propaganda; and as candidates, we could attack the political parties at meetings to which electors came. (157)

For Devlin, the equally problematic second issue, that of a young woman from Northern Ireland seated in Westminster, was of similar consequence. She describes the tendency, following the election, to neutralize her political effectiveness, as had been the case with Leila Khaled, by romanticizing her person or turning her into a fetish:

The trouble in those early weeks was that I wasn't just an MP, however ineffective, but a phenomenon: I was the big international story. Which is a very time-taking and soul-destroying thing to be. If Michael Farrell had been elected, he would just have been an MP, getting on with the job within the limits of the possible, whereas I was not only failing to do anything for the people of Mid-Ulster; I was failing to do anything for God knows whom else as well. (197)

Michael Farrell, a founder-member of Peoples Democracy, who has himself often been interned, describes in his history of the Northern Ireland struggle for social and political equality the response of the authorities, following the battle of the Bogside, to the radical politics represented by Devlin in the chambers of Parliament no less than on the terrain of Northern Ireland: "Bernadette Devlin MP was charged with riotous behaviour during the siege of the Bogside and sentenced to six months in jail, a decision calculated to enrage Catholics to whom the siege was a

65

Fig. 1. *Top:* "When we were in London last summer I found this in the boutiques and I said to myself, 'This is the chance to buy something for my maid. She can wear it when she's locked in the closet for making some stupid mistake.'" *Bottom:* "But this other thing, this 'ankle bracelet,' I said, 'We can make this locally!'" A cartoon by Egyptian artist Mohiyadin al-Labbad, reprinted from *Ruz al-Yusif*, 11 July 1988.

heroic episode" (271). Commodified, that is, like Leila Khaled, on the basis of gender, and politically ostracized on the same grounds (as her parents had been socially shunned for the combined reasons of class and religion), Bernadette Devlin suggests the need to reelaborate around the role of women in the resistance the reciprocal consequences of the categories of gender, race, and class.

The history of the contested role of women in Northern Ireland's politics as in the Republic of Ireland, figuring variously as Womanhood, Virgin, the mythic Queen Maeve, and Mother Hibernia, is critically examined in *Mother Ireland*, a videotape produced in 1988 by the Derry Film and Video Collective for Channel 4 in Britain. It considers women from Sighle Humphries, active in 1916, through Bernadette Devlin-McAliskey, to Mairead Farrell, assassinated in a British shoot-to-kill operation in Gibraltar in 1988 following ten years as a political prisoner in Armagh jail. It was also the first documentary to be censored under Britain's new censorship laws. According to Annie Goldson (1989), the supervising editor of the video, "the women within *Mother Ireland* articulate subject positions that are not only colonial, the result of living under British occupation, but also gendered, women active within a nationalist movement, Catholic by tradition, and still dominated by men" (18).

A cartoon by the popular Egyptian caricaturist Mohiyadin al-Labbad depicting upper-class Egyptian women reflecting on their summer shopping excursions in European capitals represents the necessary intersections of gender and class oppression and argues against an uncritical isolation of one analytical category from the other. The drawing, however, further asserts the historical and geopolitical dimensions to prison as a structurally endemic social and political practice, not to be rhetorically contained by self-exculpatory gestures of blame or accusation directed against each other by the "Third" and "First" worlds, nor relegated to a putatively essential repression exemplified in a "Second" World, nor politically salved by a liberal vocabulary of human rights that serves only to mask a global policing project. The current phenomenon of political prison in the United States, then, though denied, by the judicial and legal apparatus, reproduces within the nation's territorial borders the same paradigms of dependency and exploitation that are maintained by the distorted relations of military, economic, and political power between the First and the Third worlds. A listing of "political prisoners" (a category nonetheless not recognized by the penal system) in United States prisons, detention centers, and penitentiaries demonstrates the prominent place of issues of race and ethnicity in defining the lines of political oppression and the struggle against it in the United States.[6] Political prisoners, who in the past have included abolitionists, suffragists, labor organizers, members of the Communist party, conscientious objecters, and antiwar activists, now represent in significant numbers and constellations the black, Puerto Rican, Chicano, and Native American populations, as well as, more recently, antinuclear protesters and members of the sanctuary movement, which offers illegal asylum to Central American political refugees.

In 1970 Angela Davis, a black woman militant, was arrested in New York City and extradited to stand trial in California. Her *Autobiography* (1974), which opens when she goes underground following the Marin County Courthouse revolt, a response to the shooting deaths of several **67** black detainees in the San Quentin prison, is structured around her detention and trial. It posits political prison as the decisive juncture in her political development, as that experience which not only has distinguished her, but, more importantly, has aligned her with a larger exploited people. As Davis insists in the Preface:

The one extraordinary event of my life had nothing to do with me as an individual—with a little twist of history, another sister or brother could have easily become the political prisoner whom millions of people from throughout the world rescued from persecution and death. I was reluctant to write this book because concentration on my personal history might distract from the movement which brought my case to the people in the first place. I was also unwilling to render my life as a personal "adventure"—as though there were a "real" person separate and apart from the political person. (ix–x)

As in *Assata*, the autobiography of Assata Shakur, one of the Black Panthers arrested in 1973 by state troopers on the New Jersey Turnpike, so too in Davis's *Autobiography* prison provides the frame story for a narrative of resistance and struggle. The account of her prison experience, first in the New York women's detention center and subsequently in California, is counterpointed by the story of growing up in Birmingham, Alabama, attending college, studying philosophy at Brandeis University (where she was first influenced by the writing of Herbert Marcuse), and finally participating in various civil rights organizations.

Throughout her much-publicized trial, the main effort of the prosecution was to nullify Angela Davis's political offense by rendering it instead as a "crime of passion," the action of an emotional female on behalf of George Jackson, who was incarcerated in Soledad Prison and alleged by the prosecution to be her lover. As evidence for this accusation, the state produced one of Davis's letters to Jackson in Soledad Prison where he had become active as a black militant and "read" it as a convicting moment in the unfolding of an impassioned personal melodrama. The state's literary critical effort thus to control and appropriate Davis's autobiography is contested by the counterinterpretations of the letter offered by both the jury and Davis herself. The courtroom and the ongoing trial are turned into sites of critical combat over the significance of the gender narrative as "personal" or "political." Angela Davis had already addressed the issue in her opening statement, as cocounsel, to the court:

> Now he [the prosecutor] will have you believe that I am a person who would commit the crimes of murder, kidnapping and conspiracy, having been motivated by pure passion. He would have you believe that lurking behind my external appearance are sinister and selfish emotions and passions which, in his words, know no bounds.
>
> Members of the jury, this is utterly fantastic. It is utterly absurd. Yet it is understandable that Mr. Harris would like to take advantage of the fact that I am a woman, for in this society women are supposed to act only in accordance with the dictates of their emotions and passions. I might say that this is clearly a symptom of the male chauvinism which prevails in our society. (363)

68

The relationship between George Jackson and Angela Davis meanwhile had played a different, more political, role in the New York City women's prison where Davis was held prior to her extradition to California. Released from the isolation of 4B, the section of the prison reserved for mental patients, into the general prison population, Davis discovers books by Edgar Snow and W. E. B. DuBois in the prison library. Her initial surprise at finding these authors inside the prison is overcome, however, when she realizes that they must have been requested years ago by former women prisoners, prisoners such as Elizabeth Gurley Flynn and Claudia Jones, who decades earlier had been detained in the same facility. Following their example, Davis decides that her own literary legacy to the prison will be George Jackson's *Soledad Brother* (1970). And although the prison authorities refuse to allow her to donate ten copies of the volume to the prison library, she shares her copy of the book with her fellow inmates, most of them incarcerated on criminal charges for prostitution, drug offenses, and petty theft. Through the book and Davis's conversation they come to recognize the political bases of their "criminality." But the women's politicization was a social lesson for their Soledad brother as well:

> When I wrote George of the enthusiastic reception of his book among the sisters there, it gave him great pleasure to know that they were learning to relate to the movement through studying his individual political evolution. But there was one question that disturbed him: how were the sisters responding to the attitude toward Black women manifested in some of his early letters? In the past he had seen Black women as often acting as a deterrent to the involvement of Black men in the struggle. He had since discovered that this generalization was wrong, and was deeply concerned that the other women in the jail be informed of this. (62)

PART II

THE RESISTANCE IN PRISON

Recognition Scenes

Al-i'tiraf khiyana. (Recognition/admission/confession is betrayal.)

ADIL AMR, *The Shamed*

Criticism . . . is not a process of recognition, but work to produce meaning.

CATHERINE BELSEY, *Critical Practice*

"Go home, Maha" (*ruh al'-bayt*), Issam told his wife, who was standing with their son at the prison gate, and walked slowly back to his cell as his fellow prisoners, Palestinian and Israeli, sorrowfully but proudly watched him, some with tears in their eyes, and quietly applauded. The final scene of Uri Barbash's 1985 film *Beyond the Walls* culminates the cinematic story of a collective hunger strike waged by Palestinian Arab and Israeli Jewish prisoners—or in other terms, political and social/criminal prisoners—against the Israeli prison system and its authoritarian organization. In keeping with Israeli state policy, that system is managed along racial and religious lines. In order to break the political challenge of a strike that has been coordinated across ethnic divides by the Palestinian Issam and the Israeli Uri, the leaders of the respective groups, the prison authorities have brought in Issam's wife, with their young child, in an effort to tempt or seduce Issam into capitulating in a deal with the system. The Palestinian prisoner is serving a life sentence for alleged "terrorist" activity.

Issam's steadfast refusal to participate finally was not originally scripted; the film's preliminary scenario had prescribed instead the classic paradigm of family reunion and the containment of nonsectarian resistance as an appropriate closure to the prison struggle. According to Uri Barbash, director of the film, "To me it was clear that Issam must go out with the wife and child, and that was how it was written in the script. I said that in such a human moment everyone must forget the political, social statement—there is here a human interest that stands above everything. You are a man, you have not seen your wife for ten years, you do not know your son, you must go out; even at the price of breaking the strike" (Shohat 1989, 252). Issam's refusal in the film, however, is the result of another refusal, that of Muhammad Bakri, the Palestinian actor who plays Issam, to be conscripted even into acting out such a capitulation. The off-screen refusal crucially transforms the cinematic narrative. According to Bakri:

Throughout all the rehearsals I told Uri and Beni Barbash [the director/scriptwriter and scriptwriter] that it would not work. . . . If I were a leader like Sirtawi [the name of Bakri's character in the film is a reference to the PLO figure Issam Sirtawi] I would not have been broken, because I am a symbol. I told them that they would kill the utopia; that if I do something I do not believe in I would be a shit. I sat with my head between my hands and I could not do it. Here it was not a matter of being the fucker of the management. Here there appears a PLO leader, which in my eyes is the only representative organization of Palestinians; and I am for PLO leadership that argues for coexistence and dialogue with Israel and the shattering of prejudices. I am indeed not a politician but an actor, but the message is important to me. The real Issam Sirtawi was killed because he believed in dialogue. . . . Issam would not break and meet with his wife and son. . . . [When] the cameras worked, I began walking toward my wife and son in the film. All the prisoners began to cry. . . . Uri [Barbash] cried, the cameraperson cried. I finished the scene and walked crying to the dressing room, because that was the story of my life that was focused in one moment. (Shohat 1989, 253)

The critical debate between the Israeli filmmaker, Uri Barbash, and the Palestinian actor, Muhammad Bakri, a debate that culminated in the radical change in the film's ending, reverses a series of hierarchical orders—Israeli/Palestinian, prison/prisoner, author/actor—within the larger context of cinema as an interventionist political art. Furthermore—and just as significantly—it militates against a conventional reading of that final scene as representing a masculinist imperative in keeping with traditions of Arab patriarchy by posing the prisoner's final refusal as a subversive challenge to that very system and its implied complicity with Israeli military occupation authorities and prison officials. Issam, that is, not only rejects the calculations of the Israeli machination, but refutes as well the long-standing and tradition-honored convention of the "recognition scene restoration" with its ideologically reintegrative functions of conservation and of a temporarily sundered or disrupted social order restored by a sudden revealing of arbitrary or fortuitous circumstances—at least within the drama's own terms, historically unnecessary or unmotivated circumstances. Father, according to that convention, is reunited with son, lover with betrothed, husband with wife. The ruling order is satisfied that its rules are still in order—and recognized. The story can, happily, end.

Prison "recognition scenes," by contrast, work counter to this ideology of restoration. Like Issam's pained response to Maha's appearance at the prison gates ("go home") and its implicit subversion, its ironic, indeed radical, challenge in the context of the continued Israeli assault on the Palestinian struggle for a homeland, to the very concept of "home," recognition scenes in prison refuse to acknowledge the ascendancy of traditional paradigms of family and participate instead in the resistant formulation of alternative strategies of social and political organization.

Yol, for example, a controversial 1981 film written and directed by Yilmaz Guney from inside a Turkish prison, narrates the short-lived furlough of a small group of prisoners who use their leave to attempt to reassemble some of the shattered pieces of their personal lives, which have been interrupted by their respective sentences. From a wife accused of adultery to the Kurds struggling against Turkish domination, they confront anew the structured social and political relations that traverse the prison walls. In one scene toward the end of the film, and after the accused wife, who was punished bestially by her husband's family, has died in an aborted reconciliation with her husband, the bloodied bodies of Kurdish freedom fighters are brought back by Turkish authorities to their village to be "identified" by their families and neighbors. Like Lupe, who denies her husband, who was killed by the death squads in Manlio Argueta's Salvadoran novel *One Day of Life* (1980), the Kurdish villagers, paraded one by one past the wagon carrying the men's mutilated corpses, refuse the orders to "recognize" and acknowledge their own family members, demanding instead Turkish recognition of the legitimacy of their claims to liberation and national self-determination.

Widows (1984), to take another example, a novel by the Chilean writer-in-exile Ariel Dorfman, which is set in Greece under the dictatorship, rewrites as an open-ended resistance narrative the recognition paradigm conventionally used to close a story by foreclosing any further questions. When the tortured body of a man is washed up out of the river, a single woman from the town begins by claiming to "recognize" in the bruised, disfigured, and swollen features of the individual the image of her missing husband. She is followed by another woman, with the same claim, and still another, and another, until a women's chorus collectively demands recognition by the authorities of their government's crimes against the human and civil rights of its population.

Unlike these women and their proto-organization, but like Lupe or the Kurdish villagers of *Yol,* Rigoberta Menchu, an Indian woman organizer in Guatemala, knew that the authority of the inherited paradigm still maintained its threatening or fatal sway. Called upon twice by government authorities to collaborate in the ideological tyranny of the tradition of the "recognition scene," Menchu (1984) rejects its coercive hold of domesti-

73

cation and pacification over cultural and political oppositional practices. The first time that she and her family are summoned by the military to attend a recognition scene follows upon the arrest of a number of guerrillas, among whom is the Indian woman's younger brother. "Well, when we got this news, it must have been about 11 in the morning, I remember, on the 23rd, my mother said: 'My son will be among those who are punished.' It was going to be done in public, that is, they were calling the people out to witness the punishment. Not only that, a bulletin said (we'd managed to get hold of a copy) that any who didn't go to witness the punishment were themselves accomplices of the guerrillas" (175).

The second peremptory summons involves Menchu's mother, who had been abducted, tortured, and raped by high-ranking military officers when she refused to "confess" to their accusations against her and her family. "She pretended she knew nothing. She defended every one of us until the end" (198). The family's presence was thereby demanded, messages were sent, the mother's clothes were displayed in the town hall. But her children, says Menchu, stayed away. "It was very painful for me to accept that my mother was being tortured and not to know anything about the rest of the family. None of us presented ourselves. Least of all my brothers. I was able to contact one of my brothers and he told me not to put my life in danger, that they were going to kill my mother anyway and would kill us too. We have to keep this grief as a testimony to them because they never exposed their lives even when their grief was great too" (199).

When to talk, when not to talk, when to recognize, when to deny: the critical tension between "freedom of expression" and the "right to remain silent" and their overdetermination by the circumstances of history and the exigencies of political struggle inform the institutional narratives of discursive encounter in political detention between the state and its contestants. In her account to an international audience of her people's resistance, Menchu observes those protocols but reworks them as part of an oppositional praxis. The "tricks [her] ancestors used" (123), the secrets of her village, are redeployed against the Guatemalan military, but they cannot all be told. Reticence is necessary if their struggle is to continue. "This is why," she says at the end of her account, "I've travelled to many places where I've had the opportunity to talk about my people. Of course, I'd need a lot of time to tell you all about my people, because it's not easy to understand just like that. And I think I've given some idea of that in my account. Nevertheless, I'm still keeping my Indian identity a secret. I'm still keeping secret what I think no-one should know. Not even anthropologists or intellectuals, no matter how many books they have, can find out all our secrets" (247). No more than can the prison authorities or their interrogators.

"The Recantation" (or *al-Bara'a*), a poem written in 1963 by the popular Iraqi opposition poet Muzaffar al-Nuwwab, likewise insists on the function of the discursive in the urgent and critical intersection of the social and political in resisting paradigmatic authoritarian control. Responding to the prison system's brutal efforts to force from their political prisoners "recantations" of their political allegiances and commitments, renunciations that would then be published in newspapers further to demoralize **75** and discredit the progressive opposition to the new putschist regime that came to power in February 1963, Muzaffar describes the pleas of a mother and sister to their son and brother not to "shame" them through such a betrayal. In the "first image" the mother addresses her son:

> My child, I'd rather the son of a dog suckle my milk,
> than a son who throws me crumbs of bread through recantation.
> My child, I'd rather be eaten by leprosy, flesh and bone, and
> blinded, than [see] the meanness [of recantation].
> My child, these are days marked by drought, days of trial.
> My child, do not blunt our honor.

The young man's sister speaks next, in the "second image," extending her mother's appeal in a reversal of the traditional male/female role assignments that designate the woman as necessarily culpable in matters of besmirched honor:

> Brother, I faced the prison, through heat and cold, day and night.
> For your sake have I put up with assaults on my honor,
> And spent each night by my fire.
> Only at the end to have you dishonor me in a newspaper item!
> Delight your eyes, O brother of mine, for the way you have
>   rewarded my waiting!
> Is this the reward for the bread, my tears, and suffering!
> How can I face, with this recantation, every sister, who awaits
> from you, brother, revenge for her injured honor!
> How can I face, with this recantation, the mothers, and share
> my cares with them!

In the final lines of the poem, the sister denies her brother and his own denial of the political struggle:

> Oh People! The one you see, is not our son.

According to Abdul-Salaam Yousif (1988), Muzaffar's poem is, at once "appeal, . . . manifesto, a nursery poem, the voice of the collectivity, and

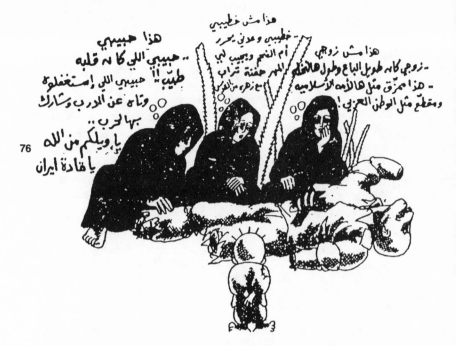

Fig. 2. *(To be read from right to left):* "This isn't my husband. My husband was strong and capable and tall as a date palm. This is all shredded like the Islamic people and broken like the Arab nation." "This isn't my fiancé . . . My fiancé promised me to liberate Um al-Fahm and promised me a handful of soil and flowers from Jerusalem as a dowry." "This is my lover, my lover whose heart was good. My lover whom they made a fool of when they made him take part in the war. Allah's curse on you, O Iranian leadership." A cartoon by Palestinian artist Naji al-Ali (widely circulated).

an ode to heroism and resistance" (222); soon after it was written it "circulated among the prisoners and was learnt by heart, and it is believed that thanks to it many political prisoners declined to sign recantations" (225). Nearly three decades after its composition, the poem remains emblematic of a continued struggle against the coercion and co-optation of language by the physical violence of authoritarian paradigms. But in challenging the structures of a repressive state power, the masculinist cult of social shame and a woman's honor must likewise be reversed. Mother and daughter, in their insistence that the political struggle be recognized, demand another recognition as well, that of their own rightful place in that struggle.

"Go home,"—*ruh al-bayt,* says Issam.

In the drawing by the assassinated Palestinian artist Naji al-Ali calling on women's testimony to the limitations and forfeitures of a male-dominated struggle, two demands for recognition are inseparably at stake, as they are in the essays that follow: (1) the recognition of the political status of the prisoners and thus of the legitimacy of their historical project; and (2) the recognition, by both the state and the resistance movement, of the political status of women.

Chapter Three

"Beyond the Pale": Strip-Searching and

Hunger Strikes in Northern Ireland

We kneel in adoration of effigies of stone
Our eyes turned to heaven, blind to what's going on
Six women hold a naked woman pinned down on the floor
Without trial or jury like a prisoner of war.
Though the rain had made the colours run the message it was plain
Women are being strip searched in Armagh and Brixton Jails.

CHRISTY MOORE, "On the Bridge"

Wars of counter-subversion and counter-insurgency are fought, in the last resort, in the minds of people   BRIGADIER FRANK KITSON, *Low-Intensity Operations*

I'll wear no convict's uniform
Nor meekly serve my time
That England might
Brand Ireland's fight
800 years of crime.

Popular rebel ballad about the men in the Maze and the women in Armagh prisons

I was strip searched, to confront me with their control, to enforce on me my own vulnerability, to degrade me. But they were not going to succeed. I saw my nakedness as an indictment against them, they thought my womanhood would help to defeat me. They didn't understand, that the strength of ideas cannot be stripped from one's mind.

Seventeen-year-old woman imprisoned in Armagh jail

On 6 March 1988, Mairead Farrell and two other IRA members, Dan McCann and Sean Savage, were shot to death in Gibraltar in an ambush sanctioned by the British government and carried out by British soldiers from the Special Air Services (SAS).[1] All three republicans were unarmed at the time of their brutal murder, "cut to pieces by bullets." Although McCann had stepped in front of Farrell to protect her when the SAS opened fire, she was "shot five times, twice in the head, three times in the body. The bullets to the head were fired into her face and exited under her left ear and at the back of her neck. The three bullets that were fired into the middle of her back exited in the region of her left breast. Her heart and liver were pulped, her spinal column fractured and her chest cavity was awash with two litres of blood" (Williams 1989, 22). Shortly after the attack, in the introduction to its report on killings by security forces and "supergrass" trials in Northern Ireland, Amnesty International (1988) expressed concern that "British security forces targeted the three and deliberately killed them without properly challenging or attempting to arrest them. Some eye-witnesses alleged that the soldiers continued to fire at the IRA members as they lay on the ground" (3). These sensational killings were, however, only the latest, if most dramatic—given their extraordinary international frame— in a series of alleged or apparent "shoot-to-kill" incidents within Northern Ireland involving British soldiers and/or members of the Royal Ulster Constabulary (RUC). An inquiry into three 1982 incidents, which was undertaken in 1984 by Manchester Deputy Chief Constable John Stalker, had been officially closed only two months before the Gibraltar case. In the meantime, Stalker, who claims that his research had been actively obstructed by the highest levels of the RUC itself, had been removed both from the investigation and from the Manchester police force, and his own record as a police officer had been challenged in a protracted investigation into his personal and professional past.

The issue of a shoot-to-kill policy, or "extrajudiciary execution," if not practiced systematically then at least sanctioned by the British occupation of Northern Ireland, raises a twofold problem: first, the elimination by assassination, a physically lethal silencing, of opponents to continued British presence in the Six Counties, and second, an ideological or discursive silencing of public critical and investigative responses to that policy. Since the beginning of the Troubles in the North, with the civil rights movement in the late 1960s and the arrival of British troops during the battle of the Bogside in Derry (and the first use of CS gas as a means of population control in Northern Ireland) in August 1969, British policy can be articulated according to periods of escalating responses to organized republican resistance. According to Hadden, Boyle, and Campbell in *Justice under Fire* (Jennings 1988), and other historical analysts, the 1969–71 period of "riots and terrorism" was followed by an initial internment operation in 1971–72. The years 1972–75 saw the expansion of internment and the establishment of the Diplock courts, where trials were heard and decided by a single judge without the presence or participation of a jury. "Criminalization" and "Ulsterization" characterized the years 1976–80: special status for political prisoners was rescinded in 1976, while policing responsibilities for the Six Counties were increasingly shifted by the British army into the hands of the RUC, which was more and more recruited from the local loyalist communities that it served. In 1980–81 were the republican hunger strikes, demanding the return of political status and the privileges that attached to it; during the strikes ten men died in the H Blocks of what was once called Long Kesh prison. Finally, 1981–85 saw the introduction of "supergrass" trials, mass convictions on the basis of "accomplice evidence," and the notorious and controversial shoot-to-kill policy. Britain, writes Anthony Jennings (1988), "has always reacted to violence in Ireland with a crude mixture of open displays of force and poor attempts to deal with an intractable problem within the confines of the law" (xv).

80

In October 1988, six months after the Gibraltar slayings, the British, consistent with their earlier implicit policy of media management of the Northern Ireland question, imposed a ban on all broadcasts that involved members and supporters of eleven Northern Ireland organizations, including the Ulster Defence Association (UDA), the Ulster Volunteer Forces (UVF), Sinn Fein, and the IRA. Previously, it was interviews with republicans that had been explicitly restricted, a restriction that Liz Curtis analyzed in *The Propaganda War* (1984) as betraying, in its invocation of the need-to-know principle, a larger project of censorship:

Clearly, there is no tangible threat to national security involved in reporting the words or deeds of "terrorists." So why does the public not "need to know"? The missing, unspoken link . . . is the authoritarian conception that the public itself presents a problem. The public's response to information about "terrorists" will not necessarily suit the authorities. Publicity alone will get the "terrorists" nowhere: it is the public reaction that matters. So "society" has to be protected from itself. (143)

The first video production to fall victim to the more explicit October 1988 ban was *Mother Ireland*, commissioned by Channel 4, a visual reading through personal interviews and documentary footage of the active and often conflicted participation of women throughout the twentieth century in the Irish struggle. Included among the dramatis personae of *Mother Ireland* was Mairead Farrell, interviewed during the brief eighteen months of freedom between her release from ten and a half years' imprisonment in Armagh jail and her assassination on the rock of Gibraltar.

Mairead Farrell's prison biography significantly summarizes a critical decade of the republican prison experience in Northern Ireland. Farrell was arrested on 5 April 1976 for planting bombs, together with two other IRA members (one of whom was killed before he could be captured), in Conway's Hotel in Dunmurray; the bombing was part of an IRA campaign against "political and economic targets" to protest the withdrawal earlier in the year of special status for political prisoners. She was found guilty and sentenced to fifteen years. She thus entered Armagh's B Wing classi-

Fig. 3. Cover of *The Captive Voice / An Glór Gafa*, which publishes writings by Irish republican prisoners (vol. 2, no. 2, summer 1990). The drawing, "Woman in Cell," is by Paul Doherty, a prisoner in Long Kesh. Reprinted courtesy of Sinn Fein POW Department.

fied as a "criminal" but was prepared to join the women's prison protest to recover status. According to Farrell (1989), "We all felt angry we were not getting status. We felt very strongly that we were political prisoners and as such shouldn't give in to the Brits attempts to criminalise us, but even worse criminalise the entire republican movement. They wouldn't recognise us, so we decided to organise against this" (18).

From 1976 to 1983 the Armagh women prisoners engaged in a no-work protest, refusing to do the prison work regularly assigned to ordinary criminals. In 1983, this action became instead a go-slow protest to stop the forfeiture of remission and privileges. Farrell, furthermore, together with Mary Doyle and Mairead Nugent, joined the aborted December 1980 hunger strike in solidarity with the male strikers in the H Blocks. Meanwhile, from 7 February 1980 to 1 March 1981, when Bobby Sands began his hunger strike, the women, who had been moved to A Wing following a riot in B, and with Farrell as officer in command (OC), had continued their no-wash protest, refusing to wash and smearing their excrement and menstrual blood on the walls of their cells.

Because Farrell refused to undergo the humiliating ordeal of strip-searching required before and after visits, she was denied her interprison visitation rights to see her fiancé in Long Kesh from November 1982, when strip-searching was introduced into Armagh by Governor Thomas Murtagh, until her release four years later. Following her release, Farrell (1989) commented to an interviewer, "I've learned a lot of self discipline and the importance of strength and resolve. I really feel as if I've never been away at all since I got out and I'm going to continue my involvement with Sinn Fein, remain politically active. Prison is really an experience I'd never have got anywhere else" (20). Months later, Mairead Farrell was assassinated, "cut to pieces by bullets," by the SAS operating "beyond the Pale," in Gibraltar.[2]

While the women's protest inside Armagh prison in demand for restoration of political status continued, the women's movement outside debated whether the demand for status was indeed a feminist issue. According to Margaret Ward (1983), in her study of women and Irish nationalism, "Many feminists were emotionally torn between their desire to support the sufferings endured by the women, and their concern lest this feminist solidarity be translated into unconditional support for the Provisionals. And, unhappily, women within Sinn Fein who are fighting for greater equality for women, isolated as they so obviously are, felt betrayed at the lack of public support by the feminist movement" (3). The underlying contradictions between feminism and nationalism that continue to riddle contemporary resistance politics—not only in Northern Ireland, but also in Palestine, South Africa, El Salvador, Britain, and the United States—are written into the longer history of women. These "unmanageable revolutionaries," as Ward designates them, the women in the Irish struggle and in the British and Irish prisons, have been persecuted throughout the twentieth century by means of the traditional imperatives imposed by Church, myth, and colonialism.

Nor is the difficult intersection between the "feminine" and the "political" peculiar to internal debates within a multidimensional women's movement; rather it is continuous with, if not derivative of, a histori-   **83**
cally dominant project of patriarchy—and academic humanism—to maintain the self-interested conveniences of an unequal division of labor. Of women's uneasily combined national and suffragist work, the poet-philosopher W. B. Yeats, for example, commented on "the way in which women could 'give themselves to an opinion as if it were some stone doll' " (Mulvihill 1989, 8).[3] In many of Yeats's poems political commitment, especially that of women, is torn between a "terrible beauty" and this "stone." In "Easter 1916" he writes: "Hearts with one purpose alone / Through summer and winter seem / Enchanted to a stone / To trouble the living stream / . . . / Too long a sacrifice / Can make a stone of the heart." And women's participation in that engaged political project is seen to de-feminize their personas, making the difference, in the same poem, "between day and night": "That woman's days were spent / In Ignorant good-will, / Her nights in argument / Until her voice grew shrill." In "On a Political Prisoner," Yeats wonders, "Did she in touching that lone wing / Recall the years before her mind / Became a bitter, an abstract thing." Finally, in "In Memoriam to Eva Gore-Booth and Con Markievicz," the poet ponders, "Dear Shadows, now you know it all, / All the folly of a fight / With a common wrong or right."

By 1921 the nationalist uprising of 1916 had been destroyed—sixteen of its leaders had been executed and more than eleven thousand republicans had been interred—Ireland had been partitioned, and the border between North and South was still to be defined. In that year Constance Markievicz, together with Maud Gonne, Charlotte Despard and other women, the mothers, wives, and sisters of prisoners then in detention, having met regularly if informally outside Mountjoy jail, joined forces to form the Women's Prisoners' Defense League (WPDL)—or the "Mothers," as they came to be known.

Kathleen Clarke, a committed Republican, visited her husband, Tom, just prior to his execution. Tom Clarke, who was the first signatory to the Proclamation of the Irish Republic in 1916, gave her, as if in a transfer of power, £3100, what was left of the Irish Republican Brotherhood's funds, to assist the dependents of those who had been killed or imprisoned during and after the uprising. Kathleen Clarke, another "unmanageable revolutionary," "was as much the dedicated republican as her husband; at their last meeting, in his death cell, she had upbraided him for having surrendered to the British. No personal matters were mentioned in this, their final conversation, which was solely concerned with the future course of the struggle, now to be carried by women" (Ward 1983, 119).

No less than Clarke, Markievicz, Despard, and Gonne all had had their own critical experiences, as women and as nationalists, on the other side of the prison wall. Constance Markievicz, the daughter of a wealthy landowner who acquired the title of countess through her late marriage, was arrested five times during the last ten years of her life. Her first arrest— and quick release—was in August 1910 for "making derogatory remarks" during the visit of King George V to Dublin. Much of the time that she was not detained in Mountjoy, Aylesbury, Holloway, or Cork jails, she was "on the run." From 1908 on she was active in the nationalist cause; she worked with James Connolly, the republican and socialist, in the trade union movement and founded Fianna Eireann, a boys club that was designed to provide a republican alternative to Baden Powell's imperially inspired Boy Scouts. This landlord's daughter also wrote a gardening column for the women's journal *Bean na hEireann*, in which she made clear, at least rhetorically, that gardening, land reform, and the nationalist struggle were not discreet spheres of engagement: "It is very hard killing slugs and snails but let us not be daunted. A good nationalist should look upon slugs in the garden in much the same way as she looks on the English in Ireland" (Haverty 1988, 78).

By contrast, arrest came less easily for Charlotte Despard. Her early work in the socialist and women's suffrage movements led her eventually, but inexorably, to Ireland (where her brother was the British commander in chief) and to the Irish national cause (in this, much unlike her brother). According to her grandnephew,

Her most salient characteristics were a habit of wearing sandals and a mantilla and a keen desire to be a heroine in the cause of women's suffrage by finding herself in jail. Unfortunately, these two characteristics got in each other's way. Authority apparently decided that it would be unseemly for the sister of the Commander in Chief (Lord Ypres) to rot in prison and the order went round debarring ladies wearing sandals and mantillas from arrest and incarceration. Aunt Lottie began to grow desperate until, tumbling finally to the reason for her lack of success, she sallied out in boots and a bonnet, and, before being identified and ejected, spent one glorious and heroic night in jail. (Mulvihill 1989, 4)

That arrest was in February 1907, for suffragist activities, but sixteen years later, when her friend and comrade Maud Gonne (who was also Yeats's unrequiting paramour) was on a hunger strike in the infamous Kilmainham Jail, she actively identified with the protesting prisoner:

Mrs. Despard, on hearing of her friend's arrest, rushed to the gates of Kilmainham in an anguish of helplessness. With so many of those who could have been relied upon to organize protests now inside, the veteran campaigner resorted instead to an individual display of solidarity. She confided to her diary that she was "moved to a sudden resolution" and she immediately sat down outside the gates of Kilmainham, remaining there through the twenty days of Maud's incarceration. (Ward 1990, 139)

85

Charlotte Despard's black mantilla and sandals, the emancipatory bequest of her widowhood, had at once enabled her social and political work and inhibited her martyrdom in a prison cell. She and her struggling female comrades made political use of their physical appearance and their garments—as if foreshadowing the assault on the female bodies of their imprisoned sisters more than half a century later, that is, the British internment policy of strip-searching its detainees.

Maud Gonne, renowned for her dramatic beauty and for hanging a black petticoat from her upstairs bedroom window when King Edward visited Dublin in 1903, was, according to her biographer, "always careless of her appearance, her beauty no more than a weapon to be used in the cause of Irish freedom" (Ward 1990, 71). Constance Markievicz, striking in her own right but without Gonne's singular beauty, eschewed as well Despard's mantillas for men's breeches when she joined the Citizens Army in 1916 in the streets of Dublin: "Constance's solution to her femininity for the moment was to disregard it, to adopt male attitudes and male practices. What she worried about was whether she should wear breeches as the men soldiers did, and whether her male colleagues were keeping vital information from her" (Haverty 1988, 133).

What to wear at the revolution was an absorbing question. It was, after all, an occasion for which there was no precedent. Constance put together an uncompromisingly soldierly rig-out—dark-green woolen blouse with brass buttons, green tweed knee breeches, black stockings, and heavy boots. She wore a cartridge belt around her waist, with an automatic hanging from it on one side and a Mauser rifle on the other, a bandolier and haversack on her shoulder. "What do you think of my rig-out," Constance asked Nora Connolly [James Connolly's daughter] who calls herself Nono in the following account:

"You look a real soldier, Madame," said Nono admiringly, and Madame beamed as if she had received a tremendous compliment.

"What's your rig like, Nono?"

"Something similar. Only I have puttees and my shoes have plenty of nails in the soles. I was thinking of wearing my Fianna hat, but maybe a tam would be better."

"This will be my hat," said Madame, putting on her best hat—a black velour with a heavy plume of coque feathers. (Haverty 1988, 139–40)

"What to wear at the revolution" would indeed be important in Armagh and Long Kesh prisons, for it was the historic right of the political prisoner to wear her/his own clothes. If there had been "no precedent" in 1916, there would be no such lack a history sixty years later, thanks to the one that was provided, flamboyantly, daringly, by republican women like Maud Gonne, Charlotte Despard, and Constance Markievicz.

86

The WPDL, which the three women had been instrumental in establishing in 1921, was banned in 1923. Following the release of republican prisoners, it was reconstituted as the Released Prisoners Committee. It re-emerged once again in 1931 as the People's Rights Association in response to Article 2A, an amendment to the Free State's 1937 constitution that gave to police the unrestricted right to detain and search anyone they chose, including women. In part at the behest of Maud Gonne, "the Women's International League for Peace and Freedom passed a resolution of protest against this, viewing with particular concern the 'moral danger' in which it placed women who could be searched and detained at will by any man in the police force" (Ward 1990, 158).

Negative stereotypes of the Irish as existing somewhere "beyond the pale" of English civilization have informed the eight-hundred-year history of British cultural and political colonialism in Ireland. These stereotypes, from the "Irish bull" to the "Fenian pest," which Liz Curtis (1984) has called "nothing but the same old story" and which Seamus Deane (1985) has analyzed in "Civilians and Barbarians," can be reread in their contemporary redeployment around the issue of gender as capturing and recontaining through mass culture the republican resistance narrative. As Bill Rolston (1989) has pointed out in his critical reading of the "images of women in novels of the Northern Ireland conflict," women characters are conventionally assigned a limited set of stereotypical roles within a plot that is always already defined by the reductive identification of the masculine republican "villain," portrayed as a "loner," who acts out of "personal need or psychological inadequacy" (42). This portrayal thereby isolates him from an organized political collective with an articulated social program. Within these dominant, male-centered, popular narratives—which borrow as well from specific traditions and images within the Irish heritage of "Mother Ireland"—the consequential options for women are restricted to those of the classic "mother" who fears the danger of random violence for her offspring (44) or the proverbial "seducer" who lures the innocent male into sinful temptations (47); alternatively, political women may be seen as "villains," revolutionaries, and therefore examples of failed womanhood: "Their curse is that, having abandoned their natural vocation of motherhood, they can never be real 'terrorists' like men" (51).

No less than mass-circulation novels, the popular film media have explicitly gendered the romantic plot paradigms of the IRA and the Northern Irish conflict. Examples range from John Ford's early *Informer* (1935), set in civil war Dublin of 1922, to Mike Hodges's contemporary *Prayer for the Dying* (1987), and include as well Ford's later romance, *The Quiet Man* (1952), Don Sharp's *Hennessy* (1975)—which, for all that it conformed to cinematic conventions, was denied distribution by two cinema organizations in Britain (Curtis 1984, 80)—and Pat O'Connor's *Cal* (1984). All five American and British films, spanning as they do half a century, depict renegade IRA men caught between the demands of their "outlaw" organization and the forces of "law and order"—although *The Quiet Man* displaces direct representation by mediating it through a western/boxer formula. For these protagonists the social and ideological alternative to their alienation/ostracism is variously incarnated in a woman, whose nurturing, caring, even passionate, assistance almost necessarily fails—*The Quiet Man* again provides the exception—to counter the untrammeled forces of violence, whether "legal" or "illegal."

The Informer, based on Liam O'Flaherty's novel and set in Ireland during the time of the rebellion and the Black and Tans, opens with a destitute and disheveled Nolan contemplating a wanted poster; a reward of twenty pounds is being offered for the IRA "murderer" Frankie McPhillip. Although the two men had worked together within the organization in the past, Frankie has been in hiding, and Gypo Nolan, for his part, has been court-martialed for failing to carry out an assignment. When Nolan, unable to provide for his girlfriend Katie, finds her soliciting on the street, he decides to turn in his friend Frankie to the Tans. The wanted poster, with its offer of twenty pounds, is insistently juxtaposed with a poster offering passage to "America" for just ten pounds—the escape Nolan and Katie dream of. Frankie is gunned down by British soldiers during a fleeting clandestine visit to his mother and sister, and Nolan squanders his reward on drink and carousing with a new-found friend anxious to help him spend his sudden wealth.

But the IRA must have its vengeance, and Nolan is summoned by Commandant Dan Gallagher. Katie tries in vain to intercede with Gallagher's girlfriend, who is also Frankie's sister, but Nolan is found guilty by an IRA court of inquiry and sentenced to death. Nolan attempts to escape, is mortally wounded, but manages to make his way to a church where he finds Frankie's mother. Finally, a Judas figure in a Christ-like death at the foot of the cross, Nolan dies with her forgiveness. Where girlfriends and

87

sisters are powerless to confront the organized male violence, proclaims the film, mothers and Mother Church provide absolution.

The Quiet Man, by contrast, allows the wife and sister to domesticate the feud between her new husband—an Irish-American boxer who has retired to his family cottage in rural Ireland after killing a man in the ring—and her brother, but only at the expense of her own independence. After opposing Mary Kay's marriage, her brother refuses to deliver her dowery, her mother's furniture, and her money. When her husband re-fuses to stand up for her and fight to retrieve it on her behalf, this Irish-colleen-cum-imminent-feminist refuses him her wifely favors. At first, to his reproach that she is greedy and materialistic and that her things mean nothing to him, certainly not enough to fight for, she insists that they are hers, her inheritance from her mother, her history, her independence—and thus stages a threatening emancipatory moment that the cinematic narrative must move to contain decisively. Thus, in the concluding scenes of the film, her husband, without recourse to violence, has become a "man," her furniture is in her home, and Mary Kay, a pregnant wife, is serving dinner to her reconciled brother and husband—the male order restored and reasserted.

"Would you die for me?" the widow of an executed Protestant police-man asks the young Cal, who has come to work on her farm and becomes her lover. She knows that her husband's death had been an IRA murder; she does not know that Cal had been the driver. *Cal, Hennessy*, and *A Prayer for the Dying* all narrate the story of a lone and isolated man, flee-ing the coercive and obsessive "terrorist" violence of the IRA, who would now die instead for the love of a woman. Hennessy has already decided to abandon the IRA when he finds his wife and daughter shot dead by British soldiers. Instead he decides to extract a personal and suicidal re-venge by blowing up the houses of Parliament on their opening day in the presence of the queen. He is killed in the end by Tobin, his best friend in the IRA, which ironically has had to work with the Special Branch in order to stop a slaughter that neither party, albeit for contradictory reasons, wants to see happen. In *Cal*, the protagonist's former colleagues harass him to reverse his decision to defect, and his father's house is burned out by the Protestants; in the end he is interned by British soldiers. In *A Prayer for the Dying*, Martin, a (former) marksman for the IRA, is pursued by the IRA and the British mafia, both of whom want his services. In the end, it is the gangsters who kill him, but he dies in the arms of a priest, the uncle to a blind girl he has fallen in love with. The priest agrees to give him absolution only if Martin will repent his murderous past. Martin's confiteor, however, absolves both himself and the Church for its official refusal to support the liberation struggle—to provide funeral masses, for example, for slain IRA members or, as in the actual case of Father Faul, to support the H Block hunger strikers during their protest for political status.

Together these five films mark the seven decades of struggle against colonialism and sectarianism since the partition in 1921 which divided Ireland into twenty-six southern and six northern counties. Each film narrates, according to the ascendant political conditions of its historical moment, an agenda that requires both the delegitimization of the IRA through its emasculation and the concomitant depoliticization of the women's role that would have contributed to transforming the repressive paradigms. This ideological project also distinguishes British propaganda, as well as the globalized mass culture. Rita O'Hare (n.d.), then director of Sinn Fein's women's department (established in 1980), who was herself shot by British soldiers in 1971, notes:

One of the biggest weapons in Britain's arsenal during its war against the Irish people has been that of black propaganda and republican women have suffered most from this.

In the early Seventies we were the "grandmothers of hate." Maire Drumm who was targeted in this way paid for it with her life, gunned down in a hospital ward. In the late Seventies and early Eighties we were the female dupes in a man's war when we raised the oppression of Northern women and the treatment of women prisoners.

During the grim year of the hunger strike, the mothers, wives, sisters and daughters of the hunger-strikers were bombarded with demands from the media, clergy and politicians to remove their support from the prisoners. Women whose opinions had never been sought before were now being wooed, blackmailed and guilt-tripped in an attempt to break the hunger-strikers before them. (84)

On 1 March 1981, the same day that the women prisoners in Armagh jail's A Wing ended their no-wash protest, republican prisoner Bobby Sands began his hunger strike in the H Blocks. Sands, who had been joined by Francis Hughes and Raymond McCreesh, died sixty-six days later, on 5 May. The funeral of Bobby Sands, who had been elected to Parliament while on the hunger strike, was attended by an estimated one hundred thousand people. He was replaced on the strike by Joe McDonnell. By the time that the hunger strike was called off on 3 October 1981, ten prisoners in all—Sands, Hughes, McCreesh, Patsy O'Hara, Martin Hurson, Kevin Lynch, Kieran Doherty (who had been arrested with Mairead Farrell), Joe McDonnell, Mickey Devine, and Tom McElwee—were dead.

The tradition of the hunger strike in which these men participated is writ long and large over the centuries of Irish history. According to the Brehon Laws of the fifth century A.D., a person could seek redress for a grievance by fasting at the door of the offending party. Over the centuries hunger strikes, although not always rewarded, remained one strategy in the ideological arsenal of Irish resistance, used again and again, from late-nineteenth-century Fenian prisoners in British jails demanding political status to Marion and Dolours Price in 1973. After 206 days of force feeding, the Price sisters were transferred as they demanded, from detention in Britain to Armagh prison in Northern Ireland.[4] In 1981, the H Block prisoners struck again for certain of the privileges that attached to "special category" status: the right to wear their own clothes; the right to refrain from penal work; the right to associate freely with other political prisoners; the right to organize their own educational and recreational facilities; the right to receive one letter, visit, and parcel a week; and the right to earn remission of sentence.

Some years after W. B. Yeats had finished his hunger-strike play, *The King's Threshold* (1904), Terence MacSwiney died on his own hunger strike in South London's Brixton jail following his arrest in 1920. Yeats altered the ending of the play, which had originally concluded with the hunger-striking poet, Seanchan, capitulating to the king for the sake of his life. The new ending, however, left Seanchan dead and his pupils, who supported his protest, themselves under sentence of death (Beresford 1987, 431).

Seanchan, the poet, has been expelled by the king from his council and in protest has been fasting to the death, in what the king calls "an old and foolish custom" (70), at the king's threshold. According to the king and his couriers, "it was the men who ruled the world, / And not the men who sang to it, who should sit / Where there was the most honour" (71). But the king also fears the insurrectionary threat posed to his rule by the popular poet's imminent death and pleads with all who might assist— the pupils, the mayor, a monk, a soldier, the princesses, and finally Seanchan's betrothed—to intervene to persuade the poet to cease his protest. Only Seanchan's own mother refuses categorically to participate in the appeal. "Your mother," the poet's servant Brian tells him, "gave no message, for when they told her that you had it in mind to starve or get again the ancient right of the poets, she said, 'No message will do any good. We cannot change him,' and she went indoors, lay down upon the bed and turned her face out of the light" (77). But while decisively excepting the figure of the mother from the clamor of the poet's cajoling detractors, Yeats's play is more ambivalent about his fiancée. As the mayor explains to the king,

> But I'll go find the girl that he's to marry.
> She's coming, but I'll hurry her, my lord.
> Between ourselves, my lord, she is a great coaxer.
> Much honoured, my lord. O, she's the girl to do it;

> For when the intellect is out, my lord,
> Nobody but a woman's any good. (80)

He suggests here that women, at least those who have not "given them-selves to a [political] opinion," can be made to act out of more personal motives. And indeed, Fedelm approaches a near-unconscious Seanchan, saying, "I will not give you up to death; no, no! / And are not these white arms and this soft neck / Better than brown earth?" (91). But the poet rallies himself and is able to persuade his beloved to embrace his cause— and his death. In the end it is the continued refusal of the institutions of the state to recognize the poet's ancient right that presides against the strength of his women, over his demise on hunger strike.

91

Whereas *The King's Threshold* dramatizes the Irish historical issue of the hunger strike though the state's efforts to mobilize its ideological appara-tus against the protester, *The Price of Freedom*, a play written in 1983 by Eoghan Mac Cormaic and smuggled out of Long Kesh prison, focuses in-stead on the frustrated attempts by a hunger striker's mother and father— but omitting a wife or fiancée—to persuade these same institutions on behalf of the fasting prisoners during the 1981 hunger strike. The prisoner speaks to his struggle:

> While in this war to be a winner
> I must gradually grow thinner
> Losing muscle and fatty matter
> So the weak can beat the strong
> In a war where rules are wrong. (37)

Neither the Free State (that is, the Republic of Ireland) nor the Church, nor the SDLP, the "Catholic" electoral party of Northern Ireland, will agree to endorse the legitimacy of the strikers' demands for political status. In addition to the hypocrisy of the Free State and the Social and Democratic Labour Party (SDLP), it is the treachery of the Church that is identified and assailed by the prisoner's play: "They vowed to sink the battle ship / By using family interventions. / . . . / As families already suffering too much / Were coaxed to say they'd intervene, / The clergy kicked away the crutch / of church support for the *cealachan* [fasting person]" (42). As Rita O'Hare (n.d.) pointed out, and as these two plays, one by the pre-mier Irish poet and the other by a republican prisoner, demonstrate in different ways, it is the political status of women—as much as that of the prisoners themselves—that is at stake in the contest between the state and the organized resistance movement.

While on hunger strike for political status in 1972 in Crumlin Road Jail, the republican prisoner Billy McKee had maintained that "this war would be won or lost in the prisons of Ireland" (Kelley 1982, 179). In a pamphlet response, a decade later, to the intervention from Church, state, and, finally, family, in the 1981 hunger strike, the "lifers" in prison attacked the hegemonically proffered idea that "the IRA can be defeated through its prisoners" (*Lifers*, n.d., 4), arguing that the "British and Irish collaborators [try to] make it seem as if it is the Republican Movement and not the British that are our jailers" (2). The issue of the family, particularly as "family" is construed through the role conventionally played by wives and mothers in defining and maintaining traditional familial coherence and ideological integrity, is central to the resistance narrative of the hunger strike. In the prisoners' press release on 3 October 1981, at the end of the hunger strike, the prisoners themselves spoke to this contested ideological space of public/private: "We, the protesting republican prisoners in the H-Blocks, being faced with the reality of sustained family intervention, are forced by this circumstance, over which we have no control at the moment, to end the hunger strike" (Bernard 1989, 155). In a 31 August 1981 "comm," or clandestine communication, to the IRA leadership outside, 'Bik' MacFarlane, the H Blocks officer in charge of the hunger strike inside the prison, had spoken to the growing family pressure, and the pressure on the family from church and state: "I think we have done everything in our power to combat this, so we can only wait and see. It wrecks me to think that the breaking power lies with those who haven't a clue what our struggle is all about. I'm serious—I'm shattered even thinking about it" (Beresford 1987, 410).

Ten Men Dead, an account of the 1981 Irish hunger strike by the *Guardian* journalist David Beresford (1987), critically combines three separate but intersecting textual and political narratives. In regular typeface Beresford presents the account of the strike itself, the family background of the ten martyrs, the ideological processes that went into their strategic selection, the debates within the organization on the evolution of the strike, and the protracted negotiations with the Church, governments, and international groups. In smaller type are the "comms" sent from inside the prison to the IRA leaders who coordinated the multifaceted support work outside the prison with the prisoners' strike. Finally, there is an italicized "fiction," continued at the end of chapters two through nine, of a prison visit during which a "comm" is passed from the republican prisoner to his female visitor, herself an undercover IRA member—and messages, tobacco, and ballpoint-pen refills are passed back in exchange.

The fictional story is generically based on the paradigm of a "day in the life" of a prisoner, beginning with wake-up and the business of starting a new day, "on the blanket," and ending with the evening's political lecture and a republican song shouted and intoned among the cells. The paradigm is extended further to reference the traditional "boy meets girl" narrative as well, one that has been necessarily forsaken by a long-term sentence and that must be reconstructed within and by the political circumstances of detention. It is Christmas time and the prisoner falls asleep, thinking to himself: "Into jail at 22, out in his forties" (396). The period of manhood and romance is rechronologized in the prisoners' daily schedule, no longer the coming of age of a man, but the routine of breakfast, dinner, and teatime, interrupted by searches, slop-outs, and punishment cells. But this day also is scheduled for a visit, and the narrative of the visit is written counter to both the repressive prison regimen and the traditional romantic paradigm—a radical alternative scenario to the conventional "boy meets girl" encounter. The sanctioned expected visit with his mother has been deferred and the prisoner will meet instead with a woman from the movement acting as a friend of his sister. 93

The "comm" from the H Block's officer in charge to the Belfast Brigade written on a tightly rolled cigarette paper, must get out that day. The means of transmission subtly but critically restructures, at the same that it uses, the narrative paradigm. In the first section, only the "tightly rolled package" (180) shoved between the prisoner's legs and the breakfast "marge"—good for "greasing your arse" (81)—indicate the political significance of the impending visit. Then the daily prison inspection and charges are interrupted by the prisoner's fantasy of the forthcoming meeting:

He grinned to himself, wondering what she would be like. It would be odd, greeting a strange girl with an open-mouthed kiss. And him stinking, like he did. Like they all did. She was Sinn Fein and should know how to take his comm first. But it could always go wrong: two tongues simultaneously pressing two packages, locked in labial combat in the middle of the room. And if he dropped the comm! The screams from the womenfolk in scramble for it. He'd head-butt the screw and they'd wrench his mouth open, trying to stop him swallowing. The beating and the silence of the Boards. The prisoner shook his head clear. (175–76)

That fantasy, which rewrites the physical relationship with a woman into a political agenda, is followed by dinner and an Irish language lesson.

Finally the much-anticipated visit takes place. The "comm," now concealed in the prisoner's foreskin, escapes the strip search and the rectal-mirror examination. When the woman at last arrives, amid the usual hubbub of the family conversations of other visits, the exchange takes place. She is adept: "They embraced and she used her body with confidence to block the line of sight from the control booth, her hand nudging into his jacket pocket. The tobacco. Their mouths met and he tongued the small package to her. No problem" (303). In addition, "her Gaelic was better than his; she said she'd learnt it doing time in Armagh—two years on a possession charge. He had to ask her to repeat herself twice, once when he got confused by her pronunciation, the second time when he lost himself in the movements of her mouth and eyes" (303). The visit is over. But the exchange has been consummated through the passing of the message from the prisoner to his visitor. He returns to his cell. The messages, the cigarettes, as well as those shared by a loyalist prisoner, are distributed. There is communal jocularity about the encounter. And the prisoner and his cellmate sleep. "Into jail at 22, out in his forties." In the meantime, inside and outside prison, the inherited roles of men and women and their prescribed relations to each other are being remade.

94

"Biting at the grave" was the description sententiously conferred by the king on the fasting poet Seanchan, who was near death at his threshold. This phrase was appropriated by Padraig O'Malley (1990) to describe "the Irish hunger strike and the politics of despair." O'Malley considers his own discursively ambivalent approach to the historical narrative of the hunger strike which he finds "both noble and perverse" (5),

I was attracted and repelled by the hunger strikers' actions: attracted by the heroic element, the steely determination to sacrifice life itself on behalf of conviction, the impulse to transcend the daily petulance of stuporific resistance; repelled because I was tired of the small gestures of impotence, the fusing of the praxis of suffering and the pretensions of idealism to evoke the easy sentimentality that too often is the hallmark of the Irish response to questions of life and death. (6)

The critical contradictions of writing placed "beyond the pale" that are exhibited in the title to O'Malley's text and his prefatory confession reiterate the complexities of Tim Pat Coogan's earlier reluctant decision to narrate the story of the H Block and Armagh prisoners' blanket and no-wash protests when the project was proposed to him: his book, *On the Blanket* (1980) "was conceived—as so many children are—by accident" (11). The laterally implicit reference here to the controversial questions of contraception and abortion in Ireland[5] critically situates the book itself and its history of the prison protest within the discursive realm, in the Irish context, of the taboo, the unspeakable, the silenced, or the unacknowledged. Simultaneously, however, it perhaps covertly implies—albeit without articulating the connections or the sequel—that if the prison protest can be narrated, then so too might other transgressive topoi: "what sort of people embarked on such a protest. What drove them to it?" (xi). When Philip MacDermott suggested that Coogan write the H Block protest book, Coogan's reaction, as he reports it, was this:

I rejected the idea out of hand instinctively, recoiling from the idea of the excrement-befouled cells. Moreover, having just completed a work spanning the last troubled decade of Irish history, I felt myself for the time being emotionally unable to cope with Northern Ireland and its intensities. However, eventually largely out of politeness to Philip I agreed to think about the proposal, and to do some preliminary research. Almost immediately I was both fascinated and appalled. (xi)

In deciding finally to take on the task and see it through, Coogan concluded: "In a faecal society, itself resembling a prison in many respects, the H Block protest began to assume a repellantly apt symbolism" (xi).

In May 1980, at the same time that Coogan was writing his book, the Irish playwright Margaretta D'Arcy joined the Armagh women for three months in prison on their no-wash protest. Her account, as she disarmingly indicates in the preface, is

95

a non-dramatic and often rather absurd story of one person who found herself in Armagh Jail for three months during the period of the long-term prisoners no-wash protest in 1980. The women in Armagh said to me: 'Tell them everything' and this I have tried to do. And since so few books have been written about Irish women's experience as political prisoners over the last two centuries, I felt it essential to put down my own small experience with all its limitations. (D'Arcy 1981, 13)

In her move "beyond the pale," D'Arcy, while experientially identifying with the women protesters in the prison, also demarcates the political and discursive differences that distinguish her position from theirs. That D'Arcy "found herself" in Armagh jail, appears to indicate a politically passive entry into prison as well as an existentially, "non-dramatic" for a dramatist, active process of self-discovery. The women incarcerated for long sentences in Armagh ask her, on her release, to write their story, and because she, unlike them, is released, she attempts to acquiesce.

That attempt, *Tell Them Everything: A Sojourn in the Prison of Her Majesty Queen Elizabeth II at Ard Macha (Armagh)* (1981), is at once the story of the women's protest and the marking of the distance, indicated by the narrator, between its transgressive acts and their transcription. As Laura Lyons (1990) has pointed out, the tension in the subtitle, following the titular imperative, between the prison's official, bureaucratically British description ("prison of Her Majesty Queen Elizabeth II") and its Gaelic appellation ("Ard Macha") with the parenthetical transliteration "(Armagh)," linguistically betrays the complexity of the conflict, both nationalist and feminist. And in no small part the limitations to the "everything" that D'Arcy would tell are because "in Britain the intimidating and expensive laws of libel and criminal libel are used by the vested interest of the state as a means of covert censorship" (D'Arcy, 9).

Margaretta D'Arcy had been among a group of eleven women arrested as part of a protest on behalf of the Armagh republican women prisoners by Women against Imperialism, but only she and one other woman, Liz

Lagura, who was British, served their sentences in jail. Indeed, the British courts, in the face of adverse publicity, proved reluctant to prosecute the southern women, much less send them to jail, and within the women's movement itself, the membership debated among and against themselves the greater efficacy of paying the fines imposed versus spending time in prison. For D'Arcy, however, it was different: "I had to get myself into that prison" (1981: 35).

Inside Armagh, the dramatic peripeties are played out around the socially and ideologically distributed character assignments between the academic writer—individualist and solitary—and the republican women —organized in long-practiced solidarity: D'Arcy writes: "My initial contact with the other prisoners made me feel like one of the villains of a Brechtian play, self-centred, individualist, used to an explosive and intensely vigorous public life" (67). The difference was marked in particular between writer Margaretta D'Arcy and OC Mairead Farrell: "I was not only an observer, I was also a participant and I had to retain my own individuality as a civilian. Mairead's task was infinitely more intricate—to ride the everchanging currents and winds affecting life in jail from society outside" (68).

On the no-wash protest, however, the intellectual D'Arcy watches her own physical integrity disintegrate—in her eyes, her hands, her vagina: "Every part of the body that can run down on you, will" (79). The special and specific problems of the female body for the organization of the protest become a sociopolitically critical issue: for example, the prison distributed towels and tampons only at the beginning of each month. "The whole problem of menstruation had been a taboo area, never discussed in the *Republican News*. Eilis talked in the yard about how the men in the Blocks were becoming educated" (80). And the women educated each other. Margaretta and Liz learned the politics of republicanism, and they eventually were asked by their skeptical fellow prisoners to give presentations on the women's movement. As Liz later reported to feminist writer and critic Nell McCafferty,

> They were bursting to discuss the women's movement with us, mainly I suppose because it was brand new and they'd been exchanging old ideas for years on end. We talked about abortion, which many of them thought was murder, contraception and sexuality. They wanted to know if we were anti-man or did we burn bras. They couldn't understand why men were not allowed into the women's movement, especially given the support between them and the men at Long Kesh. (D'Arcy, 14)

But D'Arcy also asks, "Where was the Women's Movement in 1976 when these women were rounded up, tortured, and thrown into prison?" (108).

Is Armagh, ask the women inside and outside, again and again, a feminist issue?

Sisters in Cells (Giolla Easpaig and Giolla Easpaig 1987) narrates, according to other conditions—inside prison and outside Ireland—another construction of solidarity. Aine and Eibhlin Nic Giolla Easpaig, two Irish sisters who grew up in England, were arrested in their home in Manchester in late 1974 and charged with "conspiracy to cause explosions." Their trial was held after passage of the Prevention of Terrorism Act and a series of "show trials" staged in Britain against republican actions, such **97** as that of Guildford Four and the Birmingham Six. On 27 February 1975, despite a lack of evidence, the sisters were convicted and sentenced to fifteen years in jail. They were released, with remission earned, after they had spent a decade as Category A prisoners—prisoners "whose escape would be highly dangerous to the public or police or to the security of the state"—in Durham Prison's H Wing. Their incarceration experience as Irish women in a British jail was radically different from that of their compatriots in Armagh. Rather than the highly trained, disciplined, and organized solidarity of the republican women prisoners, the Giolla Easpaig sisters had, in the midst of British "criminal" women and hostile wardresses who resented republican activities, only each other.

Prior to their trial and sentencing, they were held in isolation, separate even from each other, in Risley Remand Center. The prison term itself, then, brought its own measure of release: "Thank God that the two of us were together later on during our long sentence of imprisonment. One is grateful for small mercies in such circumstances. If some people marvel at our soundness of mind at the end of it all, it seems certain that sisters' solidarity helped us through the long hell" (52). In this hope the two women had made their appeal, through their lawyers—according to the republican practice, at the conclusion of their trial: "We did not speak but we did request, through our legal team, that if we were to spend long years incarcerated we be allowed to do our time together. *Giorraionn beirt bothar*, as they say at home. Two shorten a road" (69). On their release in summer 1985, Aine and Eibhlin wrote again of the importance of their sisterly solidarity in the cells: "All the cards are stacked against you—and you are in the hands of the police. You are on your own. That is, unless you have a sister in the same situation" (163).

"On your own" characterizes very decisively the Irish experience in British jails, if not under centuries of British control and occupation over the divided country. The very name "Sinn Fein," adopted at the beginning of this century's struggle, means "ourselves alone," and it is directly invoked by the two sisters to describe their own specific experience: "generally speaking, we said very little to anybody during our first year in

Durham. We stuck together and spoke Irish to each other. We believed that most others were hostile to us, or at the very best indifferent. The only alliance the Irish sisters had was one of self-reliance" (91–92). That collective imperative is likewise written into their text in the variable narrator pronouns that they deploy together: a combination of the first person plural "we" and the first person singular "I" followed by either "(Aine)" or "(Eibhlin)," producing a collective narrative voice against both the repressive isolation of confinement and the straightforwardly contained chronology of their prison story: "Let us begin at the beginning—as a typical policeman might say!—by introducing ourselves" (7).

Aine and Eibhlin Nic Giolla Easpaig's exemplary account begins with their family background in the Republic of Ireland, follows the family's move to England, the girls' schooling, their joining Sinn Fein in 1964, their arrest, their imprisonment, and their release and celebrated return to Ireland. But the story, published originally in Irish, is told not just for the sake of its telling; rather, as a document, it attests to the British treatment of the Irish people, and as a manifesto, it implicitly exhorts its readers, on both islands, to acknowledge their complicity in the conflict: "It is not the aim of this book to discuss these and other horrible cases in detail. But we would appeal to all readers to familiarise themselves with such cases and act on them, even if it is years too late to undo the monstrous injustices that the wrongful imprisonment of all these Irish people involves" (96).

The sisters also remind and caution their responsive readers that prisoner visits and work on prisoners' behalf are not inconsequential, either to the prisoners or to their visitants. In the Republic of Ireland, for example, "people's reputations can be undermined in court under Irish law by suggestions that those who visit prisoners in Port Laoise—a variety of prisoners, and for humanitarian reasons—are less reliable witnesses" (59). Similarly, in Britain the government exacts a price for interaction across prison walls: "Visiting Irish prisoners for no apparent reason other than distant acquaintance or simple Christian charity can be a dangerous thing for members of the Irish community in Britain, as has been proven. People have gone to jail for life for simply attempting to attend the funeral of a friend!" (118).

Indeed, in late 1988 Deirdre Whelan, the sister of Martina Shanahan, one of the Winchester Three (arrested in October 1988 on two charges of "conspiracy to murder" and released in April 1990), was detained under the 1974 Prevention of Terrorism Act while in England to attend her sister's trial. Whelan was eventually deported and finally "excluded" from returning to Britain, even to visit her own "sister in the cells." Aine and Eibhlin Nic Giolla Easpaig are determined to show through the writing of their prison book that the "barbarity" represented by the demarcation "beyond the pale" is always already located within the "pale" itself. "Let us say straightaway—because people are often quite confused about this—that people are found guilty or innocent under the legal processes that prevail *in this part of the world according to the rules*. This can have, and frequently has, very little to do with right or wrong, the truth or the whole truth" (56, emphasis added).

The Prevention of Terrorism (Temporary Provisions) Act (PTA) of 1974, according to Peter Hall's analysis in *Justice under Fire* (1988), "is commonly 99 assumed to have been born out of the killing of 21 people in the Birmingham pub bombings of 21 November 1974" (144). Revised in 1976 and again in 1984, and made effectively permanent in 1989, the act nonetheless remains in essence and effect the same legislation, providing the government with extended powers to detain persons for suspected involvement in or association with broadly defined "terrorist" activities. In addition to proscribing certain organizations, the act also prohibits displaying support for (such as flags, insignia, symbols, and so forth) or contributing to the support of (such as collecting money or aid) any of these organizations. Section 11 of the act further defines as a criminal offense the failure to disclose to the authorities any information that would allow for the capture, prosecution, or conviction of persons suspected of "terrorist" activity. This section has been used, for example, to threaten television and newspaper journalists. The PTA also grants power to the authorities to exclude from the country—as happened in the case of Deirdre Whelan—anyone suspected of involvement in "terrorist" activity. In addition, it allows extended powers of arrest and detention for the purposes of intelligence gathering and short-term internment. Originally directed against, although not restricted to, Northern Irish "terrorism," the PTA was explicitly extended in 1984 to cover "international terrorism." Hall speaks to the fears of many of critics of the act:

Where the PTA amounts to an extension of the law is not in the creation of substantive offences but in the creation of substantial powers. Without reference to any offence a person can be arrested, detained, questioned at length, and then thrown out of the country and stopped from returning. This unchecked power has been used on political activists among others and represents a form of political control and censorship of dangerous proportions. Furthermore, it can be and has been extended to cover international terrorism and thus a wide range of political activists are drawn into the net of the PTA. Still more frightening is the prospect that, as on occasions has been mooted, the Act could be extended to cover industrial or domestic 'terrorism.' (183)

Whereas the PTA grants to policing authorities extensive control over political activities, the systemic and systematic practice of strip-searching in the prisons confers on government authorities excessive power over the very bodies—especially women's bodies—of the state's internees. According to Professor Ivor Browne, "most people think of rape as a sexual act; in fact the more you go into studying rape the more clearly it is revealed as an act of hatred and violence and strip-searching has all the connotations of this" (cited in Troops Out Movement n.d.).

Systematic strip-searching was introduced into Armagh prison in November 1982, and between November 1982 and November 1985, on average 2.5 strip-searches were carried out on each of the women prisoners there. Although strip-searching has been justified by the authorities on the basis of "security needs" in the prison, the women prisoners themselves argue that the repeated searches are in fact another, and more humiliating, means of harassment. Rather than diminishing in frequency as time and criticism went on, however, the practice of strip-searching has continued to escalate, both in Northern Ireland and in Britain. In 1985, for example, two Irish republican women, Martina Anderson and Ella O'Dwyer, remanded in custody and awaiting trial in Brixton jail, were strip-searched on average 25 times a month. Martina Anderson described the experience:

> I walk to the wing knowing what lies ahead. There are two empty cells and I am ordered into one of them. Once in the cell, two prison officers order me to take my clothes off while a third holds up a blanket shoulder high. The fourth stands watching. Realising that their eyes are constantly watching me over a blanket and feeling so helpless knowing I cannot do anything I start to remove my blouse and bra. (Troops Out Movement n.d.)

Similarly, Ella O'Dwyer emphasizes the degradation that strip-searching exacts from its women subjects:

> I had to stand naked while they checked my clothes. Prison officers rub my hair and ears and like an animal I have to lift my feet so they can inspect them too. The awful dread is that I will be touched so I am stiffened to resist. They have told me they can lift my breasts forcibly if they decide to and even probe my body folds. They can touch any part of me at all . . . I know that every part of me has been touched accidently or deliberately since I arrived here. Normal physical contact has become a challenge. (Troops Out Movement n.d.)

According to its critics, systematic strip-searching is an assault by the representatives of the state not only on the personal identity but also on the political commitments of its women victims.

The "pale," that is, may need to be redefined, not just around male/female relationships, but consentaneously around the arbitrarily upheld and discriminatorily practiced distinctions between "civilian" and "barbarian"—even if the voice should grow shrill in the process of redefinition.

Chapter Four

Narrative in Prison: Stories from the

Palestinian Intifada

The story of "Um Khadr"—al-Sayyida Fatima Husayn—forms an extraordinary and exceedingly strange scenario, a scenario that no writer, however clever and however he may have searched the world of romance, could ever have imagined.

RAYMONDA TAWIL, *Women Prisoners in the Prison Country*

The stranger-than-fiction story of Um Khadr tells the life of a Palestinian woman living under Israeli occupation. When she had been married for ten years, Um Khadr's husband, Abd al-Rahman, traveled to Brazil, where he hoped to earn enough money to support his wife and their two sons and two daughters at home. Um Khadr did not hear from the man she married for another thirty years. Her youngest daughter is a deaf mute. Her first daughter was abandoned by her own husband, who left her behind with five children when he married a Syrian woman. Khadr, the Palestinian mother's eldest son, is in an Israeli prison, sentenced to ninety-six years behind bars. His younger brother, Ghazi, spent ten years in Israel's prisons. Um Khadr was herself arrested at the Allenby Bridge while returning home from a visit to Amman. Following her release from prison, her husband reappeared from his thirty-year absence in South America, unannounced, ailing, and debilitated, only to be deported to Jordan by the Israeli military occupation authorities.

The next day they took him to the bridge. I sent my youngest daughter with him. I stood with tears in my eyes and watched as he disappeared into the crowd of travelers. Then I went home, like I've always done, alone, but with my head high and strong in my faith and resolve to look for the springtime sun. Life has made many hardships for me, but what is there new in all that has happened?? (Tawil 1988, 188)

Her son Khadr had already reminded his mother that there was nothing untoward about his being in prison. Following his detention, Um Khadr had searched the Israeli prisons for an entire month to locate her missing child. When finally she found him in the Ramallah Military prison, she visited him wearing black and weeping, only to be gently reproached by her prisoner son: "What are you wearing . . . where is your love for me that I should have to welcome you in that dress. I thought you would be proud of your valiant sons. I didn't think you would be dressed in mourning" (182). The many hardships that life made for Um Khadr she reworked into a biography of resistance, a narrative that took her from outside the prison walls into its cells, where she rejoined her sons in their collective struggle. Arrested at the Allenby Bridge, she no longer feared prison: "I was neither angry nor sad. I didn't lose my faith in Allah. I will disappear behind the bars, but what does that matter? I will be like Khadr and Ghazi. Prison will bring us together" (184).

The story of Um Khadr is told in Raymonda Tawil's *Women Prisoners in the Prison Country* (1988), which recounts the personal and political histories of twenty-six Palestinian women political detainees. From Terese Halsa, who left home at the age of fifteen to join the resistance in Lebanon, was arrested in 1972, and became one of the senior prisoners whose strength continued to support the younger detainees, to Ra'ida Shahada, a schoolgirl arrested for throwing stones at Israeli soldiers, these individual women and their separate stories are part of an emergent historical compilation. Together with the popular committees, writers unions, prisoner associations, research centers, and other institutional structures, formal and informal, they represent the combined textual and infrastructural rudiments of what may become a Palestinian state, declared at the nineteenth meeting of the Palestine National Council in Algiers in November 1988.

Women Prisoners in the Prison Country was published in the spring of 1988, in the first year of the Palestinian *intifada*, the popular uprising against twenty years of Israeli occupation of the West Bank and Gaza Strip. Raymonda Tawil, the author/editor of the collection, herself spent a year under house arrest in 1976 (see Tawil 1983). She is a journalist and editor of the monthly news magazine *al-Awdah* (The Return), which was closed by the occupation authorities in May 1988. Because of the prisoner exchanges of 1983 and 1985, which released several thousand detainees, Tawil was able to interview many former political prisoners and to collect and assemble their stories into an anthology that is at once historical and visionary. Her mission to document the prison lives of these twenty-six women acquired a new relevance and urgency from the events of the *intifada*. Israeli prisons are being populated once again by the Palestinian resistance, and while exact figures are unavailable—deliberately obscured by Israeli detention procedures and the military government's calculated failure to report arrests and the whereabouts of prisoners—it is known that some twenty thousand Palestinians were arrested in the first year of the *intifada*.

Tawil here disclaims the demands, even the applicability, of scientific objectivity: "We have attempted to go beyond the bounds of statistical and academic research which merely presents and enumerates dates and figures. We have sought instead to sketch a personal and social picture of the life of the struggle" (6). Writing in 1966, before the June war of 1967 and the occupation of the West Bank and Gaza, Ghassan Kanafani too, in his study of Palestinian literature under Israeli occupation, *Literature of* **103** *Resistance in Occupied Palestine 1948–1966* (1982), found that the apparent methodological problem was itself part of the resistance movement and its historical transcription. According to Kanafani, a researcher who does not play an active part in the resistance is not in a position to write its history. History and the historical record, that is, are both made by and constitutive of the course of events themselves, and presentist preoccupations confute necessarily the academic injunction of historical objectivity. If, for Kanafani, accepted or conventional academic standards have been displaced by the material pressures of the history of resistance, those same pressures argue, according to Tawil, for a curricular revision of academic practices. "Perhaps," she writes, "our universities should assign a course of study in prison history, one that would acquaint the students with the real history of peoples' struggle through their heroic efforts inside the prisons" (9). Such an investigation, however, with its efforts to introduce the lessons of prison into the school system, breaches the disciplinary and institutional boundaries that maintain the regulated ordering of social structures. Israeli prison officials, seeking to maintain that hierarchical order, attempt to reenforce the distinctions that separate researcher from subject, and prevent Tawil from pursuing further her inquiry. They ask: "But what could be lacking? You enjoy a comfortable and pleasant life. You're an educated lady. Why would you want to sink down to the level of street life?" (5).

Ferial Sama'an Salim was another of the women prisoners interviewed by Raymonda Tawil. Prior to her arrest, Salim had been a history teacher in the Ramallah Girls School, where the secondary school curriculum legislated by the occupation authorities found no relevance in the lived history of the students. Ferial Salim confronted in her own way that dilemma, the dilemma of "what does a history teacher say . . . about the true realities of history made material in the roar of army vehicles, the whistle of bullets from Uzis and the clang of metal . . . the bark of loudspeakers, the rifle shots . . . and the tear gas?" (108). For Ferial Salim, "the road was clear before [her]" (108), and she was arrested for planting explosives in Jerusalem. The Palestinian historical narrative, in activist contrast to the Israeli school curriculum, is punctuated by a sequence of critical moments, written on the land itself, drawn onto its map, and marking defeats and setbacks no less than triumphs: the Balfour Declaration of 1917, the 1936–39 popular revolt, the creation of the state of Israel in 1948, the June 1967 war, the October 1973 war, Land Day of 1976, and the Israeli invasion of Lebanon in 1982; 1988 defines the first year of the *intifada*, or uprising.

104   *Intifada* in Arabic means a shiver, a shudder or tremor, and derives from the trilateral root n-f-d, which connotes shaking, shaking the dust from. In an essay entitled *"Intifada* or Revolution [*Thawra*]" (1988), part of a longer analysis of the recent events in the Occupied Territories, the Egyptian intellectual Abdelwahab Elmessiri discusses the significance of the 1988 Palestinian uprising and its connections both to previous Palestinian and Arab-Islamic history and to other exemplary "revolutions," in the combined ideological effort to redefine the specificity of Palestinian historicity and to dislocate it from an international historical narrative of resistance struggle.

> Formulas do not exist in a vacuum, but within a conceptual framework that incorporates a system of conventions. . . . Some writers have tried to drop the word *intifada* and replace it with the word *thawra* [revolution]. The word *thawra*, however, as a general term is, to my mind, inappropriate for what is happening here in that it simply assimilates this as part of world culture. The *intifada* has its own specificity which must be expressed.[1]

Elmessiri's anti-orientalist argument, however, premised as it is on a still-unreconstructed East/West dichotomy and thus requiring that a peculiarly Arab-Islamic terminology assert itself against Western-dominated political conventions, ultimately elides the global consequences of the Palestinian resistance movement in favor of an Islamic program and ends by reasserting an "orientalism in reverse." However, if, as Perry Anderson (1988) has pointed out, *revolution* is a term with a precise meaning, and if, according to Armand Mattelart (1979), following Lenin, the "revolutionary moment" is that moment "where the ruling class can no longer maintain its domination in an unchanging form and conditions become intolerable for the oppressed masses, who intensify their struggles" (117), then the Palestinian *intifada* must claim a place of its own in the narrative of revolution. The term *intifada* itself makes that place a critical locus for examining the new possibilities for such a narrative.

Whereas the Israeli government and its ideologues are seeking to prevent the Arabic word *intifada* from entering the Hebrew lexicon, the Palestinian vocabulary has proclaimed its own initiative and insisted on producing its own narrative construction of events. In Europe and the United

States, "modern" literature is often designated "post–World War II" literature. That same effort at a literary-historical narrative is articulated differently in the Arab world, where contemporary writing is distinguished as
"post 1948" (post *nakba,* or disaster) or "post 1967" (post *naksa,* or setback).
Following the 1982 Israeli invasion of Lebanon, the two-month siege
of its capital city, and the departure of the PLO from Beirut, Arab writers
generally and Palestinian writers in particular found themselves enjoined
to reassess the critical role and place of the intellectual within the resistance movement (see Harlow 1984). In the summer months of the first year   **105**
of the *intifada,* Arab writers from Morocco, Egypt, Lebanon, Syria, and
elsewhere, met in Sanaa, Yemen, to discuss their own revised relationship
of alternating compromise and active support for the Palestinian struggle.
Nizar Qabbani's poem "Children of the Stones," which first appeared in
December 1987 and was quickly reprinted in publications throughout the
Arab world, had provided a preliminary critique of the Arab failure to
"shake the dust" from its own social hierarchies.

> They fought for us . . . until they were killed
> While we sat in our coffeehouses
>
> .   .   .   .
>
> Ay . . . o generation of betrayals . . .
> O generation of brokers . . .
> O generation of discards . . .
> O generation of debauchery . . .
> You will be swept away—however slow is history—
> By the children of the stones.

In the months that followed the publication and rapid dissemination of
Qabbani's celebrated verse, more and more poems commemorating and
celebrating the *intifada* appeared in news weeklies and daily newspapers
as well as in literary journals, creating an "anthology" in its own right,
and producing and reproducing variations on the image of children confronting the amassed military apparatus of the Israeli Defense Forces.
The Arabic poetic tradition rallied round the *intifada,* captivated by its
symbolic power and capturing that power in its symbols, and providing,
according to that other tradition of resistance poetry, the mobilizing formulas for its popular audiences living in Arab lands beyond the borders
of the Occupied Territories. "The children of the stones" of the international newspaper headlines became poetic figures, heroes in the epic
tradition, but even the longer poems, such as "Death on the Sidewalk"
(1988), by the Egyptian colloquial poet Abd al-Rahman al-Abnudi, a poem
that appeared in six installments in the Cairo weekly *Ruz al-Yusif,* emphasized the imagistic dimension of the *intifada,* seizing and suspending,
even reifying, the historical narrative in the spellbinding and compelling

vision of the "stone," the *hijara*, wielded by children as both weapon and building block.

The conflicted relationship, however, between poetry and resistance was at the same time being submitted to a new scrutiny by poets and writers. Within such a debate in the pages of *al-Ahali*, a leftist opposition newspaper in Egypt, Ibrahim Nasrallah, a Palestinian poet, remarked, "If I am against anything here, it is the transformation in creative works of the *intifada* into a dessicated analogy without any soul, which is what is happening in 95% of the poems. . . . In this torrent of *ghazals* [poetry], all you see is the substitution of the word 'stones' [*hajar*] for the word 'dawn' [*sahar*] or any other woman's name, and there you have a poem" (3 August 1988). As Asʿad al-Asʿad said in a similar debate in the Damascus-published *al-Hadaf*, "it is not a matter of stones [*al-hajar*] but of throwing stones" (19 June 1988).

The *intifada*, even as it was altering historical circumstances on the ground, generated generic differences for its poets and writers. The narratives that emerged from the concatenation of events in the Occupied Territories were stories, anecdotes, accounts of elderly women confronting soldiers, of neighbors sharing food, and informal classes held in homes when the schools were closed, that circulated by word-of-mouth, acquiring in the telling renewed impetus, new settings in different villages and refugee camps, and alternate casts of characters. One such tale, repeated in numerous places at various times, was the story of the child Ammar (or Ahmad, or Ghassan, or Muhammad), six years old, caught throwing stones by an Israeli soldier. The soldier asks the boy, now in his custody, who has told him to throw those stones. Finally, under pressure, the child answers, "My brother Mansour." Thinking he has perhaps found one of the legendary leaders of the uprising, the soldier orders Ammar to take him to his brother. When they reach his home, the child calls to his brother, who eventually appears at the door, "a child of three years old, with his eyes shining and carrying a balloon in his hand."[2] Thus these stories of collective participation in the opposition to occupation authorities involve home as well as street, domestic space no less than public places, and have worked complex infrastructural reorderings in a traditional Palestinian society and in the organization of its resistance movement.

The florilegium of imagery that characterizes the poetry of the *intifada* is historicized in the documentary materials, from the *bayanat*, or communiques issued by the Unified Leadership, to reports on prison conditions, all produced out of the sustained resistance of the more than one and a half million Palestinians living under occupation. The critical importance of the documentary as a literary genre to the narration of the *intifada* is emphasized by the writers themselves. In a series of interviews conducted early in the uprising, in spring 1988, by *al-Hadaf*, the weekly magazine of the Popular Front for the Liberation of Palestine (PFLP), Arab writers were asked to respond to the question "How is the *intifada* reflected in your writing?" (19/26 June 1988).

For Salman Natur, in the same discussion, what was significant was the "recording of small realities, the kind that give body to the humanity of the *intifada*." For Natur, however, Arabic literature was not yet adequate, **107** for reasons of circumstance, to the theoretical and creative demands being made on it by the *intifada*: "I believe that our literature is not up to the level of the *intifada*, but then that is only natural, for the time made by the *intifada* is still very short." The historical positioning of the intellectual within the course of events is rendered similarly problematic by Asᶜad al-Asᶜad. Yet unlike Ghassan Kanafani, who two decades earlier had insisted that the committed participation of the writer and critic in the very events being narrated was a criterion for the historicity of her/his account, al-Asᶜad sees that the failure of historical distance inhibits literature's rendering of the uprising: "the *intifada* will leave a much greater mark [on literature] in the future than in the present. The finest writings are those not written directly from within the events" (1988).

The historical placement of the writer is further complicated by her or his geopolitical location. The articulation of Palestinian literature over the last forty years into a literature of exile (*manfa*) and a literature under occupation (*taht al-ihtilal*) participates in the recent historical trajectory of the Palestinian people—the flight and expulsion of significant numbers of the population in 1948 and again in 1967, the mass exoduses regularly reinforced by Israel's systematic policy of deportation. The *intifada* represents now a crucial transformation in the relationships of power between "inside" and "outside." Whereas Kanafani was much criticized in 1966 for his decisive presentation and analysis of the long-neglected Palestinian cultural production under Israeli occupation (inside the 1948 borders), at a time when the PLO functioned as the leadership in exile, the burden of momentum has now shifted to the Occupied Territories and the popular uprising. Perhaps like the exiled African National Congress (until its unbanning in 1990), which continued its organizational operations in Tanzania and the "frontline" states of southern Africa and its diplomatic operations in Western capitals, often in response to mobilizing developments from within South Africa itself, the Palestine National Council (PNC)/PLO issued its historic 1988 declaration of an independent state, testifying to the ideological and political transformations in the resistance agenda occasioned from the "inside" by the *intifada*. The Lebanese writer and intellectual Elias Khouri (1988) insisted after the first month of the uprising:

The Palestinian national experiment is today in the most serious of its historic turning points, having reached a stage of maturity which allows it to express itself on its own land, to establish a partial pattern for its historical trajectory and to lay the basis for a horizon of liberation deriving from its own internal developments.

Thus it is necessary that Arab and Palestinian thought not bypass the *intifada* as an ordinary event. It is a call for a fundamental review of Palestinian structures on all levels, a call to the resistance organization to rebuild itself according to priorities coming from inside—toward the establishment on new bases of a unity between the Palestinian inside and outside. The outside, the refugee camps in the countries neighboring Palestine, is being transformed into a replacement for the inside and a bridge from which is expressed the Palestinian struggle for an Arab nationalist cause, its heart and central point.[3]

The formal questions of genre posed by writers "outside," as well as the organization of Palestinian literature along the axis of exile/occupation, are being critically revised by the material force of historical circumstance and the consequences of geopolitical conditions as these are reworked by the *intifada*.

As historical events force the formal limitations of literary genre to give way to new political agendas, the institutional affiliations of even generic conventions are made to subvert the inherited ideal of the autonomy of literature and the sectarian interests served by such an ideal. *The Road to Birzeit*, a novel by Edmond Shahada published in summer 1988 and perhaps the first full-length "fictional narrative" to come out of the *intifada*, relies on a set of narrative paradigms and received plot structures that the novel itself is, finally, no longer able to resolve according to generic standards. *The Road to Birzeit* narrates a conventional romantic triangle formed by an older lover and a younger rival competing for the attention and affection of Wafaa, an attractive Birzeit coed. The coherence of that romance, which depends on a certain configuration of familial structures and a legacy of traditional patterns, is inhibited and ultimately transformed by emergent social formations within Palestinian society under occupation, organizational formations such as writers unions, universities, prisons, and the resistance movement itself.

Shahada's novel opens with a scene cited from a novel of the same title being written by Basil, the protagonist of *The Road to Birzeit* and a professor of educational psychology at Birzeit University in Ramallah. That scene, which has just been completed by Basil and is being transcribed by Wafaa, his student/secretarial assistant, represents an Israeli military roadblock (*hajiz ʿaskari*) in the Occupied Territories and a conversation between two soldiers on duty at the blockade. Each soldier figures a different ideological position within the Israeli political context. For the younger recruit, there is only horror at the murder of Palestinian civilians, but the older soldier provides the clichéd justification to his junior colleague: "The only good Arab . . . is a dead Arab" (6).

The opening scene of the novel critically transgresses the "green line," the geographical marker of the division between the state of Israel and the Occupied Territories, in two ways. On an ideological level, the Palestinian writer situates his narrative within the context of debates internal to the Israeli political program. On a territorial level, the border has been crossed by the occupying Israeli army. The function of the roadblock within the novel is to subvert its own militaristic purpose of monolithic control in the political arena. The roadblock becomes instead the site of confrontation on which the contradictions inherent in the conflict are to be renegotiated.

These larger political contradictions of state and resistance contend with and further enable the still-problematic romantic-involvement narrative and family-drama paradigm on which the plot is conventionally premised. Basil, the professor and political activist, has fallen in love with his much younger student and assistant Wafaa. To her he entrusts the completed manuscript of his novel, for her to see to its publication in the event that he is arrested and detained—a fear that is eventually realized.

In the meantime, however, Basil and several of his compatriots have been meeting secretly at the Young Men's Christian Association in West Jerusalem with Hananya, an unofficial representative of the Israeli "peace camp," in order to discuss, if only informally, potential negotiating positions around a resolution of the Palestinian-Israeli conflict. These clandestine "diplomatic" exchanges on the part of senior Palestinians are both countered and complemented by the public activities of the students in the streets, throwing stones and confronting Israeli soldiers, and marking through generational differences the historical developments of the Palestinian resistance movement:

after the occupation and numerous demonstrations, confrontations and even interactions as well, the inhabitants of the Occupied Territories had come to learn that the Jewish soldier was an ordinary person. He could be brave or cowardly, victorious or defeated. He could advance or retreat. The October War, or the Yom Kippur War as it is called by the Jews, had seriously eroded the legend of the invincible Israeli soldier, and as a result the confrontations between the people and the Defense Forces had become very different from what they were during the first years of the occupation. (38)

Both the possibility for negotiation and the potential of active resistance have assumed new dimensions in recent years, so that while Basil met with Israelis at the YMCA, "Muslih and Fawaz challenged the soldiers with determination and perseverance. The students were no longer frightened at the sight of the security men and responded to their provocations with provocations of their own.

When Basil's friend Salah is arrested, Basil realizes that his own detention is imminent and begins to prepare for that eventuality. These preparations are both material—he must arrange his house, deposit his manuscript with Wafaa, and settle his responsibilities—and psychological—he must be ready for the effect of prison on his own self-perceptions as well as on the various reactions of his associates, friends, and colleagues. Why has he been detained? What has he done? How will he respond, react, under the pressure of interrogation, isolation, torture? The combined specter and vision of prison as an almost inevitable moment in a Palestinian autobiography under occupation is at once realized and romanticized in *The Road to Birzeit*: "prison" is a dream that Basil, as if smitten with its heroized resonances, almost wills to come true, as well as an institutional reality maintained by the Israeli state apparatus of military occupation.

The conflicted relationship between the Arab intellectual and the *intifada* is central to the novel and its reconstruction of events around Basil's personal itinerary. Crucial in that narrative reworking of events is the anticipation of prison that animates Basil's decisions. Basil's (self-)image is informed by the ideological significance that attaches to the writer in prison as well as by the social and historical significance of "prison" (*al-sijn*) within the consciousness of the Palestinian population under occupation (30 percent of that population had passed through Israeli prisons at that time). Basil drives to Jerusalem and wanders about the Old City, attends prayers at the Dome of the Rock, and visits his old friend, the woman poet Abir. In his nostalgic meanderings, prison is reconceived as a potential work of art with Basil himself as the central persona: "He smiled somewhat bitterly as he imagined himself behind the prison walls, a smile that resembled that of the *Mona Lisa*. If he were standing now before Signor da Vinci, would he be able to turn his smile into a unique creative canvas?" (84). On his return to his home in Ramallah, as he is preparing his morning coffee, the soldiers arrive to fulfill Basil's expectations, if not the projected work of art.

With Basil in prison, Wafaa carries out his request to pursue the publication of his novel, and in the process she meets his friend Taysir, to whom she becomes engaged. After six university students plan and carry out the assassination of Said al-Batl, whose role as an Israeli collaborator has been exposed, the meetings between the Israeli mediator Hananya and Basil and his friends, are revealed as well. When Basil is released

110

from prison to return to his position at the university, he is reviled and physically attacked by a large group of students. While the Hebrew newspapers attempt to turn this incident into evidence of the lack of democracy among the Palestinians, the six students are arrested on charges of murder and "national zealotry." When one of them, Ayman, dies in suspicious circumstances in prison, the authorities fear that the funeral will give rise to further and still more violent confrontations. That fear is realized when Israeli settlers arrive to transform the funeral demonstration into a conflagration that leaves six more dead and dozens wounded. At the conclusion   **111** of the novel, Taysir and Wafaa are married and Basil's novel is published. The novel is the subject of a conference at Birzeit University and the object of banning orders issued by the military government. Basil is rearrested for the crime of being its author.

The Road to Birzeit, even as it narrativizes the events preceding and during the *intifada* according to the generic conventions and plot paradigms of the acculturated form of the novel, subjects those same formalities to a rehabilitating analysis of the internal debates and constitutive contradictions that animate the *intifada* and its development in relation to the PLO "outside." Those controversies, such as the traditional familial structures of authority, class imbalances, generational conflicts, collaboration, the role and function of leadership, "inside" (*dakhil*) and "outside" (*kharaj*), wrest the romantic/heroic paradigms from their foundations and relocate them within the force field of historical circumstance and political debate. In so proceeding, the novel confronts, rather than avoids, what Stuart Hall et al. (1978) have described as the "problem of actually engaging with the analysis of a really contradictory field, of intervening in a real field of struggle, by simply assigning the people whom you hope to rescue permanently to one or another of the poles" (71).

The importance for historical agency of a critical acknowledgment of apparently failed unanimity had already been emphasized in the months immediately following the Arab-Palestinian defeat in the June 1967 war. Ghassan Kanafani had written a series of critiques of an ostensible petrification around these contradictions within the Palestinian resistance agenda, critiques that focused especially on the patriarchal bases (*al-qaʾida al-ubuwa*) of Palestinian society and their consequences for the structure and organization of the resistance movement. "The danger in a time of defeat," according to Kanafani, "is that it contains within itself the simultaneous potential for both construction and demolition" (1990, 139). The role of critique is crucial to the renewal of the resistance, and that critique, Kanafani insists, using a metaphor of the "circulation of blood" (*al-daura al- damwiyya*) (143), must come from a younger generation. Warning that the absence of "new blood" in the centers of power threatens a cleavage between the infrastructure and the superstructure of the resistance, Kanafani goes on to claim that "the political party is only one form among several for the effective organization of powers in society"; he includes among the other possibilities unions of peasants, workers, and professionals, as well as cultural associations (153). The failure of such a circulation becomes manifest in what Kanafani refers to as the reified "language of the blind" (*lugha ʿamyaʾ*): "it seems that what we most need now is a revaluation of terminology" (146).

112   The narrative events and images that derive from the *intifada* suggest that such a revaluation is currently taking place. That revaluation is made radically explicit in *The Road to Birzeit* in the dialectically productive confrontations between the older intellectuals, such as Basil, and the more spontaneously organized students. Neither alternative is righteously vindicated or exonerated; rather, the mutually contradictory interaction, like the roadblock that dismantles, as always already operative, the monolithic inside/outside dichotomy in the first pages of the novel, is rendered immanently constructive of new organizational forms.

The tension in *The Road to Birzeit* between a romanticization of political prison and the political detainee and an ideological critique of the cult of an autonomous sphere of culture is critically elaborated around the question of leadership and generations as expressed in the vision of prison that impels Basil. Kanafani's "language of the blind" and the "dialogue of the deaf" (*hiwar al-tarshan*) that accompanies it cannot be made a literary school. Basil succeeds in completing his novel, a novel that will cause his reimprisonment as a result of its publication and popular success. The insistence of this conclusion, however, is not on posterity or a posthumous revival, for the "death of the author" can no longer sanction or be sanctioned by a transcendent literature or literary achievement. Rather, according to the novel's implicit, if ambivalent, argument, the institution of prison confers historical significance on the literary work and historical agency on its author.

In the introduction to *Policing the Crisis* (1978), an analytical reconstruction of "mugging, the state, and law and order" in Britain in the 1970s, Stuart Hall and his coauthors speculate on the potential reactions on the part of their prospective readerships. Common to the response of nearly all constituencies—police, media, academics, even liberal reformers— they suggest, will be an objection to its apparent bias and lack of balance. Most of their readers, they expect, will no doubt be worried that no solutions or remedies that follow from the analysis are proposed. The authors go on to critique such a demand: "if someone says to us: 'Yes, but given the present circumstances, what are we to do now?', we can only reply,

'Do something about the "present conditions".' . . . The practical remedy involves taking sides—struggling with the contradictions" (x).

While the Palestinian *intifada* is to be distinguished from the phenomenon of mugging on the basis of its material specificity within the historical narrative of imperialism, Zionism, and orientalism and the concrete conditions of settler colonialism and military occupation to which the uprising responds, the challenge it poses both to law and order and to literary critical disciplines resonates within the same configuration of issues of resistance to domination, the state's criminalization of political opposition, **113** and the contemporary global crisis following on the era of national liberation and decolonization. For Harris and Wallace, who examined the 1980 Bristol "riot" in *To Ride the Storm* (1983), the "process of reconstructing a coherent and comprehensible account of an event [was] the essential first stage in defining, understanding and explaining it" (3); so too the historical demand made on "narrative" by the *intifada* is itself a critical redefinition, around a crisis of state and popular resistance, of conventional narrative tactics.

The Palestinian *intifada* generated various written responses and cultural contributions to its collective political momentum. This literary participation in the historical process is not limited to generic formulas and the forms of poetry, novel, short story, and anecdote; it includes as well the documents that chart the course of events. Texts written from prison on the lining of a trouser pocket; appeals from detainees held in Ansar III in the Negev Desert to the international community to protest the inhuman conditions of the prison camp; the report on the Dahriyyah detention center prepared by al-Haq, the Ramallah-based commission of jurists; requests from the Palestinian Union of Women's Work Committees to assist women political prisoners; and the documentation of efforts of human rights organizations to trace the very whereabouts of the detainees—all are part of a collective enterprise to resist the Israeli government's attempt to contain the historical narrative within the walls of its extended prison apparatus. Interviews with released prisoners, victims of Israeli violence, and families of the martyrs contribute additional dimensions to this narrative reconstruction of an ongoing historical event, dimensions that are themselves part of the events and their making. Likewise, the "society pages" of the Arabic-language newspapers in East Jerusalem report, instead of the conventional social and biographical moments of birth, marriage, and death, rather the incidents of arrest, release, and deportation, and announce as well the constantly changing visiting hours at different prisons and holding centers in Israel and the Occupied Territories, thereby reconstituting a social narrative around the locus of prison rather than home and family. These reports and their documentation, however "presentist" their preoccupations—perhaps because of that very "presentism"—are reworking the historical narrative.

The texts contributing to the history-making record of the Palestinian *intifada* provide an analytical site, less of the Debordian "situationist" type with its emphasis on "spectacle," than of a historical conjuncture whose critical possibilities transgress the disciplining of formal boundaries and institutionalized border controls. While Fredric Jameson's proposal (1988) of a "new organisational concept—that of the *situation*" suggests an important reordering of the priorities of literary critical approaches to cultural history, his proposition that "culture itself as a system, but also the individual texts and works of art and literature that are 'included' in it, are both best grasped as responses to situations, as solutions to contradictions, as answers to questions" (19) perhaps too holistically closes these works off from intervening on their own terms within the historicizing internal contradictions of the resistance movement. Instead, it is these very contradictions that can be made to animate—rather than fracture— the critical development of the resistance in its own terms on its own terrain as well as in the global arena. Closure, that is, whether in narrative or detention, is law and order's response through policing to what Stuart Hall referred to as crisis or "moral panic."

The tension or contradiction produced by the border transgressions that underwrite the history of the Palestinian *intifada* is reproduced again in *Silencing of an Opposition: The Case of "Derech Hanitzotz"*, a report published in November 1988 by the Jerusalem-based Hanitzotz Publishing House. In February 1988 the publisher's Hebrew/Arabic newspaper, *Derech Hanitzotz/Tariq al-Sharara*, had been closed, and in the following months six of its writers—Ribhi al-Aruri, Yakov Ben Efrat, Ronnie Ben Efrat, Michal Schwartz, Hadas Lahav, and Assaf Adiv—had been detained. Al-Aruri and Lahav were later released, and the trial of the other four prisoners began in October 1988. In the meantime, however, on 29 May, the two women prisoners, Michal Schwartz and Ronnie Ben Efrat, had been transferred from the Moskobiyya detention center in West Jerusalem to Neve Tertza women's prison, where they were held with Israeli women criminal prisoners, who immediately—and continuously— attacked and brutalized them. Following the repeated requests of the women and their lawyers that they be removed to the political wing of the prison and held with the Palestinian detainees, Schwartz and Ben Efrat were eventually put in isolation cells. Later, in the course of the trial proceedings, it was disclosed that Shin Bet collaborators among the criminal prisoners had been used to instigate the systematic beatings of the two Israeli women political prisoners.

The interim document by Hanitzotz Publishing House, released after the first weeks of the ongoing trial, contains chronologies, judicial rulings for and against release of the prisoners on bail, press dispatches, messages from the prisoners, previously published articles by the detained journalists, and an introduction written by Yakov Ben Efrat from his cell in Jalame prison. The critical interpretation of this case and its historical placement in the Palestinian-Israeli narrative is of crucial importance to Ben Efrat, who insists that both the issue of censorship and the event of the newspaper's closing be reinterpreted within the history of the *intifada:*

115

It would be a sorry mistake to try and limit the issue of "Derech HaNitzotz" exclusively to a matter of freedom of the press. It is chronologically correct that the story began with the closing of the paper by administrative order in February of this year. However, the arrest of its editors and the severe charges brought against them constitute an escalation and came in the framework of an attempt to obliterate all political opposition to official policy. It is impossible to divorce the issue of "Derech HaNitzotz" from a series of unusual steps taken for the first time in 20 years against Israeli citizens, Jews or Arabs, who work for a change in the official policy towards the residents of the Occupied Territories, against the background of the Intifada. (5–6)

The further effect of the Palestinian *intifada* within Israel, according to Ben Efrat, has been to disengage the Israeli opposition from the "traditional perspectives of the Labor Party" and to relocate them on the "other side" of the green line: "It depends first and foremost on the Palestinian people to continue its struggle" (7).

Michal Schwartz, in her 1987 article "Children behind Bars" (reprinted in the Hanitzotz Publishing House document), had already demarcated that trajectory, one that demanded not just a territorial restoration but a reconstruction of personal itineraries confiscated by military occupation. According to Anton Shammas (1988), the Israeli Palestinian writer of novels in Hebrew:

The state of Israel hasn't only confiscated the land from under the feet of the Palestinians in the occupied territories; it has also taken away their childhood. For twenty years now officially there has been no childhood in the West Bank and the Gaza Strip. The word "child" is never used in military announcements: they refer to either an infant or a youth, but never a child. So a ten year-old boy shot by the military forces is reported to be a "young man of ten."

This insistence on restoring the once-truncated collective Palestinian biography and historical narrative is reiterated in the title to al-Mutawakkil Taha and ʿAmr Samha's study of Palestinian national culture in the occupied land after twenty years of occupation, *After Two Decades . . . and a Generation* (1988). For Taha and Samha, at stake in Israel's attempted suppression of Palestinian national culture are not cultural artifacts alone but the institutional and infrastructural history of their production and distribution, "in the sense that the Israeli occupation is endeavoring to efface, destroy, distort and pillage the sites of culture and not just the individual. It is attempting furthermore to blockade and close the routes by which the culture is transmitted from these sites to the individual" (3). Both *After Two Decades . . . and a Generation*, written a year before the outbreak of the *intifada*, and Ghassan Abdullah's *Freedom of Expression . . . the Crime*, issued in 1988 by the Palestinian Writers Union in the West Bank and **116** Gaza, prefigure the new cultural forms, actors, and situations that will emerge from the popular uprising to lay claim to a place in the political struggle.

Poetry, too, long a force in mobilizing the resistance, will challenge even the seats of government, as did Mahmud Darwish's poem "Passers among the Passing Words." First published in Arabic in the newsweekly *al-Yaum al-Sabiʿa* in March 1988, the poem was soon translated into Hebrew and quickly created a furor in Israel. The ten (out of fifty-two) lines of the poem calling for "withdrawal" were taken as ultimate evidence that negotiations with the Palestinians were henceforth, as they had always been, out of the question. In interviews Darwish repeatedly maintained that his poem referred to the Occupied Territories, but the Hebrew translations insisted on rendering his lines to reiterate the call by Ahmad Shuqayri, the first leader of the PLO, who was deposed by Fatah in December 1967, to "drive the Jews into the sea." Darwish's poem entered the chambers of the Knesset and was quoted in a speech given by Prime Minister Yitzhak Shamir that demanded more vigilant repression of the *intifada*. According to the Israeli newswriter Haim Guri, writing in *Davar*, "the poem returns us to the true demons. It speaks truth; poems do not lie" (*International Herald Tribune*, 17 March 1988). "Passers among the Passing Words," with its own titular insistence on historicity and temporality, was thus narrativized and became part of the transgressive historical narrative of the *intifada*, engaging even literary critics in government politics and politicians in the art of textual interpretation (see Darwich 1988).

The Palestinian *intifada* is proposing, as integral to its resistance to Israeli occupation and the struggle for self-determination, alternative strategies for narrating history and reading narrative. The struggle over narrative is waged historically in the struggle to control interpretation. As the Palestinian lawyer Walid al-Fahum observed:

Many are the imprisoned writers who have shredded or burned their writing in prison at the moment of a search. And many are the papers and literary texts that have been seized even as they are being concealed. Despite all this, the Israeli government fears that literary production of any sort might escape the cell, interpreting all literary output in only one way, by reading between lines and overturning letters, periods and paragraphs, as if hidden beneath each letter was a bomb, in every period a rifle, and in every paragraph an airplane. (Tawil 1988, 101)

The Palestinian *intifada*, like Um Khadr's story, is a historical series of events, stranger by far perhaps than fiction, but yielding in the end the possibility of another narrative.

Chapter Five

Sectarian versus Secular: The Case of Egypt

Aziza looked with satisfaction at the washed floor with its dampness so agreeable in that hot season and at the strip of foam matting rolled up in the corner and reflected contentedly from her solitary iron bed on the political prisoner, one of those who get brought to the prison from time to time without any reasonable explanation for her sentencing or why the government should want to push her head in amongst their heads. This political prisoner seemed very nice to Aziza and had greeted her once while crossing the corridor when she was standing there with Azima the Tall. Aziza plucked up her courage and approached her in order to learn her story. The political smiled a broad welcoming smile. Aziza guessed that she must be either a communist or from the Muslim Brotherhood since those were the only kinds of politicals that Aziza had met during her stay in prison.

> SALWA BAKR, al-ʿaraba al-dhabiyya la tusʿadu ila-l-samaʾ
> (*The Golden Chariot Won't Ascend to the Heavens*)

Twelve Women in One Cell (1982) is Nawal al-Saadawi's dramatization of her three months in al-Qanatir women's prison in the fall of 1981. Al-Saadawi, a prominent Egyptian physician, feminist, and writer, was among the more than fifteen hundred individuals of all political persuasions arrested in early September of that year by Egypt's president Anwar Sadat. One month later, and only days before the Islamic Aid al-Adha, or Feast of the Sacrifice, on 6 October 1981, Sadat was assassinated by members of an Islamist group within the military, as he presided over the annual parade commemorating the October war of 1973. In late November, most of the prisoners detained prior to Sadat's assassination began to be released under the new presidency of Hosni Mubarak. On 25 November al-Saadawi was among the first to reenter the busy tumult of the streets of Cairo, still under a state of emergency and military rule.

Although it is set in the midst of a concatenation of political events that momentarily traumatized Egypt, al-Saadawi's drama opens with the arrest of Sabah, a woman who has been charged with nothing more than illicit begging. The prison, however, and its organization have changed since Sabah's previous sojourn, and the beggars' cell, as the garbage collector there tells her, has now been given over to the political prisoners (10). The former beggars' cell itself has been reorganized, as the stage directions imply; on one side (significantly the right side) are located the veiled women, the *muhaggabat* and the *munaqqabat*, depending on the degree of veiling, while on the left are found women without veils (12). From the opening scene, *Twelve Women in One Cell* questions the bureaucratic **119** distinction between criminal and political prisoners and raises the ideological issues that divide the political detainees among themselves. The massive arrests, on charges ranging from spying for the Soviet Union to "sectarian sedition," carried out by Sadat's *mukhabarat*, or secret service, in September 1981 did not distinguish between right and left, Muslim and Christian, sectarian and secular, or even male and female. Al-Saadawi's play, with prison as its setting and women as its protagonists, dramatizes recent Egyptian history and its major currents and conflicts.

Soon after Sabah arrives in the prison, Fahima, the female warden, enters the political prisoners' cell to announce that the director and his cohorts will arrive soon for still another search of the cell. She warns the women that they must get rid of all the "forbidden things." "You know," she says, "what all is forbidden . . . no money, no newspapers, no radio, no paper and no pens." On hearing this admonition, Salima, one of the veiled women, responds immediately: "Alhamdulillah, praise be to God, I don't have any paper and pens and I don't even know how to read and write" (15). The implicit critique of the illiteracy and political ignorance of the Muslim detainees that is exemplified in Salima's self-vindication before the authorities is elaborated again in the charged discussion over who will do the work of cleaning out the cell. Samira, who is also veiled, insists that "there are people in the cell who don't read the Quran, who don't pray, and who have nothing else to do. Let one of them clean out the cell" (16). Labiba, however, who is unveiled, tells the warden that she is no more able to do the work than are her devout Muslim sisters: "Really, Sitt Fahima, I have at home three maids." Class, just as importantly as religion, functions in maintaining the conflictual relationships among the various women in the political prisoners' cell. The warden's proposed solution to the political dilemma serves only to redistribute the responsibility. She will, she suggests, bring one of the women criminals, the prostitute Zaynab, for example, to do the cleaning and regular washing for the politicals. Fahima's suggestion is in turn met with horror and repugnance by the Muslim women, who consider this introduction of a prostitute into their midst as an abomination, a contaminating affront to the purity of their environment. Will they ever be able to pray once the cell has been thus defiled and sullied?

Throughout the play, it is the leftist, unveiled women detainees who, despite their own class differences, establish reciprocal relationships with the various female criminals—prostitutes, beggars, drug dealers, and murderesses—who enter their cell. These relationships in turn serve to educate each group to the specific needs and analyses of the other's situation. Significantly for the play, it is within the prison walls and under the unwitting supervision of the prison bureaucracy that the leftist intellectuals discover the immediacy of the "people's" social and individual problems, and that these criminalized women for their part encounter a political analysis of their imputed crimes.

Twelve Women in One Cell is divided into two acts. Act One opens with the arrest of Sabah, the beggar, and develops through the internal conflicts created within the prison society by the opening of a political section to hold the new detainees. Act Two is introduced by the arrival of Aliya among the political prisoners. Aliya distinguishes herself, even among her fellow prisoners in the political cell, by her stubborn refusal to cooperate with the prison authorities, a refusal that is complemented by her willing participation in the other prisoners' lives, be they criminal or political. Self-conscious, critical, resistant, she transforms the cell by her example, as when she learns from Zaynab, the peasant murderer, to plant a garden in the prison courtyard. Even Basima, the senior political prisoner who has criticized Aliya for her inability to work with the party or the political organization, participates in the agricultural efforts of her cellmates.

The final emphasis of the play, as the title suggests, is on the common humanity, *insaniyya,* of all the prisoners as against the repressive bureaucratic machinery of the dictatorial government, its security forces, and its prisons. That common humanity endorses a common struggle against an oppressive authority, whether religious or governmental, from above, *min fawq.* Hovering over the stage throughout the play is a "large portrait of a man in a gold frame" (7). (Anwar Sadat was well known for his propensity to public portraiture and display, and his picture appeared everywhere in Egypt, in newspaper advertisements, on billboards, in coffeehouses, shops, and offices—so much so that Hosni Mubarak, on assuming the presidency of Egypt following Sadat's assassination, forbade the use of his own portrait and attempted to discourage the ostentation of public appearance that had been one of the hallmarks of the Sadat era.) The portrait in the play, however, represents contested authority, and when the prison director claims that the legitimacy of his orders comes "from above," *min fawq,* the Muslim women challenge him with another idea of "on high."

Indeed the very masculinity of that authority is caricatured when Fahima insists to the Muslim women who want time to veil themselves before the prison director enters their cell for the announced search that their fears and modesty are irrelevant in any case: "that's the general director, not a man" (25).

Al-Saadawi's play is dedicated to "all those who know repression in the home and in prison." The overwhelming significance of prison even in the daily life of the ordinary Egyptian population is evident in a recent popular film by the Egyptian director Mohammed Khan, *Dreams of Hind and Kamilia* (Ahlam Hind wa Kamilia), which opened in summer 1988 to a broad spectrum of reviews, from critical to laudatory, in the mainstream and opposition press. Critics either condemned or hailed the ruthless realism of its portrayal of the underside and the backsteps of the Cairene social order. The film tells the story of two maids who find common cause in their mutual exploitation by their brothers, uncles, husbands, and middle- and upper-class employers. The solidarity of Hind and Kamilia is finally assured when Hind's husband, and the father of her child Ahlam, is sent to prison for his dealings on the black market. The enforced absence of men consolidates the two women's independent organization of their lives and their livelihood.

Although *Dreams of Hind and Kamilia* offers a scathing social and political critique of the discrepant economic relationships and the gender oppression of modern no less than traditional Egyptian society, it is unable in the last analysis to provide a resolution to the indigenous problems and inherent inequities that it exposes. The social narrative gives way in the end to an idyllic conclusion borrowed from the conventions of bourgeois comic romance and television melodrama, conventions reinforced by the penetration of multinational capital into the Egyptian system. The same money that sends Hind's husband to prison provides the two maids an escape on the shores of Alexandria. Critical to the film, for both the success of its analysis and the failure of its conclusion, is the intersection of capital and patriarchy, exemplified by the prison, in historically conditioning the political fates of Hind and Kamilia.

The conflicted history of Egypt in the decades since the Free Officers Revolution brought independence in July 1952 can be articulated through the history of its political prisons. The Egyptian historian Salah Aissa, in his study of what he describes as an impending disaster, cites the Lebanese journal *al-Adab*:

The Arab world is one great prison . . . a prison which contains all tendencies and opinions. . . . It confines in huge numbers divided ideas and their contradictions. A confusing phenomenon in the Arab world is that Arab countries have opened their prisons to the Muslim Brotherhood, the Communists, the nationalists, the radicals, the liberals, the supporters of imperialism and the opponents of imperialism . . . all at one time, and for years on end. (cited in Aissa 1987, 28)

Aissa goes on to refer specifically to the case of Egypt:

> This has happened in the past and it will happen again tomorrow. Nagib Mahfuz described it in the period between the twenties and the forties when he put two brothers, Ahmad Shawkat the Marxist and Abd al-Munaym Shawkat the Muslim Brother in a single cell. When Abd al-Munaym asked, "Did they imprison me because I serve God?" Ahmad answered in sarcasm at the whole comedy, "So what is my sin then? That I don't serve him?" (28)

While Egyptian prisons have persisted continuously since independence, their differential use over time represents as well the narrative of struggle between the government and its popular opposition, whether the various leftist movements and the Communist party or the right-wing Muslim Brotherhood, *Ikhwan Muslimin,* and its offshoots, such as the various *jama'at islamiyya.*

Both 1954 and 1959 saw massive arrests by Gamal Abdel Nasser of the communists as well as the Muslim Brothers, many of whom spent sixteen or more years in prison. A less severe onslaught of political detention occurred in 1973 following the student demonstrations in the Egyptian universities. September 1981 marks another moment in Egypt's prison history. In 1988, two groups in particular were subject to the harsh threats and brutal realities of political detention: the Islamic Jihad and Thawra Misr (Revolution Egypt). The latter, under the leadership of Nasser's son, had been responsible for many of the attacks on Israeli diplomats and official representatives in Egypt since the conclusion of the Camp David Accords. These two cases, the Islamic Jihad and Thawra Misr, ensured the ongoing discussion, particularly in the opposition press, of torture in the prisons and the abuse of human rights. The experience of such treatment by opposition activists, both inside and outside the prison, has in turn influenced the internal ideological and political development of the various political groups to which they belong. The historical narrative of these developments is recounted in large part in the prison memoirs of the political detainees themselves.

Legion are the communists imprisoned by Nasser in 1954 and again in 1959, an attack that severely weakened an already-divided movement composed of several different subgroups. Each group was represented in the prison population, which was dispersed among the various concentration camps, prisons, and detention centers. Their prison experiences are recounted in such novels as Sherif Hetata's *Eye with the Iron Lid* (1984) and Fikri al-Khuli's *Journey* (1987), and such memoirs as Ilham Sayf al-

Nasr's *In Abu Za'bal Prison* (n.d.), Tahar Abd al-Hakim's *Bare Feet* (1978), and Mustafa Tiba's *Letters of a Political Prisoner to His Beloved* (1978–80). Muin Basisu's *Descent into the Water: Palestinian Notes from Arab Exile* (1980) records the experiences of Palestinian communists from Gaza held in Egyptian prisons. Political prison has entered the domain of popular culture as well, in such feature films as *al-Karnak* about the labor camps in Upper Egypt and *We're the Ones from the Bus*, starring the Egyptian comic actor Adel Imam and telling the story of two men who are arrested for disturbing the peace on a Cairo bus and mistakenly become detainees **123** in Nasser's prison camps. Poetry by the colloquial writer and activist Ahmad Fuad Nagm and paintings by the feminist Inji Aflatun contribute further to the record of the incarceration, torture, and political confrontation that characterized in critically important ways the first fifteen years of Egyptian independence.

Those writers, artists, and leftist historians imprisoned in the 1950s who have survived continue to function today as prominent intellectuals and active political thinkers. (Many of them, despite their prison experience under his regime, remain loyal, if critically so, to Nasser's political vision.) Their prison memoirs, documentaries, and literary texts recount a particular moment of the history of the Egyptian left and the internal debates and controversies concerning its political orientations, allegiances, goals, and organizational strategies. According to Rifaat Said, a member of the Communist party and the author of a multivolume history of the left in Egypt, prison constitutes a particularly brutal formative element in that history, so brutal and so specific that his own historical account must relate its place in only tangential ways.

In the volume concerned with the years 1957 to 1965, Said (1986) writes:

the first of January 1959 found the regime engaged in a desperate attempt to finish off the communists. Government announcements blackened all the newspapers and all its resources were devoted to the battle against them. The communists collectively were either imprisoned or had fled. . . . [Yet] at the beginning of this book I indicated that my object was not to discuss the period of prison. Prison is a tragedy which cannot be discussed in passing or in some relative way. It is a crime which can only be discussed in detail, by investigating those responsible for it, its executions, its real aims and its ultimate cost. . . . Prison has its specific conditions and characteristics. (192)

The emphasis of Said's account then falls on the trials and the testimonies of the defendants, who used the public occasion to bear witness to their political affiliations and patriotic loyalty, such as their defense of the nation during the 1956 Suez crisis, and to provide a contemporary critique of current government policies. The prison experience, he implies, is most adequately told from within the prison itself and in genres other than history. Prison and its writing in turn contribute in unique ways to the reconstitution of the historical and political narrative.

Both Tahar Abd al-Hakim and Mustafa Tiba waited some twelve years before undertaking the transcription of their prison experiences as Egyptian communists in the 1950s and 1960s. Their different reasons for this deferral form an integral part of their respective narratives. For Abd al-Hakim, the political and historical conditions in 1964, at the time of his release, did not warrant the publication of such an account, which must necessarily excavate the controversial relationships internal to the movement and between it and Nasser's government in the larger context of pan-Arabism. In the introduction to *Bare Feet*, the former political prisoner even then writes that "this book is not an indictment of the Nasserite system. Rather it is only a record of the relationship between that system and the communists at a given moment—the years between January 1958 and May 1964" (23). Mustafa Tiba also recounts the inhibitions that deterred the writing of his prison years. The introduction to his two-volume *Letters of a Political Prisoner to His Beloved* is in the form of a telephone conversation between the writer and an anonymous caller who summons up his prison years and asks him to record his experiences for a new readership. When Tiba hesitates, the caller insists:

Don't you have confidence in the people?
All the confidence in the world. But I don't have the tools for research and
    publication.
Look for them and you'll find them.
Where?
With those who shared in the making of the journey.
But they were all different.
Only the dead have no differences . . .
But the differences were deep and radical.
Look for the reasons why.
Where?
In everything they say and do.
It will just be a record then.
Record first and then analyze afterwards. (1:6–7)

The ideological complexities of incarceration that at first inhibit the composition of the prison memoirs of political detainees are also the basis for their historical necessity. Tiba's letters are a dramatic and compelling rendering of both the daily struggles among the various leftist groups in the prison and the open conflicts, manipulated like the internal divisions within the movement by the prison authorities, between the communists and the Muslim Brotherhood. Thus the second volume of the *Letters* opens with the writer's transfer with other communists to al-Mahariq prison in the desert, a consequence of his and his fellow prisoners' refusal to take sides with the government against the Brotherhood.

Critical to *Letters of a Political Prisoner to His Beloved* is the connection between the formal decision to reconstruct the prison experience through a sequence of letters to an unidentified recipient and the conditions of political detention itself. There are sixty-six letters in all, dated from 5 January to 11 October 1977. Their assemblage produces a relational genre, addressed specifically to a woman, *habibtihu*, however hypothetical she may be, and thus locates personal relationships within the political context of prison. The prison experience in turn educates those relationships anew. At a certain point in the narrative, after the transfer to al-Mahariq prison and after a protracted argument with a nonetheless sympathetic prison official, who finally acquiesces and allows the prisoners to keep their "forbidden things," even to acquire glaze and other materials necessary for a kiln they have built to make pottery from the clay and sand of the prison grounds, the officer admits to the prisoners: "There are only two things which I cannot get for you." To which one of the prisoners replies, "Release is the first thing. What is the second?" "Women," the officer answers (2:18).

The somewhat ironic connection between women and freedom cursorily suggested in the officer's remark is elaborated more consequentially and rendered problematic in Tiba's following reflections: "Most of us are in our thirties, approaching forty. *How old will we be when this period of punishment is over?* How old will we be when we leave the prison? More than forty? Will we find women who will want us? And if we find them will we have anything to give them?" (2:18). For the younger man with whom he is speaking, the problem Tiba faces seems less urgent, preoccupied as the former is with generational differences and questions of seniority among the prisoners. After twelve years in prison, however, the question of reentering civilian society is critical. Perhaps it is too late to reintegrate into the social order according to the conventional paths provided for by custom—from school to marriage, children, and family.

The effect of prison, especially long-term, on inherited social and family patterns is radical, and the issue of women in the prisons is crucial, contested between the prisoners and the detention system itself. William Isaac is an artist who was detained with Mustafa Tiba in the political prison of al-Mahariq. His abilities are at one point described to a visiting officer, who immediately demands that William paint him a portrait of a nude woman. When William refuses, the officer insists, ordering him to do the painting. Still William refuses, and the officer must depart, frustrated finally in his desires by the different analyses of gender and art proposed by the prisoner artist. This simple incident exemplifies the fun-

125

damental ideological differences that separate the prison authorities from the political detainees and places the role and concept of woman centrally within these differences. The very genre of Tiba's memoirs contains the attempt to investigate, not only political party differences and conflicts, but also the transformed gender relational possibilities that have been produced by twelve years of continued political detention.

126 Tahar Abd al-Hakim's *Bare Feet* represents a similar indictment, despite its disclaimers, of the Nasserist prison system and the social and political policies that it implemented in seeking to coerce the prisoners, through physical brutality and psychological humiliation, into renouncing their own political commitments and subscribing to a political identity provided for them by the government. The collective interrogation procedures practiced by the prison authorities required that the detainees, for example, sing patriotic songs in praise of Gamal Abdel Nasser, or declare before their comrades that they were not communists. The prison regime sought in its interrogations to manipulate as well the concept of woman and a certain regressive ideal of masculinity prevalent in and sanctioned by traditional bourgeois society, a cult such as is later caricatured in Nawal al-Saadawi's play *Twelve Women in One Cell*. According to Abd al-Hakim (1978), "They would openly ask their victim to deny his manhood and say 'I am a woman' [*ana maraʾa*], since the bourgeoisie in our countries still looks at women with a feudal mentality or with the mind of a slave trader as if she were a shameful creature good only as an instrument of pleasure and gratification" (127). The men's female relatives outside the prison are in turn manipulated, both to suppress their solidarity with the prisoners and to introduce conflict into the social ties that bind the inside of the prison with its larger counterpart beyond the walls. The single expression "I want the body of my son" (*urid juththa waladi*) epitomizes the experience of many mothers and suggests the prototype of contemporary committees of mothers in Argentina, El Salvador, South Africa, and Palestine. It is the title to the story of Muhammad Uthman, a prisoner who died in the custody of the police and whose burial place the authorities later refused to reveal to his mother (Abd al-Hakim, 51–2). Eventually the prison officials resort to persuading the wives of the prisoners to write letters to their husbands threatening them with immediate divorce if the men do not submit to the will and decisions of the government and thereby secure through capitulation their release (243).

Two major issues inform Tahar Abd al-Hakim's narrative of prison: the incessant efforts to undermine the sociopolitical identity and affiliations of the political prisoners, efforts to which the traditional patriarchal concepts of womanhood and masculinity are critical, and the history of the Egyptian prison system itself. The lineage of Nasser's prison camps is traced back to Turkish rule in Egypt and then continues through Napoleon's invasion and British imperialism. Prison—in its very edifices such as the Citadel, and the system of discipline and punishment that it substantiates—serves as a critique of the Nasserist regime and challenges its claim to revolutionary independent rule in Egypt by aligning that rule directly with the previous centuries of foreign imperialist control and domination. The narrative analysis provided by *Bare Feet* insists on the intersection, in prison, of the reciprocal repressions of imperialism, gender discrimination, and bourgeois patriarchy, and the resistance to their systemic deployment waged from within the prison walls by the political prisoners.

127

If the prison memoirs written by members of the Communist party and other leftist organizations can be read as contributing to a reconstruction of the movement, a similar development is to be found within the Islamist groups incarcerated in significant numbers during the same period. When Hasan al-Banna, the founder of the Muslim Brotherhood in Egypt was hung along with five other Brotherhood leaders by the Nasser government in 1954, the Brotherhood was suddenly deprived of its spiritual leader. According to Gilles Kepel (1985), "Islamicist thought was reconstructed after 1954 primarily in the concentration camps, which were felt by [Sayyid] Qutb [another prominent member and ideologue of the Brotherhood] and his disciples to symbolize the relationship of the state to the society" (27–28). Indeed Sayyid Qutb (who was himself executed in 1966) composed his most important manifesto, *Signposts* (1980), during his years in prison. Rather than a documentary history or a historical narrative such as those written by leftist or communist prisoners, *Signposts* proposes instead an outline of the future Islamic society as envisioned by its author and charts the necessary stages of *jihad* through which that society will be achieved. The generic differences among these various prison writings signals as well the radical ideological discrepancies that separated the religious or sectarian and the secular oppositions in Egyptian politics through the decades of struggle for national independence and that continued after independence.

Distinctions of genre characterize too the prison memoirs of Zaynab al-Ghazali, the only woman, it seems, to have committed to a written memoir her prison experiences during the 1950s and 1960s.[1] Zaynab al-Ghazali, the leader of the Society of Muslim Ladies, which not only held seminars and discussion groups but also tended to the needs of released Muslim prisoners in the late 1950s, was herself arrested in the summer of 1965, along with Sayyid Qutb (who had only just been released a year earlier), Abd al-Fattah Ismail, and others, on charges of conspiring to assassinate Abdel Nasser and overthrow the government. *Days of My Life*

(1984) [Ayyam min hayati], the story of her imprisonment, opens with
an account of Nasser's recent attacks on the Muslim Brotherhood and its
members and the history of al-Ghazali's own affiliations with the movement, which she traces back as far as 1937 and which include her spiritual
relationship with Hasan al-Banna. In 1955, however, her active public
work on behalf of the released prisoners had led her, as she relates in
her memoir, to participate more fully in the organization and its efforts to
reconstitute itself following its dissolution by Abdel Nasser. Particularly
important is the program, undertaken with Abd al-Fattah Ismail following
a pilgrimage to Mecca in 1957, of mass education throughout the country
and the gradual preparation (in thirteen-year stages) for the establishment
of an Islamic state (in contrast to the call from others for its violent and
immediate creation). The volume closes with a description of her trial, her
sentencing to life imprisonment, her stay in al-Qanatir women's prison,
and her eventual release following Sadat's amnesty in 1971. The historical and historicizing framework to al-Ghazali's autobiographical prison
writing is necessitated by her urgent need to legitimize, as a woman, her
position of leadership within the Brotherhood.

128

Historical referencing and autobiographical chronicity provide a crucial context for the central and substantially larger part of *Days of My Life*,
which focuses on al-Ghazali's interrogation and torture and emphasizes
her steadfast refusal to submit to the inherent line of questioning presented consistently by her inquisitors. The role of the woman and her
ideologically assigned place in Egyptian and Islamic society are central
to the Muslim sister's confrontation with a prison system whose strategy
of attack is to subvert her belief in the religious integrity and personal
loyalty of her Muslim brothers. At various moments her interrogators
cleverly attempt to persuade her that the men have already confessed to
the charges and furthermore that they have implicated her directly in the
alleged conspiracy: "You are only burning yourself," they tell her, "for
the sake of individuals who have all repudiated you. You should change
your position. . . . The men know their own good and are making sure to
secure it by throwing all the blame on you" (152). The relentless thrust of
the interrogation is thus to manipulate what the prison officials construe
as the insecurity of her position as a woman both in the Brotherhood and
in Egyptian society as a whole. Their concern to extract from her a confession of her own participation in the plot, one that would implicate the
others as well, by insisting that all her cohorts have already confessed,
is repeatedly met and discursively challenged by Zaynab al-Ghazali, not
with the desired confession, but with a sermon, a *khutba*.

The central narrative of *Days of My Life* takes on an almost ritualis-
tic structure built around interrogation—sermon—punishment and its

repetition. This ritual and its repetition as if ultimately establish, indeed consecrate, al-Ghazali's legitimate participation in the Brotherhood. They furthermore sanction the historical framework of her memoir and herself as its author and writer, a preacher and user of words. Zaynab al-Ghazali's struggle is waged on three specific but mutually articulated fronts: against the "infidel" authoritarianism of the Nasserist government, against the masculinist ideology of a particular interpretation of Islam, and against the traditional patriarchy of her Egyptian bourgeois society. An earlier struggle with her husband over her activities in the Brotherhood is re- **129** produced in her incarceration as a Muslim woman in Nasser's prisons: "There is something in my life," she had told her husband, "that you must learn since you are going to be my husband. Inasmuch as I agree to marry you, I will tell you about it now so that you won't ask me about it later. My preconditions with regard to this matter I will not abandon. I am the president of the Central Committee of the Society of Muslim Ladies . . . and if ever your personal interest or financial work conflicts with my work in Islam and I find that my life as a wife is an obstacle in the path of the call and the establishment of an Islamic state, on that day we will part ways" (34). The formal tension in *Days of My Life*, between the historicized framework and the ritualized interrogation and response in prison, reproduces the contradictions of her own feminine role within the Ikhwan Muslimin and the personal conflict between the *da'awa li-l-taharrir* and the *da'awa li-l-tahajjib* (the "call to liberation" and the "call to veiling").

Gamal Abdel Nasser, the charismatic Free Officer of the 1952 revolution and the hero of pan-Arabism as well as the person ultimately responsible for the prison camps and detention centers of Egypt in the 1950s and 1960s, died in 1970. His rule, which had witnessed the Tripartite Aggression of 1956, the aborted federation with Syria, the debilitating efforts to assist in the Yemen war, agrarian reform, and the nationalization of banks and private companies, culminated in the disastrous defeat of the Egyptian army by Israeli forces in the June war of 1967. Nasser was succeeded by Anwar Sadat as president of Egypt, and in May 1971, Sadat launched what came to be known as the "corrective revolution." Sadat's effort to come out from under the imposing shadow of Nasser and to establish his own bases of authority included the release of many of the political prisoners detained by his predecessor. The many prisons of Egypt were not, however, put out of commission, or even put to other uses, during the decade of Sadat's rule. There were collective arrests following the student demonstrations in 1973 (see Abdalla 1985), and again after the bread riots in January 1977. Members of the Islamic groups were regularly detained, although repression of the Nasserist magnitude was less common under Sadat. In 1979, however, opposition from both the religious and the secular leftist organizations to the signing of the Camp David Accords by Egypt, Israel, and the United States initiated a new wave of government controls and censorship, much of it the result of pressure from the United States and Israel and of Sadat's desire to maintain his newly acquired media image in the West.

The final five years of the Sadat regime, from the January 1977 bread riots to the September 1981 arrests, provide the chronological structure for Farida al-Naqqash's prison memoirs, *Prison: Two Tears . . . and a Rose* (1985) [Al-Sijn: Dama'atan . . . wa warda]. In it the intermittent arrests of herself and her husband, Husayn Abd al-Raziq, counterpoint each other with metronymic regularity, climaxing in their combined imprisonment in the sweeping detentions in September 1981. Was it the result of their opposition to the Camp David Accords? Nawal al-Saadawi, in her *Memoirs from the Women's Prison* (1986), realized only during her interrogation that what had once again brought together in Egyptian cells members of the right and the left, Christians and Muslims, women with veils and without, was their combined opposition to Camp David: "Is Israel the reason for our presence in prison? Had it wanted to suppress the voices which oppose the Israeli cultural and economic assault that has taken place under cover of the label 'normalisation of relations?' What sort of deception has been taking place behind the screen of National Unity, Social Peace, Protecting Egypt from the Sectarian Rift and Protecting the Values of the Village from Shame?" (al-Saadawi, 161).

Opposition to the Camp David Accords and Egypt's separate peace with Israel was expressed on many fronts and in varied arenas, cultural, political, and economic (see Harlow 1986). Israeli presence at the annual Cairo International Book Fair in 1980 and 1981 brought about a boycott by many Arab and Egyptian publishers as well as demonstrations at the fairgrounds itself. Government pressure on intellectuals, university professors, artists, and other professionals to participate in official exchanges with their Israeli counterparts resulted in the formation of the oppositional Committee in Defense of National Culture and the publication of the journal *al-Muwajaha* (Confrontation) challenging cultural dependency. Refusal to participate in the "normalization" process could nonetheless result in loss of job, other governmental reprisals, and censure.

Opposition to the Camp David Accords betokened not only a patriotic commitment to Egyptian cultural and political integrity but also support for the Palestinian resistance movement and Palestinian rights to self-determination and an independent state. Support for the Palestinians, however, could represent widely discrepant ideological positions, from the combined vision of the Egyptian left of Arab and Palestinian nationalism and the ideal of a "democratic secular state" to the Islamist appropriation of the democratic secular/nationalist goals of the Palestinian resistance to serve the aims of an Islamic state secured by the waging of a militant *jihad*. This disposition is found at the conclusion of Safinaz Kazim's *On Prison and Freedom* (1986): "You ask me why I don't write about Palestine. Didn't I write about Palestine? Every line I wrote was for Palestine and from Palestine. Our hope begins and ends with Palestine. . . . 'Democratic secular state'! Down with such a vision and those who raise it, let them drink their own blood. The ugliest of atheisms!" (237). **131**

Three accounts of prison by Egyptian women of different political backgrounds, all held in al-Qanatir women's prison in the fall of 1981, reveal very different constructions of that historical conjuncture and its consequences for subsequent political and cultural formations in Egypt. Their conflicting voices, heard in Nawal al-Saadawi's *Twelve Women in One Cell*, critically complicate the two-act drama and its simplified distribution of roles, even as they reinforce the political contradictions implicit in the prison system itself. Farida al-Naqqash, a member of the opposition Hizb al-Tagammuᶜ, or Progressive Union party, was arrested in March of that year. Her narrative, *Prison: Two Tears . . . and a Rose*, describes Nawal al-Saadawi and Safinaz Kazim's arrival in prison, with myriad others, in early September. Al-Saadawi, who later founded the Arab Women's Solidarity Association, followed her play with a volume of her own prison story, *Memoirs from the Women's Prison*. Safinaz Kazim, an erstwhile Marxist and the former wife of the popular colloquial poet Ahmad Fuad Nagm, had been fired for political reasons in 1979 from her position at the publishing house of Dar al-Hilal and was now an Islamic militant. In 1986 her collection of essays on the significance of her prison experience, *On Prison and Freedom*, was published.

Critical to all of these texts, and the one thing that they all have in common, is the cautious, even surreptitious, announcement in the prison of the assassination of Sadat on 6 October, and the collective jubilation from cell to cell that followed the confirmation of the death of the Egyptian president. When she first heard the report from a prison warden, Safinaz Kazim says, she "jumped up and grabbed her hand: 'Is he dead?' Hurriedly and laughing all the while, the warden answered, 'Inshaᵓ Allah [God willing]" (225). By evening, the report could no longer be denied, and while prisoners throughout the prison clasped the bars of their cells and chanted patriotic songs, Safinaz Kazim intoned, "Allahu akbar, Allahu akbar [God is great]." "I couldn't find a political song," she writes, "in all the songs I knew—which so well expressed our collective situation in the face of this overwhelming shower of beneficence" (226).

Nawal al-Saadawi recounts a different tumult when finally the British Broadcasting Corporation report from their clandestine radio tells the women that "Sadat has died." Ideological preferences give way to uninhibited instincts:

> The bodies exploded into the air, as the radio fell to the ground. No one paid any attention to it. . . . I became aware, suddenly, of a strange scene: Boduur whirling around, minus *niqaab* and cloak, whirling and dancing, surrounded by her cellmates who usually wore *niqaabs*, dancing with hair uncovered, without face-veils or head-coverings, bodies rocking violently, waists bending, bellies quivering, heads swaying, hair flying.
>
> And another bizarre scene: Fawqiyya, who had never in her life performed a single ritual prayer sequence, was kneeling on the ground, raising her hands to the sky and shouting, "I give praise to You, O Lord." Around her, the other cellmates were kneeling, praying, calling out in unison, "O Lord we give praise to Thee." (1986: 174)

For the political consciousness of Farida al-Naqqash, however, the long history of government censorship and media control plays a cautionary role even in the momentous announcement and its tidings of liberation:

> Radio Cairo said that Sadat was struggling for his life and had been transferred to the hospital. We couldn't get any other station, so we believed Radio Cairo. That was at three in the afternoon. . . . They closed the cell doors and the warden said that maybe he had died. We wanted neither to believe nor disbelieve, and our question remained once again unspoken, suspended. Our distress only increased at the vagueness of the news until finally at 5.30 pm we tuned into Radio Israel which announced the news of the decease of Sadat. (1985: 303)

The fact that Radio Israel here betrays the news of Sadat's death suggests both a bitter critique of Egyptian censorship and an ironic commentary on Sadat's foreign policy of dependency: Israel, whose reception of the Egyptian president in Jerusalem four years earlier had assisted in the remaking of Sadat as a Western media hero, now tolled his death knell to the Egyptian opposition to Camp David.

In each of the three texts the announcement of Sadat's assassination signals the writer's impending release from prison and the conclusion of her writing of prison. Yet the preliminaries that prepare for that historic terminus ad quem vary from text to text, and the issue of genre, of how to write prison, is critical to all three compositions. Generic and formal choices condition and are conditioned by the envisioned historical analysis. *Memoirs from the Women's Prison* opens with the proverbial knock at the door, the unannounced arrival of the security forces, which immemorially in Egypt and elsewhere heralds the arrest and detention of political prisoners. At the time of her removal to prison, al-Saadawi is at work on a new novel, a work that is radically interrupted by her detention and is displaced, at least temporarily, by the prison memoirs themselves. Political forces of circumstance thus transform the self-styled autonomy of the creative task and relocate it in a historical narrative.

Memoirs from the Women's Prison nonetheless observes certain classical conventions of tripartite plot construction: arrest—imprisonment—release; and once inside the prison, the documentary framework is fictionalized when the cellmates are named on arrival. Latifa al-Zayyat, Amina Rashid, Safinaz Kazim, Shahinda Muqallid, Farida al-Naqqash, and Awatif Abd al-Rahman are subsequently seconded by artificially designated personas: "We began to give our accounts of all that had taken place, as all our colleagues in the cell joined us. We were fourteen women, one still a girl—of different generations, ages and outlooks on life" (35). At this point al-Saadawi's narrative draws in two fictional characters who will focus the peripeties of prison life under Anwar Sadat: Boduur, the veiled Islamic militant, and Fawqiyya, the leftist activist. These two fictional characters will act out the drama of political detention as it is organized around a chronological sequence of critical conjunctures in al-Saadawi's prison experience: 6 September, arrest; 28 September, interrogation; 6 October, assassination of Sadat; and finally 25 November, release. "The Final Part," however, proposes a visionary, if still immanent, innovation to the dominant conventions of narrative and the standardized rules of historical chronicity. Following her release and return home, Nawal al-Saadawi returns with her husband, Sherif Hetata, to visit her former cellmates who are still in detention and to agitate for their release.

On Prison and Freedom, by contrast to the straightforward narrative complicated only by the combination of fiction and documentary that characterizes al-Saadawi's account, is a collection of essays—autobiographical, literary, critical, journalistic—that recollect the impact of prison on the personal and public lives of Egypt and Egyptians. The first article sets the historical stage for the political conflict that informs the following analyses. "The Euroamerizionist Age and the Age of Islam" elaborates the theoretical basis, beginning with dependency theory and concluding with religious imagery and citation, for the Islamic resolution to the Egyptian dilemma as epitomized in the prison system: an Islamic state. Safinaz Kazim's personal history, her conversion from Marxism to Islam, is elliptically narrated in the sequence of essays, culminating perhaps in the mosaic of letters penned to an unnamed male recipient in which she finally says: "You don't know the depth of religion in my life. You don't understand that my outburst, my boldness, my love, my revolution and my ardor all come from the growth of Islam with which Allah has honored me by making it dawn inside me. All praise to him. Perhaps you laugh but it makes me sad. Why do you want to explain my religion as if it were an inadequacy, an escape, a regression?" (183). Kazim's prison essays are at once a confessional apologia for her own personal itinerary and an analytical outline of a future religious trajectory for Egyptian and Arab society.

The fragmentary theologized historicity of Kazim's *On Prison and Freedom* is reworked in al-Naqqash's *Prison: Two Tears . . . and a Rose*, a complex collage of historical narrative and political analysis, combining letters from prison, anecdotes and stories of fellow prisoners, trial reports, and social commentary. It documents the history of Egypt from 1977 to 1981, as seen from and against the vantage point of prison, a state institution that both mobilized and shattered Egyptian family and political party life: the woman in prison, her husband at home; the man in prison, his wife at home; both husband and wife in separate prisons, the children in the care of family and political colleagues. "Why," Farida al-Naqqash writes at one point, "did we continue to place ourselves in opposition to Sadat in all events and discussions during those seventeen months of freedom [when neither was in prison]? . . . You have to ask that question, and it will be asked in part by all those who look in this book for human anecdotes and the experiences of a woman and mother in prison and who are surprised to find all this politics" (157).

Prison as a personal and political phenomenon provides for al-Naqqash the premises from which to examine critically the multiple affiliations— to political party, to husband and children, and to fellow prisoners, criminal and political—and their intersections, all of which condition the biographical self-accounting. These premises demand a different form of writing, one that knows, for now, no historical closure; the clichés of romance and melodrama have been rendered anachronistic and invalidated by the prison experience, and history has not yet provided the ending: "or so it seems . . . my book will remain open, with no conclusion, until popular democracy brings down the laws restricting freedom and closes the prisons forever, ending the state of emergency and heralding the abolishment of torture in the prisons—and not like the feeble soap opera staged by Sadat in 1971 when he burned the tape recorders only to install others in people's homes . . . only a popular celebration will succeed in bringing true democracy for all to enjoy" (352).

In *Days of My Life* (1984) Zaynab al-Ghazali described prison and torture as *jahannam*, "hell," and defined the writing of her prison memoirs as a mission, at once proselytizing others and purifying herself (7). The material fact of the prison, based as it is on the erection and maintenance of walls, physical and ideological, in the lives of Egyptian women, especially politically active women, results in an active redefinition of those very premises that the state seeks to maintain by means of its institutional apparatus. The prison memoirs of political detainees rework not only the basic inside/outside distinction but other ideologically structured dichotomies which the spatial metaphor subtends: political/criminal, private/public; these memoirs thus allow for an analysis of the hegemonic sociopolitical system that the structure is designed to contain and prevent.

Nawal al-Saadawi's *Twelve Women in One Cell* is dedicated to "all those who know repression at home or in prison," and her memoirs, from that same women's prison in which the play is set, establish the necessary connection between the brutal smashing of the door to her apartment in Giza **135** by the security police who have come to arrest her and the "open door" economic policy (*infitah*) launched by Sadat in 1973, which opened Egypt to the greed of foreign enterprise and the predations of multinational capital:

The third knock on the door.

It must be the concierge, I thought, but I will not open the door for him. This concierge respects none of the residents of the building except its owner. He would never consider knocking on the landlord's door three times, or with this violence. People in Egypt have changed. The only ones who are respected any more are those who own blocks of flats or office buildings, dollars, open door firms, farms producing Israeli chickens and Israeli eggs, or American chewing gum. (3–4)

For Safinaz Kazim, however, prison is the "absence of Islam" and the specific details of her prison experience remain but one dimension in her larger critique of the prison that is modern irreligious Egypt. Her memoirs are dedicated to "Sanaa," one of the Islamic militant women who carried out a suicide bombing mission against Israeli targets in Lebanon on 4 April 1985.

For both Safinaz Kazim and Nawal al-Saadawi, prison in Egypt is, as Farida al-Naqqash (1988) similarly maintained in an interview, "a picture in miniature of Egyptian society" (64). Like the ordinary struggle of daily life, the endlessly unfinished and unpaved streets (Kazim, 134), or just turning on the oven to bake a *fatir*, or crepe, political prison requires its own practiced forms of courage. Safinaz Kazim (1986) assimilates the inefficiency and inadequacy of state-provided services to the intransigent and implacable machinery of its prison and security system: "To my mind the butagaz oven could explode in my face at any moment, so that even cheese *fatirs* take daring" (142). To reconstruct the experience of political prison through the minutia of daily life as much as through the trauma of political upheaval enjoins for each of these women, albeit differently according to their own political agendas, a vision of dismantling the prison machinery and the government that it protects.

Political prison more and more provides the analytic tools for such a project, which, according to Farida al-Naqqash in the opening lines of

Prison: Two Tears . . . and a Rose, can only be undertaken collectively: "It is not in order to paint a resplendent portrait of heroism, of myself or anyone else, that I present this book. It is become all too ordinary a matter that the prisons seasonally open their doors to hundreds of intellectuals and workers concerned with the urgent problems of the country, so much so that it would be strange indeed for anyone from my generation involved in politics to have escaped the experience of prison. Prison has now become an integral part of the public nationalist sentiment" (9). The

136 overwhelming fact of prison thus requires the elaboration of an alternative political and personal modus vivendi that would resist the ruthless incursions into daily life of the prison apparatus. Al-Naqqash writes:

My own limited experience dates to 1977, and since that time my small family has lost any feeling of safety and security. My husband and I, my children, our family and friends, have had to make a special kind of security for ourselves, to surround our lives with pleasure, affection and psychological fortifications which would incite us against the continued terrorization in all its different forms over these past years. We have been obliged to give our children large doses of political concepts well beyond their years and to fill their lives with the mind and soul of courage and steadfastness. We have shortened their childhood and its pleasures. As contemporary parents we wanted to leave them strong enough to make their own discoveries, not just inherit ours. (9)

In the meantime, the children must learn to live with an overnight bag packed with the few essentials of mental and physical hygiene for their parents, in anticipation of the eventual "knock on the door" (11).

Safinaz Kazim, by her own account and others, spent her days in prison reading the Quran and devoting herself to prayer. Prison, for her, is the will of Allah. In *On Prison and Freedom* she writes: "When I found myself en route to the Barrages [al-Qanatir], to prison and detention, I was neither surprised nor sad, but told myself, it must be that Allah wants happiness for me in this direction. I turned my imprisonment into an account of total submission" (29). Kazim furthermore prefers the discipline of isolation and solitary confinement to the company of her fellow prisoners (30), and, she claims, would refuse any offer of assistance from human rights organizations. Allah will ensure the protection of those who remain faithful (28).

If prison becomes a private spiritual exercise of withdrawal for Safinaz Kazim, it is instead a socializing experience in which their interaction with the women criminals is crucial for Farida al-Naqqash and Nawal al-Saadawi. The state-ordered separation of criminals and political prisoners is only partially effectual in al-Qanatir women's prison. As she reports in her *Memoirs*, the daily exercises that Nawal al-Saadawi performs in the courtyard to the cell soon attract a number of prostitutes, beggars, and murderers who participate across the separating fence in her self-disciplined regimen of physical hygiene and fitness. The political detainee in turn begins to learn from Fathiyya, a peasant woman who murdered her husband with a hoe when she found him sexually abusing her daughter, the careful nurturing details of agriculture and ends by planting a small garden in the same courtyard where she exercises and writes in the dirt the daily incidents of prison life. The hoe and the pen, the *fallaha*, or peasant woman, and the intellectual, find common cause in inaugurating the outlines of a counterculture that will resist the bureaucratizing **137** influence of the state's apparatus of repression and degradation.

The lessons in social consciousness that she learns from her fellow prisoners—the prostitutes, drug traffickers and petty thieves—most of them in prison for the second, third, or fourth times, Farida al-Naqqash (1985) shares with her children. In one of her letters to her son, Gasir, she writes, "I want to talk to you tonight about Firyal, one of my friends in prison" (73), and goes on to tell him the very ordinary story of a very ordinary woman who toils against the systemic deprivations of lower-class Egyptian life. In the context of the prison memoirs, it is Firyal's very ordinariness that becomes exemplary for the political prisoner. The prison, as al-Naqqash writes to Mahmud Diab, confers a new significance on the committed intellectual's endeavors. It is above all a reminder of the public responsibility of the artist: "I agree with you that absence from the public arena isolates one from the people, that our presence in the information apparatus is necessary and that we must strive for it, since these are the people we write for and these are the means to reach them. But remember too, that this isolation was not of our choice, but was imposed on us" (91). (In the months before the arrests of September 1981, Sadat had ordered the closing of most of the opposition press.) From within the isolation of prison, enforced by state censorship and media control, another kind of community temporarily develops, and the distance between intellectuals and the "masses" is collapsed for the moment.

According to Farida al-Naqqash, she rediscovered creative writing in prison. In a 1988 interview with Nuha Samara she reports that "one of the joys of prison for me was to return to writing stories" (64), and in the many letters to her husband, Husayn, which make up a significant part of her prison testimony, al-Naqqash (1985) narrates the writing of a novel in which she is engaged. The myriad stories of her fellow prisoners that counterpoint the letters and documentary are themselves a collection of intimate anecdotes that propose an implicit narrative, one that, like the film *Ahlam Hind wa Kamilia*, as yet knows no ending. The experimentation with writing is critical to the experience of prison.

In *Prison: Two Tears . . . and a Rose*, the stories develop gender and political relations internal to the women's prison, and the letters to friends, husband, children, and political associates elaborate new forms of social organization and personal solidarity: "At first I wanted to write you a love letter" (81), she writes to her husband; or to her friends, "I hadn't intended to write you a political letter" (86). The history of these relationships, however, has been embedded in a history of political commitment and activity, much as prison itself is integral to the historical narrative of the left in Egypt. "We are lucky to have you as friends," she writes in the letter to her comrades. "A friend once asked me about what happened to the children of members of the opposition when they went to prison for an extended period of time. Did they go hungry? I thought about it and told her confidently that the progressive political movement in Egypt had attained a sufficient degree of maturity and strength to prevent family vagrancy or children's hunger. This situation no doubt forms a basic part of the confidence, security and strength of the fighters. It makes the other problems easy" (86).

Amina Rashid, who also spent three months in political prison in the fall of 1981, reports that these problems of social support are less easy for the younger, especially lower-class, women new to the political movement and to the prison.[2] The families and neighbors of these women still exercise the traditional direct and indirect forms of social and psychological control over their daughters and neighbors. What do the people think when they see the dreaded security officers escorting a political detainee to the local police station and thence to prison? And what do the other members of the party think? These two questions initiate Farida al-Naqqash's testimony (1985: 12–13). Political prison is an arena in which the answers to the questions are not given, but are elaborated, reworked, and resubmitted for further questioning.

Egypt in 1988 once again witnessed the eruption into the public domain of the issue of political prison and allegations of torture and brutality by the prison authorities against both the Islamic Jihad and the Thawra Misr, which had carried out a number of attacks on the Israeli diplomatic presence and official representation in Egypt. In an editorial on 20 July 1988 in *al-Ahali*, the weekly opposition paper of the Hizb al-Tagammuᶜ (Progressive Union Party), which recalls her own prison testimony, Farida al-Naqqash found it necessary to write again, "Don't say, we didn't know!"

Chapter Six

Negotiating/Armed Struggle: South Africa

Lieutenant Prins, then head of prison on Robben Island, once made an irrelevant analogy to express the official attitude on the question of prisoner morale. I had gone to him to complain about some passage I was instructed to rewrite in one of my letters. The letter was to someone in Botswana. In the letter I had wanted to know about the results of the previous elections in the country (Botswana). When the letter came back with the message underlined in red, I saw red. Prins was not ruffled. He told me: *'Look, Dingake, would you regard it as a sound policy and practice if the prisons department brought the women into the cells of convicted rapists?'* The analogy was far-fetched. But the point Prins was trying to convey was that in prison, political prisoners were to be made to forget politics in any form. Mention of politics of any kind was dangerous, it was morale boosting. Prins said so in plain language when I ridiculed his analogy. Prins was naive in the extreme. Not his fault. He represented naive policies. [emphasis added]

MICHAEL DINGAKE, My Fight Against Apartheid

The attitude of the prison authorities toward child detainees is callous. I was told by my client [a sixteen-year-old girl] that one night, unable to bear the thought of being detained any longer, she broke down and cried. Some of the other detainees followed suit. The prison warder's response to this, needless to say, was a total lack of concern. *Their attitude was that the detainees were in need of male company and that is why they were upset.* [emphasis added]

VANESSA BRERETON (Port Elizabeth lawyer), cited in Children of Resistance

Lieutenant Prins of the Robben Island administration may appear naive, even to Michael Dingake, a member of the ANC arrested in 1966 and sentenced to fifteen years imprisonment, but the apartheid policies of detention that he represents are indeed summarily contained in the disingenuous query put to his prisoner (Dingake 1987, 170). Nor is the analogy entirely "far-fetched." Women detained by the security forces in South Africa are indeed held and interrogated in the "cells of rapists." Those rapists, however, are members of the police and prison apparatus who have yet to be "convicted," for all that they stand accused by international human rights organizations and indicted by the public outcry of many of the country's own citizens, both enfranchized and disenfranchized, and including lawyers, doctors, and members of the Detainees' Parents Support Committee (DPSC). But the analogy, that women are to rapists as politics is to the political prisoner—that is, dangerous, inciting, and taboo—also enjoins the reading proposed by Dingake, according to which political prisoners are considered to be as inimical to the correct and upright practice of the political as rapists are to the coveted righteousness of women.

140   The apparent identification in the analogy of women and politics is undermined, however, by the very presence in the cells of women political prisoners, whose own identification with political work must be categorically denied by their warders. As Vanessa Brereton's client reported, the warders respond to the women's plaints with the self-justifying explanation that "the detainees were in need of male company" (Brittain and Minty 1988, 64–65). No less than Lieutenant Prins's rhetorical dismissal of Dingake's argument against prison censorship, the warder's apparently absurd statement here speaks to the immediate brutality of the conditions of South African prisons where the availability of "male company" is a dire, significant problem for the detainees, both female and male.

Elaine Mohamed, a Coloured woman arrested in 1981 for designing and distributing posters marking the sixtieth anniversary of the South African Communist party, describes in an interview the acutely threatening role of "male company" especially for women prisoners: "The way women experience detention is totally different from the way men do. I burst into tears when a security policeman said to me, 'I really enjoy interrogating women. I can get things out of them and do things to them that I can't do to a man'" (Russell 1989, 37). Does the warder's analysis of the young girls' position—suggesting even ironically, that the girls in fact need more of the "male company" of interrogators and torturers—imply that they have not been adequately "disciplined"?

On 11 February 1990, ANC leader Nelson Mandela was released from twenty-seven years of imprisonment, bringing a new conjunctural crisis to the South African history of the political detention of the opponents of apartheid. The previous fall, eight other long-term prisoners had been released, including Walter Sisulu, another ANC leader sentenced with Mandela in 1963. Previously illegal organizations were unbanned: the South African Communist party (SACP) which had been underground since the Suppression of Communism Act in 1950; the ANC and the Pan-Africanist Congress (PAC), both banned in 1960 following the Sharpeville massacre; the United Democratic Front (UDF), formed in 1983 and declared illegal in 1988; the Detainees' Parents Support Committee (DPSC), established in 1981; and twenty-eight other anti-apartheid organizations. The three decades of struggle defined by the dates of Mandela's incarceration articulate as well the historical and political development of the liberation struggle, from a policy of nonviolent resistance to the practice of organized armed struggle, from a resistance movement grounded on its own territory to a movement leadership in prison and in exile, the emergence from within the schools of new generations of activists, and renewed mass mobilization in the townships, the mines, and the bantustans. **141**

The turn-of-the-decade from the 1950s to the 1960s was demarcated by two infamous and sensational trials. In the Treason Trial, from 1956 to 1961, 156 Congress alliance leaders stood accused of high treason and planned violence against the state; they were eventually acquitted on all charges. In the Rivonia Trial, in 1964, Mandela, Sisulu, and other ANC and Umkhonto we Sizwe leaders were found guilty and sentenced to life imprisonment. Between the long years of the Treason Trial and the arrest of the underground leadership at Rivonia in 1963, the political and material conditions of both the apartheid regime and the organized opposition had been subjected to radical and brutal pressures. In 1960 tens of demonstrators were massacred in Sharpeville when South African police opened fire on a mass protest and work stoppage carried out against the pass laws, which required all Africans, men and women, to carry with them at all times identity documents indicating their "right" to be where they were. And on 16 December 1961, Umkhonto we Sizwe (or "Spear of the Nation"), the newly formed armed wing of the resistance, carried out its first coordinated act of violent sabotage against key South African state installations.

At the Treason Trial the apartheid state had been unable to prove that violence and armed struggle had been a constitutive or integrated part of the ANC program of resistance. And correctly so. In 1961, however, following protracted and vexed internal debate, the Sharpeville slaughter, and a crucial realization of the intransigent nature of state violence against nonwhite South Africans, Umkhonto we Sizwe was formed, not as a wing of the ANC itself, but as a separate and independent entity, albeit with overlapping membership, to undertake armed sabotage against the official institutions of apartheid. As Nelson Mandela proclaimed to the court in his statement from the dock at the conclusion of the Rivonia Trial: "Experience convinced us that rebellion would offer the Government limitless opportunities for indiscriminate slaughter of our people. But it was precisely because the soil of South Africa is already drenched with the blood of innocent Africans that we felt it our duty to make preparations as a long-term undertaking to use force in order to defend ourselves against force. . . . The fight which held out the best prospects for us and the least risk of life to both sides was guerrilla warfare" (Benson 15).[1]

When the South African government in 1976 designated Afrikaans as a mandatory language of instruction for most subjects in "Bantu" schools, most of the organized resistance leadership was, as a result of the arrests and sentences during the previous decade, in prison, in exile, in hiding, or inactive. A new generation of activists rose up, however, as the schoolchildren of Soweto took to the township streets on 16 June 1976, the day on which the Afrikaans language was to be enforced in the schools, to protest this further attempt at appropriation by the government of their already restricted educational facilities. The youths' nonviolent march was met that day by police and armed forces with teargas and then with gunfire, leaving more than forty children dead in Soweto on that first afternoon alone. Many more would be killed, thousands of the protesters wounded, and still greater numbers detained in the ensuing months, marking still another decisive juncture within the history of the South African resistance and what has been called the apartheid government's "war on children." The Soweto uprising, begun on 16 June 1976, would henceforth be commemorated, and continued, as a critical transformation of the developing parameters of the popular struggle.

The Public Safety Act of 1953 had granted the state president the power to declare an emergency and to impose emergency regulations on part or all of the country for up to one year. Such an emergency had been declared in the aftermath of Sharpeville in 1960. It was declared again in July 1985 to contain the popular unrest, of students and workers especially, that had resurged in 1983; again in June 1986, in anticipation of the tenth anniversary of the Soweto uprising; and once more, in June 1987. When Nelson Mandela was released in February 1990, South Africa continued under the imposition of renewed emergency regulations. An end to this state of emergency and the repeal of its attendant regulations were part of the demands made and conditions claimed, including as well the release of all political prisoners still in South African prisons, for the proposed negotiations between the newly liberated leadership of the resistance and the South African government. In the historic speech made on the day of his release, Nelson Mandela announced his continued support for previously banned organizations such as the SACP and maintained the uncompromised position of the ANC in his refusal to renounce armed struggle as one of the means still available to the liberation of South Africa.

The issue of negotiations itself remained, as it had over the past three decades, subject to ongoing debate. In a poem published in 1972 in the collection *Cry Rage* (Matthews and Thomas), for example, "dialogue" had been eschewed as "a bribe offered by the oppressor."

> Dialogue
> the bribe offered by the oppressor
> glitters like fool's gold
> dazzling the eyes of the oppressed
> as they sit at the council table
> listening to empty discourse promising
>   empty promises
> beguiled by meaningless talk
> they do not realize ointment-smeared words
> will not heal open wounds
> the oppressor sits seared with his spoils
> with no desire to share equality
> leaving the oppressed seeking warmth
> at the cold fire of
> Dialogue.(John Matthews, cited in Shava, 86)

143

Nearly three decades later, in an article in *The African Communist*, a journal then published by the SACP in London, Phineas Malinga (1990) warned that although "struggle must always be given forms appropriate to the concrete political situation," a "negotiations bandwagon" was not without its own perils in that the "enemy aims at a 'compromise' settlement which will preserve the essentials of the present system and this is to be achieved by pushing the liberation movement into premature negotiations—negotiations at a stage when the balance of power still remains with the regime" (26–29). The debate over the strategic priorities of negotiations and/or armed struggle confronted by the South African liberation movement in 1990 informed and was informed by its longer history of resistance, a history that is written from within and without the territorial boundaries of the South African state, inside and outside the state's prison appartus, and by women no less than by men.

A week after the release of Nelson Mandela from his twenty-seven years in prison, first on Robben Island and then in a mainland government compound, Christopher Wren, the *New York Times* correspondent in South Africa, wrote a feature article on Nelson's wife, Winnie, under this headline: "With Return of Mandela, His Wife Is Rescued from Political Oblivion."

A year ago, Winnie Mandela was held in disgrace by the anti-apartheid movement for condoning what was widely described as bullying and brutality by her young bodyguards.

Today, she is visibly back at the heart of the struggle as the dutiful wife of Nelson Mandela. When the world watched the black nationalist leader leave prison last Sunday, she was walking by his side.

Mrs. Mandela's political rehabilitation was made easier by her husband's return to the domestic leadership of the struggle against apartheid, ending the surrogate's role that she played so prominently during her husband's 27 ½ years in prison. (*New York Times*, 12 May 1991)

144 Referring here to allegations that Winnie Mandela's young bodyguards, once part of a local football team, had engaged in unwonted violence resulting in the death of a fourteen-year-old boy, the *Times* reporter not only participates in a particularly sensational version of the dominant South African narrative of "black-on-black violence," but complicitly uses the vaunted release of the ANC's legendary leader to recontain women in a subsidiary role, as a "dutiful wife . . . walking by his side," within the liberation struggle. The phrase that is employed to describe Mandela's release, his "return to the domestic leadership," in its very ambivalence—conflating in the word "domestic" the home front with the struggle inside South Africa—further suggests the imperative of disciplining the woman activist within her proper sphere.

In the next day's issue of the *Times*, Wren carried out a similar editorial attempt at displacement and discreditation, this time enlisting the rhetoric of anticommunism (which the United States and South Africa have in common), by asking what now would be the role of the South African Communist Party and its leader, Joe Slovo, with the rehabilitation and reinstatement by the state of the traditional patriarchal figure. Wren's two articles demonstrate, however, the discursive strategy of an attempted, if belated, hegemonic control over the emancipatory social and political transformations envisioned by the resistance movement. Joe Slovo nonetheless appeared at Mandela's side in the ANC delegation when it arrived in Cape Town in May 1990 to discuss "negotiations" with the South African government. Ruth Mompati of the ANC executive was there as well, as was Cheryl Carolus—the only women, however, out of a group of eleven.

According to *Cries of Freedom*, a report on women in detention in South Africa prepared by the Detainees' Parents Support Committee in 1988, "women comprise only 8 to 12 per cent of the total number of people detained in the crackdown against organisations which have spearheaded resistance to apartheid" (1989: 7). The authors of the report attribute this apparently small representation of politically active women in detention to "the fact that women are located principally among the rank and file of popular organisations and few have yet risen to leadership positions" (7). Ruth Mompati in an interview with Diane Russell in Lusaka, Zambia, at the ANC-in-exile's international headquarters, suggests a contrasting explanation for the limited number of women executives of the ANC: "The National Executive is outside the country. One of the reasons there are only three women [out of thirty-five] on it is that very few senior women have left the country" (Russell 1989, 116). But as Russell pointed out, "The second edition of Shelagh Gastrow's *Who's Who in South African Politics* (1987) lists only six women, two fewer than the 1985 edition" (27n). *Prisoners of Apartheid*, a biographical list of political prisoners and banned persons in South Africa published in October 1978 by the International Defense and Aid Fund (IDAF) in London, lists only 5 women among the 322 political prisoners. By contrast, 25 women are identified among the 139 banned persons, suggesting perhaps that the South African penal system discriminates between males and females in setting the forms of punishment.

Statistics, lists, catalogues, and figures notwithstanding, women activists have had a distinguished record within the struggle for the liberation of South Africa (see the IDAF's booklet *To Honour Women's Day* [1981], with its profile of thirty leading women in the South African and Namibian liberation struggles). Hilda Bernstein's *For Their Triumphs and For Their Tears* (1978) recounts the particular pressures, from state and society, that coerce the lives of South African women under the apartheid regime. The women themselves, both black and white, have narrated the histories of their own ordeals of political detention, as well as their experience of the imprisonment of others: Winnie Mandela, *Part of My Soul Went with Him* (1985); Norma Kitson, *Where Sixpence Lives* (1986); Hilda Bernstein, *The World That Was Ours* (1989); Frances Baard, *My Spirit Is Not Banned* (1986); and Helen Joseph, *Side By Side* (1986). Ruth First's *117 Days* (1989) tells of the arrest of a white woman activist in the ANC and the SACP under the 90-Day Detention Law at the time of the Rivonia Trial in 1963, whereas Caesarina Kona Makhoere's *No Child's Play* (1988) is the narrative of a black woman student in her twenties sentenced in 1976 to five years' imprisonment under Section 6 of the Terrorism Act.

First's *117 Days* opens with a quasi-obsessive description of the brutally transformative effects of solitary confinement on the physical and intellectual identity and ontology of the prisoner. "For the first fifty-six days of my detention in solitary I changed from a mainly vertical to a mainly horizontal creature. A black iron bedstead became my world. It was too cold to sit, so I lay extended on the bed, trying to measure the hours, the days and the weeks, yet pretending to myself that I was not" (15). Was not what? Or simply was not? The material specificity of the prison experience remains here suspended, the political activist as if deactivated,

145

between the meticulous marking of time, the calculations of temporality, and existential denial. First goes on, in a Kafkaesque evocation, to express the anticipated threat of a total loss of her recognizable physical self: "Left in the cell long enough, I feared to become one of those colourless insects that slither under a world of flat, grey stones, away from the sky and the sunlight, the grass and people" (15). She recognizes herself as having become a prisoner according to the long written tradition of political detention: "Yet, not an hour after I was lodged in the cell, I found myself forced to do what storybook prisoners do: pace the length and breadth of the cell" (15–16).

First's intellectual faculty here takes over as the prisoner reads the proverbial "writing on the wall" of the prison cell, the personal messages from young girls, common law or "criminal" prisoners, who admit to having slain their babies or to being in love, and the political slogans, *Mayibuye i'Afrika* ("Let Africa Come Back"), from the women prisoners of the Sharpeville Emergency (16). This intellectual function, which allows even the retrospective representation of her physical responses and reflexes, informs Ruth First's account of her 117 days in a South African prison and her calculated efforts to counter the verbal and psychological assaults of her interrogators. Like Draupadi, the woman guerrilla of Mahasweta Devi's story, Ruth First projects the details and scenario of the inevitable forthcoming inquisition and questions her strength to withstand their probing. "What did They know? Had someone talked? Would their questions give me any clue? How could I parry the interrogation sessions to find out what *I* wanted to know, without giving them the impression that I was resolutely determined to tell them nothing?" (19). While she does not propose, as Draupadi had momentarily planned, to bite off her own tongue, First does mentally seek for ways to frustrate the interlocutor's aggressive attempt to wrest from her his wanted information. "Calm but sleepless, I lay for hours on the bed, moving my spine and my legs round the bumps round the mattress, and trying to plan for my first interrogation session" (20). In a determined and concerted effort to regain her self-control on that first night in prison, she concludes her preparations for the impending confrontation: "At the first interrogation session, I decided, I would insist on saying nothing until I knew whether a charge was to be preferred against me" (20).

The South African government did not, as it turned out, charge Ruth First during that period of detention in the women's cells in Marshall Square. The prison was already vaguely familiar to her from her previous brief stay there in 1956, at the start of the Treason Trial, in which she was one of the 156 defendants. Nineteen years later, however, the Pretoria government apparently sentenced her to death: she was assassinated on

17 August 1982 by a parcel bomb sent to her in Maputo, Mozambique, where she was working as a researcher at the Eduardo Mondlane University.[2] The introductory self-examination prior to her interrogation in Ruth First's prison memoir signals the radical crisis of subjectivity that characterizes political detention and its eventual manipulation by the state penal apparatus, as it endeavors to realign an oppositional political position within its dominant ideological framework. In the Foreword to the 1989 edition of her memoir, issued twenty-five years after the original publication and seven years after her death, Albie Sachs points out that First's **147** work and critical position stood as a dramatic contradiction and challenge to that framework. Sachs, himself an ANC activist and former detainee, describes her as "white in an overwhelmingly black movement . . . an intellectual of middle-class background in a struggle dedicated to the emancipation of the workers . . . [and] a critic in a movement that required a high degree of discipline" (8–11).

At the time of her arrest, First, a historian and journalist who had covered the bus boycotts and had investigated the exploitative conditions for peasants in the rural areas, had been banned by the South African government. She was working as a librarian trainee in a university library. A prominent member of the ANC, the SACP, and the earlier Congress of Democrats, she had edited or worked for various of their publications, each in turn banned, and including *The Guardian*, *New Age*, and *Fighting Talk*. That first night in prison, First berated herself for carelessness because the security forces had found an illegal copy of this last publication in their search of her house at the time of her arrest. Her husband, Joe Slovo, himself a leader of the SACP and of Umkhonto we Sizwe, had meanwhile fled the country in the month just preceding the government sweep of Rivonia and the mass arrests of the opposition leadership.

If the formation of Umkhonto we Sizwe was, as Sol Dubula described the event on the tenth anniversary of the organization's founding, "a qualitative break with the traditional methods of mass political action and mobilisation and . . . influences directly or indirectly every aspect of political and organisational activity" (Dubula 1971, 388), the Rivonia raid was no less crucial, from a negative perspective, in temporarily dismantling those structures. Hilda Bernstein, whose husband, "Rusty," was among those arrested but later acquitted, wrote in her retrospective *The World That Was Ours* (1978):

There came a time when it seemed as though the ground was no longer firm beneath our feet; as though the world had tilted and we were uncertain about each step.

But this was not only a personal concern. The same sense of disorientation existed in the organizations within which we worked. It was not so much a loss

of direction; there was no doubt about what we believed, what we were looking for; no hesitation in political aims. The uncertainty arose from the blows we
had received, as though we were concussed by the widespread arrests, the jail-
ings and bannings, the loss of those who had escaped across the borders to safer
countries; the iron clamps placed on speech, publications, activities, even social
associations . . .

And the disorientation we felt was the experience and outcome of the Rivonia
Trial that was dealing blows to the liberation movement as a whole. (vii)

148 The personal transformations recounted by First in the opening pages of
117 Days were, therefore, more than subjective hallucinations or solipsistic
self-scrutiny; rather, they represented a critical and substantive reponse
to the larger, organizational crisis enacted upon the liberation struggle by
the state's security apparatus.

The Rivonia Trial itself was one of the more publicized of South Africa's
"political trials." It was further distinguished by the fact that the accused
did not plead innocent to the charges against them; instead they retook
the courtroom as an arena in which to present from the dock an alternative
history and political analysis, one that exposed the exclusivist ideology of
race that underwrites the South African apartheid regime. In the recent
film *A Dry White Season* (1989), the lawyer MacKenzie (played by Mar-
lon Brando) tells an indignant Ben Du Toit: "law and justice are not on
speaking terms in South Africa." But if political trials are "part of a long
and violent process in which the label of criminality is forced on those
struggling for freedom," then detention, as one lawyer has claimed, is
"a witness factory, a place where evidence is manufactured for court"
(South Africa—The Imprisoned Society, 7). On her first night in solitary
confinement, and all the subsequent nights as well, Ruth First's expressed
concern with her interrogation and her need—as well as her ability—to
withhold information from her examiners is grounded in the legal and
systemic expropriation of justice in South Africa.

As a trained sociologist, historian, and journalist, First collected and
distributed information. Her active political commitment gave that information, derived from outside the traditional archival research space, a
transitive effect that also extended beyond the academic sphere. She wrote
in the Preface to *South Africa: The Peasants' Revolt* (1964), by Govan Mbeki,
a Rivonia defendant sentenced to life imprisonment (and released with
Sisulu and six others in the fall of 1989), of their collective work: "it all had
to be written under cover, both to secure the manuscript and to guard
ourselves against arrest, prosecution, and imprisonment for writing in
defiance of the government ban" (11). Mbeki's study of peasant revolt,
begun as a "manual for members and organizers of the African National

Congress" (9), was continued in prison on two rolls of toilet paper; First arranged for its publication when she reached exile in London after her release from prison in December 1963.

Belinda Bozzoli and Peter Delius (1990), of the University of Witswatersrand's History Workshop, see a historiographical ambivalence in the apparent "contradiction between the theoretical analyses which proclaimed the death of 'race' on the one hand, and on the other, the social movements of 1976 onward—movements which were based in communities as well as at workplaces, which erupted in townships as well as through trade unions, many of which were black, youthful, and implicitly or explicitly nationalist in orientation" (28). This ambivalence has a material history of its own, one that is conditioned by struggle and as such raises significant questions for the institutional disciplining of the historian and the task of history. In prison her state interrogators demand that Ruth First contribute to a punitive narrative that will be deployed in order to incarcerate for life the Rivonia activists—if, that is, they are not given the maximum death sentence. Her intellectual contest with her interrogators must prevent that history from being written and carried out. Her self-imposed antithetical role as counterhistorian informs her account of prison and struggle in *117 Days*.

Given her political commitments and engaged intellectual participation in the South African struggle against the state institutions of apartheid, Ruth First, on finding herself as a detainee, must redefine her theoretical role as historiographer and investigative reporter against the coercive constraints of detention and interrogation. The articulation of a new and alternative resistance strategy of active discursive disengagement, which would not signal abdication, nor presume abandonment of the resistance, nor betray her partisan function, becomes crucial to First's prison exercise. As a white and a woman, furthermore, she is less subject to wanton physical brutality from her captors than her black male and female or white male counterparts, the official representatives of apartheid in prison still being loathe to relinquish their traditional reverence and respect for the sanctity of white womanhood, even when it has, as in her case, turned treacherous. As an activist intellectual, then, Ruth First redeploys differently inside prison the same words and information that she has used as weapons in the struggle outside the prison. Prison, as an institution, both reinforces and at the same time necessarily remakes the very role and conventional practices of the intellectual. First collects words where she can and rewrites them behind walls designed to contain and foreclose the elaboration of oppositional counterinformation.

From the writing on the walls of her solitary cell to the partially visible

149

newspaper placard posted by the black newsvendor on the pavement out-side her tiny window, the writer activist must again piece together, from scratch, the events of the world and her committed place in them:

> To me it looked like this:
>
> QUA
I
RHO
>
> RHO had to be Rhodesia. But what in Rhodesia? Quarrel? Newspaper posters were getting vaguer than ever. Qualms? Ditto. Quads? Well, I suppose so, but they must have been special to merit a poster. (It never struck me that it was a QUAKE in Rhodesia. I never thought of Rhodesia as earthquake-prone.) (47)

The Bible, at first the only reading material allowed her in solitary confine-ment, is also enlisted to undermine its sanctioned use in her discursive strategies against the security system's assault on her political position:

> I read the Book, from first page to the last, first the Old Testament, then the New. When I reached the last page I started again with the first. I memorized psalms and proverbs:
>
> > A fool's mouth is his destruction
> > And his lips are the snare of his soul
>
> and
>
> > Confidence in an unfaithful man in time of trouble
> > Is like a broken tooth, and a foot out of joint
>
> memorizing and storing up references to my predicament at the hands of informers and the Security Branch. (70–71)

First even transforms physical nourishment into mental and intellec-tual energy: "Even better . . . was the ration of brown sugar that started to arrive every few days, for the six or eight ounces were rolled in a cone of paper, printed paper, torn from old magazines. This way I feasted on a few torn paragraphs from *War Cry*, organ of the Salvation Army, and once only, tantalizingly, I got a short jagged piece from the *Saturday Evening Post*" (78). The tattered shards and fragments of text are reinscribed in a transgressive, if still hypothetical, counternarrative of resistance: "Around this extract I tried to improvise a version of a serial *à la* James Bond in which all the action centred around a jail break from Pretoria Central— my cell" (78). Writing projects, no less than reading, are thus redevised within the prison. Against the generic grain of reportage, First, a histo-rian and journalist, becomes a novelist rewriting her own personal past and reviewing the story of the resistance as part of a still-obstructed and incomplete emancipatory narrative of the future.

> I devised a plot for a novel. The characters were me and my friends, all cast in heroic mould. We planned and organized in opposition to the Government, called

for strikes and acts of civil disobedience, were harassed and chivvied by the police, banned, and arrested. Then we were locked in prison cells and here I was again, grappling with life in a cell. I did better than that. I spent hours getting behind the political declarations of my characters, dissecting their private inclinations, scrutinizing their love affairs and marriages, their disillusionments and idle talk. When my imagination faltered I turned again to the Bible. (77)

The conditions were still not right for bringing the story to a close.

The calculated use by the Security Branch of information against First is, by contrast, directed in malicious design, and its experience with interrogation informs that design, at two ideological fronts: First's organizational allegiances and her filial loyalties. "Even now I cannot write how it happened but shortly after this I was given two pieces of information that froze my limbs. First leak: a delegate present at a meeting I had attended at Rivonia with Mandela, Sisulu, and others had blurted information to the police. . . . Second leak: the Security Branch was investigating my father and my mother" (61). The detainee's concerted sense of self, already challenged by detention, interrogation, and solitary confinement, is further exposed to question in this surreptitious and impending attack on the conflicted relations between "self" and "other." That conflict becomes physical again.

During my first weeks in the cell I had been impudently buoyant. I was determined to find the stamina to survive this war of attrition. But now I began to feel encumbered by diversionary actions. My parents, and through them the children, were being pulled into the line of fire. What was the Security Branch planning? Who else was on the list to be detained? Who else had turned informer? I lay and worried, before full awakening in the morning, all day, even in my sleep. I was no longer sleeping well. (62)

While First's concern for the well being of her parents is probed by her interrogators, her worry about the welfare of her children haunts her imagination: "I had to stop thinking about the children. I needed all my concentration to handle my own situation . . . but of course I couldn't stop thinking about them" (63).

First's two daughters have renarrated that obstructed thinking and have rewritten their mother's prison experience from a retrospective, outside point of view. Shawn Slovo's film *A World Apart* (1988), directed by Chris Menges, elaborates the contested outlines of the mother-daughter relationship and the conflicting political forces that rework these ties. Refused visits to her mother by the prison authorities, "Molly" is taken by Elsie, the "Roths'" family servant whose own brother Solomon will die in detention, to visit Elsie's family in the black township where they live. Whereas *A World Apart* is contained within the narrative frame of the 117 days that Ruth First spent in detention, *Ties of Blood* (1989), Gillian Slovo's epic novel, traces the struggle of three generations of women as political activists in two families, one black and one white. Toward the end of the novel, the white father Jacob reflects, "Some times, Jacob thought [toward the end of the novel] as he wiped his forehead again, revolutions are simpler than families" (492). Addressing these complications that revolutionary change imposes on a traditional family order, the chapter entitled "Detention and the Family" from *Staying Strong in Detention*, a manual written and distributed in 1989 by South African Committee for Higher Education (SACHED) Trust to help people prepare for detention and cope with problems after arrest, warns:

152

> Children can get very anxious or scared when a parent or brother or sister is detained. It is wise to prepare children for the event of detention. Parents who think they might be detained should explain now to their children. If no-one explains to the children that a parent is in detention, they often think the parent is either dead or has left because he/she does not love them anymore.
>
> If both parents could be detained, establish a support structure which will take care of the child if that happens. Single parents and the parent left behind should do this too. (73)

Her interrogators nonetheless confront First not only with family issues but with the complications of "revolution" as well. Released at the end of ninety days, only to be rearrested as she stepped outside the Marshall Square Station, Ruth First must begin again her intellectual exercise of discursive resistance. Told that others had informed on her, told too that the others believed that she had informed on them, First sets out to re-strategize her role in the interrogation process: "I lay awake the whole night. I worried without stop about the news that B. was talking. This, I thought, introduced a critical change into my own position" (119). She agrees to answer questions, to make a statement, but insists on her profession as a writer in refusing to allow the use of a tape recorder. Still, she rearranges the mental compartmentalizing of her information: "Into a strong-room labelled 'NEVER to be divulged' I stored everything I knew— and I knew so much that I was heavy with it—which would provide trails to information the Security Branch so wanted" (120–21).

Like the projected novel imaginarily composed during her original "ninety days," First's statement proposes a history, at once personal and political, of her emergence within the resistance as an intellectual worker, her schooling and degrees, the miners' strike of 1946, police raids and arrests, her own banning orders, the Defiance Campaign of 1952, her travels in the Soviet Union and China, *Fighting Talk*. In the end, when her legal activities have been exhausted, Ruth First breaks down: "It was madness for me to think I could protect myself in a session like this, in any session with them" (128). She refuses to continue the statement. "That was all I thought the entire night: literally two words 'NO STATEMENT NO STATEMENT NO STATEMENT' over and over again in my mind" (130). She forgets to put on her makeup. She wonders whether she should continue her hunger strike. The Security Branch will claim to her comrades that she has turned "informer." To forestall their attempted character assassination— perhaps, like Bhuvaneswari, thinking that death alone will certify and attest to her loyalty—Ruth First momentarily abandons her intellectual exercise for the physical resistance of self-denial. Her attempted suicide is thwarted by the authorities and after 117 days First is released.

> I don't know why I was released. Perhaps they just didn't have enough evidence. Perhaps they had made up their minds that I would not talk after all. Perhaps I was approaching another cracking-point, a cracking not wide open to them, but of myself, and they might have seen it coming . . .
> When they left me in my own house at last I was convinced that it was not the end, that they would come again. (150)

Before they came again, however—for the final time in 1982, in Mozambique—Ruth First went on to rework the task of the political historian/ activist: in a biography of Olive Schreiner, coauthored with Ann Scott (1980); in *Power in Africa* (1970); in her editing of the works of the still-imprisoned Nelson Mandela, *No Easy Walk to Freedom* (1973); in *The South African Connection* (1973), with other authors; in the posthumous and collective *Black Gold* (1983); and in her own prison memoir, *117 Days*. In this memoir her individual story of personal confrontation with the apartheid system is reconstructed through the narratives of her fellow prisoners: the prison escape of Rivonia detainees Arthur Goldreich and Harold Wolpe; the detention and sentencing of Dennis Brutus; a smuggled diary; the first death in detention, of Looksmart Solwandle Ngudle, banned after his death to prevent an exposé of torture in the cells; and finally Albie Sachs's successful demand for reading and writing material in the prison.

Ruth First was in exile in London and the Rivonia prisoners were serving life sentences on Robben Island and in Pretoria Maximum Security Prison when the Soweto student uprising against Bantu education, catalyzed by the newly won independence in neighboring Mozambique and Angola, swept through the townships of South Africa in 1976. Twenty-year-old Caesarina Kona Makhoere, with a young child at home in the care of her mother, was back in school at the time. Arrested as an "agitator," she waited after a year to be charged and served five more years in various of South Africa's prisons. The title of her prison memoir, *No*

153

Child's Play (1988), belies the sentimental, or even sensational, representation of the emergent cadres of South African resistance from within the schools, a new generation of black activists. Many of them may have been children, but their childhood had been denied by the legal, economic, and political structures of apartheid that oppressed them and their people, the majority of the population of South Africa.

The nonetheless enduring grip on the popular imagination outside South Africa of the compelling image of "children in revolt" is dramatically displayed in films such as *Cry Freedom* (1988) and *A Dry White Season* (1989),[3] both of which are framed by panoramic visions of gathered schoolchildren chanting, carrying banners, and demonstrating in the barren and dusty township streets in confrontation with the amassed military might of the state. Tear gas cannisters are fired from the armored phalanx of the security forces; they are followed by machine gun shots into the crowds of young people fleeing in panic. *Cry Freedom*, a British feature film directed by Richard Attenborough and based on Donald Woods's book *Biko*, tells the quasi-documentary story of the 1977 death in detention of the Black Consciousness leader Steve Biko and reporter Woods's public investigation into and exposure of the brutal circumstances of that death. The Hollywood production of Euzhan Palcy's *A Dry White Season*, by contrast, fictionalizes the consciousness-raising encounter of a well-to-do Afrikaner businessman with the penal system when his gardener is said to have "committed suicide" in prison. Both films, however, through their framing scenes, reference their narratives to the Soweto uprising.

No less powerful is the impact of Soweto on the more critically analytical and less imagistic South African novels, such as Sipho Sepamla's *Ride on the Whirlwind* (1981) and its sequel *Third Generation* (1986), and Mbulelo Mzamane's *Children of Soweto* (1982). In these texts, however, the dramatic composite image of "children in revolt" that is contained by the two feature films is analyzed around issues of gender, the role of women in the struggle; race, the complex place of white South Africans in the struggle and the allegiances of "Blacks," "Asians," and "Coloureds"; generation, the recalcitrance or quiescence of parents against the explosion of anger from their children; and class, the treacherous and self-interested complicity of black township residents with the state's security apparatus.

Caesarina Kona Makhoere was betrayed into the hands of the South African police on 25 October 1976 by her father, a black policeman who, as she writes in the first chapter of *No Child's Play*, "was trapped and could not help pointing out where I was hiding when I was on the run" (1). Afterwards, she goes on, he "tried to get me out on bail but this was refused. He suffered a lot of mental torture. There he was, visiting me, yet he was the one responsible for my being behind bars" (1–2). Her father broke down and cried the day she was sentenced to five years in prison, and that, according to Makhoere, was "the last picture of my father I carried to prison" (2). Later, in the middle of a struggle with the prison authorities over prison food, when she is told by one of the female wardens that her father has died, the young prisoner only cursorily acknowledges the tragic news before returning to the political work of prison:

And they started, "Caesarina, we have something to tell you." Me, I was only concentrating on the food issue. "What is it?" "We have bad news for you. Your father is late; he was buried yesterday."

I could not believe it. Man, my father was buried yesterday. Anyway, I retorted, "Aaiiee, what can I do? Okay, I've heard that. There is nothing I can do. Let's come back to the issue of food." (81)

The disintegrating legitimacy of the family patriarchy that Makhoere introduces in the first chapter of *No Child's Play* is radically left behind in prison.

Makhoere quickly undertakes the urgent work, even from within a partial solitary confinement, of remaking an organized social order of resistance and struggle among the women prisoners. The critically theorized verbal confrontation between Ruth First and her interrogators is transformed and complimented here, a decade and a half later, through escalating mobilizational activity. To begin, the struggle over the land of South Africa waged by the state against its black population—through laws such as the Group Areas Act of 1950; the bantustan, or "homeland," policy relocating Africans to "tribal" reserves; and the razing of black townships like Sophiatown to make place and remake space for white suburbs—is fought again inside the prison over the peach tree growing in the center of the exercise yard.

We decided that peach tree belonged to the people, meaning us. It would bear peaches, golden, round and juicy. And as far as we were concerned the peaches were ours, only. We got no fruit in our official diet. We agreed that black male prisoners who mowed the lawn should take the peaches with the understanding that we were suffering the same fate. But let any white warder or wardress try it and we would scream through the windows: "Hey! What are you doing. Leave our peaches alone!" Eventually even the wardresses accepted that it was more peaceful to ask our permission to eat those peaches. (19–20)

Land, for the moment, is retaken from the state for the people inside the prison.

The peach tree incident signals the beginnings of organized protest in *No Child's Play*. Challenging the institutional forms that conscript their identity as women with minds of their own and asserting a radical critique of the state and its policies, the women detainees refuse to wear the regulation prison clothes for black women: heavy men's shoes, "white apron, sky-blue denim overalls, navy-blue jersey, brown shoes, navy-blue socks and red doek [headscarf]! These people had decided to treat us like mad people, but all identically mad, a uniform insanity" (21). They further refuse to abide by the different diets presented to black and Coloured prisoners and stage a hunger strike: "Our strategy went like this: we complained and complained and complained, so that we should have sufficient grounds. And then we acted" (32). Makhoere challenged the ritual practice of the "morning parade" as well, and a work refusal began. "Dis"—for disregard—was what the women called their tactics. They used illicitly acquired information to bribe the prison officials into compliance with their demands. "After all," Makhoere writes, "there is one thing I have learned about this system of the South African government. When you talk soft, they don't listen to you, whatever you say. Until you take action, action in the true sense of the word, where people are fighting physically, not verbally. It is only then that they believe that we mean business. You must hit them hard" (41).

In prison Makhoere meets Thandi Modise, an ANC guerrilla fighter—"a trained MK [Umkhonto we Sizwe] cadre, a woman!" (88). The historical example of armed struggle is important to the young prisoner: "We the generation of 1976, we admire the heroes and our heroines of *Umkhonto We Sizwe*, the MK. I admired what Thandi had done; breaking away from the traditional role of the female in our society of supporting the male. Thandi Modise—a fully fledged soldier of the people" (88–89). That example reinforces her commitment to active resistance against the prison regime. "The apartheid rulers leave you with no alternative but action, direct action. They do not understand anything verbal" (91).

The women prisoners attack Mbomvana, a sadistic female warden: "We stabbed her several times with those mathematical instruments. We had made up our minds that this person was not going to treat us like this; we wanted to kill her, there and then. Let us kill her and they can hang us. Because we have had enough of her. We assaulted her for a long time, stabbing her in the face, on the head, on the body, all over. She was bleeding on to the passage floor. After we had satisfied ourselves we went back to our cells" (64). The decades-long debate within the South African liberation struggle over passive resistance, defiance campaigns, work stoppages and boycotts, sabotage and armed struggle, is recapitulated by the prisoners themselves, informed by their generational experiences and reciprocal collaboration, inside the prison confines. Prison, like liberation, is, as the text maintains, "no child's play."

According to testimony and documentation presented at the 1987 Harare Conference on Children, Repression and the Law in South Africa, between 1984 and 1986, 312 children had been killed by the police, more than one thousand children had been wounded, and an estimated 11,000 children had been detained under the emergency regulations (making up 40 percent of all detainees). (Brittain and Minty, 1988) Schools were raided by security forces and entire classes were arrested. On release, many of the children were treated for "post-traumatic stress syndrome." But, as Dr. Kevin Solomons, a psychiatry registrar from Johannesburg, explained to the Free South Africa's Children Symposium held in Washington, D.C., in 1987, "as stressful as detention was, children coming out of detention **157** were going back into township situations which were equally and sometimes even more traumatic, stressful, and threatening than the detention experience itself" (Human Rights Quarterly, 1988 76).

The last prison in which Makhoere was held before her release on 26 October 1982 was Klerksdorp prison, situated in the area of South Africa where the largest mines are located, and housing mainly prisoners convicted on pass-law offenses. Here, in her last stage of prison, the former student holds literacy classes for her fellow prisoners and redistributes her own meager resources among the other women. If the peach tree incident on her arrival in prison reenacted the struggle to liberate the land, her sojourn in Klerksdorp Prison proposes the outlines of a visionary scenario of the new South Africa: "We shared out the soap, creams, all that, even my Christmas sweets. I was practising the Freedom Charter, not only theorising about it: 'The people shall share in the country's wealth,' even if at that point it was only the section's wealth" (112).

Ruth First, who in detention sought to derail the duplicitous "negotiations" of her interrogators, was present in Kliptown in 1955 at the popular ratification of the Freedom Charter, a document that the state would hold as treasonous at the Treason Trial the following year; two decades later Caesarina Kona Makhoere gave up "child's play" to struggle in prison against her captors so that the same Freedom Charter might yet be realized. Two generations, two women—both mothers, both activists, both detained, one white, the other black—both were part of the struggle to liberate a larger prison, apartheid South Africa, a country in which, according to Terry Sacco, "children have become the brunt of vigilante action and they have become refugees in their own country. They no longer can live at home. They no longer can experience family life. When children phone home and say, 'Mother can I come home?', a mother has to say, 'No, my child' " (Brittain & Minty, 94).

Chapter Seven

Carceles Clandestinas: Interrogation, Debate, and Dialogue in El Salvador

I write you
from the 5th Bartolina
of our Central Penitentiary.
I couldn't write you before
because with a playful bubbly liberty
one can't elevate one's words
to the height
of the ancient imprisoned
who showed how to see jail
as one minuscule
stepping stone more
on the road to
deserving a little
the future freedom
of all.　　　　　ROQUE DALTON, "Letter to Nazim Hikmet"

Our poetry cannot afford to be enamored with the moon when we have bomb craters in our own land dropped by one of the biggest and most powerful nations of the planet. Our poetry can take the luxury of reminiscing about a sleepy lake or volcano, but we cannot consent to being complicitous to the dangerous game that proliferates sleepy consciousness.　　ANONYMOUS, "We Cannot Afford to be Enamored with the Moon"

We arrive at the conclusion that one form is no more or less formative or deformative than another; that the task of being a revolutionary in the country or the city does violence to the individual; and that a revolutionary can transcend this threat of self-violence only if he possesses a clear idea of why he does violence to himself, what he is giving his life to—in sum, when he perceives the full grandeur of the cause.

CLEA SILVA, "The Errors of the Foco Theory"

At least thirty thousand peasants and Indians, according to official estimates, were killed by the Salvadoran military, commanded by the country's newest dictator, General Maximiliano Hernandez Martinez, in the 1932 *matanza*, or massacre. Dr. Alfonso Rojas, a young Nicaraguan physician practicing medicine in the Salvadoran town of Santa Ana at the time, is one of the characters in *Ashes of Izalco* (1989), a novel originally published in Spanish in 1966 by Claribel Alegria and Darwin Flakoll. Thirty years after the massacre, his daughter Carmen, in one of the novel's multiple narratives, returns from the United States to her family home for her mother's funeral. She describes her father:

For years Dad has spent his free hours writing speeches and articles, sending bales of telegrams to the five presidents urging them to take this or that step which would further the cause of unity. In his office there are boxes full of news clippings, letters, communiques, grandiose projects for overthrowing the Somoza clan. (56)

159

The issue of Central American unity still remains contested half a century after the massacre. The contest has been waged over the last decades through the armed struggles of the national liberation organizations, especially in El Salvador and Nicaragua, and has most recently been staged there in what Edward Herman and Frank Brodhead (1984) have referred to as "demonstration elections," or "elections organized and staged by a foreign power primarily to pacify a restive home population, reassuring it that ongoing interventionary processes are legitimate and appreciated by their foreign objects" (5).

In El Salvador, the right-wing National Republican Alliance (ARENA) party, whose reactionary political pedigree can be traced back from its contemporary figurehead Roberto D'Aubisson to the military government of General Martinez, came to power in March 1989, in an election in which two-thirds of the eligible voters did not vote. Less than a year later, in February 1990, Daniel Ortega, president of Nicaragua's revolutionary Sandinista government, after more than two decades of struggling against the government of Anastasio Somoza and nearly ten years of resisting a U.S.-supported counterrevolution, acknowledged electoral defeat to the United Nicaraguan Opposition (UNO) coalition headed by Violeta Chamorro. Within these political developments, Alegria and Flakoll's *Ashes of Izalco* and *La mujer habitada* [The Inhabited Woman], the first novel by the Nicaraguan poet Gioconda Belli (who also worked in the information service of the Sandinista government), mark perhaps the culmination of a particular historical moment. However, in their narrative review of specific articulations of that history, they suggest retrospectively new possibilities for its necessarily critical reconstruction.

Ashes of Izalco, written in alternating voices by Salvadoran Alegria, who, like Dr. Rojas, was born in Nicaragua, and her U.S.-born husband and translator, Flakoll, not only narrates the complex historical processes that continue to distinguish the 1932 *matanza* as crucial to the Salvadoran political struggle—the funeral of Carmen's mother is immediately followed by that of Colonel Gutierrez, one of the military participants in the massacre—but insists furthermore on the larger "American" context of that struggle. Carmen's mother has bequeathed to her daughter as a legacy the diary of one Frank Wolff, a North American writer and recovering alcoholic, who visited El Salvador in late 1931 in search of a new significance to his derelict life and met, in the provincial town of Santa Ana, Isabel, Carmen's mother and Alfonso's wife. Frank's journal writings from that time thus provide a counterpoint to Carmen's contemporary reminiscences of her return thirty years later, yet both documents, from their different historical and geopolitical positions, must come to terms with the subordination of women and their marginalization within the domain of the political.

Frank's emergent relationship with Isabel, an association that is made possible by her own frustrated and romanticized ambition to escape her domestic situation in Santa Ana, is itself frustrated and ultimately terminated by the violent military suppression of the peasant uprising. The date set by Frank for his escape with Isabel coincides with the very date of the *matanza*, and in the end the socially confined Isabel is no more able to change her domestic situation than Frank is able to grasp for himself the political consequences of the brutal history into which he has unwittingly intruded and with which he is now complicit.

Like Frank, but for reasons of class that are more marked for their want of national difference, Lavinia, the *mujer habitada* (or inhabited woman) of Belli's novel, is isolated from the social and political revolutionary challenges being raised around her. The well-educated daughter of a wealthy Nicaraguan family, now a professional architect, Lavinia becomes the lover of her office colleague Felipe. Living in a house of her own as part of her program of personal independence, Lavinia is roused late one night by Felipe, who asks temporary refuge for the seriously wounded Sebastian. In assenting to the request, Lavinia for the first time encounters the Movimiento, the national liberation movement. By the end of the novel she will have become a commando in one of its major actions: the hostage-taking at the housewarming party at General Vela's residence, which she herself has designed.

Dedicated to Nora Astorga, the FSLN partisan, known for her role in the execution of a leading Somozista, and loosely based in its final act on the Christmas 1974 Los Robles action in which three women commandos participated,[1] *La mujer habitada* is the narrative of the political growth of its heroine. The conventional paradigm for that growth, one that attributes women's political partisanship to romantic involvement, while it is not dismantled by the plot, is nonetheless redeployed in a layered self-critical account. The first-person voice of an Indian woman in the resistance to the Spanish conquest that merges finally with the third-person relation of Lavinia's political development suggests, too, a deeper history to the question of gender, ethnicity, and politics in Central America. As an architect and a daughter of an aristocratic family, Lavinia is asked to play herself as her undercover role in the movement: *"Aparentemente, para lo unico que iba a servirle al Movimiento era para ser quien era"* (173). [Apparently the only thing that would serve the movement was to be who I was.] Whereas forty years earlier, in neighboring El Salvador, Isabel had seen no escape from her social identity and domestic confinement beyond an imagined and aborted romance, Lavinia has her very class and gender positions enlisted by the resistance—and materially transformed.

161

In November 1989, El Salvador's FMLN launched a major offensive in the capital city of San Salvador. The ARENA government had yet to agree to full negotiations with the resistance. Then, in December 1989, the United States military invaded Panama to restore an "elected" government to power. And when the UNO coalition took over the government of Nicaragua in April 1990, the Sandinistas became again, as President Daniel Ortega said following the February elections, the "opposition." The English translation of *Ashes of Izalco* and the publication of *La mujer habitada* in 1989 could not, any more than Dr. Rojas in his dreams of Central American unity, have prefigured these historical developments in the region. Their critical renarrations of the past, however, propose now significant contributions to rethinking the immediate future, particularly the role of women—and North Americans—in new global and regional contexts.

In 1989, following the ARENA-won elections and nearly three years after a devastating earthquake that destroyed major sections of San Salvador (and substantially damaged the United States Embassy, whose counterinsurgency fortifications had served only to make the building more earthquake-prone), large segments of the capital city's displaced urban poor were still living in makeshift shantytowns and barrios of *champas* (huts). United States government relief aid had been differentially distributed by the government of Jose Napoleon Duarte; perhaps following the example of former Nicaragua's Somoza who, after the 1972 earthquake in Managua, used the international economic assistance to the country to rebuild the military and business sectors of the city against the increasingly pressing demands of the Nicaraguan people and the organized resistance.

In El Salvador, in 1989, popular organizations, such as the National Union of Earthquake Victims in El Salvador (UNADES), continued to assist the still-affected portions of the population, often with the help of nongovernmental support from abroad, such as the Women's Caravan, which had traveled overland from the United States in late spring of 1989. This "international aid" was one of the topics pressed by the Treasury Police interrogators in their questioning of three Salvadoran women—Carmen Rivera, age thirty-seven and a member of UNADES, Lucia Ramirez, age thirty-four and the treasurer of UNADES, and Ana Araceli Lopez Melgar, age twenty-seven and a former member of COMADRES, Committee of Mothers of the Disappeared—arrested in a search-and-seize raid at the UNADES office in San Jacinto on 18 July 1989.

162

The women were held incommunicado for the legally mandated seventy-two hours by the Treasury Police, then transferred to Ilopango Women's Prison. Their testimonies were taken there on 23 July by Cynthia Curtis, director of Building with the Voiceless of El Salvador in Washington, D.C.[2] The women's brief accounts are not necessarily unusual or exceptional within the narrative and procedural pattern of interrogation that has been established in El Salvador's detention centers: psychological intimidation, physical brutalization, the *capucha*, or hood, often filled with lime or soaked in kerosene, placed over the head of the prisoner. The testimonies disclose as well the interrogators' particular stratagems systematically practiced against their women victims: the threat, or act, of rape; assaults on the women's sexuality and sexual parts; the suggestion that their children too will be made to suffer for the "subversive" activities of their mothers, who, according to the militarized patriarchal customs of the society, do not know their proper place as women in the home. Carmen Rivera reported: "The interrogator pulled my hair and ran me about the cell. He said I should collaborate with them, because there are many people like me collaborating with them. '*Even machos talk here,*' he said. The beating continued until they got bored" (emphasis added).

In addition to insisting on links between UNADES and the FMLN, and pretending that women were not capable of resistance, the police were especially determined to discover more about the "international aid" that was assisting UNADES in its work. In their search of the office premises, according to Rivera, the police had already begun "to take out the material aid that was in our office, the aid from the Caravan. They said it was going to the Military Hospital and the Cuartel." Later, while Rivera was being questioned, her captor "mentioned the Caravan aid and said that it was aid that came 2 years ago and had been guarded for the guerrillas. I said no, and he said that he would kill me." According to Ana Araceli Lopez Melgar's testimony, that material aid was in fact reaching the people. She told Cynthia Curtis, "At the time of the capture, I had been at the office to receive a pair of shoes from the Caravan aid."

The police interrogators were especially aggressive in their questions to Lucia Ramirez, the organization's treasurer. She reported to Curtis:

Since I am the Treasurer of UNADES they kept me asking me questions about money. They had taken the bank account information out of the office, and asked me about deposits and withdrawals. In particular they asked me about a withdrawal for 5000 *colones*. They said it had gone to the guerrillas. I said that it had gone to buy construction materials for some "champas" (lit. huts). I told them that the receipts were in the office. They asked me where the money came from, if it came from the international level. I answered "yes, we got help from Building with the Voiceless of El Salvador in the United States." I was asked who is in Building with the Voiceless of El Salvador, and I said that I did not know, just some gringos. **163**

The testimonies of the three Salvadoran women from the UNADES office to their North American compiler and solidarity worker produce a counterdialogue to that elicited by force during their police interrogation, a counterdialogue that itself contributes to the establishment of a multidimensional activist front whose very sociopolitical articulations constitute the alternative cultural narrative against which the military government has launched its predatory attack: politically active women, the organized resistance movement, and international solidarity. The testimony taken by the human rights worker translates the police examination and torture into a different and resistant register, rewrites interrogation as dialogue, and reconstructs the assault on the individual as a necessarily collective oppositional project.

Against the allegations raised by Salvadoran military authorities and government officials of terrorist conscription of the peasants and the urban working class emerge the countering popular accounts of personal trajectories that have led Salvadoran women to enter the disputed public arena of political activity. One Salvadoran nurse, for example, described her own experience: "My son was one of those who *disappeared* [following a massacre in a San Salvador park in 1977]. . . . Two months later, I *joined* the Committee of Mothers of the Disappeared (COMADRES). I began to *travel,* to really *see* my country for the first time. I began to *understand* that what had happened to my son was not an isolated incident. I *saw* many similar cases, and many that were even worse" (Carter et al. 1989, 40–41, emphasis added). The sequence of verbs—disappeared, joined, travel, see, understand, saw—that structure this testimonial excerpt transcribe a mother's itinerary that leads her to a new kind of seeing, an itinerary that proceeds from the absence of her son ("disappeared") at the hands of a politically repressive authority to an analytical comprehension of the social issues that confront the country. The trajectory passes through collective action ("joined"), traverses geographical space ("travel"), and maps an ideological process of conscious political development ("understand"). The nurse's personal history of her engagement in collective resistance challenges the authoritarian imposition of the hegemonic constructions of a narrative of "modernization" as the basis of "progress," a narrative that is critiqued in a 1981 position paper by the Women's Association of El Salvador (AMES):

164

> In order to avert the threat of a genuine change in the role of women and our active participation in the liberation processes which would follow upon a massive increase of female consciousness, many governments have promoted "modern-ist" or "developmental" solutions. They point to the betterment of general living conditions in capitalist countries and to the introduction of new technology; they claim that this economic prosperity offers women the possibility of participating in the labor market and, consequently, of having "access to and participation in social life."
>
> These seductive conceptions of women's liberation are almost always asso-ciated with conservative or reformist values which are not conducive to effective changes in social relations. These values provide a basis for exalting the role of women within the family, an institutional outgrowth of the capitalist system— macho, repressive and based on the commercialization of human relations. (Carter et al. 1989, 85)

Indeed, the AMES paper goes on, "To advocate our 'insertion' into devel-opment, without determining what kind of development, resolves noth-ing" (85).

Within that dominant narrative, metropolitanly practiced and just as centrally preached to and within the periphery, women have been cus-tomarily and historically assigned various subsidiary support roles, as Cynthia Enloe (1990) points out, as tourists, sexual companions, domestic servants, military spouses, and diplomatic wives, to the main male actors on the political stage. Describing the helpmeet characterizations ascribed, for example, to wives of diplomats and government personnel, Enloe insists on the structural necessity of gendered power relations and the traditional bourgeois marriage to the maintenance of metropolitan poli-tics: "Thousands of women today tailor their marriages to fit the peculiar demands of states operating in a trust-starved international system. Some of those women are married to men who work as national-security advi-sors; others have husbands who are civilian weapons-engineers working on classified contracts; still others are married to foreign-service career-ists. Most of these men would not be deemed trustworthy if they were not in 'stable' marriages. Being a reliable husband and a man the state can trust with its secrets appear to be connected" (10).[3] The Latin American writer and poet Cecilia Bustamante (1989), however, writes from the perspective of political exile:

Because of her dependent condition, woman has usually identified with the minorities' movements. She is training *herself* in the reality of our time: direct violence, death. Such an involvement would seem contradictory to her human nature and her balancing function in the social structures. It can only be explained in part, because she easily identifies with suffering and discrimination and her sensitivity has not been numbed. When politicized, woman tends to become radical, depending on the status in her own society. Her operativity is antagonistic to the system, she is then a revolutionary. She is coming into being. Like the new language, she is setting categories, forging individual access to new aspects of reality and trying her alternatives to integration. (126)

For Bustamante, "Absolute authority practiced in woman its power and rule" (123).

The modern Latin American history of autocratic rule and military dictatorship is writ large in El Salvador. The peasant revolt led by Anastasio Aquino in 1833 was violently suppressed by the creole elite, and its hero and leader was summarily executed. Nearly a century later came the 1932 *matanza,* under the direction of General Martinez, whose brutal dictatorial rule was to last, with United States assistance, until 1944, when he was forced into exile following a general strike in San Salvador. With only intermittent respites, El Salvador would remain under the violent sway of military juntas and *los quatorce,* the aristocratic families who control the largest share of the country's land and resources—and power, for the next four decades, until the "election" of Jose Napoleon Duarte in 1984. The year 1989 and the "election" of the right-wing ARENA party reintroduced undisputed, if de facto, military control over the country and its population.

The statistics invariably invoked to describe the socioeconomic situation of El Salvador crudely testify to the socially distorted demography of this small nation (roughly the size of Massachusetts, in a comparison commonly cited). For example, 2 percent of the population owns 60 percent of the arable land; or in 1980, 8 percent of the population received 50 percent of the national income; or illiteracy stands at 50 percent; or the infant mortality rate is four times the U.S. level (which itself ranks notoriously high in world comparisons). The repeatedly cited statistics can serve a different function, however. According to the Salvadoran poet Jose Roberto Cea, "In the Place of Facts" (in Zimmerman 1988, 259):

> The statistics reveal
> rates of mortality

> that in spite
> of their euphemism
> stand the hair on end
> of the most ignorant bald man.
> In 1979, for example,
> of 174,183 children born
> 32,961 of them died before
> reaching one year of age
> and this from the figures
> of the Ministry of Public Health and Social Aid

Joan Didion (1983), the U.S. writer who visited El Salvador in 1982, commented derisively on such figures: "Actual information was hard to come by in El Salvador, perhaps because this is not a culture in which a high value is placed on the definite. . . . All numbers in El Salvador tended to materialize and vanish and rematerialize in different form, as if numbers denoted only the 'use' of numbers, an intention, a wish, a recognition that someone, somewhere, for whatever reason, needed to hear the ineffable expressed as a number" (61). But then, as Didion imperiously goes on, it is not just the numbers, but words as well that are faulty here: "Language has always been used a little differently in this part of the world" (64). Perhaps it is history itself that the North American would cancel in the peripheries. According to Didion, "Five years is a generation in El Salvador, it being a place in which not only the rest of the world but time itself tends to contract to the here and now" (71). Unlike her colleague and compatriot Carolyn Forché, who visits the countryside, the prisons, the encampments of the resistance movement, Didion interviews United States embassy personnel, Salvadoran government officials, and foreign correspondants and concludes that El Salvador is a "state in which no ground is solid, no depth of field reliable, no perception so definite that it might not dissolve into its reverse" (13) and that "the texture of life in such a situation is essentially untranslatable" (103). The resistance organization that gives political definition to the struggle had already been similarly and casually dismissed by Didion, as letters, acronyms, with no history, no agency, no consequence: "the FMLN-FDR, which is what the opposition to the Salvadoran government was called this year . . ." (32).

Carolyn Forché's brief "aide-memoire" (1983), by contrast, following her several visits to El Salvador at the encouragement of Claribel Alegria, whose poems she had been translating, describes the radical transformation in her own poetry and poetic vocation wrought by the impact, even when mediated, of the Salvadoran history of repression and resistance. After trying in vain to maintain the distinction between the traditionally dual tasks of poetry and journalism, Forché concludes: "I have been told that a poet should be of his or her time. It is my feeling that the twentieth-century human condition demands a poetry of witness" (107).

The urgent contemporary struggle of Central American writing, according to the Guatemalan novelist Arturio Arias (1989), is located within a "central contradiction," that of the "obligation of speaking of a historical drama that is developing simultaneously with its writing." For Arias, for the Central American writer, "the historical process of writing, the historical process of reading, and the historical process of social transformation accompany each other, encounter and intertwine with each other" (57). It is furthermore an ultimately dangerous contradiction that the writer must contend with, according to the Salvadoran novelist Manlio Argueta, for "the artists have chosen the difficult role of enemy. That role now forms part of our culture" (in Zimmerman 1988, ix). "But more than that," writes the Salvadoran poet Mirna Martinez in her poem "If Only Someday" (in Anglesey 1987, 237–39), these same risked contradictions must be made emancipatory—liberatory of the people and the poetry alike:

> but more than that
> it will be an essential poem
> borne from historical contradictions
> the poem desired above all
> that evidently i might not get to
> unless i finish real fast
> this silly poem.

The very question of watching and witnessing, the observation and control that are no less a part of the "politics of punishment" than of testimonial literature and poetry, is manipulated by the prison and its personnel, who make it integral to their procedures and techniques. In *Secuestro y capucha* (Kidnapping and hooding) (1982; first published in 1979), Salvador Cayetano Carpio's narrative of his detention in El Salvador in the early 1950s, the former prisoner, a trade unionist who would subsequently become Commandante Marcial in the Fuerzas Populares de Liberacion (FPL),[4] raises the question of a counter "prison perspective," describing both its limitations and the alternative perspectives that these limitations elicit. There is a strike in the city and widespread demonstrations are taking place beyond the prison walls. Indeed, this unrest is the purported reason for Cayetano Carpio's arrest and the massive repression that has been unleashed by the state against the trade union activity of the workers of El Salvador. From within the walls, the prisoner hears the agitation in the streets and reflects on its significance: "But at that moment I could not gauge in all its magnitude the strength of the repression against the democratic sectors. For that I would have to be in the streets, see the display of armed forces, the arrests, the raids on homes, the searches, the terror released simultaneously in multiple cities; the weeping, the suffering of children, mothers, brothers, wives, at seeing their loved ones torn from their arms. I would have to be in all the cells and see the noblest of the Salvadoran people crowded like plunder into the prisons" (21). *Secuestro y capucha* relates the efforts on the part of the detained union leaders to reconstruct for themselves, from inside the prison, the events taking place beyond the walls of their detention. Their own "prison perspective" is critical to that reconstruction and its renewal of historical possibilities of organized collective resistance that the prison system assaults and attempts to isolate.

168

Personal relationships among prisoners, as well as their links to social formations outside, are exploited by the interrogators to subvert the political resistance of the detainees. Cayetano Carpio describes one such scene in his memoir. His wife and child have been arrested with him, and part of his torture during interrogation is to witness his wife's brutalization at the hands of his guards. "They brought her closer. She was just a meter away from my shoulders. I heard her breathing in gasps, like a nail. I felt her gaze in my body, in the back, in the waist, in the feet. . . . I could almost hear the beating of the heart of my beloved *compañera*" (46). The tense intimacy, the surveillance and covert contact, produced by this scene of torture, both as it displays the efficiency of the prison system and as it reveals the possibilities of concerted challenge to that oppression, is crucial to the history of resistance engendered—and gendered—from within the prison.

Despite its long history and development through world "civilization," torture today has acquired new ends and a radical technologization of its means. In addition to the information that the system of power is concerned to extract from its victims, torture in political detention is calculated to produce propaganda and intimidate, if not destroy, the human and political constitution that continues to resist. The witnessing of torture by the tortured yields, however, another kind of information, the clandestine testimony of the political prisoner who survives, testimony such as Cayetano Carpio's prison memoir, which bears witness to the ruthlessness of the Salvadoran regimes and, even in the 1950s, its U.S. support. Detained at one point in the same cell with other union leaders, workers, and university staff, Cayetano Carpio tells how the detainees narrate and memorize their respective experiences. These will be important later, *"para que, por lo menos, el pueblo se de cuenta . . ."* (so that, at least, the people will know . . .) (175). The narratives of prison are an integral part of the Salvadoran resistance itself. They not only recount strategies of resistance; they are themselves one such strategy. A young woman, nicknamed Beatriz, alias Ticha, a partisan in the Salvadoran resistance, reflects to herself in Manlio Argueta's novel *Cuzcatlan* (1987): "If the [North American] advisors knew our history, would they still treat us the same? I don't know. Besides our history is sad and boring. Maybe they're not interested in hearing about it. We're interested though, because it gives us strength. It teaches us to survive" (5).

The political prisons and secret detention centers of authoritarian regimes, such as that of El Salvador, despite themselves, perhaps because of their purpose to police dissent, have engendered counterorganizations and become training grounds for the resistance. Inside the walls, across those walls, are elaborated strategies for survival and active opposition to the prison and the system it represents. I. G., for example, was twenty-six years old in 1987 when she was charged with working with COMADRES (the same COMADRES whose offices were bombed in May of that year and who in 1984 were denied U.S. visas to receive the Robert F. Kennedy Peace Prize that had been awarded to them) and sentenced to an indefinite term in Ilopango Women's Prison just outside of San Salvador. In July 1987 Ilopango prison housed thirty political prisoners and thirteen children between the ages of one month and three years, most of whom were born in prison. The right to have their children with them in prison was won by the women prisoners after a long hunger strike. Another successful hunger strike gained for the political prisoners the right to remain, even after the prison had been rebuilt, in the outdoor tents to which they had been moved following the massive earthquake in fall 1986. In Ilopango prison at that time, it was not uncommon for women criminal prisoners to request transfer to the political section, where the detainees had organized for themselves the daily routine of their detention to include exercise, hygiene, socialization, and literacy classes. A bulletin board announced the intersection of political activity and personal life: proclamations from the FMLN, a demand for amnesty for all political prisoners, and instructions of hygiene, *salud,* and the disposal of garbage, to prevent mosquitos and the spread of disease.

While male political prisoners too struggle inside the prison, the women have a particularly complex and urgent role to play in transforming the structures of gender and ethnicity as they are manipulated both by the state apparatus and within the cadres of the resistance organization. The decisive encounters might be fleeting, such as the moment of tortured intimacy between Cayetano Carpio and his wife, or the scene described by the Argentinian writer Alicia Partnoy in *The Little School* (1986): " 'Slap his face. Make him pay for his bad manners,' said Loro, placing my still untied hand on the prisoner's chest. I caressed his face" (131). Such confrontations are also evidence of the larger impact of women's political resistance on the resistance organizations themselves, as manifested in the education that Molefe Pheto received from the female "criminals" he encountered during his prison sojourn in South Africa. According to Ximena Bunster-Burotto (1985), "socializing women in particular modes and then using that very socialization as a method of torture" is a crucial part of the government's modus operandi (297). Bunster-Burotto goes on to describe, for Latin American military regimes, the "primary form of sexual torture for men [which] is directed toward their sexual confidence; their humanity is debased by placing them in powerless situations [as in the case of Cayetano Carpio], where they cannot defend a female political prisoner—usually a wife, daughter, lover or friend—from brutal sexual torture performed in their presence" (306). This torture is different from that practiced against women:

> The sexual violence unleashed against women political prisoners is seen as the key in controlling them, through punishment and interrogations. Gang rape, massive rape becomes the standard torture mechanism for the social control of the imprisoned women. Politically committed, active women who have dared to take control of their own lives by struggling against an oppressive regime demand such torture—as do the women who have stood by their men in an organized political effort to liberate their country and themselves from a coercive military regime. (307)

The women prisoners, in turn, have elaborated, within their political contexts and formations, their own specific forms of resistance.

In an interview from Mexico City with Radio Farabundo Marti, following the cease-fire that concluded the major FMLN military offensive in November 1989, Ana Guadalupe Martinez (1989), a member of the FMLN Political Diplomatic Commission, maintained that the "offensive continues. We are in another phase and are not necessarily going to maintain the same tactical military planning with which we started the offensive." Nor had the military offensive been without significant results, she went on: "I think that the most important lesson that Alfredo Cristiani and the armed forces have learned is that the analysis they had in the last few years—that of a strategic weakening of the FMLN—is absurd. It was this mistaken analysis which would not permit the dialogue to advance because they thought that the FMLN had come to the negotiating table to surrender" (6). At the time of her arrest in 1976, however, twenty-four-year-old Guadalupe Martinez was a member of the Ejercito Revolucionario del Pueblo (ERP), formed in 1970, when these militant groups that favored armed struggle against the Salvadoran regime separated from the reformist-oriented Salvadoran Communist party. Ten years later, the ERP and the FPL reconstituted themselves by joining in a united front with other groups, representing both militant and popular ideological groundings, to form the combined military-political FMLN-FDR, in which Ana Guadalupe Martinez would eventually serve as a high-ranking comandante with its political wing.

Guadalupe Martinez's prison memoir of her six months in El Salvador's "secret prisons," *Las carceles clandestinas de El Salvador* (1980), first published in Mexico, is presented as a practical contribution, to be "used" but not "copied," to the "ideological, political and military development of the revolutionary movement" (14). Its fifty chapters, which treat of the conditions of her incarceration and her release in an exchange arranged by the ERP for the kidnapped Salvadoran aristocrat Roberto Poma, propose as well, on the basis of her prison experience, an inquiry into the theoretical and structural questions that marked the ERP at a particular historical and organizational moment. Thus the former detainee's opening description of her arrest on 5 July 1976 is explicitly linked to her political commitment to armed struggle as the most effective and appropriate means to national liberation and the seizure of state power. Her personal disempowerment by her captors is identified with her physical disarming: "This moment was very special since I felt as never before the importance of not being able to defend myself, the necessity of my weapon, and I understood fully that it is only with weapons in hand that one can confront the enemy" (15). 171

In prison, however, with no weapons to hand, other means of self-defense, no less than the defense of the movement, will have to be devised, and it is these alternative strategic lessons that Guadalupe Martinez presents to her reader, *"si llegaras a caer preso, camarada"* (if you should be taken prisoner, comrade):

At the time of my capture and that of other *companeros,* the scant experience that our young organization and the revolutionary movement had had with the problem of how prisoners should deal with torture and prison, meant that this was a totally new and unknown terrain for many of the captured. This is not meant as a justification for weaknesses committed but to locate us in the situation in order to be more objective in the process of correction in the coming years of struggle. The absence of practice and lack of experience contributed to the mistakes that were made and that without a solid ideological grounding can lead to the weaknesses of informing and even betrayal. (245)

Such a betrayal had already been committed at the time of Guadalupe Martinez's arrest by one Valle (Juan Jose Yanez), who had become a collaborator with the prison apparatus and who helped to identify her when she was brought to the prison, assisting the interrogators' practiced if illegal use of voter registration lists and archives to locate people whom they considered to be "subversives." Other prisoners, however, more resistant, help Guadalupe Martinez over the coming six months to withstand the sexual and political assaults deployed against her revolutionary commitments—and for her part, she contributes to the education of new prisoners. As is "customary" with women prisoners, the sergeant who is on duty rapes her one night. "Days later," she reports, "when I did not begin to menstruate at the usual time, I was tormented, obsessed, by a single idea: to abort if it was a pregnancy. The mere thought of it produced an indescribable despair" (76). Several months afterwards, when the problem persisted, the doctor held in a nearby cell gave her, across the distance created by prison architecture, his professional counsel: "He gave me instructions on how to give myself a physical examination: do this, do like this, like that. Afterwards, when I described to him the results, he said that it was almost 99% certain that it was not a pregnancy, but was what in medicine was called *stress* [in English in the text] due to the body's tendency to adapt itself to surrounding conditions" (159–60).

In turn, Guadalupe Martinez shares her slowly and painfully acquired knowledge of the prison with Ana Gilma, a newly arrived prisoner in an adjoining cell: "That afternoon I taught her how to see through the little hole in the metal plate of the door and told her that in this way I could see pass by a multitude of people who had been captured and brought here like us" (182–83). From then on, the two women divide between them the monitoring work of listening and watching and interpreting the ephemeral but decisive signs of the prison. Guadalupe Martinez also teaches the new prisoner to see beyond the prison, to catch a glimpse of the tree tops outside. The prisoners develop still other collective projects: a game called "Improve Your Vocabulary" imitated from the *Reader's Digest*, narrating films to each other—not unlike Molina in Mario Puig's *Kiss of the Spider Woman*—and reading sessions, using the scraps of newspaper provided to the prisoners for use as toilet paper.

And as with the "bembas" in Argentinian prisons analyzed by Emilio de Ipola (1983),[5] these Salvadoran prisoners were "semiologists" of the prison system, whose collective discursive strategies of resistance "served as a continuous renovation of the circuits of communication" (219). The military interrogators wage a different discursive battle in the attempt to extract information from the prisoners and to introduce destructive disinformation into their operational communications network. To talk, Guadalupe Martinez learns, is to collaborate: "*quien hablar, colabora, y esto constituye una dura derrota a la moral del prisionero, no importa que fue lo que dijo*" (whoever talked, collaborated, and this was a hard blow to the prisoners' morale, that it didn't matter what one said) (75). No less important to the interrogators than the information that they extract from their victims is the divisive disinformation that they are able, by making use of the internal debates of the movements themselves, to insinuate into the prisoners' minds. "One of the elements most used by the enemy to demoralize and create a lack of confidence in the prisoners, make them collaborate and inform, is the internal problems and ideological struggle between the revolutionary organizations" (109). One example of this discursive machination occurs when her interrogator describes to Guadalupe Martinez a telecommunications system alleged to have been developed by the FPL. " 'See,' " he tells her, " 'you don't have a technical capacity like this.' " As the prisoner realizes, "in this way they thought they could pique my self-esteem for the ERP and that I would give away some piece of useful information to them" (151). More critical, however, to this ideological counteroffensive of political fragmentation are her own movement's conditions for the release of the prisoners in exchange for their kidnapped hostage, conditions that reveal the crucial difference between the prisoners' political unity inside and the ideological discord of the organizations outside: only ERP prisoners are to be included in the exchange. Ana Guadalupe Martinez will be released, but FPL activist Lil Milagro will remain behind in the *carceles clandestinas*.

Guadalupe Martinez's release from El Salvador's secret prisons is won at the cost of another political lesson, a lesson that is written into her prison memoir and that will eventually be realized in the course of the historical development of the Salvadoran resistance: "The contradictions, the subjectivisms that accompany our organizations dominate a political necessity: the unity and maturity of the revolutionary forces. We felt here so strongly its lack in those captured from all the organizations and understood how manipulating the contradictions between [the organizations] has helped the enemy to advance its project of destruction and liquidation against the country's revolutionary movement" (214).

For Roque Dalton, the Salvadoran poet and revolutionary, writing in 1968, it seemed that "possibly 50% of the theory of the Latin American Revolution would be at the same time the history of the Latin American Revolution" (114). The necessary connection, argued here by Dalton, between theory and history in the development of a revolutionary practice in Latin America, was presented in his collection of essays, *¿Revolucion en la revolucion? y la critica de derecha* (1970), written as a contribution to the international ideological controversy that had been generated among communists in particular and on the left generally by the publication of Regis Debray's account of *foquismo* as a guerrilla strategy, *Revolution in the Revolution?* (1967). Dalton referred to this study as a "*bomba ideologica*" that had been dropped into a "serious theoretical vacuum" (21). For Dalton, "given the polemical quality of this work, the only way to approach it is through a critical analysis, even passionate if you like, that will make its pages function in the way their author conceived them: as an element of marked perturbation in a period of crisis of the Latin American revolutionary movement in which quietism—both intellectual and material—or tendencies toward quietism pose fundamental dangers" (22).

Debray, a young French journalist, had joined Che Guevara in Bolivia. Much influenced by recent tumultuous events in Europe and by the Cuban revolution, Debray argued that the latter had shown definitively and in a practical way that non-communists were capable of overthrowing capitalism and further that the Cuban revolution could itself serve as a model for the resistance movements of other Latin American countries on how to seize state power. His analysis was made still more contentious for the more traditionally oriented Communist parties of the Third International in that Debray, in referring to Che Guevara's theory of the *foco*, or revolutionary vanguard operating in the countryside, maintained that the urban struggle of the working class needed to be reprioritized and relocated in reference to the rural revolutionary bases.

Debray's slim volume itself quickly became the focus of protracted debate, with significant contributions—constructive, self-critical, and petulant—representing the ideological spectrum as well as the political divisions within the international revolutionary left. Dalton's review of this literature argues, while engaging in the very terms of the debate in critical support of Debray's theses, that the debate itself is of primary consequence for the Latin American revolution, that in this discursive and polemical context is articulated the necessary and reciprocal relation between theory and history.

At the time that Debray's book was being so furiously debated, the Frenchman was in a Bolivian prison. With his booklet as the major evidence for the prosecution, he had been sentenced to thirty years as a result of his role as its "intellectual author," in Che's organizing work in the Bolivian countryside, work that ended with Che's murder in a confrontation with the Bolivian military. In his contribution to a special Debray issue of the U.S. leftist journal *Monthly Review*, Juan Bosch, the former president of the Dominican Republic, who had been ousted from office with the assistance of United States intervention in that country, argued against Jean-Paul Sartre's assertion that Debray had been jailed for having written *Revolution in the Revolution?* Bosch (1968) claimed that "it would seem the contrary must be true: he is alive because he wrote this book" (105). In other words, for Bosch, the international notoriety that accrued to the European through his booklet had spared him the death that a Latin American would have inevitably faced in the same situation.

In more stylistic readings, other of Debray's critics cited the geopolitics of the metropolitan-periphery divide, in their claim that in his analysis, "French prose [had been enlisted] in the service of Cuban thought" (cited in Dalton 1970, 169). For Dalton, however, it was precisely these necessary contradictions—discursive, theoretical, political—that gave to Debray's work its significance as an *"elemento de perturbacion."* According to Dalton, arguing against parochialism and out of the immanence of newly emergent global configurations, "Regis Debray inaugurated a new form of saying things that are at the core of the Latin American Revolution. He has reclaimed the role of the thinker towards the popular masses . . . and revitalized the political essay as a genre of the masses" (168). Against the impending danger of rigidification and dogmatism, the Debray book and its ensuing debate came to constitute a major and crucial conjuncture in the processes of historical change and military-political development of the Latin American revolution. For Dalton, that is, in 1968, "Given the conditions of theoretical vacuum existing on the [Latin American] continent, the historical method is one solution" (60).

175

Two years later, Roque Dalton would be among those cadres who broke with the Salvadoran Communist Party to form the ERP. The critical processes of historical development represented as political essay in *¿Revolucion en la revolucion? y la critica de derecha*, also elaborated, for example, in Ana Guadalupe Martinez's prison memoir, would find further development in the subsequent history of the Salvadoran resistance movement. The letters FMLN-FDR, that is, represent historically, theoretically, and substantially more than "what the opposition to the Salvadoran government was called" in the year that Joan Didion visited El Salvador.

In the final pages of her prison memoir, *Nunca estuve sola* (I was never alone) (1988), Nidia Diaz, an FMLN comandante, briefly sketches the history of her participation, beginning in the early 1970s, in her country's political struggle. She recalls her passage from "legal" to "illegal" activities, her first weapon, and the friendships frustrated by the demands of the organization and its projects. She evokes too her anticipation of what her future work would lead her to: "When I joined the organization, I always believed that I would be clandestine, that my name would never be publicized" (211). On 18 April 1985, however, Comandante Nidia (Maria Valladores M. de Lemus) was wounded and arrested in an army helicopter raid on FMLN guerrilla bases in the mountains of San Vicente. Her captor was a *"yanqui,"* one of the advisors provided by the United States as part of its "aid" to the Salvadoran government and its armed forces. Nidia Diaz, unlike thousands of disappeared and murdered prisoners in El Salvador before her, survived her capture and detention, "because of the happenstance," according to Maria Lopez Vigil in her introduction to

Diaz's prison account, "of being taken prisoner in a conjuncture where it was not convenient to kill captives" (7). But in a poem, "Tierra heroica," written two months after her arrest, while she was being held in Cerros de San Pedro, Diaz questioned self-critically the reasons and consequences of what had happened to her (24):

> Was it misfortune?
> Was it adversity?
> Was it chance?
> Or was it the result
> of an error of method
> in revolutionary work?

176

Some six months before her capture, Nidia Diaz had participated prominently in the historic meeting at La Palma between representatives of the combined Salvadoran resistance organizations, the FMLN-FDR, and president Napoleon Duarte's Christian Democratic government of El Salvador. This charged encounter, with FMLN-FDR leaders in exile returning to the country with promises of "safe passage," was to open the way for longer-term political negotiations between the government and its popular and armed resistance. Instead it saw the elements of a peace proposal offered by the FMLN-FDR representatives blocked by the Duarte government. At one point in her prison story, Diaz reflects on this thwarted exchange: "So many times I've asked myself why we dialogue with the government, why we continue fighting to dialogue with an enemy like this one," but immediately she goes on to answer her own question: "What is happening to you, Nidia? We dialogue because we are dedicated to peace, because we believe in a political solution to the conflict. One after another, we have presented initiatives for dialogue" (162–63).

The issue of "dialogue," of discussion and negotiations between a repressive state and its political opponents, structures Nidia Diaz's account of her 190-day prison experience, from her capture on 18 April by the *"yanqui"* to her release on 25 October as part of a prisoner exchange for Ines Duarte, the kidnapped daughter of El Salvador's president. The "dialogue" takes different forms, from psychological torture and interrogation, to verbal abuse by her guards, to press interviews with both progovernment and independent journalists, national as well as international, and each of these discursive modalities in turn contributes within the narrative to the political detainee's own examination of the necessary reconstruction of an oppositional political stance within the extreme structural constraints imposed by incarceration.

The prisoner's interrogation, using both information obtained from collaborators and the threat that she too will now be seen by her comrades as a traitor, seeks first of all to elicit from her a betrayal of her *companeros* and the present and future plans of the resistance organization itself. Under the pretense of wanting to inform her relatives of her whereabouts and her "safety," the interrogators demand information about her family. "Go to the front," she tells them, "that is my family" (35). On another occasion, visiting government officials insist that they have come not to interrogate her, but to have a conversation, *platicar*. "Why then," she demands, "don't you remove my blindfold?" (79). Trained interrogators say that they want **177** her life history (53), but Nidia Diaz's biography is the story of the Salvadoran resistance itself. Later still she refuses to cooperate with the prison doctor, Bottari, who claims to need background information from her for a book he is writing about a "guerrilla who gets tired of fighting" (139). Her vigilance is momentarily challenged by Vazques Becker, who maintains that he is doing a study of "women's participation in the struggle" (210), but she does not relent. To at least one press conference, Nidia Diaz denounces her captors and the conditions of her detention. At another, recognizing her interlocutors as progovernment reporters, she demands, "Why have you come to pose the same questions as my interrogators?" (85). Her final interview is held aboard the plane transporting her, the other released prisoners, and evacuated wounded guerrillas, to Panama and on to Cuba.

What emerges in *Nunca estuve sola* out of these different encounters, and with the La Palma meeting as their immediate background, is a political counterdiscourse. Through its engagement with the personal itinerary of the *guerrillera* and the historical trajectory of the Salvadoran resistance, this counterdiscourse challenges the very premises of the ostentatious rhetoric of democracy, a rhetoric sponsored by the United States military aid that underwrote the Duarte government's repression of the people of El Salvador and that underwrote the 1989 elections, which brought the right-wing ARENA party with its death squad connections to power.

But, like Ana Guadalupe Martinez, who in prison became practiced in new resistance strategies of self-defense, Nidia Diaz too learns to struggle from her cell. "This," she writes, "will be my trench" (105). Diaz tells Maria Lopez Vigil about her friends' responses to her prison memoir: "They told me that the book contained more revolutionary ideology than my personal emotions. But in prison, if you don't hold on to your convictions, to your ideology, you are lost. You can't show anything personal to your captors. Nor did I want to. And afterwards, when I got out, it was this that made me write. This is how I lived prison, minute by minute, enduring, resisting" (8).

It is not only political prison, however, but participation in the resistance movement that transforms the self and its personal relationships, "does violence," according to Clea Silva (1988), "to the individual" (29). Thinking momentarily, even longingly, about her distant husband while she is in prison, Diaz reflects:

> We watch the qualities of each one of us grow and develop along this singular path. But it is not possible to love everyone, to give them our affection as a woman [como mujer]. How many compas are alone? How many of them have had the privilege of loving, of being loved, of going on loving? How many have suffered disappointments and reverses in love? Ideas of life, our mentality, are to eliminate pettiness and egoism. When a relationship or an engagement is broken off, it hurts us, but no rancor or trauma remains, if one learns to assimilate it with maturity. The revolutionary's situation helps us to understand why a couple didn't work out. Shared interests strengthen the affective bonds of comradeship. Other problems are more important. (50–51)

For Diaz, "intimate relations among us are subject to the circumstances and the concrete situations in which the struggle develops" (51). And these collective bonds are made and remade inside the political prison.

Unlike Ana Guadalupe Martinez, whose capture had come as a surprise for which neither she nor the movement was adequately prepared, Nidia Diaz knows what to expect, and the FMLN itself has its own contingency plans for just these recurrent eventualities. One of her interrogators, for example, relying on the past divisions rather than the new forms of the organization, seeks to intimidate her by asking: "Look, Nidia, with all these documents that we have found, how many years has the revolution lost?" She answers straightforwardly, "That's what you would like. But the revolution will not lose ground, because the FMLN is the full expression of the maturity of our people, and all its risky aspects have been changed." But the interrogator persists disparagingly, "No, mamaita, they're not capable of that." And the prisoner answers again, "Do you think that we haven't foreseen that one day one of the cadres of the directorate might be captured? Many people are aware of my capture. And they know that I had papers" (39).

Nunca estuve sola is part of a lineage of prison memoirs from El Salvador that Nidia Diaz herself refers to as being her only previous experience with political detention: Salvador Cayetano Carpio's *Secuestro y capucha* and Ana Guadalupe Martinez's *Las carceles clandestinas de El Salvador*. The three texts, written out of political detention and taken in context, constitute an important dimension of the history—and theory—over the last four decades of organized struggle against a succession of brutal dictatorships in El Salvador. The additional dimension elaborated in *Nunca estuve sola* to the "dialogue" between political detainee and the state's prison apparatus is a popular one. The participation of representatives of international and Salvadoran human rights organizations and prisoner associations, from Amnesty International and the International Red Cross, to the Church-sponsored Tutela Legal and Committee of Political Prisoners in El Salvador (COPPES), are evidence of an enlarged mass mobilization and the impact of political detention on the society as a whole. As Diaz acknowledges, "the popular struggle allowed me to live. It was the national and international pressure of yesterday, today and tomorrow. But fundamentally it was the people. I owe nothing to the regime, absolutely nothing. It is not a gift of the Duarte government that I am still alive. It is not a gift of the '*yanqui*.' It's the result of that popular history" (98). The publicizing of the name of Nidia Diaz, like the publication of her prison memoir, *Nunca estuve sola*, testifies again to the critical significance of unrelenting "dialogue" in terms of popular resistance.

Chapter Eight

On Trial: The United States

It is true that [prisoners] often lose touch with reality. They are not realistic about what is politically possible. It is very hard to convince them that they can get any sympathy or respect whatever from the system or the law. And, in a way, it is very important for them not to allow themselves to be convinced. Prisoners who actually think that they can get justice from the system are usually the ones who go mad.

FAY STENDER, *Maximum Security*

Dear Comrades,
After pondering the discussion we had concerning the term "prison reform" I have concluded that more people will support our cause and you will avoid apathy by centering your efforts around the title that has already been established "political prisoners."

JOHN CLUCHETTE, *Maximum Security*

Sister Fay,
Today, Friday November 13, 1970 is a day I will long remember, our hunger strike has ended, two weeks of self inflicted punishment, all of which was in vain. All we actually won with the exception of Mr Alvarez leaving here, was soup at lunchtime—at least this is the only immediately visible gain. Many here including myself have never participated in any form of meaningful protest before, perhaps we expected too much . . .

LEROY NOLAN FLEMING, *Maximum Security*

From 7 to 10 December 1990, the United States government stood publicly accused of the violation of the human rights of political prisoners incarcerated in its penal institutions. An indictment on behalf of more than one hundred political prisoners and prisoners of war in the United States was brought against the government of the United States; George Bush, president; Richard Thornburgh, attorney general; William Sessions, director of the Federal Bureau of Investigation; William Webster, director of the Central Intelligence Agency; Michael Quinlan, director of the Bureau of Prisons; the director of the Federal Parole Board; and the governors, directors of the prisons, and directors of the parole boards of each state wherein political prisoners and prisoners of war are incarcerated.[1] The defendants and their predecessors were charged with

the denial of self-determination, failure to comply with fundamental laws and principles of international law and human rights, and using their criminal justice system to imprison and repress those who seek national liberation and/or oppose U.S. foreign and domestic policies. The indictment also charges the defendants with illegal and arbitrary arrests and detentions, denial of fair trials, cruel, inhuman and degrading treatment of prisoners and conspiracy to commit the above acts. **181**

The International Tribunal on the Human Rights Violations of Political Prisoners/POWs in the U.S.A., held in New York City, was presided over by a panel of nine international jurists, and the case was prosecuted by long-time defenders of political prisoners in United States courtrooms, including Lennox Hinds, Jan Susler, and Bruce Ellison. Among the petitioners were incarcerated members of the American Indian Movement (AIM), the Black Panther Party (BPP), the Republic of New Afrika (RNA), the Puerto Rican independence movement, MOVE, the Resistance Conspiracy case, the Ohio Seven, as well as Silvia Baraldini, an Italian woman whom the federal government has refused to extradite to her native country, and Joe Doherty, an IRA member whom the federal government had been attempting for nine years to extradite to Great Britain. One of the plaintiffs, former Black Panther and MOVE supporter Mumia Abu Jamal, was awaiting execution on death row. Alan Berkman, one of the Resistance Conspiracy "defendants," was dying of cancer in the Marion Control Unit, where he had been denied parole. Geronimo ji Jaga Pratt continued to serve a life sentence for a crime he did not commit, likewise denied parole until he agreed to denounce the political ideals of the Black Panther Party.

At the conclusion of the tribunal, and following a day's deliberation, the panel of judges hearing the case determined that, as charged, the criminal justice system of the United States was being used in a harsh and discriminatory way against political activists. It called for the release of all prisoners held for exercising their legitimate rights of national liberation and self-determination, and for the United States government to cease all acts of interference in the exercise of those legitimate rights.

The staging of the tribunal followed months of preparation that included an international symposium the preceding April and a poetry reading two months prior to the event, as well as the more traditional litigational work of assembling evidence, locating witnesses, and preparing cases. The tribunal ultimately achieved far more than an indictment of the United States criminal justice and penal systems, or a set of temporary role reversals, (casting defending attorneys as prosecutors and prisoners as plaintiffs), or even a challenge to certain legal terminological conventions, such as those that characterize "expropriation" or "liberation" as "stealing." The tribunal practiced a structural and critical retaking of the legal apparatus itself, transforming the courtroom into an arena for hearing and negotiating a United States political history of opposition that the courtroom procedure has long been used to police and finally criminalize.

Representatives of organizations that had been victimized by the FBI's **182** *COINTELPRO* (counterINTELigence PROgram) activities against the BPP and other dissident organizations narrated that covert oppression. Others recounted continued harassment by state and federal authorities, rendering proof positive that *COINTELPRO*-type operations continue today. MOVE member Alberta Afrika described two miscarriages that she had suffered as a result of police beatings while she was in detention and told the long history of confrontations between MOVE and Philadelphia officialdom that culminated in a brutal massacre in May 1985 and the destruction of an entire city neighborhood. Rafael Cancel Miranda, a Puerto Rican *independentista* only recently released following a long campaign on his behalf, had been sentenced to eighty-one years for an assault on the United States Capitol in 1954. Like that of Alberta Afrika, Cancel Miranda's testimony, a life history of struggle, was received by the audience in attendance at the tribunal with ovations and acclamation. Bobby Castillo, a former prisoner and member of the Treaty Council at the United Nations, together with author and activist Ward Churchill and AIM representative Bob Robideau (who had been arrested with Leonard Peltier), related the legal and illegal acts, the violence and economic depradations committed by the federal government against American Indian peoples. Former Black Panther Dhoruba bin Wahad, released in May 1990 after nineteen years in prison, argued that for people of color to obey the laws of a racist society was tantamount to suicide.[2] And Patricia Levasseur, one of the Ohio Seven, described her years in prison on charges of "harboring a fugitive," her husband, Raymond, himself currently serving a forty-five-year sentence.

For two full days, interrupted only by evening poetry readings and cultural performances, the formal witnesses to the creative contributions of political work, testimony was heard from former United States political prisoners and prisoners of war. It was supplemented by the questioning of expert witnesses, such as lawyer Michael Deutsch, who testified on the abuses of justice in the United States court system, the grand jury process as a form of "political internment American style," the ostentatious use of "courtroom security" paraphernalia to undermine the only independent actor in the courtroom (i.e., the jury), and the calculated manipulation of the trial site to ensure that defendants will be judged according to the determinations of the government prosecution, as in the case of

Fig. 4. A poster.

the Puerto Ricans standing trial in Hartford, Connecticut on charges relating to a Wells Fargo robbery. Attorney Mary O'Melveny testified to the disproportionate sentences given to political activists, citing the case of Laura Whitehorn of the Resistance Conspiracy trials, who was sentenced to twenty years, despite an advisory committee's recommendation to the judge that she be given probation and community service. Law professor Francis Boyle provided further expert testimony on the constitutional right of civil resistance and its defense under international law, as well **184** as the applicability of the protections guaranteed by the principle of self-determination to specific cases within territorial United States borders. In the end, the Tribunal, by its very enactment, as much as by its findings, was a visionary argument that it was still possible, indeed imperative, to practice law against the system and on behalf of "liberty and justice for all."

According to *The Fortress Economy* (Lichenstein and Kroll 1990), a report prepared for American Friends Service Committee to "commemorate" the 200th anniversary of the opening of the first United States penitentiary in Philadelphia in 1790, the United States has the "third highest rate of incarceration in the industrialized world, surpassed only by South Africa and the Soviet Union" (4). Meanwhile, a report published only a few months later, in January 1991, by the Sentencing Project, revealed that the United States had now surpassed both South Africa and the Soviet Union to become "number one," with more than one million Americans in jail—at an annual cost of sixteen billion dollars. Furthermore, states *The Fortress Economy*, the prison population is itself systematically distorted along race and class lines: 53 percent of low-income defendants, for example, received prison sentences, as opposed to 26 percent of high-income defendants. African American males, who make up 6 percent of the country's population, comprise nearly 50 percent of its prison inmates and receive sentences that are 20 percent longer than those of whites for similar crimes. Sixty percent of incarcerated women are African American or Latina. United States prisons, the report argues, "have a far greater impact on communities of color, because of their disproportionate representation in prison populations" (11).

The larger consequence of this discriminatory detention policy has been the criminalization of substantial sectors of the United States community, a criminalization that has been extended to stigmatize and penalize the political activism of individuals and organizations that have sought to reform and to transform the social system regulating its own inequities. If the extralegal lynchings of black men—and women—in the decades following "Reconstruction" were, as Manning Marable (1983) and others have maintained, merely legalized in the racially biased criminal justice system of the United States, or if the lynchings practiced by the Texas Rangers against Mexican Americans were only recreated, as James Cockcroft (1986) and Ramon Saldivar (1990) have argued, in the immigration legislation enacted throughout the twentieth century, then contemporary United States history is scarred with the legal and illegal repression by government agencies of political dissidence and dissidents. From the Palmer Raids in 1919 and their aftermath, to the union busting activity of the 1930s, the surveillance of citizenry in the 1940s, McCarthyism in the 1950s, the FBI's *COINTELPRO* operations through the 1960s and their continuation under other names since 1971, United States citizens and their foreign guests opposing government policies of discrimination at home and imperialism abroad have written an alternative history in struggle, one that has established a dialectical counterpoint, against that promulgated by approved school textbooks and official accounts disseminated for public consumption.

185

Much of that other history is summarized in the exemplary narrative of Elizabeth Gurley Flynn's autobiography, *The Rebel Girl* (1986), and echoed in the circumstances of its composition. Written while she was a "political prisoner" in the Federal Women's Reformatory at Alderson, West Virginia, from January 1955 to May 1957, as a communist convicted under the Smith Act, Flynn's first volume of her life story rewrites again the traditional female biographical trajectory as combined party history and labor organizational development. Women's emancipation is consolidated in and through worker resistance and trade union struggle. Flynn identifies herself as a member of the Industrial Workers of the World (IWW or "Wobblies"), and the transformative events that punctuate her narrative and rearticulate her autobiography are constellated in its opening chapters, entitled "Childhood and Early Youth" and "Socialist and IWW Agitator."

Beginning as the conventional story of a young girl growing up in an Irish American family, *The Rebel Girl* is already overtaken by the politics of labor organizing against the pressures and exploitation of capital and government. Not only is the female labor agitator's life changed by her political involvement, but the very form of her narrative is subjected to a reworking around that history. The subsequent chapters are named accordingly: "The Lawrence Textile Strike" and "The Paterson Silk Strike." In between, from 1912 to the end of World War I, her own tale is told through prison visits to fellow organizers, attendance at their trials, and public speaking at occasions called for by the continued efforts of the authorities to suppress worker struggle and silence dissent. The volume ends provisorily with "Sacco and Vanzetti" and the frustrated attempts by their lawyers and supporters to prevent their execution on trumped-up charges in 1926.

Elizabeth Gurley Flynn did not live to complete the second volume of her autobiography, the story of her life as a member of the Communist party, but the last paragraph of the first installment suggests that its continued itinerary began counter to both traditional women's stories and sanctioned public history. For Flynn too, "where a woman belongs" is no longer a received idea but a space still to be constructed:

186

Years later, in 1940, after my son's death, I saw LaGuardia then Mayor of New York City out at Flushing Meadows. He said, "Elizabeth, I hear you joined the Communist Party! I said, "Yes, Fiorello, don't you remember you told me to leave the Italian anarchists and get back where I belong?" He laughed his hearty, roaring laughter and said, "Well, I'd rather see you with the Communists than with those freaks!" But I had not been able or willing to take his advice in 1924 because I was then too deeply involved in a battle for justice for two anarchists who were not freaks but honest workers. I was fighting against a damnable frame-up in Boston, Massachusetts—fighting for the lives of "the good shoemaker and the poor fish peddler"—Sacco and Vanzetti. (335)

"It did happen here," thirty-four victims of "political repression in America" told Bud and Ruth Schultz (1989). "*Testimonios*" of a particular kind, located within and informed by the specificities of a territorial United States historical and political narrative, these "recollections" of dissent and its suppression constitute a critical and dramatic dialogue that engages the formulas and conventions of trial and courtroom procedures, of examination and cross-examination, and links them within a discursive field extending from the extreme of the human rights issues of torture and interrogation to the civil rights questions of freedom of speech, petition, and assembly. While the United States government and its various law enforcement agencies historically have not eschewed extralegal physical violence and/or material invasion against person and property, undertaking assaults ranging from phone taps to assassination in order to maintain their own semblance of law and order, their enlistment of the legal and judicial apparatuses of the criminal justice system to these same ends continues to distinguish the maintenance of the official United States historical narrative. In his Foreword to *It Did Happen Here* (Schultz and Schultz 1989), Victor Navasky comments, for example, on the "Are you now or have you ever been . . . ?" questions that are written into the United States bureaucratic process, in House Un-American Activities Committee hearings as on visa applications. He describes the imperious demand for "naming" and "informing" as a "degradation ceremony" (xvi–xvii), a rite of passage of an ignominious sort that guarantees to the civilian at once the official cooptation of her/his political dissent and the discreditation of her/his political independence.

Testimony on the witness stand, crucial to a United States governmental appropriation of opposition discourse, functions critically in many of the *"testimonios"* collected in *It Did Happen Here* as the different narrators reenact the discursive agon staged in HUAC hearings or in courtrooms. The combined rights to freedom of expression and to remain silent, protected by the First and Fifth amendments to the Constitution, are negotiated and challenged as defendants struggle, experimenting with strategies of verbal contestation, with their inquisitors. Scott Nearing, for example, lost his job at the University of Pennsylvania's Wharton School **187** for his public speaking on behalf of child labor legislation. He was also indicted for his opposition to World War I, as expressed in a pamphlet entitled *The Great Madness*. Nearing recalls:

We had a meeting of interested people in New York about the indictment. We said, now here's a chance to publicize our views about the war. Because the pamphlet was part of the indictment, we used it in presenting our case. When I was on the stand, my attorney, Seymour Stedman, said, "Mr. Nearing, turn to page three of this pamphlet. Would you read paragraph two?" And so I read that. Then he said to the jury, "My client will now defend this paragraph." We spent eight days going through the pamphlet, paragraph by paragraph, and I gave a detailed explanation each time. The newspapers and magazines were full of it. (Schultz and Schultz, 12)

Half a century later, Dr. Benjamin Spock, famous to several generations of mothers and children for his writing on child-rearing, was arrested with four others for their opposition to the war in Vietnam. Having endorsed the Call to Resist Legitimate Authority by urging young men to refuse the military draft, the Boston Five were charged with conspiracy and brought to trial. For Spock, as for Nearing, it was important to retake the courtroom proceedings: "To me, it seemed perfectly clear that this was a political trial. We had been doing the things we had been charged with for political reasons. Then why not use the trial politically, as far as we could? I didn't feel like being docile" (Schultz and Schultz, 97–98). Pete Seeger, the folk singer, had offered to sing his songs to the HUAC hearings, those that had been found objectionable, as further evidence for the prosecution. When this offer was refused, Seeger chose to remain silent. Although he might have regretted not doing "what [Paul] Robeson did" (19), accusing his accusers of un-American activity, Seeger concludes: "Historically, I believe that I was correct in refusing to answer their questions. Down through the centuries, this trick has been tried by various establishments throughout the world. They force people to get involved in the kind of examination that has only one aim and that is to stamp out dissent" (20). Edward Lamb, a print and broadcast journalist, who was accused of being a Communist and therefore was denied licenses for his stations, used his trial to expose the government's exploitation of an informer system against its own citizenry (377–91).

Literary critical prowess and sophistic interpretive skills, as Gil Green relates, can serve as lethal weaponry in the discursive contest of judicial examination and cross-examination. Green, a leader of the Communist party, was convicted with ten colleagues in 1948 under the Smith Act in a trial where the principle evidence consisted of books studied and taught by the defendants. According to the prosecution's "expert" witness on reading socialist literature, the principles of the Communist party—scientific socialism and Marxism-Leninism—"were codewords for the violent **188** overthrow of the government. It was 'Aesopian language' and those 'on the in' knew that the paragraph in the [Communist party] constitution that decries force and violence means the opposite of what it says" (79).

In the lengthy deportation hearings of activist, writer, and feminist Margaret Randall over thirty years later, Randall's disciplinary credentials in literature, conferred by accredited institutions of higher learning, were used against her.[3] Randall, considered a "subversive" on the basis of her writings on women and revolution in Cuba, Vietnam, and Nicaragua, had been denied her United States citizenship under the McCarran-Walter Act and threatened with deportation. Authors, scholars, and writers joined forces to defend both Randall's work and her right to work, and Adrienne Rich was invited by the defense to testify at the hearings to the critical significance of her literary contributions. But, Randall reports:

When Adrienne Rich was being introduced as an expert witness, our lawyer asked a few questions to establish her credentials. Adrienne was the winner of the National Book Award, distinguished scholar at Stanford, and writer of I don't know how many books. Then my lawyer said to the judge, "I move to qualify Professor Rich as an expert on writing, poetry, and literary interpretation." Guadalupe Gonzales [the prosecuting attorney] jumped to her feet: "Your honor, I don't think there are any experts in that area." (Schultz and Schultz, 188)

In the end, in spring 1990, Margaret Randall won her case, if only on a "technicality"—that she had never really given up her United States citizenship. The politics and the status of literary interpretation remained undecided. In the meantime, although apparently neither the reputed conventions of "literature" nor the putative bonds of "feminism" can be argued and re-constellated with impunity within the boundaries of the United States criminal justice system, the personal testimony recorded in *It Did Happen Here*, like the tribunal, challenges the decisions, if not the decision-making process, of that system.

The available and still-accumulating social and scientific literature on United States prisons—sociological, criminological, institutional, even architectural—is massive, constituting a field unto itself, with its own call numbers and Library of Congress designations. The literature of political dissent, by contrast, enjoys no such categorical distinction or acclaimed classical status, and with only rare exceptions, such as Thoreau's *On Civil Disobedience* or perhaps, although more disputably, Thomas Paine's *Rights of Man*, remains largely marginal to both the curriculum of penal practice and reform and the literary canon alike. Indeed, political prisoners are themselves not recognized as such by the United States judicial process. Formally defiant, by definition "subversive," "extremist," or more recently "terrorist," the literature of political detention stands as categorically and generically unassimilable within the systemic paradigms that regulate and guarantee the United States polity and its manifest social and cultural order. Even the story of the historic international tribunal of December 1990, covered by journalists from Spain, Germany, and Australia, received no mention or acknowledgment in the dominant United States media. Indeed the "newspaper of record" carried in its stead a pre-Christmas human-interest story in its metropolitan section entitled "Busing Family Love to Prison Walls" (*New York Times*, 10 December 1990), telling of the laudable but entrepreneurial efforts of a former inmate to provide transportation services for families to and from New York's correctional facilities. By humanizing, personalizing, familializing, even mythologizing the issue of incarceration and its sociopolitical ramifications, the mainstream mass media, through public culture, aid and abet the more nefarious covert action programs against political dissent of the FBI and its attendant services, both local and federal. **189**

Within the discretionary terms of the Freedom of Information Act (FOIA), that policy of covert action, and in particular *COINTELPRO,* was exposed for a time to public scrutiny and even congressional critique. A recent trilogy, enabled by archival finds among the FBI files of reputed dissidents, elaborates a preliminary groundwork for a new field of interdisciplinary critical study and research.[4] In *Agents of Repression* (1988), Ward Churchill and Jim Vander Wall, drawing on this evidentiary material, narrated and detailed "the FBI's secret wars against the Black Panther Party and the American Indian Movement." This volume was followed by Brian Glick's *War at Home* (1989), at once academic and practical, a guide to "covert action against U.S. activists and what we can do about it." Finally, in *The COINTELPRO Papers* (1990), Churchill and Vander Wall go on to provide both the documentation and the instructional lessons, a new paleography, in how to read and interpret the manuscript evidence, made available upon request by the FOIA, with regard to FBI efforts to "disrupt, misdirect, discredit or otherwise neutralize" the Communist Party of the United States of America (CPUSA), the Socialist Workers party, the Puerto Rican independence movement, the black liberation movement, the New

Left, and the American Indian Movement. The authors' project, as they maintain, is to "reproduce secret FBI documents to allow the Bureau to document its own lawlessness" (1).

The documents themselves, however, given the reinscriptions and emendations made to the texts prior to their release by the FBI, in the interest of "national security," are not immediately legible upon receipt, and the first chapter of *The COINTELPRO Papers* renders the background and paleographical techniques necessary to "understanding deletions in FBI documents." The eventual purpose of this disciplinary exercise in bibliography, archival research, and textual editing is to begin "to create a readily accessible mini-archive which will ultimately say more than we ever could. We have felt a responsibility to do this because the sad fact is that *COINTELPRO* lives. We must all learn its face. Only in unmasking it can we ever hope to destroy it and move forward to our more constructive goals and objectives" (20). Interpretation, in the form of new strategies of reading, is crucial to the discursive politics of the struggle waged in the United States between the "right of the government to 'defend itself' from dissent" and the "rights of citizens to 'privacy and free expression' " (300).

The FBI's "secret war" against the Black Panther party is the most thoroughly documented in the now-available records from the bureau. Founded in Oakland in 1966 by Huey P. Newton and Bobby Seale, the BPP quickly but surely launched a series of projects in cities across the country oriented toward community organization and popular control. They eventually included, in addition to self-defense and economic self-sufficiency projects, Free Breakfast programs for children, education courses, and an antiheroin campaign. So effective were these initiatives that by 1968, FBI director J. Edgar Hoover had identified the Panthers as the "greatest [single] threat to the internal security of the country" (cited in Churchill and Vander Wall 1990, 123). The previous year Hoover had already ordered a massive *COINTELPRO* against them. This protracted operation, involving 233 admitted actions against the BPP between 1967 and 1971 (Churchill and Vander Wall 1990, 164), included the by now classic stratagems of eavesdropping, bogus mail, "black propaganda," disinformation, infiltrators and agents provocateurs, "snitch-jacketing" or creation of informers, and assassination (Churchill and Vander Wall 1988, ch. 2). Just as crucial to this agenda were harassment arrests on spurious charges and prolonged trials designed to "harass, increase paranoia, tie activists up in a series of pre-arraignment incarcerations and preliminary courtroom procedures, and deplete their resources through the postings of numerous bail bonds (as well as the retention of attorneys)" (Churchill and Vander Wall 1988, 44).

Four celebrated trials took place in the early 1970s: the New York Twenty-one; Bobby Seale and Ericka Huggins in Connecticut; Angela Davis in California; and Assata Shakur in New Jersey and New York. Against the secrecy of the covert operations of United States counterintelligence programs that led to the arrests of the defendants, the remade publicity of their trials retook public space in a series of collective counterdemonstrations that involved defending attorneys, the prisoners themselves, popular support committees, and finally, the juries which— for a time—displayed the active independence of public opinion. The **191** trial of the New York Twenty-one in 1971 on charges of planning a sequence of bombings in New York City department stores ended in their acquittal. Bobby Seale and Ericka Huggins, on the basis of manufactured evidence provided by an FBI informer, were charged with the murder of another Panther, Alex Rackley; they were released in May 1971 when the judge who had been hearing the case for seven months declared it a mistrial, with a hung jury at its conclusion, and dismissed all charges. In 1972 Angela Davis was found innocent by the jury on all three counts of kidnapping, murder, and conspiracy involving the shootout with sixteen-year old Jonathan Jackson, George Jackson's brother, at the Marin County Courthouse during the trial of the Soledad Brothers. Assata Shakur, arrested on the New Jersey Turnpike in 1973, was repeatedly acquitted on various charges of bank robbery. Finally convicted on a murder charge and sentenced to life imprisonment, she escaped from prison in 1979 to Cuba, where she was granted political asylum and continues to live today, still on the FBI's "most wanted" list.

The four trials from the two coasts also produced a series of books that rehearsed, from multiple perspectives and within different places of the dramatis personae of the trials, the events and the courtroom exchanges, each contributing thereby to a counterhistory, a configuring of a literary tribunal, a generic experimentation in writing the system against the system. *Look for Me in the Whirlwind*, presented as the "collective autobiography" of the New York Twenty-one, constructs a combined narrative that traces the larger historical trajectory of black struggle in the United States in which the multiple defendants had participated. As Haywood Burns writes in the introduction to *Whirlwind*, "In the processing, packaging and presenting of news involving group political trials, the mass media so often, perhaps inevitably, squeeze out the personal and human aspects of the defendants and they become numbers—Presidio 27, Chicago 8, Panther 21—cardboard, stereotyped one-dimensional composites." But, he goes on, "it is impossible to lump them in the cold isolation of the grand jury's indictment 'People of the State of New York v. . . .' They are part of 'the people,' members of a community that swirls around them, protects them, beleaguers them, fortifies them, debilitates them, spurs them on to action" (vii–viii).

The suppressed histories told in *Whirlwind* traverse the divides between the rural south and the urban north, between male and female. Like Elizabeth Gurley Flynn's autobiography, they recount a political growth that recuperates the patterned conventions of "growing up," of personal history, within a programmatic political project: from school days, ghetto gangs, and military service, to Malcolm X, the Black Panther party, and prison, where the struggle reconstitutes itself. As Joan Bird writes from the Women's House of Detention in New York City: "The sisters in there are actually very beautiful. Because they are all from the colony and they know about how rough it is and how hard it is to survive. And they know about how to use different methods to get around and survive. When you are in there you learn to do some time, you learn that you can't actually control what is happening out there in the street. So you have to deal with what you are confronted with, and that is basically the Women's House of Detention" (318).

Such a book was itself imperative, despite its mediate place on/off the street, according to Afeni Shakur in a letter written from prison and reprinted in *Whirlwind*, if the politics of history were to be reclaimed:

> March 20, 1971
>
> A letter to Jamala, Lil Afeni, Sekyiwa, and the unborn baby (babies) within my womb.
>
> First let me tell you that this book was not my idea at all (as a matter of fact I was hardly cooperative). But I suppose that one day you're going to wonder about all this mess that's going on now and I just had to make sure you understood a few things. (360)

Prison and the courtroom, the trials of "political prisoners" in the United States and the narratives that they generate, elaborate historical sites in which the popular bases and structures of political dissent can in turn be reconstructed and renegotiated for the future.

From her own solitary cell in a California prison, Angela Davis wrote to Ericka Huggins, held across the country at the Niantic State Farm in Connecticut:

> Dearest Ericka, Sister, Comrade,
> All your messages have been beautiful and inspiring.
>
> It's been a long time—over two years—since our last meeting. I recall, however, as if it were yesterday, that cold, rainy evening, submerged under sadness and rage, those agonizing hours we were stationed in the parking lot outside Sybil Brand [a UCLA building], anxiously awaiting your release from jail. The outrageous assassination of Jon [Huggins] and Bunchy [Carter] had come so unexpectedly, engendering an atmosphere of shock, incredulity and ungovernable

anger. But our paramount concern was you Ericka. Your husband, closest comrade in struggle, your love, the father of Mai, your new-born child, had just been slain by the bullets of our foes. You had been immediately arrested on a manifestly fabricated charge—conspiracy to retaliate, or something equally ridiculous. We were hurting with your pain. (Davis et al. 1971, 107–8)

Ericka, whose husband Jon had been killed in a shootout at the University of California, Los Angeles, the year before by members of Ron Karenga's US, at the time of this letter was on trial with Bobby Seale in New Haven, Connecticut. The story of that trial is told in Donald Freed's **193** *Agony in New Haven* (1973). Unlike *Whirlwind*, which emphasizes chronology, Freed's narrative is framed by the temporal space of the trial, but moves ceaselessly in and out of the courtroom. The constant juxtapositions—of Ericka Huggins's poetry, the history of African Americans in the United States, programs and agendas of the BPP, biographies of the major protagonists (defendants Huggins and Seale and lawyers Charles Garry, Katie Rorabach, and David Rosen), the impoverished economic and demographic situation of New Haven with wealthy Yale University in its midst, and newspaper headlines from the trial of Lt. William Calley for the My Lai massacre in Vietnam—are articulated across ever shortening sections: "The Jury," "The Trial," and "The Verdict."

Freed's narrative structure thus places in the foreground the voir dire, the jury selection process, which in New Haven proved to be the longest in history: "the defense insisted on making a record for appeal and for history. Everyone knows that in the future this pretrial ground breaking would be of historic importance, and the representatives of the State banked on it to vindicate the system and their dedicated defense of it" (82). At issue in the prolonged questioning of prospective jurors were such contested problems as their position on the death penalty, attitudes toward black people in general and the Black Panthers in particular, and ultimately whether it was possible for Huggins and Seale to receive a fair trial in New Haven. The trial itself, in comparison to these preliminaries, was brief, and the jury's deliberations shorter still. They could not agree collectively to convict the defendants on the charges brought against them, and Judge Harold M. Mulvey was obliged in the end to dismiss the charges. Written into this teleological collage, a textual counterpoint to the judicial reportage, is Ericka Huggins's self-presentation in verse, her life in prison, in the movement, the lives of others who have served time with her. Freed's volume concludes in her words: "not dead / not living / not asking for freedom— / but free / Ericka" (332).[5]

In her letter from prison to Huggins, Angela Davis had written of the urgency of reconstructing the politics of women and prison: "So much work remains to be done around prisons in general—pending revolutionary change, we have to raise the demand that prisons in their present form be abolished. As an inevitable by-product of a male-oriented society and consequently still largely male-oriented movement—which women are however increasingly contesting—sufficient attention has not been devoted to women in prison" (Davis 1971, 109). Davis's own experience of incarceration and trial, told in her *Autobiography* (1974), enjoined the necessity not only of resisting the institutional racism that oppresses black people and other people of color in the United States, but of counter-

194   ing in writing and practice the prosecution's attempts to recuperate her political activism as no more than female infatuation with the masculinism of resistance. Her trial—then her acquittal—was as much a defense of a woman's specific role in the struggle as it was a critique of the United States judicial apparatus.

Bettina Aptheker, a long-time friend of Davis, a legal investigator for her team of attorneys, as well as a member of the Committee to Free Angela Davis, described that multidimensional contest in *The Morning Breaks* (1975). Like *Agony in New Haven*, Aptheker's account is divided between pretrial preparations, in this case the fight for bail and the defense motions to have the trial moved to another, more hospitable venue, and the trial itself. Equally critical to the pretrial arguments was the inadmissability as evidence of Angela Davis's letters to George Jackson, of which two were confiscated by the FBI in a search of Davis's apartment and one was intercepted by the prison censors reading Jackson's mail, and eighteen pages from her diary to the Soledad Brother murdered in San Quentin just before her trial.

Angela Davis's trial and the charges against her are situated in the context of the struggle in the early 1970s in and against the United States prison system. Davis, who had just been removed from her teaching position in the philosophy department of UCLA for membership in the Communist party, was a member of the Soledad Brothers Defense Committee. George Jackson, Fleeta Drumgo, and John Cluchette, inmates in Soledad, were being tried for the murder of a prison guard. On 7 August 1971 Jonathan Jackson was killed in a firefight while trying to aid the prisoners at the courtroom where the three were being tried. On 21 August George Jackson and five other prisoners were shot dead from a watchtower in the yard at San Quentin, and on 13 October Angela Davis was arrested in New York City and subsequently extradited to California for her alleged participation in the 7 August courthouse shooting. Her motive, according to the prosecution: her passion for George Jackson.

On the basis of her letters and the diary "edited" by the authorities, prosecutor Albert Harris argued: "Her own words will reveal that beneath the cool academic veneer is a woman fully capable of being moved to violence by passion. . . . Her basic motive was not to free political prisoners, but to free the one prisoner she loved. . . . The motive was not abstract. It was not founded . . . on any need, real or imagined, for prison reform. It was founded simply on the passion that she felt for George Jackson" (Aptheker 1975, 166). One of Davis's attorneys, Doris Walker, argued that to edit the text of the diary, written in "stream of consciousness," was to destroy it.

Just as important in this literary/legal struggle over interpretation, according to Aptheker, was attorney Leo Branton's closing statement. Branton began carefully, meticulously, to recount to the jury the history of black people in the United States. Having thus provided a crucial lesson in the politics of race, Leo Branton went on to examine the new political parameters given to traditional romance paradigms in the conflicted arena of the liberation struggle: **195**

Leo prepared to move on to the issue of the diary. It was Harris' characterization of it, and of Angela's love for George that formed the lie upon which the presumption of guilt hung. The diary had to be lifted from defilement. It had to be lifted from even the amenities of judicial etiquette with which Judge Arnason had treated it. The jury had to be able to confront Angela's love for George: to comprehend in some small way the beauty of its intensity; and the courage of its passion. They had ultimately to seek identity with it, as they would seek to identify with any other human experience. (Aptheker 1975, 262).

The jury did something of that when they found Angela Davis innocent: "The jury was being escorted out. They were smiling now and some of them were crying. We didn't know what to do. Howard [Moore, a lawyer] stood up, raised both fists and shouted, 'All Power to the Jury!' We started to applaud, louder and louder" (273).

The several jury selection processes function just as importantly in Assata Shakur's narrative, *Assata* (1987), of the seven trials to which she was subjected; she was finally convicted at the last and sentenced to life imprisonment. Texts within the text, plays within the play, the voir dires serve, as in *Agony in New Haven*, to interrupt and temporarily reverse the charges and reframe the trial proceedings as an inquiry into racism in the United States. Stopped by state troopers in 1973 while traveling on the New Jersey Turnpike with two comrades, Zayd Shakur and Sundiata Acoli, Assata Shakur, (once known as Joanne Chesimard) was seriously wounded in the shootout that ensued. (Zayd Shakur was killed, and Sundiata Acoli is still in prison.) Her autobiography opens as she lies semiconscious, chained to a bed in a heavily guarded hospital room, recalling the incident: "There were lights and sirens. Zayd was dead. My mind knew that Zayd was dead. The air was like cold glass. Huge bubbles rose and burst. Each one felt like an explosion in my chest. My mouth tasted like blood and dirt. The car spun around me and then something like sleep overtook me. In the background I could hear what sounded like gunfire. But I was fading and dreaming" (3). Shakur, who had been underground, moving between safe houses, since the FBI's *COINTELPRO* activities had fractured and decimated the BPP, emerged from the nether space of unconsciousness into still another world of suppression—incarceration—the frame for her autobiography.

Like *Look for Me in the Whirlwind*, which details the southern origins of several of the defendants, one of *Assata*'s narratives recalls her growing up in the South, her move to New York City to attend high school, college years, an emergent political consciousness, and finally the organized work with Panthers. Like Angela Davis's autobiographical reconstruction of a classic biography, Shakur's itinerary is reframed and reworked by another narrative, one that in *Assata* traces the chronology of arrest, trials, prison, sentencing, and ultimately escape to Cuba. Like *The Morning Breaks* too, the text dramatically rebuts the paradigmatic traditional separation of women from the political sphere in its reenactment of the lover/mother archetypes. Assata Shakur had a child while she was in prison. After long stretches of being held in solitary confinement, and as a result of a series of interventions into the courtroom exchanges by herself and her codefendant Kamau, Shakur and Kamau were incarcerated in adjoining chambers:

> Talking to Kamau was so good for me. Solitary had affected me really badly. I had closed up inside myself and had forgotten how to relate in an open way with people. We spent whole days laughing and talking and listening to the kourtroom madness in between. Each day we grew closer until, one day, it was clear to both of us that our relationship was changing. It was growing physical. We began to touch and hold each other and each of us was like an oasis to the other. For a few days the question of sex was there. Then, one day, we talked about it. Surely, it was possible. But, i thought, the consequences! Pregnancy was certainly a possibility. I was facing life in prison. Kamau would also be in prison for a long time. The child would have no father and no mother. (92)

The child, a daughter, was born in prison—and was raised outside by Shakur's mother and grandmother. Many years later, at the very end of the book, Kakuya would visit her own mother in Cuba.

Assata's two complementary narratives, bildungsroman and trial drama, inextricably enjoin each other, redeploying thereby the endemic relation of penal and legal institutions to the personal histories of African Americans in the United States, a relation that is still reflected in today's prison population. In narrating that inherent relation from the perspective of asylum in Castro's Cuba, however, Shakur self-critically recalls three "mistakes" that she had made in the course of her own political de-

196

velopment and disciplinary evolution. The first error occurs early in that trajectory, during a visit to California in the 1960s, and is pointed out to her by a Red Guard cadre whom she and her companions encounter while carelessly smoking marijuana in a public park: "You guys should really be careful with that grass, especially when you've got leaflets or newspapers on you. A lot of good comrades have been busted like that." And Shakur recalls "feeling guilty and stupid, silly and politically backward" (202). Two other analytical lapses attend upon her arrest and trial and are recognized only in hindsight. The one she apologizes for in a radio address from prison:

I want to apologize to you, my Black brothers and sisters, for being on the new jersey turnpike. I should have known better. The turnpike is a checkpoint where Black people are stopped, searched, harassed, and assaulted. Revolutionaries must never be in too much of a hurry or make careless decisions. He who runs when the sun is sleeping will stumble many times. (52)

The other occasion, however, can only be recalled in the course of writing the book: "Participating in the new jersey trial was unprincipled and incorrect. By participating, i participated in my own oppression. I should have known better and not lent dignity or credence to that sham. In the long run, the people are our only appeal. The only ones who can free us are ourselves" (252).

The trials of the New York Twenty-one, of Ericka Huggins and Bobby Seale, of Angela Davis, of Assata Shakur, like their written narratives, all culminate in freedom. But there is an important difference between the trials of Shakur and those of the previous three, to be located perhaps in the recontainment of the judicial process and the courts by the government's prosecution, which Shakur's final self-critique addresses. Her liberation had to be seized, rather than accepted, in a prison escape enabled by the Black Liberation Army. The details of that escape, however, go unnarrated in *Assata*—as if to observe the right to "remain silent"— as if to allow it to happen again, for some other political prisoner—and are replaced by a visionary dream of freedom that Shakur's grandmother reports to her during a prison visit: "I drilled her for more details. Some she gave and some she didn't. Finally, after i had asked a thousand questions, my grandmother let all authority show in her voice. 'I know it will happen, because I dreamt it. You're getting out of this place, and I know it. That's all there is to it'" (261).

Silvia Baraldini and Susan Rosenberg were arrested in 1982 and 1984, respectively, on charges and indictments that included their alleged involvement in the liberation of Assata Shakur from prison in 1979. Silvia

197

Baraldini was sentenced to forty years plus three years, and the extradition to her native country requested by the Italian government has been denied by the United States. In Italy, Baraldini would serve less than one-quarter of that prison sentence for the same charges of expropriation and refusing to collaborate with a grand jury. Susan Rosenberg was convicted for possession of explosives, weapons, and false identification and was sentenced to an extraordinary fifty-eight years without parole. Both women were eventually assigned to the Lexington High Security Unit (HSU), a federal maximum-security control unit for women prisoners opened in October 1986. It may be that Baraldini and Rosenberg's alleged contributions to Assata Shakur's freedom played a role in that particular assignment, since among the criteria for the placement of women prisoners in the HSU, according to Rosenberg's attorney Mary O'Melveny, are that their "confinement raises a serious threat of external assault for the purpose of aiding the offender's escape" as well as "serious histories of assaultive, escape-prone or disruptive activity" (O'Melveny 1989, 51). However, as O'Melveny goes on, citing a 1987 letter from Bureau of Prisons director J. Michael Quinlan to Representative Robert Kastenmeier, the specifically political bases for the Bureau of Prison's incarceration of the women in the Lexington facility eventually became clearer: an inmate is selected on the basis of her "past or present affiliation, association or membership in an organization which has been documented as being involved in acts of violence, attempts to disrupt or overthrow the government of the U.S., or whose published ideology includes advocating law violations in order to 'free' prisoners" (51).

The Lexington HSU, an underground facility that was designed to hold sixteen women and was built, at a cost of several million dollars, below the existing correctional institution in Lexington, Kentucky, was closed twenty-two months after its opening in August 1988, following court appeals by its inmates and a campaign involving human rights organizations, prisoner-support groups, and Amnesty International.[6] Among the conditions that characterized this "prison within a prison" and that were denounced by Amnesty as constituting "cruel and degrading punishment" were sleep and sensory deprivation, denial of privacy, small-group isolation, hostility and sexual harassment from guards, and twenty-four-hour camera and visual surveillance. According to Dr. Richard Korn, a clinical psychologist, in a report for the American Civil Liberties Union, the Lexington "experiment" could be designed only "to reduce prisoners to a state of submission essential for their ideological conversion. That failing, the next objective is to reduce them to a state of psychological incompetence sufficient to neutralize them as efficient, self-directing antagonists. That failing, the only alternative is to destroy them, preferably by making them desperate enough to destroy themselves" (cited in O'Melveny 1989, 52–53). For Susan Rosenberg (1989), the twenty-two months that she spent in the HSU before it was closed and its five inmates were transferred were tantamount to "being buried alive": "Everyone who wrote us asked how we felt about what was happening and how we resisted it. It was never an easy question to answer, and it still isn't. Small-group isolation is a form of mental/psychological maltreatment, recognized by the tortured and torturer alike. The isolation, the sensory deprivation, the constant inactivity, and the forced dependency for basic life necessities on jailers who both hate you and fear you mean that existence is a constant confrontation where the four walls become the world" (50). **199**

In 1988 the Department of Psychology at the University of Puerto Rico in Rio Piedras held a public forum to discuss the case of Alejandrina Torres, then "housed" in Lexington with Rosenberg and Baraldini, and more generally the larger question of state violence against its political prisoners. Ester Vicente pointed out the punishing paradoxes that distinguish such carceral practices especially when directed against women: "When we women leave the private sphere and participate actively in the tasks necessary to the vital transformation that society deserves, they punish us doubly: for our insolence in posing questions and for having left the private sphere in which we have been contained for centuries" (*Brutalidad*, 14). High-security detention U.S.-style is made to distort abusively what have traditionally functioned as both private and public arenas, enlisting as integral to its design the very conventions that have historically circumscribed a woman's personal space and her political activity. Confined underground, and denied access to normal channels of communication with colleagues, families, even lawyers, the women in the Lexington HSU were at the same time on relentless twenty-four-hour "public" display to their guards, their correspondence open to the prurient view of the prison readers, and their every private move visible to the concupiscent gaze of the watchers of the films recorded by the surveillance cameras.

The University of Puerto Rico forum itself, in its combined expert, scholarly analysis of the psychophysiological effects of prison and its political advocacy on behalf of Puerto Rican prisoner-of-war Alejandrina Torres, proposed one means from within the academy of countering the prison's usurpation of the legitimacy of a woman's human and political rights. Alejandrina Torres acknowledged the importance of the forum's intervention into her case in a message sent to the meeting and its participants: "You don't know the immense joy and gratitude that I owe you for undertaking this activity that represents a serious and deep analysis of the impact that the brutality of psychological torture has on a human being. I am very happy that these things are being discussed by academics of my native country [*suelo patrio*]" (*Brutalidad*, 55).

Alejandrina Torres's health suffered serious deterioration as a result of the nearly two years spent in the Lexington HSU. A Puerto Rican *independentista*, born in Puerto Rico and schooled in New York City, she was convicted on charges of "seditious conspiracy" to overthrow the United States government. Torres refused to renounce her claim to POW status and argued at her 1985 trial that the "conspiracy was not to overthrow the authority of the government of the United States but to win the independence of Puerto Rico; the authority that is to be overthrown is the authority of colonialism" (*Brutalidad*, 20).

Ever since the United States acquired the island of Puerto Rico in 1898 as a result of the Spanish American War, the national status of the colony has been continuously contested by its inhabitants, who have fought the equally continuous, if conflicting, economic, military, and political designs on its people and resources by the government in Washington, D.C. In 1936, for example, following the police shooting of five student demonstrators at the University of Puerto Rico in Rio Piedras, independence leader Pedro Albizu Campos was sentenced to two to ten years on charges of seditious conspiracy. In 1947 the United States government took over the area of Vieques as a military base (used as a staging position in the 1983 invasion of Grenada), destroying the natural life of the area and the culture and livelihood of its inhabitants (see Lopez 1987). In 1954 Lolita Lebron and Rafael Cancel Miranda, together with two *companeros*, managed to wage an armed assault on the United States House of Representatives. They were released from prison twenty-five years later.

More recently, the Puerto Rican independence movement has been a major target of the FBI's continued *COINTELPRO*-type activities. In 1978, in what Manuel Suarez called the "requiem on Cerro Maravilla," two young *independentistas* were ambushed in a remote area of the island, tortured, and assassinated in a police operation that was enabled by an FBI informer. In August 1985, with the help of the United States military and SWAT teams that invaded homes and ransacked offices, 350 FBI agents arrested thirteen people in San Juan on charges related to a Wells Fargo robbery in 1983 in Hartford, Connecticut. Eventually known as the Puerto Rico/Hartford Fifteen, these fifteen men and women would stand trial in Hartford in a court that "went along in part with the government's claim that there should in effect be a 'political organization exception' to the probable cause requirement of the Fourth Amendment, sanctioning the search of any alleged member based on evidence that some member of the organization might possess the items sought" (Deutsch and Harvey 1989, 43).

No less egregious in this century-long colonial history, indeed central to it, is the period from 1948 to 1957, the period of the "gag law," or *ley de la mordaza*, which went even further than its model, the Smith Act, in criminalizing any *expression* of disapproval of government policy or functioning. In her study of this decade of *mordaza*, Ivonne Acosta (1987) presents a multidimensional history, at once cultural and political, of the setting for that gagging and its judicial and penal enforcement. Her own methodology, itself necessitated by the continued consequences of the law— such as the removal of relevant documents from archives in the interest of **201** "national security" and the persistent fear of witnesses in Puerto Rico— challenges, in much the same way as the investigations through the FOIA into the FBI's *COINTELPRO*, the imposition of a coercive silence on readers and writers of an alternative United States historical narrative.

That alternative history is being composed on many fronts by a "conspiracy of voices," a phrase that also serves as the title to a collection of writings by the four women of the Resistance Conspiracy case that continues the countertradition of United States prison writing. Susan Rosenberg, Laura Whitehorn, Linda Evans, and Marilyn Buck, together with Tim Blunk and Alan Berkman, were charged with conspiracy and a number of bombings of military and government buildings. But because the "government does not know who did any of the bombings, . . . they construct[ed] the indictment so that they only have to prove the defendants are associated through common politics and/or clandestine work, in order to convict them of aiding and abetting the bombings" (Whitehorn 1989, 48). The women's *Conspiracy of Voices* (Rosenberg, et al. 1990) tells of joy at the release of Walter Sisulu from South African prisons, solidarity with the Sharpeville Six and the Palestinian "children of the stones," despair and pride in secretly sewing bookmarks in the cell to be sold to earn money for the Sandinista election campaign, anger at United States "democracy," and the importance of visits to the prisoners—"sitting amidst / a space that we carve / clandestinely out of their / criminality and restrictions" (Rosenberg, 34)—from people outside to challenge the prison apparatus's authoritarian assumption of its prerogative to define inside and outside.

Such a "conspiracy of voices" must be raised to help in "hauling up the morning" (*izando la manana*), a phrase taken from a prison poem by Salvadoran Roque Dalton to Turkish Nazim Hikmet and used as the title of an anthology of writings by sixty-five United States political prisoners and anticolonial prisoners of war (Blunk and Levasseur 1990) with an introduction by Assata Shakur. According to its incarcerated editors, that work was "born of a desire to fight a lie: the US government's incredible assertion that it holds no political prisoners" (xix). Most of the contributors to the project of "hauling up the morning" were among the plaintiffs in the international tribunal, demanding a hearing for their history, its past and its future. Linda Evans, of the Resistance Conspiracy case, comments on prison writing:

> I've rebelled against writing a journal or writing articles because I've viewed them as accepting the unacceptable isolation of imprisonment. Since the readers are unknown, or maybe only myself, there isn't even a pretense of dialogue or delayed discussion. I realize that it's this imprisonment, this isolation that I am rebelling so fiercely against, not the writing itself.
>
> Better to view written words as tools with which to organize, a way to keep fighting, a means of communicating free ideas with unknown comrades-to-be. In fact, writing can *overcome* our enemy's attempts to isolate us, words can be turned against our captors. So—I will write! (But I do wish I had a typewriter!) (Rosenberg, et al., 32)

PART III

MY HOME, MY PRISON

Chapter Nine

The Tyranny of Home versus "Safe Houses"

After the establishment of the state of Israel in 1948, the Palestinians, who were driven or fled from the territory of pre-1967 Israel, left behind immoveable property with an estimated value of 100,383,784 Palestinian pounds. This property included extensive stone quarries, 40,000 dunums of vineyards, 95 percent of Israel's present olive groves, nearly 100,000 dunums of citrus groves, and 10,000 shops, businesses and stores. They also left behind 19,000 Palestinian pounds worth of moveable property. . . . In 1950, the Israeli Knesset passed the Absentee Property Law by virtue of which a custodian was appointed to manage this property. The Development Authority (Transfer of Property) Law, also of 1950, established a Development Authority in Israel, which was permitted to buy the lands placed by the earlier law under the control of the Custodian of Absentee Property.   RAJA SHEHADEH, *Occupier's Law: Israel and the West Bank*

The very first time that Salim Bakri, in Costa-Gavras's 1983 film *Hannah K.*, returns to Israel/Palestine in an attempt to reclaim the property lost by his family in 1948, when they were obliged to flee their home in Kfar Ramanah, the Palestinian is arrested and, following a brief trial, deported across the bridge to Jordan. Salim was found by Israeli soldiers, assisted by their dogs, hiding in a well outside an Arab house near which a small group of alleged Palestinian "terrorists" had just been captured. Before Salim and the other detainees are taken away from the scene in an army jeep, the Israeli soldiers demolish the house with explosives, while its inhabitants and their neighbors, surrounded by the few belongings and pieces of furniture they have salvaged, look on silently. A short while later, Salim returns to his country a second time, bringing deeds, titles, and documents, and with the same purpose, to reclaim his family's property. On this occasion he is arrested again, tried, and sentenced to eight months' imprisonment as the result of a deal struck by the court, the prosecuting attorney, and Salim's Israeli woman lawyer, Hannah Kaufman. According to the bargain, Salim is to be sent to South Africa upon his release. From there, if he still so desires, he can begin again his efforts to reclaim the family home. Six months later, however, Salim, near death after several weeks of a hunger strike, is released, in an unusual move (and this is just one of the many ways in which Costa-Gavras's film "fictionalizes" Israel's military law and its application), into the custody of Hannah, who provides him shelter in her own home.

Hannah K. opens with the first arrest of Salim and the demolition of the Palestinian home. The final scene of the film displays Hannah's house, surrounded by a heavily armed unit of the Israeli army. In the course of the cinematic narrative of Salim's struggle for his rights as a Palestinian, from the destruction of one house to the siege of another, *Hannah K.* represents, however cursorily, the three major institutionalized measures of repression regularly deployed by the Israeli military occupation against the Palestinian people: imprisonment, deportation, and house demolition and sealing. These acts violate international law and are part of Israel's policy of annexation of the Occupied Territories of the West Bank and Gaza Strip.

Prison, in particular, has become an endemic feature of Palestinian daily life under Israeli occupation, with over 30 percent of the population having passed through Israeli prisons. "Under the Israeli Military Orders relating to the Occupied Territories," states Paul Hunt (1987), "a soldier may arrest any person who has, or is suspected of having, committed a security offense" (7). Salim's experience is in no way unusual or extraordinary, except perhaps in the leniency of his plea-bargained sentence and his premature release, given that nearly every Palestinian family in the last twenty years has undergone the incarceration of at least one of its members.

Deportation, while practiced less often than detention, is no less central to the occupation. Furthermore, as Joost Hiltermann (1986) has pointed out, "Deportations in Israel are a form of extra-judicial punishment, violating due process, since they are based on an administrative decision in which no formal charges are brought against the deportee, no trial is held, and the person is deported on the basis of evidence to which neither he/she nor his/her lawyer can have access" (2–3). Although Salim's banishment to Jordan would not be construed strictly as "deportation," according to official explanations of Israeli policy, in that he has been convicted of being an "infiltrator" (defined in 1969 by Military Order 329, article 1, as a "person who knowingly enters the Area contrary to Proper Procedures, after having resided in the East Bank of the Jordan, or in Syria, or in Egypt, or in Lebanon, after the Determining Date"), his expulsion dramatically illustrates within the context of the film the larger practice of mass and individual deportation characteristic of Israel's treatment of the Palestinians living under its jurisdiction.

More dramatic perhaps than even imprisonment and deportation is the demolition of houses belonging to families of persons suspected of or alleged to have committed "security offenses." According to official Israeli figures, 1,265 Palestinian houses were blown up in the first fifteen years of occupation (since 1967), after which the demolitions occurred less frequently for a time, only to increase intensively several years later. At least 786 homes were destroyed or sealed in the first fifteen months of the Palestinian *intifada*, which began in December 1987. House demolition is considered a form of collective punishment, in violation of the 1949 Fourth Geneva Convention Relative to the Protection of Civilian Persons in Time of War, a punishment that leaves entire families, who have been given **207** one-half hour to two hours notice to evacuate their belongings, destitute and homeless. According to legal researcher Emma Playfair (1987), "The land on which a demolished or totally sealed house stood is forfeited and frequently declared a 'closed area,' meaning that no one can enter or leave without permission, and the family may not even be allowed to remain on the land" (7).

At stake in these punitive and repressive practices of the Israeli occupation and the Palestinian popular resistance against that occupation are the land itself and the right of the Palestinian people who live on that land or in exile to their self-determination. In *Hannah K.* the struggle for the control over the land is materially symbolized in the sequence of four distinct and ideologically marked houses against which the courtroom and prison scenes are elaborated. The demolished Palestinian home of the opening scene is followed by Salim's family house, discovered by Hannah with the help of the prisoner's old maps and documents as part of her preparation for his approaching trial. Kafar Ramanah, the original name for the town in which the house is located, has now become Kifar Rimon, an Israeli settlement, and the Bakri house functions as a "museum" visited by foreign tourists who are curious about the quaint family customs of the Arabs of another era. There are also the stone ruins and structural skeletons of the abandoned refugee camp in which Salim's family lived when they were first obliged by the fighting in 1948 to flee their home. One day, after Salim has been released from prison and is living under Hannah's supervision, she follows him there, secretly she thinks. The Israeli lawyer's charged encounter, through Salim, with all of these buildings provides her with a condensed and summary narrative of Salim's biography and of recent Palestinian history. That narrative to which she is made privy, however, trangresses the restrictions of the official Israeli accounts of security and statehood. Finally, Hannah's own home, the site now of these government trespasses, and symbolizing the connection between women and land and their mutual subjection to masculinist authority, is placed under military siege by the Israeli army.

In the end, however, *Hannah K.* subsumes the Palestinian historical narrative into the romantic plotting of Hannah's conflicted love affairs, with her French husband, Victor, her Israeli lover, Joshua, and the Palestinian prisoner, Salim, and her feminist claims to personal independence and a life of her own. The film genders the Palestinian-Israeli conflict in its ultimate emphasis on Hannah Kaufman, and while the reified issues of national identity are challenged by the counterparadigms of an emergent romantic involvement between the Israeli woman lawyer and the Palestinian prisoner whom she is defending, the weight of the argument around gender and its theoretical and practical contributions to altering existing power relations is exclusively concentrated on the Israeli side of the ideological and territorial borders. Except for the silent portraits of the family members who stoically look on at the destruction of their home in the opening sequence, there are no Palestinian women in *Hannah K.*. Indeed, Salim is the only significant Palestinian character in the film. His singular, almost alien presence—as an "infiltrator"—forces an unwonted realignment within the domestic configurations of the Israeli sociopolitical setting. Through Hannah's insistence on the demands for a public speaking voice, as a lawyer in the courtroom, and an independent private life, the film not only stereotypes the Palestinian struggle as a masculinist movement, but also mutes the argument of the one Palestinian male whose case is presented in court by the woman lawyer and whose cause is rendered through her coming-to-consciousness story.

The second time that Hannah encounters Salim is occasioned by his second arrest, when he requests that she defend him in the new trial proceedings. The lawyer, meeting her client in the prison, is accompanied by an interpreter, whose assistance she has applied for. Eventually Hannah realizes that the detainee is replying in Arabic to her questions without waiting for their translation. Still she addresses herself to the interpreter: "He answers before you have a chance to translate," and then, "Why doesn't he speak to me directly?" The translator replies, "You were the one who asked for an interpreter."

Hannah K. goes on from this scene of failed communication to tell the story of the growing, if thwarted, understanding between the two protagonists: male and female, Palestinian and Israeli, political prisoner and state's attorney. Their love story, however, serves finally to conflate the political significance of these categories of gender, nationalism, and the state, and their mutual interaction, by obfuscating as melodramatic background the complex and multidimensional history of the Israeli military occupation and the Palestinian popular resistance to it. The "green line," which separates "Israel" from the Occupied Territories, is itself effaced, and with it the tentacular military apparatus that supports a repressive occupation. Prison, deportation, and house demolition are refigured, not as instruments in a state policy of dispossession of a people, but as mo-

208

ments in an unfolding romance. In the end, the armed siege of Hannah's house, called in by Joshua, her former lover, the father of her child, and the state's prosecuting attorney, is calculated to punish her alone in her home for her dual social transgression, first as a "single" mother, and second as a Jewish woman cohabiting with a Palestinian male. The political significance of the collaboration between lawyer and political prisoner is elided. Salim, the "infiltrator," leaves before the arrival of the army. Unlike Victor, however, who can come and go at will through Ben Gurion Airport in Tel Aviv, Salim remains even more a prisoner of Israel's concept of "security" and national borders than is Hannah in her home surrounded by soldiers of the Israel Defense Forces, who have been assigned to safeguard the patriarchal integrity of their theocratic and racially identified state.

209

Israel's practice of demolishing Palestinian houses in the Occupied Territories as a collective punishment for alleged security offenses is only one aspect of its larger occupation policy designed to implement eventual annexation of the territories that its military occupied following the June 1967 war. Together with imprisonment and deportation, house demolition violently assaults the social structural bonds that have historically maintained the cohesiveness and the coherence of Palestinian society. The three practices—which, according to a certain territorial logic, might be considered analogues of each other—operate an infringement, a transgression or breach, of traditional concepts of home, the individual, and the integrity of private or domestic space. The actual destruction of the home carried out by the explosives or bulldozers in a house demolition is ideologically refigured in narratives of detention by the "knock on the door," already a near-classical topos of the writing of political prison.

If They Come in the Morning, the 1971 collection of essays and documents edited by Angela Davis et al. around the arrest, prosecution, and incarceration in the late 1960s of members of the Black Panther party, opens up an agonistic narrative of political resistance to a state apparatus of counterinsurgency. It begins with the crossing of a threshold, the entry of the police or secret service agents into the protected space of domicile and autobiography. The political resonance of the title is already embedded in an extended history of political detention, from Rex Stout's thriller *The Doorbell Rang* (1965) to Elizabeth Gurley Flynn's prison memoir. *The Alderson Story* (1976), Flynn's sequel to the first part of her autobiography of her years with the IWW, opens with the account of her arrest:

On a hot morning in June 1951, the bell of our apartment on East 12th Street in New York City rang insistently. A knock came on the door, too soon for anyone to have climbed the three flights of stairs after we had pressed the button to open the downstairs door. There were two groups apparently, one already waiting outside our apartment. My young niece was preparing for school. My sister Kathie was cooking breakfast. She opened the door and I heard her scream out indignantly.

Three FBI agents, two men and a woman, roughly pushed their way past her. They stated they had a warrant for my arrest. (9)

Three decades later, in September 1981, the Egyptian writer and feminist Nawal al-Saadawi was working at home on her latest novel when she was interrupted by Anwar Sadat's *mukhabarat*, or secret service, who had come to arrest her. Al-Saadawi's prison narrative, *Memoirs from the Women's Prison*, opens with that insistent "knock on the door," so violent this time that the door to her apartment is itself physically damaged. The knock ruptures the constitutive nexus of her multiple relations to children, to husband, and to writing, and the physical premises, her home, on which these are grounded.

Within the narrative of political detention, which is the attempted physical appropriation by the state of the political and personal identity of the detainee, the "knock on the door" can be reconstrued as a political variant of the more blatant practice of "house demolition." Other variants include the concomitant operations of surveillance, intelligence, and the government's bureaucratic archivalization of political opposition, in what Herbert Mitgang (1988), in his study of the FBI's covert war against United States writers, has labeled "dangerous dossiers." Mitgang cites Chief Justice Louis Brandeis's dissenting opinion in the 1928 Supreme Court case *Olmstead v. United States*, which declared that evidence obtained through wiretapping was legal and admissible in court. Justice Brandeis stated: "Subtler and more far-reaching means of invading privacy have become available to the government. Discovery and invention have made it possible for the government, by means far more effective than stretching upon the rack, to obtain disclosure in court of what is whispered in the closet" (Mitgang, 6). So prevalent has this kind of surveillance become in the United States in the decades since *Olmstead v. United States*, and so desecrated the domestic and organizational territory of political belief, that the Center for Constitutional Rights (CCR) in 1985 issued an instructional pamphlet outlining in brief the rights that an individual still has even "if an agent knocks." According to the CCR, "A major job of FBI agents is to convince people to give up their rights to silence and privacy" (6); its recommendation: "Politeness aside, the wisest policy is never to let agents inside. They are trained investigators and will make it difficult for you to refuse to talk. Once inside your home or office, just by looking around, they can easily gather information about your lifestyle, organization and reading habits" (8).

Political detention, while it can be specifically located within a configuration of ideological confrontations between what Western literary historiography terms the individual and society, rearticulates the narrative of those confrontations instead as the state versus an organized political opposition. The symbolically overdetermined significance of "home" and identity remains central to such conflicted narratives.

Critical to the contested construction of "home" is the position a woman occupies in it, a position to which she may be confined as much by the resistance as by the state. The concept of "home," with its attendant philosophies of female domesticity and female sexuality, can be appropriated or violated, even in the valiant, if adventurist, efforts to defend it. For example, in *Gringo Justice* (1987), a history of the legal and economic dispossession of Mexican American citizens in the United States, Alfredo Mirande cites the description by Tiburcio Vasquez, a nineteenth-century California *"bandido,"* of the initial impulses to his personal history of rebellion. Vasquez said:

211

My career grew out of the circumstances by which I was surrounded. As I grew up to manhood, I was in the habit of attending balls and parties given by the native Californians, into which the Americans, then beginning to become numerous, would force themselves and shove the native born men aside, *monopolizing the dance and the women*. This was about 1852. A spirit of hatred and revenge took possession of me. I had numerous fights in defense of what I believed to be *my rights* and those of my countrymen. (cited in Mirande 1987, 77, emphasis added)

The history of Mexican "banditry" to which Vasquez belongs, traced by Mirande and others,[1] thus serves both the dominant interests of the United States in criminalizing Chicano opposition movements and the oppositional construction of a heroic counternarrative of a *machismo*-type liberation struggle.

The "tyranny of home" that is written perforce into this Chicano counternarrative, often in unacknowledged complicity with its "gringo" counterpart, is at once exposed and challenged from within in the work of contemporary Chicana writers. "Neighbors," a short story by Helena Maria Viramontes (1985), condenses in the history of Aura Rodriguez a larger narrative of the Chicano population in a major United States urban center, a narrative that displays the indigenized internal generational and gender contradictions as these are reproduced and exacerbated by the topographic and demographic alterations engineered by what are euphemistically referred to as "urban renewal" programs. For example, Fierro, Aura's neighbor of many years, must now take the freeway's pedestrian overpass in order to reach the Senior Citizen Luncheon Center. "The endless freeway," he thinks to himself in crossing it, "paved over his sacred ruins, his secrets, his graves, his fertile soil in which all memories were seeded and waiting for the right time to flower, and he could do nothing" (106). Aura's past and her memories, however, are planted in her front yard: the chinaberry tree, the chayotes, gardenias, and rosebushes, some of them "twenty years old, having begun as cuttings from her mother's garden" (111). Aura's garden was her last bastion, her refuge against the encroachments of both the expanding metropolis and the neighborhood's burgeoning younger generation: "Aura Rodriguez always stayed within her perimeters, both personal and otherwise, and expected the same of her neighbors. . . . Like those who barricaded themselves against an incomprehensible generation, Aura had resigned herself to live with the caution and silence of an apparition . . . without hurting anyone, including herself" (102).

212

These storied barricades, however, which Aura has erected of chayote and chinaberry trees, are not impregnable, and one day, when the elderly woman can no longer tolerate either the noise of the boys from the street or their empty beer cans in her front yard, Aura calls the police. The boys are arrested, even Toastie, on whom she closes her door when he tries to flee apprehension, only to be quickly released, to take the revenge that Ruben had threatened her with "as the patrol cars drove off" (109). Aura wakes one morning to find her many plants, like Fierro's memories, uprooted. But it is her own neighbors this time, not the urban planners, who have wreaked the damage and painted the walls of her house with Bixby Boys *placa* and graffiti. By summoning the police in a defiant act of self-defense, Aura has doubly transgressed the externally imposed internal codes of her riven community. Neither the police nor the "barrio warriors" can protect her from the historicized conflicts of gender and exploitation. Aura, despairing and defeated, descends into her dark cellar to rummage among the damp, decayed remnants of her past to retrieve the gun that has been hidden away there these many years. To what buried history of a forgotten resistance does Aura appeal in her recovery of the gun? And to what end? The implicit question goes unanswered, but when, at the end of the story, Aura finally fires the weapon at the unidentified caller on her front porch, it is not clear whom, if anyone, she may have hit. Was it perhaps the strange woman who had come from nowhere to live with her neighbor Fierro, and who was at that moment seeking help for Fierro, who has just died following an unusual meal of beans, chilies, and tortillas? It may be that the police cars will next visit the neighborhood for Aura, who, alone, needed to protect her home.

The history of the "tyranny of home" in which Aura Rodriguez is shown to have self-destructively collaborated in Viramontes's story "Neighbors" is constructed again through the individual pieces of a collective narration assembled in Sandra Cisneros's semi-autobiographical

House on Mango Street (1984). The women of Mango Street are "prisoners," each in her own way, of the reification of their traditional past in their present circumstances, and it is the dream of Esperanza, *Mango Street*'s child-narrator, to escape the coercive confinement of her home in the Mango Street neighborhood. In this neighborhood others, "those who don't know any better," are scared, but outside of it, in a "neighborhood of another color," it is instead Esperanza's "knees that go shakity-shake" (29).

Esperanza's great-grandmother, the girl says, "looked out the window   213
all her life, the way so many women sit their sadness on an elbow. . . . Esperanza. I have inherited her name, but I don't want to inherit her place by the window" (12). On Mango Street, women like Esperanza's great-grandmother, who as a girl was carried off by her husband-to-be with a sack over her head (12), are tyrannized by their husbands, who will not let them go out. When Rafaela's husband plays dominoes on Tuesday nights, for example, she asks the children in the street to bring her coconut and papaya juices from the store to alleviate the bitterness of her confinement. Other women, like Rosa Vargas and Minerva, have been abandoned by their husbands, but the many (too many) children left with them create still other restrictions. In Sally's case, it is her father, first of all, who refuses to allow his daughter egress into the world outside. Sally's early escape into marriage, however, only reproduces the closed structures she thought to have left behind.

For the woman who has only just arrived from Mexico with her infant son, after her husband had saved enough money, however, that same "new world" outside is forbidding: "Whatever her reasons, whether she is fat or can't climb the stairs or is afraid of English, she won't come down. She sits all day by the window and plays the Spanish radio show and sings all the homesick songs about her country in a voice that sounds like a seagull" (74). Outside the protective custody of home wait perhaps the police or, more threateningly, La Migra, the agents of the United States Immigration and Naturalization Service (INS), authorized to patrol the national borders and protect the country's internal security from "illegal aliens."

If *The House on Mango Street* is an exposé of an inherited masculinist tyranny over women, it is furthermore a critique of the exploitative contradictions built into the "American dream" and its failure to accommodate within its conflicted panorama the challenges to its hegemonic dominion that come from beyond its self-defined borders.[2] The house that Esperanza plans for herself proposes a counterblueprint to that drawn with freeways and defended by the police system: "I want a house on a hill like the ones with the gardens where Papa works. . . . One day I'll own my own house, but I won't forget who I am or where I came from. Passing bums will ask, Can I come in? I'll offer them the attic, ask them to stay, because I know how it is to be without a house" (81).

The same edifices, the "homes" that have been made to contain tyrannically women in their domesticated solitary confinement, are ideologically reconstructed to other ends, liberated, as it were, by organized guerrilla and resistance movements looking to locate themselves and their operations strategically within a populous urban context. The calculated use of "safe houses" is critical to the program of an armed struggle against a military dictatorship or a police state. These "safe houses" provide, however temporarily, a base of operations in selected population centers from which to carry out attacks on specific vulnerable targets that symbolically or materially represent the regime and its state apparatus of repression. Following such public attacks, "safe houses" can also function as intermediate retreats or refuges, transitional passages underground for the individuals who have perpetrated the deeds and who must eventually regroup with the organization itself. Since "safe houses" remain safe only so long as they remain unknown as such to the military or police force, they thus require the witting or unwitting cooperation and tacit assent from the other inhabitants of the neighborhood.

The selection of buildings to serve as "safe houses," when not the fortuitous consequence of emergency circumstances, is perforce of utmost significance to the resistance organization. In making such a designation, the organization must adequately assess and integrate the material factors of physical location with the ideological issues of the nature and development of the relationships between, on the one hand, the revolutionaries and commandos and, on the other, the popular masses on whose support, even when it is passive, the organization must rely.

The sociopolitical issues attaching to "safe houses" arose, for example, when the Ejercito Revolucionario del Pueblo (ERP), one of El Salvador's armed resistance movements, decided in 1976 to kidnap Roberto Poma, a prominent figure within the nation's oligarchic elite, in order to arrange his exchange for members of their own organization held by the military in one of El Salvador's secret prisons. The need for an appropriate "safe house" was essential to the success of their plan. Ana Guadalupe Martinez (1980), one of the exchanged political detainees, describes the choice of a location in the second part of her prison memoir:

One of the many problems to be resolved in this kind of operation is the arrangement for holding the prisoner. The tasks to be done have their own characteristics and require solutions to such problems as: that the personnel be the best for maintaining the premises; that conditions be such as to prevent the escape of the prisoner; that conditions allow for an eventual retreat; and that there be all the features of normality of an ordinary family in keeping with the characteristics of the house and the area in which it is situated. (281)

Guadalupe Martinez goes on to describe the effective and purposeful ideological transformation of the selected house: "After having rejected several houses, one was located that combined all the conditions necessary for its conversion into a People's Prison [*Carcel del Pueblo*]. It was paradoxical that a house normally inhabited by the bourgeoisie should in the space of a few short months be converted into a prison for one of the most powerful representatives of the country's bourgeoisie" (281). Part of that material transformation is the mimicry enacted by members of the ERP, who had to establish themselves as acceptable residents of the neighborhood. The house is rented formally and legally from one Dona Marta Guillen Alvarez de Milan, of El Salvador's coffee families, and the lease is signed in the presence of a lawyer and a notary (whose assistant, Guadalupe Martinez indicates, was subsequently arrested and brutally tortured by the police).

At a certain point, the guerrillas-cum-bourgeoisie begin to fear suspicion about the real nature of their activities, and they decide to escalate the artifices of their assimilation into the mores of the area:

obviously the house needed a lot more normal life, and so the collective decided to stage a party one Saturday night to complement the naturalness of its movements. A mariachi band was hired for the party who were somewhat amazed at the friendly and confident way in which they were treated. Scandalous parties are normal events for these people so it was quite certain that such an attitude would confirm for any witnesses to the party that the customs of the house were those of good bourgeois and thus of good neighbors. (285)

The ERP guerrillas' charades succeed, Poma is kidnapped, and Guadalupe Martinez and her fellow prisoner "Marcelo" are released and flown to freedom in Spain. Only later is it revealed that Poma had died in captivity of wounds received during the abduction, and Guadalupe Martinez analyzes the specific theoretical and ideological dangers with which sensational, even if apparently successful, actions like "Operation Roma" can be fraught, emphasizing especially the problems of vanguardism and militarism within the organization. At stake in her analysis are both the necessary relationship between the guerrillas and the people whose interests they claim to represent and the internal structural dynamics of the organization itself.

The contention over houses—the difference between the "tyranny of home" and "safe houses"—as it is played out in the armed political

215

struggle between the government and its opposition, as well as within the resistance organization, operates a sequence of ideologically charged displacements invested with the signficance of gender and class identifications. The combat of the military and the police to retake the "safe house" is thus also a combat to restore the authoritarian order of "domestic tranquility" and "national security."

Salvadoran Manlio Argueta's short story "Taking Over the Street" (1988) initiates a tense attempt to narrate these contested ideological contradictions intrinsic to the resistance organization's political agenda. The story is composed almost entirely in incomplete sentences that begin with "when . . .": "When it's Saturday. When she sees me as if she didn't want to. . . . When people talk about the secluded house in the San Jacinto barrio" (140). Written in the tenuous, inquiring voice of a man in hiding in a "safe house," "Taking Over the Street" testifies to the precarious temporariness of "safe houses," their tactical placement within the framework of a particular set of guerrilla operations whose consequences have yet to be played out, whose goals have yet to be realized.

The man in the story is bored. Time passes tediously. He is visited by the young girl Genoveva, who brings him water and coffee, and he is briefly tempted to respond more physically to her presence in his isolation. But Genoveva leaves, and back in the street, she is accosted by men in a patrol car. "When she refuses and they drag her to the car. When they ask her where she's coming from. When they knock loudly on the front door. When I leave through the patio in the back by the basin under the lemon tree" (142). Even then, however, the story is unable to tell its end: "When I take over the street and confront a November wind that makes one shed all the salt water, all the victories, and all that backward-upside-down freedom" (142). The "safe house" allows the *companero* to escape, but the street, still patrolled by government security agents, violently reclaims the young girl who has ministered to the guerrilla. The refuge offered by "safe houses" is yet tenuous, marking a still immanent private space within a popular domain. Inside that space the organized resistance movement must continue to expand its program beyond the limitations of its own internal structures to include popular mobilization and social transformation.

In two stories by Chicana writers, each based on the narrative and political manipulation of a discourse of boundaries, the apotropaic distance granted the First World critic by the very term "Third World" is strategically collapsed and its political complicity in the dominant ideology is exposed. "The Ditch" (1979), written by Rosaura Sanchez, is the story of an INS raid on migrant workers picking in the cotton fields. Alerted to the approach of the officials, the pickers run. The short narrative which tells the tale of their flight toward the ditch and safety, places the personal fate of the "illegal aliens" from south of the border within the context of the larger historical narrative of United States predations in Vietnam:

He ran fast, head down, stepping on whatever was in his path, be it cocklebur or thorny plants. He saw himself running through the field as others before him had run through rice paddies in Vietnam, as he himself had run when he crossed over the wire fence on the border. (182)

The historical consciousness of the "illegal aliens" acknowledges the political duplicity of a hegemonic language of nationalism: "It was an often repeated scene. They had only recently set up the radars on the border: it was hardware left over from the Vietnam War" (182). That same consciousness further reveals the agenda of destruction concealed in the duplicity: "Immigration officials were planning to clear the thicket with a little Napalm, left over as well from Vietnam" (183).

"The Ditch" is premised on the historical continuity between First and Third worlds, concealed in and by United States policy and the complicity of its "domestic" and foreign agendas; it thus collapses the dichotomies from within the system itself. In contrast, Helena Maria Viramontes's "The Cariboo Cafe" (1985) makes the border between the United States and its Central American "neighbors" a site of contestation. In Viramontes's story, borders become bonds among peoples, rather than the articulation of national differences and the basis for exclusion enforced by the collaboration of the United States and Salvadoran regimes. Borders, that is, function as a site of confrontation between popular and official interpretations of the historical narrative.

"The Cariboo Cafe" is set in an unnamed United States city that numbers Salvadoran refugees among its populations. Much as these refugees transgress national boundaries, as victims of political persecution who, by their very international mobility, challenge the ideology of national borders and its agenda of depoliticization in the interest of hegemony, so too the story refuses to respect the boundaries and conventions of literary critical time and space and their disciplining of plot and genre. No markers indicate the narrative breaks and shifts from the United States to El Salvador, and history remains to be reconstructed. Implicit in Viramontes's storied narrative, as Sonia Saldivar-Hull (forthcoming) has pointed out, is a documentary critique not only of the United States INS and the Salvadoran semiofficial paramilitary death squads, but of their active collaboration as well. This story of the Salvadoran woman refugee, self-expelled from her country when her son is abducted, and of the Chicano children, locked out of their home when they lose the key, thus

217

enjoins a historical awareness and a political reading from its audience no less than from its characters. It proposes, too, another historical narrative. Restructuring the traditional family order, "The Cariboo Cafe" assigns to women the task of a reformulation across borders of gender and race and insists on their place in the construction of identity and political struggle.

The tripartite structure (Guatemala/Mexico/Los Angeles) of Gregory Navas's film *El Norte* (1983), rather than representing a classical dialectical trajectory of development, a historical movement forward from **218** Third to First World cultural and political systems, critiques instead the very dichotomy between First and Third worlds as itself underwriting a dominant narrative of linear development. Rosa Xuncax and her brother Enrique flee their Indian village in Guatemala for "*el Norte*" when their father, a *campesino* and one of the leaders of the nascent peasant organization, is murdered and their mother abducted by the Guatemalan military in their massacre of the village. The violence and the exploitation of their village are only reproduced in Mexico, however, where the two young people are "conned" and mistreated by the Tijuana *coyotes* who, for a fee, lead migrants across the border, until at last they meet Raimundo Gutierrez, whom one of the villagers at home had recommended as experienced in the ways of border crossing. Gutierrez manages Rosa and Enrique's own passage across the border into the United States through abandoned, rat-infested drainage pipes, and further arranges work and a place for them to stay with one of his contacts in southern California. But here too, in the United States, "*el Norte*," the young pair's brief experience of refuge and a "safe haven" is destroyed by ethnic conflict when Enrique, working as a waiter in a plush restaurant, is exposed to La Migra by a Chicano coworker who is envious that "Ricky" has been promoted over him. Rosa, who has collapsed at her work as a domestic in a wealthy suburban home, dies of noninfectious typhus from the rat bites suffered in the border crossing, in a hospital that she feared to go to lest she be recognized as "illegal" and deported back to Guatemala.

The structures of exploitation and oppression, grounded in the intersecting and mutually reinforcing differences of gender, race, and class, are produced and reproduced in the three parts to *El Norte*.[3] In Guatemala, the Xuncax family, as Indians and *campesinos*, is victimized by the landed *ladino* classes. In Mexico, the brother and sister must conceal their Guatemalan identity and pose as Mexican Indians from Oaxaca so as not to be discovered by the Mexican authorities. And finally in the United States, the historically and systemically manipulated class and ethnic differences brutally disable any solidarity among Enrique's fellow restaurant workers.

As it goes beyond the issues of race and class, the death of Rosa at the conclusion of the film is not solely an aesthetically conditioned closure. Rosa's development as a politically engaged participant in her fate began in Guatemala, where it had always been the men who organized politically while the women worried at home about their safety. The development represented by her decision to accompany her brother into exile must be contained. Unlike Enrique's smitten reaction to the lures of the "American dream," her steadfast refusal, like her resistance to the traditional female subjection in Guatemala, is shown to be intolerable, even north of the border. The three-part structure of *El Norte*, with its apparent use of the dialectical model, instead employs that model precisely in order to subvert the teleology it implies. The Enlightenment paradigm of progress as practiced from within the metropolitan centers of power is revealed as illusory, a calculated deception designed to obfuscate the repetitiousness of exploitation across borders, whether based on national boundaries or on distinctions of gender, race, and class. Neither "progress" nor the "luck" that Enrique insistently invokes can save him and Rosa.

The "border culture" that is developing along the nearly two-thousand-mile divide that separates the United States and its neighbor Mexico is premised on a system of material exploitation and human abuse implemented by the combined and complementary self-interests of multinational capital and the foreign and domestic policies of the United States. South of the border are the *maquiladoras*, the cross-border factories with their underpaid female labor force, and chemical waste dumps for U.S. industry; north of the border are *colonias*, the migrant settlement camps, and INS holding centers for "illegal aliens," such as El Centro in California or Port Isabel in Texas. The multiple dimensions to this "border culture" and the narratives that are generated out of it testify significantly to the material and political implications of First World economic agendas in Third World social and cultural production. The "border" demarcates a critical space for restaging the categorical geopolitical distinctions that function rhetorically to separate First and Third worlds. Such "border crossings," with the very real risks that they entail for their perpetrators, threaten as well the enormous political apparatus constructed around an ideology of the "defense of national borders." Those borders, alternately opened and closed to migrant labor over the past century as the economic needs of United States industry and agriculture have required, are being submitted now to the more political imperatives of another interpretation as increased numbers of refugees from civil war, repression, and persecution in El Salvador and Guatemala transgress their definitions.

As part of the program of national defense, immigration policymakers in the United States have sought, in response to this human influx, to implement a constructed distinction between economic migrants and political refugees that would selectively allow asylum to refugees from countries, such as Castro's Cuba, Khomeini's Iran, and Sandinista Nicaragua, whose governments the United States has attempted to subvert, but would deny political refugee status to applicants from countries with United States-backed regimes, such as El Salvador and Guatemala as well as discriminating against Cambodians, Vietnamese, and Haitians, to name but a few applicants. Despite the intensified border vigilance and the continued policing of the citizen population, the persistent presence of "illegal aliens" in the United States constitutes what has been termed **220** an unprecedented act of civil disobedience. According to Peter Schey, a Los Angeles attorney originally from South Africa who specializes in immigration law:

This country saw massive anti-war movements. This country saw a massive movement, a grass-roots movement, to support the rights of Black persons. I do not think that North America has ever seen the kind of civil disobedience that is going on with the mass of undocumented persons that are here today. It is the biggest single act of civil disobedience in the history of North America. (cited in Lewis 1979, 124)

What Alfredo Mirande critically called "gringo justice" is epitomized in the epithet "illegal alien," an integral part of the rhetoric of the "defense of national borders" and attached by the Border Patrols to "border crossers." "El Ilegal" (The Illegal) was the defiant title to a poem found in a notebook belonging to Rosario Caldera Salazar. It portended ominously, however, the fate legislated for those who broke with the system. Caldera Salazar, age unknown, was one of the eighteen Mexican nationals who suffocated to death in a railroad boxcar on 3 July 1987 in El Paso, Texas. A poetic eulogy to Salazar appeared in the *El Paso Herald Post* (3 July 1987):

How beautiful is the United States
Illinois, California and Tennessee.
But over in my country,
A piece of the sky belongs to me.

Goodbye Laredo, Weslaco and San Antonio.
Houston and Dallas are in my song.
Goodbye, El Paso. I am back Chamizal.
Your friend, the illegal, has returned.

If the "illegal alien" movement may be deemed the "biggest single act of civil disobedience in the history of North America," the six-year-long prayer vigil in Tucson, Arizona, on behalf of Central American refugees, which began on 19 February 1981, has been called by Anne Crittenden (1988) in her study of the sanctuary movement "the longest running continuous demonstration in the United States" (26). The sanctuary movement is a loose coalition of church and lay workers that formed in 1981 (and consolidated nationally in 1982) to provide assistance in the United States to Central Americans fleeing persecution in their home countries. Its work has been compared to that of the "underground railroad," which assisted United States slaves escaping to freedom a century earlier. Sixteen of its members were charged in Arizona on several felony accounts of smuggling and transporting "illegal aliens." Following a six-month trial, fourteen of the defendants were found guilty on various charges on 1 July 1986 in a United States court in Tucson, Arizona.

Since its cautious, grass-roots emergence in Tucson's Southside Presbyterian Church and, subsequently, its more spectacular, media-covered defeat at the hands of federal judges and prosecutors, Sanctuary has been the subject of several important studies, each of which has chosen to emphasize a particular aspect of the movement. Miriam Davidson's *Convictions of the Heart: Jim Corbett and the Sanctuary Movement* (1988) constructs its heroized account around Jim Corbett, one of the most prominent figures associated with Sanctuary. By contrast, *Sanctuary: The New Underground Railroad* (1986) by Renny Golden and Michael McConnell, both members of the Chicago Religious Task Force on Central America (CRTFCA) and both "conductors" on the "underground railroad," is elaborated around testimony from the refugees themselves, those who have accepted public sanctuary and agreed to tell their story to a larger audience. Robert Tomsho's *American Sanctuary Movement* (1987) elides these more problematic alternatives in his more straightforward narrative, reporting simply on the evolving opposition of United States citizens to their government's policies in Central America. Finally, in *Sanctuary: A Story of American Conscience and Law in Collision* (1988), Anne Crittenden divides the Sanctuary story into the popular narrative of its local development in Arizona and a reportage of the federal government's machinated assault on what it saw as a domestic threat to its own civic authority and national-political hegemony. The apparently academic or literary differences in point of view, character, plot, and setting that distinguish these several accounts represent, however, important critical debates both within the movement itself, between religious and political priorities and the respective roles of Sanctuary workers and refugees, and between Sanctuary and the United States public around the strategic efforts to construct a coherent historical counternarrative.

To dislocate the refugees' personal narratives of physical violence and political dispossession from the Sanctuary story is to reproduce discursively and from within the very site of North American "sanctuary" the same brutal disenfranchisement in their home countries from which the exiled have fled. The significance of those narratives is primarily to ground the historical consequence of Sanctuary in a larger geopolitical arena.

Moreover, the refugees' accounts of persecution and escape signal new conditions of cultural production, challenging the aesthetic, generic, and disciplinary cordons that have sought to neutralize, and when necessary to control, the political consequentiality of literary/critical work. In an asylum application, for example, the political refugee must demonstrate that serious physical danger awaits her/him in the country of origin if the request is denied and the asylum seeker is thereby deported. The INS I-589 forms and the affidavits attached to them impose new standards and criteria of style and composition, emphasizing legality and bureaucratic admissibility, on narrative and autobiographical reconstructions of personal itineraries. These "travel narratives" require the active, if untoward, collaboration of lawyers, translators, writers, and the refugees themselves. Neither (strictly and generically speaking) *testimonio* nor autobiography, the application for political asylum and the accompanying affidavits, elaborate, even if secondarily, new possibilities for literature and its criticism as part of a collective written assault on the legal structures and political institutions of the state.

Similarly, for those refugees who have agreed to accept, often at considerable risk to themselves, "public sanctuary"—who have agreed, that is, to narrate publicly, in churches and town meetings, their personal histories in order to educate a United States audience about the situation in El Salvador or Guatemala—the challenge of authorship is inescapably implicated in the challenge to authority. Often, out of fear for their own safety or that of their families, fear of the retaliation that might come from their exposure and identification, the refugees make their public statements from behind masks. The bandanas covering the lower part of their faces recreated for some observers the image of the old *bandido*. Rather than criminalizing the political refugee, however, this fortuitously symbolic appropriation provides intepretative possibilities for rethinking an earlier "social banditry" in political terms.

The refugee testimony, perhaps more than even the sanctuary movement itself, is anathema to the United States government and its combined geographical and ideological border-defense mechanisms. Thus when preliminary preparations for the Sanctuary trial were taking place, Judge Earl Hamblin Carroll, in compliance with the request of prosecutor Don Reno, precluded the defense from introducing as evidence any reference to either the religious convictions of the defendants or the background and current plight of the political refugees. Indeed the term "refugee" was itself to be excluded as prejudicial from the court's proceedings. The judge not only ruled against any discussion of United States foreign policy or immigration restrictions, but also dismissed a priori any "alleged episodes, stories or tales of civil strife, war, or terrorism that may have occurred or are occurring in Central American countries, and particularly in El Salvador" (220). According to Anne Crittenden (1988), Reno "knew that if the trial got into discussions of refugee policy and definitions of what a refugee was or what religious freedom was, he'd be a certified loser. His first task, then, as he saw it, was to convince the judge to see the case at its simplest level: Did these people engage in a conspiracy to smuggle aliens into the country? He had to curtail seriously what the defense could say in the courtroom or, he feared, he would have a fiasco on his hands" (219). The judge concurred.   **223**

To whom can, or should, political refugees be allowed to narrate their stories? In his pretrial ruling, Judge Carroll, on behalf of the United States government and its current judicial apparatus, actively intervened in the processes of history-making to eradicate these narratives from the public record. Thus, not unlike the self-appointed protectors of the literary canon, he acted to suppress the *testimonio* as a valid genre, as an authoritative report of personal and historical experience, as autobiography, or as admissible evidence in a public trial in a United States courtroom. Both institutionalized and accredited positions work to produce an expurgated and sanitized version of United States immigrant history.

Unlike the Sanctuary trial in Arizona, the trial of the Winooski Forty-four in Vermont did allow for the use of the "necessity defense" in presenting the case for the defendants.[4] On 29 March 1984, forty-four people were arrested and charged with illegal trespass, having occupied for three days the offices of United States Senator Robert Stafford in Winooski, Vermont. Their trial took place in November 1984, and twenty-six of those charged entered a plea of "not guilty" on the grounds that they were acting against a United States-sponsored war in Central America in order to prevent a still greater harm to the peoples of the region than that occasioned by the Vermonters' actions in their senator's local offices. In allowing for the necessity defense in this case, Judge Frank A. Mahady allowed too for the radical reconstruction of a larger historical narrative that incorporated earlier United States traditions of popular dissent and civil disobedience, international law, political *testimonio*, and expert witness on CIA involvement in Angola and destabilization of the Sandinista government in Nicaragua.

Por Amor al Pueblo: ¡Not Guilty! (Bradley et al. 1986), the transcript of the week-long trial of the Winooski Forty-four, dramatically re-presents, as document and as script, that contested narrative. The prosecution in the trial sought only to establish whether an act of illegal trespass had been knowingly committed by the defendants and whether they believed that the public meeting with Senator Stafford that they demanded "would have stopped the war in El Salvador." The defense, however, moved to reconstitute through its series of witnesses the possible scenarios of causality that would eventually link such a public meeting with the outcome of the war in El Salvador. Calling on witnesses that included Salvadoran refugees Sonia Hernandez and Gladis Sanchez, distinguished professors of law and political science such as Richard Falk and Howard Zinn, former CIA officer John Stockwell, former attorney general Ramsey Clark, epidemiologist Richard Garfield, and experts on Central and South America such as Janet Shenk of North American Congress on Latin America (NACLA) and anthropologist Philippe Bourgois, the defense succeeded not only in obtaining a verdict of "not guilty" and acquittals for the twenty-six defendants, but in contributing as well to rewriting a contemporary United States policy of global domination, particularly that of the Reagan regime, into a multivocal geopolitical narrative of contestation and resistance.

The questions of political asylum, of "safe houses," and of sanctuary collectively propose strategies of resistance to various "tyrannies of home." Critical to these strategies is the articulation, from out of that tyrannized space and across borders, of a counternarrative to a modern truncated history that continues to underwrite and legitimate systemic and systematic domination, dispossession, and exploitation. The consequences of such testimonies, inimical as they are to the repressive regimes, are nonetheless incontrovertible. In *Forced to Move* (Camarda 1985), a collection of testimonies from the Salvadoran refugees displaced and relocated in Honduran camps, thirteen-year-old Felicita, a Salvadoran refugee in the Mesa Grande camp, states: "In that same way they have taken other people quite a few times and we, the children, have gone to follow them, but there's times when they do it and we don't see them, and then the prisoners can't be found any more" (30).

A German woman medical doctor reports on what she has learned from the women at Colomancagua camp:

I also learned that, yes, machismo is strong there, but the women organize also, in the midst of such a difficult situation.

As a woman, I was accepted, but perhaps differently since I was a foreigner. In reality I lived like a man: I wasn't washing any clothes, I didn't have children, my life was all oriented towards work which was not domestic, whereas the refugee women had to do two things: they worked in the workshops and the health centers and they also had to work in the tents. They would always ask me about my life in Germany, because they wanted to know what the women did there. (Camarda 1985, 48)

The "tyranny of home" must eventually be located as part of the rhetoric of the "defense of national borders."

Chapter Ten

Prison and Liberation

Household management lost its public character. It no longer concerned society. It became a private service; the wife became head servant, excluded from all participation in social production. . . . The modern individual family is founded on the open or concealed domestic slavery of the wife and modern society is a mass composed of these individual families as its molecules. In the great majority of cases today at least in the possessing classes, the husband is obliged to earn a living and support his family, and that in itself gives him a position of supremacy, without any need for special legal titles and privileges. Within the family he is the bourgeois and the wife represents the proletariat.   F. ENGELS, *The Origin of the Family*

. . . the foremost need to break this role of housewife that wants women divided from each other, from men, and from children, each locked in her family as the chrysalis in the cocoon that imprisons itself by its own work, to die and leave silk for capital.
                         MARIAROSA DALLA COSTA AND SELMA JAMES,
                         The Power of Women and the Subversion of Community

How often do women awake
in the prison of marriage,
of solitary motherhood
      alone and forgotten.
. . . .
And how short a step it is
      —for us—to the more obvious imprisonment
      of bars and concrete
      where our sisters lie
      alone   forgotten.
                         ERICKA HUGGINS, untitled poem written in prison

All right, good bye then, one can't even inquire about one's blood relations any more.
                         MANLIO ARGUETA, *One Day of Life*

"The Woolen Sweater" tells the story of a Palestinian mother who, after days of searching, finally finds her son in an Israeli prison. He has sent her a message, complaining of the cold and the prison conditions and asking that she knit him a sweater to wear in prison. When next the mother visits her son, she finds him in shirtsleeves and an Iraqi prisoner clad in the sweater she has made. The boy explains to her that he allows his fellow prisoner, who has been arrested as a partisan of the Palestinian resistance, to have the sweater at night, while the son wears it during the day. "Tears of joy came to the mother's eyes at this, that she could help out the *fidai* who had travelled from a distant land to sacrifice his blood." "The Woolen Sweater" is included in *Night . . . and the Grand Dawn* (Abd al-Majid 1982), a collection of reports, stories, and letters from women in prison and their families outside.

It is a simple anecdote, this story of a mother who learns from her imprisoned son the lessons of resistance, but it demonstrates the contestatory connections that can be practiced across institutional walls and national boundaries. It proposes as well an immanent analysis of the hegemonic ideological system of gender and ethnic distinctions and the state apparatuses that support it. This complex system of the imperialist domination of Zionism and the complicity of the reactionary Arab regimes, together with traditional patriarchy, exploits both mother and son, as well as the Iraqi participant in their liberation. The implied strategies of resistance, as the mother learns, are necessarily collective.

The political education of the mother by her son in prison is told again in Izat al-Ghazawi's short story "The Woman Prisoner" (1985).[1] In this tale, Um Saber, an elderly Palestinian woman living under Israeli occupation, must find her way by bus to the prison south of Jerusalem where her son is being detained. A peasant or *fallaha* who does not know how to read, she is unable to identify the bus by its number or the destination indicated on the placard placed over the front window. Assisted by a man in the bus station, Um Saber locates the correct vehicle, only to find herself uncertain where to disembark. She counts the stops to herself exactly as she has been told to do and eventually finds her son in his imprisonment. The short story narrates only the beginnings, one episode, of an arduous journey for Um Saber, a journey on which she will be obliged to transgress again and again the boundaries of tradition that have long domesticated her. She reviews her past, considers the story of village weddings, and thinks her lesson to herself as she faces her son Saber in the prison: "I wonder, are you the prisoner or am I? We are both prisoners, my son. But your prison is less confining than mine. I wonder what your world is like now? You said last time that prison is another world to which one becomes accustomed with time. As for my world, it's you even though you have made me enter worlds larger than my comprehension. Perhaps, Saber, that was the secret of my power to withstand."

The experience of prison and political detention is a systemic and endemic fact of daily life in much of the contemporary Third World. Well-established and alarming statistics and documentation by concerned individuals and international organizations attest to the brutal disruption of people's lives practiced by systematic state oppression against various populations. In Argentina, for example, at least thirteen thousand people "disappeared" between 1976 and 1983 under the dictatorship of the generals and the army. A new word was thereby added to the international political lexicon: *desaparecido*, disappeared, and the verb "to disappear" acquired a transitive usage. To take another example, approximately 30 percent of the Palestinian population living under Israeli occupation had passed through the Israeli prison system prior to the *intifada*. And in South Africa, some fifteen thousand individuals, many of them children, were detained between 1986, when the state of emergency was declared, and 1988. Rare, then, are the families in these and similar contexts whose integrity and cohesion have not been violated by detention, disappearance, or imprisonment.

The political and historical fact of prison and political detention has in turn had a significant effect on the strategies for women's organizing in those countries where it is most egregious. In Argentina Los Madres de la Playa, the Mothers of the Plaza, consolidated the efforts of individual women to locate their missing family members. Meeting one another day after day, in the corridors and anterooms of government offices, army headquarters, and police stations, the women eventually joined ranks, finding common, public cause in their private searches, and took to the streets. The white scarves that they wore and the placards and photographs of loved ones that they carried weekly transformed the Plaza de Mayo, surrounded by government buildings and banks, into a contested space of popular political challenge to bureaucratic authoritarianism. In Israel and the Occupied Territories Palestinian mothers of the detained, the *ummahat al-ghaʾibin*, gathered to demonstrate each Friday in front of Israeli prisons, often lending their support to the prisoners' coordinated hunger strikes protesting abusive prison conditions and the lack of visiting privileges. In El Salvador, COMADRES, the committee of mothers, several times occupied the Metropolitan Cathedral in San Salvador, only to be violently evicted by police and military force. In May 1987, their offices, which housed their documentation and information concerning the detained and the disappeared, were bombed and destroyed, obliging the women to seek temporary premises with the National Union of Salvadoran Workers (UNTS), the organization of Salvadoran trade unions. Many of the political prisoners in Ilopango, El Salvador's women's prison, are there because they are accused of participation in COMADRES ac-

227

tivities. The South African apartheid government similarly acknowledged the effectiveness of women's organizations by making it illegal in March 1986 to demonstrate in support of political prisoners, thereby hampering the work of the Detainees' Parents Support Committee.

These committees of mothers, alike in their collective challenge to a dominant ideology and repressive regimes, yet different in their specific historical and material conditions, have emerged to play a vanguard role in reorganizing traditional social structures and the ascendant relationships of power in those countries where they have developed in response to crises of oppression. Included in these patterns is the very concept of "mother" as promulgated by patriarchy, the bourgeois nuclear family, and an extended kinship network. The "contemporary global crisis," according to Michele Mattelart in *Women, Media and Crisis* (1986), must "find a solution to a number of specific contradictions which arise from the unrest among women, to whom—because of their restricted autonomy—the ruling culture has assigned a regulatory or pacifying role, and responsibility for maintaining a balance in society" (1). From country to country, and in rural and urban settings, this role is being transformed by organizations of women protesting prison.

Following the Israeli invasion of Lebanon in 1982, the male population of southern Lebanon, both Lebanese and Palestinian, was decimated by massive detentions in the Israeli prison camp that came to be known as Ansar.[2] *Zahrat al-Qandul* (Wild Flower), a 1986 film by the Lebanese directors Mai Masri and Jean Chamoun, documents, through a combination of interviews, newsreel footage, and restaging of events, the resistance organized by the women during the absence of their men. The film is structured around a journal kept by one of the women and her reading of it to her recently released husband. She herself has been imprisoned as a result of her activities with the women, and her recitation is frequently intersected by the narratives of other women from the village—grandmothers, mothers, and teenagers—telling tales of stone-throwing, homes bulldozed, children killed, and efforts to visit male relatives detained in Ansar. The film refuses the paradigmatic conclusions legislated by the social traditions of patriarchy and the conventions of bourgeois romance. It continues beyond the weddings celebrated upon the release of the prisoners, beyond also the birth of new children to the reunited couples, and ends with the various women discussing the multiple systems of exploitation to which they have been subjected. The final words of resistance, spoken by the diarist-prisoner, not to her husband but to the audience, reopen the issue of the ending.

Prior to the collective resistance exemplified by COMADRES or these women of southern Lebanon, (prior if not chronologically then in terms of the ideology of a conventional itinerary leading *from* an individual coming-to-consciousness *to* the establishment of affiliative ties among women and the organized resistance of women and men) is the narrative of the woman—mother, wife, sister, daughter—leaving the confines, at once re-assuring in their traditional familiarity and historically constricting, of her domestic space for the public arena of political conflict. The story of the mother who, like Um Saber or the maker of the woolen sweater, visits her son in political detention and discovers there, outside her home and behind those other walls, the grounds of her own potential liberation has **229** acquired the status of a locus classicus within the literature of prison. That liberation is figured, in all its permutations from culture to culture and at the risk of reducing a historicizing process to the simplifications of formula, in the several pieces to the mother's story: the journey itself from home to prison, a rite of passage with its own sequence of obstacles to overcome and trials to undergo; the exemplary encounter with the male child—or with the fact of his disappearance; and finally, the return to a social order that must in its turn change to accommodate the critical and conscientized transformations of its mothers—or suppress their demands.

"She Affirms Her Right to Self-Determination" (1989), a short story written under the pseudonym of Angela T. Magsilang, recounts the visit of a Filipina mother, Aling Gabriela, to her son Jerry, who has been detained and is now held in the military stockade of Camp Crane.[3] Refused permission by the young guard at the camp gate to see her son because he is an "activist" (therefore "it's prohibited for him to be seen"), Aling Gabriela challenges the guard, his automatic carbine, and the bureaucratic system that he represents. "It's the people in the government who are wicked," the old woman shouts in outrage. Her loud protests are heard by the bystanders and passersby who have slowly but insistently collected in a crowd around her. While Aling Gabriela remains "completely oblivious" to the growing audience to her personal challenge, her individual defiance has its own mobilizing consequences. When the mother violently accuses the prison system of having killed her son, the guard strikes her "shriveled chest" with the butt of his gun. The old woman turns and runs from the compound, shouting her accusation, but at each corner, at every intersection, more and more "people are congregated" (96).

The charges of this mother, denied visitation rights to her activist son, the political prisoner, had to be silenced: "They needed to cut short her shouting, they needed to drown her words so that people would not hear what she was saying." The story ends when Aling Gabriela is shot to death in the street: "Aling Gabriela fell and crumpled on the sidewalk, but countless people saw what happened. And many hundreds more heard and knew. . . ." The elliptical conclusion, however, proposes a sequel, one that will follow from the mother's exemplum. The ellipsis itself formally marks the political potential inherent still in the story, the material manifestation of its immanent historical transformation. E. San Juan (1986b) has written of the special tension in the poetry of Jose Ma. Sison, a Filipino writer, revolutionary, and political prisoner: "Sison's poems are thus incomplete, denied organic closure, because the materialist textualization of struggle escapes from the prison-house of language to emancipate itself in the discourse of physical combat" (18); the pseudonymous story of the Filipina mother in search of her detained son promises another kind of emancipation, that of the mother from her home and the mobilization through her death of a popular resistance.

Jose Ma. Sison was perhaps the premier political prisoner of the Philippines under Ferdinand Marcos. Arrested in 1977 on charges of subversion and rebellion, and alleged by the government to be the founding chairman of the Communist party of the Philippines, Sison was held for most of his period of detention in solitary confinement. Even under these dire circumstances, he continued to develop in his vocation as a political poet. Many of the poems composed in prison and published in *Prison and Beyond* (1986) answer significantly to the newly evolving gender relations under the pressure of political struggle. "Wisdom from a Comrade" (70), written in December 1977, asserts the still undeveloped potential of women to comprehend the politically committed message of their men:

> A Red fighter had died in the battle
> And his sweetheart was grieving.
> A comrade went over to her and said,
> "He was my best pal and I am also sad
> But I am happy too and proud of him
> For he was to the end a revolutionary
> And nothing can ever change that"

A few months later, Sison speaks directly to his own wife, in "You Are My Wife and Comrade" (99), urging her to meet the challenge imposed by the dictatorship on their relationship:

> You are my wife and comrade.
> It is harsh that we are kept apart
> By a bloodthirsty enemy with many snares.
> We care for each other's welfare

Mila D. Aguilar (1987), detained by the Marcos regime in August 1984, constructs in complementary contrast to the poems of Sison the same transformed gender patterns, according to the new relationships enabled by the resistance movement among women.[4] Aguilar's poem "Someone There Is" (16) elaborates an altered version of the mother-daughter paradigm in politicized terms:

> Someone there is
> whom you cannot forget:
> the way she'd slide her hand in yours
> how soft her bosom
> to your beginner cadre's woes.

In "After Not Seeing Him Three Years" (19), Aguilar suggests too that renewed relational possibilities of gender have been adumbrated within the resistance against its own dominant masculinist orthodoxy by the ideological and physical rigors of political activism:

> How you've changed, Comrade,
> from the self-importance
> and the garrulousness of the past.
> What the revolution could do to us, indeed . . .

When Mila Aguilar was arrested she had only recently assumed a position in the Extension Service Center of Saint Joseph's College. In the "Message on the Launching of 'Why Cage Pigeons?'" (1987), her collection of prison poetry, she comments on the "irony" of her political situation:

I even remember being constantly reminded through the years that nobody, certainly not the men and neither the women, can at this stage of our history accept a woman as a top-ranking leader: what's more as *the* most top-ranking! . . . So it seems ironic to me now—in fact satirical—that just eight months after I had taken a perfectly legitimate job in preparation for taking charge of my son, I should suddenly be levied with charges as glamorous as that of being *chairman* of the NDF [National Democratic Front] and a member of the CCP [Chinese Communist Party] Executive and Politburo! I am getting to think that mine is a case of irony upon irony; for those who adamantly maintain these charges despite all evidence to the contrary are—you guessed it—men! (44–45)

The historical connection between women's liberation and organized social movements traced by Sheila Rowbotham in *Women, Resistance and Revolution* (1974), from the insubordination of Anne Hutchison in Massachusetts Bay Colony to the participation of women in the national liberation struggles of Cuba, Algeria, and Vietnam, is thus exemplified in the emergent personal relationships among women, the resistance, and the imprisoned members of their families. And the traditional paradigms of plot that have been constructed around the sociopolitical institution of family are deconstructed by that other institution, prison, in order to be reconstructed eventually in the arena of political resistance, exposing in the process the connections between what Ericka Huggins referred to as the "prison of marriage" and the "more obvious imprisonment / of bars and concrete."

The perduring parameters that define traditionally and in terms of the family the properly female space are again recognized as continuous with the domestic policies of the government in the short stories of the Iraqi Kurdish writer and former political prisoner of Saddam Hussein, Haifa Zankana. For example, in its narrative of detention and interrogation, "1972-8-4" effaces the categorical distinctions between women's veils, family home, and prison walls, as one becomes imperceptibly the other. Like the anonymous Iraqi mother who told the story of her effort to recover her son's body from prison to the London-based Committee against Repression and for Democratic Rights in Iraq (CARDRI) (1986), Haifa Zankana elaborates a careful critique of the Iraqi regime's complicitous manipulations of the traditions of patriarchy and ethnic domination.

Meanwhile, the now paradigmatic figure of the mother seeking her son in the government prisons is dramatized in the CARDRI interview: the sequence of factual questions of detail give way to the narrative constructed in response to them. Amir was a fourth-year medical student when he was arrested in Basra on 29 December 1981. When he did not return home from school, his mother sought him first through petitions to the governor's office, then in repeated visits to the transit center in Gizaiza, and subsequently at the Abu Ghraib prison in Baghdad, where officials continued to deny any knowledge of her son. Finally, on the morning of 7 September, the mother is visited at home by security men, who order her to "go to the Medical City Mortuary and collect the carcass of [her] son" (111).

At the mortuary later that same day a crowd of families searching to reclaim the bodies of their relatives had gathered. Each claimant, before receiving the body he or she had come for, was submitted to the artifices of an ordeal of recognition and denial. Amir's mother describes her own experience of the political struggle over the definition of mother-son relationships:

> Then they called for the person who had come for Amir so I went into a room. I was asked by the person in charge there if I was Amir's mother. I said I was. He asked me for my full name and asked if I lived near. . . . I said I did. Then he immediately said "Your son is a criminal." I said to him "I did not bring up a criminal." Then he said "Your son is a traitor." I said "I did not bring up a traitor." He said "It looks as though you have been crying." I said "I am a mother . . ." Then he said "Even if you are a mother, he is a traitor and you should not cry for him; if you cry we will not give him to you." I said "I will not cry, just give him to me." He then said "I am your son." I said "Somebody else's son is not my son." Then he again said to me "He is a traitor . . ." He then wrote down my age, my full name and told one of the security men to go and give my son to me. (112)

The Iraqi mother is then obliged to identify and retrieve her son's mutilated body from another room and from among the scattered and scarred remains of eight other individuals placed there. For this mother, however, her son's body becomes hers again, if only to bury. The government's policy toward such claims later changed and other mothers were bequeathed only the government's record of their child's demise. The mother tells the CARDRI interviewer:

This campaign went on for about a month and a half without interruption. Corpses were returned in this horrifying manner in Basra and all over Iraq during this month and a half. There were people from the other towns of Iraq such as Karbala, Najaf, Baghdad itself, Hilla, Kut, the North of Iraq—Kurds and Turkomans. Literally every part of Iraq. Now they have stopped giving the bodies to the parents and only papers, like receipts, are given. The households that receive these death certificates are threatened with dire consequences if they talk, create a commotion or wail for their dead ones. Only papers are given. (114)

Family as a contested sociopolitical institution is thus central to the issue of political detention. The imprisoned literary narratives, drawing on documentary materials and constructed around the experience of political prison, in turn necessarily rewrite the emplotments of the traditional family romance and redetermine as well the conventional distribution of character roles, particularly as these have been delimited according to gender. In an oligarchic country like the Philippines, for example, where aristocratic family lineage has historically been consonant with combined economic and political power and hegemony, the ideological challenge of the opposition radically disrupts the privileges of genealogy. And if Imelda Marcos's shame was once her less-than-distinguished class background, Corazon Aquino's elite family ties have threatened to undermine her own capacities—and credibility—as the defender of democracy in the Philippines.

Such genealogical disruptions and distortions structure the epic anti-romance told in Ninotchka Rosca's novel *State of War* (1988), where the frame story is the assassination by the popular armed resistance of a prominent military figure at an annual festival on one of the many islands of the Philippines. The framed story, whose telling is enabled by the carnivalesque setting of the frame,[5] is that of the already-contaminated family histories of the nation's ruling elite. The plotted rupture of the Filipino familial structure is finally consummated and disclosed in the key recognition incident of the novel. It results from the arrest of Anna, wife of the traitor Manolo, lover of the wealthy heir Adrian, and an active member of the resistance organization, from her interrogation (and the consequent death of her unborn child), and from her eventual release. It is for Anna that the narrative has reserved the visionary possibilities of a counter-romantic alternative to the conventional closures of the literary generic romance. Rosca's novel can thus be read, through its disrupted narrative and interrupted genealogical patterns, as an argument for a "materialist textualization of struggle" in order to "emancipate itself in the discourse of physical struggle," similar to that which E. San Juan (1986b) had critically read in the poems of Jose Ma. Sison.

Perhaps even more than the Philippines, El Salvador is noted for the oligarchic control, the power exercised by its famous "fourteen families," or *las quatorce*, over the country's political and economic development—and underdevelopment—despite changes in government both military and **234** "democratic." At the same time, however, as these few wealthy landed families wield brutal control over the majority of the Salvadoran population, the extended family network has traditionally provided almost the only material recourse for the dispossessed lower classes of workers and the peasantry. According to Marilyn Thompson (1986),

Family relations continue to be very important both economically and socially in El Salvador. For the poor, the family network represents a crucial welfare system and for the rich, access to political power is determined by family ties and influence. The Salvadorean oligarchy is still a closed circle of families which over generations have intermarried to maintain their wealth and privilege within their own small group. (30)

But, Thompson goes on, "Most women must live in open contradiction with their own moral code, for while they regard marriage as a fundamental aim in life, El Salvador has one of the lowest marriage rates in the hemisphere" (30). Furthermore, she writes,

The civil war has aggravated this situation, causing a breakdown in family life, such as it was. Both men and women have left home to join political or military organizations and families have been separated by death, imprisonment or enforced exile. Among the refugee committees, new forms of collective living arrangements have been organized. Many women have permanently or temporarily children from other families and are establishing community child-care facilities. (31)

Manlio Argueta's novel *One Day of Life* (1980) is constructed out of the labored pieces of the working day of just such a Salvadoran *campesina* as these pieces are implicated in the larger segments of Salvadoran history—from the 1932 *matanza* to the occupation of the cathedral in San Salvador in 1978—that have claimed the members of her family. Lupe's day, and with it the novel, begins ordinarily at 5:30 A.M., when she is alerted to daybreak by the *clarinero*'s clamorous shriek outside her hut. This "one day" of her life, however, will end at 5 P.M., with the brutal death of her husband, Jose (or Chepe, as he is often called), at the hands of the National Guard. Argueta's novel thus confutes the orthodox distinction that conventionally associates men with historical change and women with the repetitive monotony of the everyday. The story is told primarily from Lupe's point of view, in chapters that are denoted by the times of her day; it is intersected by the voices of other women in her family— her daughter Maria Pia and her granddaughter Adolfina—and marred by the occasional intrusion of "them," "the authorities." *One Day of Life* condenses in its narrative of the daily life of these women the multiple means of repression practiced by the Salvadoran government against its peasant population: detention, disappearance, and death squads. The reconstruction, at once documentary and fictionalization, of this systematic violation of civil and human rights is in turn the story of Lupe's "conscientization" **235** as it is effected through the influence of her husband and his work in the village cooperative and peasant organizing, and at the conclusion, of her ultimate emergence as a spokesperson for the combined rights of women and the peasantry when she refuses to identify for the guardsmen her husband's mutilated body.

Lupe's narration of the events of that day and their connection to the historical past is otherwise punctuated by her avowed recognition of Jose's political acumen: "I ask myself these questions. Or I ask Jose. . . . Lately Jose has learned many things" (56–57); "Once I asked Chepe what being aware [*estar concientizado*] meant" (88); "And sometimes I participate a little; well, the truth is that Jose really does everything while I stay home with the children. It's hard for me to get out" (101); "Without Jose we would be lost. . . . Where would I be without Jose?" (126); "It's nice to be aware [*tener conciencia*]. One suffers less" (171); and finally, "At first, I didn't understand why he used to leave us abandoned; it wasn't that he'd go away, but that he wouldn't give us any attention—only the work of the organization existed for him. He would explain his reasons to us. 'This way of being, it is having conscience,' he tells me. And, you see, it is a complicated thing, it can't be defined by a single word. Conscience is all the things we do for the benefit of others without seeking our own interest. And I say: Chepe is my conscience" (173). When Jose is killed, Lupe assumes his awareness: "Now it will be up to me [*Ahora me va a tocar a mi*]" (200).

One Day of Life is set in the late spring of 1978, in the days just following the failed meeting between peasant representatives and the president of the Agriculture Development Bank, to discuss loans and economic assistance in purchasing seeds, fertilizers, and farming equipment. When the bank president refused to attend the scheduled meeting, the peasants held a series of demonstrations in the streets of San Salvador that were violently broken up by the military and the police. Later in the day, a bus carrying peasants out of the capital en route to their homes was attacked by the army, leaving five more peasants dead. In the novel Lupe's granddaughter Adolfina was on that bus but managed to escape in the company of another young girl, Maria Romelia. Like Adolfina's father, Helio, Maria Romelia's father, Emilio Ramirez, has been captured and is being held by the National Guard. Maria Pia, Adolfina's mother and Helio's wife, herself threatened by the Guard, has left home, taking her three youngest children with her, to sleep in the hills where the men have gone into hiding. Adolfina is sent in the meantime to stay with her grandmother, Lupe. She is there when the guardsmen finally bring her dying grandfather, Jose.

236   Three generations of Salvadoran *campesinas*—Lupe, the grandmother; Maria Pia, her daughter; and Adolfina, her granddaughter—are thus made to bear witness in Argueta's novel to the government's assault on their families. Years earlier, Lupe's first son had died as a child from dehydration. Justino, her second son and an organizer for the new peasant federation, had only just been killed by paramilitary death squads operating in the region. Helio, her son-in-law, is perhaps still in prison, but the authorities continue to refuse to acknowledge him. And now, in this "one day of life," Chepe, her husband, has been assassinated. Each of the women responds differently to the pressures of daily violence: Maria Pia leaves her home in fear; Lupe, remembering the advice of Jose, confronts the Guard; and Adolfina, the youngest, recalls, "My mother says I'm too rebellious, but my father has always told me one shouldn't call that rebelliousness but awareness. I'm unable to put up with those people called authorities" (115–16).

In the ten years since the events described in *One Day of Life*, through military dictatorship, the "democratic" government of Jose Napoleon Duarte, and in 1989 the rule of the right-wing ARENA party, El Salvador has been torn by civil war. The consolidation in 1980 of the various resistance movements into the FMLN-FDR has more recently been accompanied by the creation in both the city and the countryside of a network of popular committees, the Poderes Populares Locales (PPLs). The question of the "promised land," examined by Jenny Pearce (1986) in her study of peasant rebellion in El Salvador, as revealed through oral histories collected in 1984 in Chalatenango, is no longer a question of a utopian vision to be redeemed in an afterlife in another world, but the popular triumph in history over the broken promises from successive Salvadoran regimes of land reform, the reappropriation by the peasants of the land on which they have toiled. For that to happen, Lupe realizes, the Salvadoran women—mothers, wives, daughters—must also be liberated. Both land and gender roles will have to be redistributed.

You can't expect more from the men. From their point of view we peasant women are slaves, but it is not their fault. At bottom we help produce the wealth of the landowners when we take care of the children by ourselves, because we are also giving men the time to work in peace from sunup to sundown. That is to say, we are giving our time to the landowners so that our husbands can produce more, can be better exploited. (204)

According to the Association of the Women of El Salvador (AMES), however, "A woman's decision to become a politically conscious militant implies a much longer and more difficult process than that taken by a man" (Pearce 1986, 280).

One Day of Life, by its insistence on the necessary intersection of the historical and the everyday, rewrites the melodramatic paradigms that conventionally structure women's romances. The violent pressures exerted on the everyday lives of the fictional women by detention and disappearance, ruthlessly practiced against them and their collective families by a repressive government and its police and military apparatus, necessitate structural transformations in the organization of social and gender relations as well as in traditional constructions of narrative plot. Jean Franco (1986) has pointed out that romantic fiction addressed to middle-class women readers asks them "to sacrifice their intelligence," while in the comic-strip novels that appeal to a proletarian female readership, women often "sacrifice romance" (123). Neither of these genres provides an adequate response to the historic demands of systemic and institutionalized violence and an emergent popular resistance to it. If Michele Mattelart (1986) is correct in stating that "in times of crisis, the theme of the family once again comes to the fore" (2), then the specific material and ideological crises in the political order, which the threatened government "solves" by political detention, highlights the institution of family and the placement of women in it as crucial to that crisis.

Like *One Day of Life*, or *State of War*, Isabel Allende's novel of Chile under Ugarte Pinochet's military dictatorship, *Of Love and Shadows* (1988), records the radical and active disintegration of the family structure and undermines thereby its ideological function of legitimizing an oppressive and autocratic regime. During the three years, from 1970 to 1973, that the Popular Unity government of Salvador Allende initiated a democratic and socialist experiment in Chile, the country's conservative and right-wing establishment, in alliance with the traditional bourgeoisie and eventually with the military, waged a continuous assault on the reforms—from land redistribution programs to the nationalization of industry—gradually introduced by Allende's regime. Not only was there a massive and well-financed information campaign (with considerable economic assistance from the United States) in newspapers and magazines and on the radio and television, but in 1972 the transportation bosses and magnates, in a paradoxical reversal, staged a strike against the growing influence

237

of the workers. The strike virtually paralyzed the country's industry and the distribution of food and other resources and, by aggravating already precarious living conditions, seriously eroded Allende's fragile bases of support.

In the meantime, from the very first year of the Popular Unity government, middle-class women were conscripted out of their homes by the right-wing opposition to stage public protests in the streets, such as the "March of the Empty Pots and Pans" in 1971, in which well-dressed **238** housewives, often accompanied by their maids, beat their kitchenware along the grand avenues of the capital decrying the food shortages and the "communist takeover" of the country. These same women also threw corn kernels at the soldiers, implicitly accusing them of being "chicken" (cowardly) and not living up to their long tradition of *machismo* and masculine authority. According to Mattelart (1986), "The bourgeoisie was able to hide its class interests behind the protests of mothers and housewives, behind demands which appeared unrelated to class strategy because they encompassed areas traditionally marginalized from the political sphere, such as the home, family organization, rearing and education of children" (85). Protection of the national security and of the family, with women as its icon, then became the alibi for the military coup that overthrew Allende and his Popular Unity government in September 1973 and launched in its place a repressive regime of bureaucratic control and unchecked terror, in which, as Mattelart describes it, "the emblem of the mother and the child exorcises its reverse, the widow and the orphan" (98).

It is against this historical background of a crisis of bureaucratic legitimacy and familial disruption that *Of Love and Shadows* is written. Like *State of War*, Allende's novel is an anti–family saga, a critical demonstration of both the contemporary currency and the bankruptcy of the genre. Unlike *State of War*, however, with its final dispatch of the heroine into an uncertain but perhaps more self-determined and autonomous future, *Of Love and Shadows* preserves in its conclusion the formula of a "happy ending" in the romantic union of its two exiled lovers, Irene Beltran and Francisco Leal. Although in the dedication to the novel, Allende describes her work as "the story of a woman and a man who loved one another so deeply that they saved themselves from a banal existence," *Of Love and Shadows* does not fully subscribe to the conventional injunctions of melodramatic discourse, which, Mattelart (1986) notes, "invalidates any form against social inequalities (the existence of which is admitted) by means of this diffuse explanation: only love can cross class barriers" (13). What actually redeems the existential "banality" of Irene and Francisco's romance is its narrative development through the search for the body of Evangelina

Ranquileo, which leads to the discovery and exhumation of a mass grave in the abandoned mine at Los Riscos.

In the novel the three families—the respectable Leals, the "ideal" family of mutual love, domestic care, and nurturing; the aristocratic Beltrans, whose patriarch has absconded, leaving behind his daughter and wife, herself one of the women of the "empty pots and pans"; and the peasant Ranquileos, who have lost a son to the military and a daughter to the arbitrary violence of the *carabineros*—mark not only particular class formations but differing political positions as well. With the traumatic un-   **239** earthing of fifteen corpses at Los Riscos, their individual trajectories are shown to combine historically in a collective and popular opposition to the "general's" regime.

On the morning of 30 November 1978, the Chilean lawyer Maximo Pacheco received an invitation from the archbishop of Santiago, Cardinal Raul Silva Henriquez, to attend a meeting at noon that same day at the Vicaria de la Solidaridad. The occasion for the meeting, attended by six other men—including two priests, another lawyer, and two journalists—was, according to Pacheco (1980), the cardinal's report that "a priest had received from an individual an accusation concerning 'the existence of a cemetery of cadavers [*cementerio de cadaveres*] in the region of Lonquen'" (7). *Lonquen* is the documentary history compiled by Pacheco of the subsequent dramatic public investigation into the mass deaths, the conviction of the military assassins, and their later amnesty by Pinochet. Pacheco published the document because, he says, "I believe that the investigated facts are of such seriousness that it is absolutely necessary to make them known, in a totally objective form, by means of textual transcriptions of the most important parts of the trial, in order that public opinion can be made aware and draw its own judgement" (10). From December 1978 through September 1979, the inquiry and later the trial continued, culminating not only in the arbitrary amnesty of the convicted *carabineros* but in the last-minute refusal, as the people were assembled for a funeral mass in the cathedral, of the government to return the exhumed remains of the victims to their families. The public protest that the archbishopric issued at this official affront to its citizens is the final document in *Lonquen*: "The Church of Santiago cannot do less than raise its voice and denounce this display of insensitivity and inhumanity towards the grief of the families. What right is there to bury someone without the authorization of that person's relatives?" (300).

Lonquen, which includes direct testimony from neighbors, families, and friends of the victims, depositions from the military officers involved in the detentions in the area in September and October 1973 (immediately following the military overthrow of Salvador Allende), forensic reports, medical conclusions, ballistic findings, lists of *desaparecidos*, the charges brought by the families of the victims, as well as the decisions of the civil and military tribunals, provides the documentary material for Allende's *Of Love and Shadows*. The detailed narrative that emerges out of the meticulous proceedings and their scandalous outcome in *Lonquen* is rewritten as political romance in the novel, which, at its end, cites nearly verbatim from the documents. *Of Love and Shadows*, however, narrates that segment **240** of the history, its source, otherwise protected by the sacramental secrecy of the confessional. Who revealed to the priest the "existence of a cemetery of cadavers"? The love story of Irene Beltran and Francisco Leal is the fictionalized narrative, behind that historical revelation, of how the young couple came to find the mass grave and, in finding it, found each other and the political commitment whereby "they saved themselves from a banal existence." The relationship between fiction and documentary is more than a formal or generic question. The historical issue is raised by the novel itself:

Afterward, Irene and Francisco would ask themselves at what precise moment the course of their lives had changed, and they would point to the fateful Monday they entered the abandoned Los Riscos mine. But it may have been before that— say, the Sunday they met Evangelina Ranquileo, or the evening they promised Digna they would help in her search for the missing girl; or possibly their roads had been mapped out from the beginning, and they had no choice but to follow them. (Allende 1988, 187)

The mothers of "The Woolen Sweater" and "She Affirmed Her Right to Self-Determination," the wives and daughters of *One Day of Life*, and the lovers in *Of Love and Shadows*, together with other women and men within and beyond the prison walls, in contending with the fact of prison, assassination, and disappearance, are producing the historical bases for an organized liberatory counternarrative to the dominant paradigms of domesticity and romance by which traditional literary history has aided and abetted the containment of women's political agency.

NUNCA MAS

PART IV

Chapter Eleven

Writing Human Rights

. . . no moral or physical coercion may be exerted on a prisoner of war in order to induce him to admit himself guilty of the act of which he is accused . . .

Article 99, Third Geneva Convention

Everyone has the right to freedom of opinion and expression; this right includes freedom to hold opinions without interference and to seek, receive and impart information and ideas through any media regardless of frontiers.

Article 19, Universal Declaration of Human Rights

At the height of the repression known as *el proceso* (for Process of National Reorganization) under Argentina's military rule from 1976 to 1983, when "disappearances" of Argentine civilians into clandestine interrogation centers and prisons were an everyday event, regimes elsewhere in the world, as well as the Catholic Church, were reluctant to interfere in any significant way in the affairs of Argentina's ruling junta. The French government did protest briefly, albeit unsuccessfully, when two French nuns were kidnapped in 1977, as did the Swedish government when eighteen-year-old Dagmar Hagelin was shot and abducted. But, as Jo Fisher argues in *Mothers of the Disappeared* (1989), "To treat events in Argentina on the basis of individual cases of human rights abuse only permitted the military to divert attention away from the organized and systematic nature of the repression and to respond in terms of isolated 'errors' or 'excesses'" (72). The systematic basis of this seven-year regimen of terror was officially exposed only in the years following the 1983 election of Raul Alfonsin as president and the restoration of civilian rule in Argentina. Even then, a military trial merely exposed the junta's leaders but did not bring them to justice, argue the Mothers of the Plaza de Mayo. This organization, since its first public appearance in the Buenos Aires Plaza de Mayo in 1977, has sought information about the fate of the disappeared children, the thirty thousand

and more *desaparecidos*, and an explanation for the injustices committed against the Argentine people.

Jo Fisher's *Mothers of the Disappeared* and Latin American poet Marjorie Agosin's *Mothers of Plaza de Mayo* (1990), through collective *testimonio* and intimate conversation, engage the recent history of popular opposition waged by the mothers movement in Argentina, together with other groups such as COMADRES, the Detainees' Parents Support Committee, and the *ummahat al-ghaʾibin*, to "forced disappearance" as a political practice deployed against their own populations by governments engaged in what are justified as "wars against subversion." Not only is the systematic, bureaucratic, and even routine character of the military junta's repression represented by these texts, but the gradual emergence and consolidation of mothers of disappeared persons as the Mothers of Plaza de Mayo, an organized force for resistance, is counternarrated. In their persistent refusal to understand their own private losses and personal griefs as "individual human rights abuses," the Mothers instantiated through their weekly silent presence in the plaza the popular imperative of collective and public pressure for the accountability of their government. First against the clandestinity of the junta's operations, and then in response to the Alfonsin government's only limited indictment of those responsible for ordering and carrying out the "disappearances," the Mothers continue to insist on a public accounting of and for the atrocities as vitally necessary to a continued struggle for human rights.

Human rights reporting, itself a genre in the contemporary world of writing and rights, entails both documentation and intervention. Fisher (1989) presents her book with the "sole aim . . . to give a voice to the Madres de Plaza de Mayo." It is, she writes, "a history of collective struggle rather than . . . a series of testimonies of individual women" (ix). Just as the systematic nature and basis of the repression must be denounced, so too the organized and collective dimension of the Mothers' work must be documented and transcribed. In *Mothers of the Disappeared*, the women themselves, in their self-representation, provide that documentation, glossed only intermittently by Fisher. She turns over her text to the Mothers: the stories of their own backgrounds; the lives and presumed deaths of their children; their futile searches at government offices, army headquarters, police stations; their frustrated appeals to the church; their demonstrations; and finally, their own organization. The very format of *Mothers of the Disappeared*, its collocation of narratives alternatively suspended and reprised, suggests the urgency of the now-critical injunction that the work of "writing human rights" transgress and transform traditional authorial paradigms. As Hebe de Bonafini, the Mothers' president, tells Fisher about her own public speaking, "What do I need to prepare if I'm here all day? Those who aren't fighting something all day have to write things down." But, de Bonafini goes on, "in this way we changed the language for a lot of people" (77).

In *The Mothers of Plaza de Mayo*, Marjorie Agosin presents the ways in which her own poetic language has been altered through her month-long meeting in Buenos Aires in 1988 with Renee Epelbaum, the mother of three disappeared children and a founder of the Mothers. The Mothers' own "feminine poetic imagery" (21)—their white kerchiefs and the photographs of the missing that came to distinguish their weekly vigils—is **245** translated by Agosin and Epelbaum into "a conversation between two women joined by a common goal: defense of human rights and raising the world's consciousness about respect for human life" (n.p.). The shared encounter is premised, as Epelbaum says in a letter to Agosin following her departure from Argentina, on the need to "keep the collective memory from forgetting"; more important, she goes on, "This does not simply involve historical anecdotes. Each life is irreplaceable. We have to prevent other human beings from experiencing this pain. You and I discussed how important it is to put oneself in someone else's place" (63). Against the junta's systematic denial of its victims' personal identity and refusal to recognize the writs of habeas corpus presented by the families, Agosin and Epelbaum struggle to elaborate and defend an alternative construction of identity: an identification with others, on behalf of human rights. As Epelbaum tells Agosin, "To choose me or another mother will give exactly the same results, but I will tell you my story as if we were two friends talking or two friends crying" (25). Whether it is "Renee speaking," describing her grief, her children, or her commitment, or "Marjorie speaking," asking Renee how one mourns the missing, at stake is the need for an accounting, the demand that the authors of Argentina's thirty thousand disappearances be held accountable for the histories that they massacred.

In December 1986, the Alfonsin government passed Law 23.492, which decreed a "final point," a *punto final*, to that account. In May 1987, there followed Law 23.51, *obediencia debida*, "obedience to superiors," effectively granting amnesty to all those who had carried out the kidnappings, torture, and murders "under orders" from their superior officers. The Mothers of Plaza de Mayo, now knowing all too well that their missing children must be presumed dead, continue, even in the pages of these two volumes, to raise their demand for *aparicion con vida*, "reappearance with life." According to Graciela de Jeger, "We don't want the names of the victims. We know who they are. We want the names of the murderers. We want them to tell us what happened. They have to explain what they don't want to explain. This is the meaning of *aparicion con vida*" (Fisher 1989,

129). Such an explanation demands another strategy—at once popular and collective—for writing human rights.

Ronald Dworkin, a United States jurist, agreed with the demand of the Mothers of the Plaza that "the world needs a taboo against torture" (xxvii). In his introduction to the English-language edition of *Nunca Mas* (1986), the report of the inquiry by the Argentine National Commission on the Disappeared (CONADEP), Dworkin concludes that

246

the Mothers of the Plaza de Mayo, and others who call for prosecution of all torturers and murderers in the military ranks are right—not because they are entitled to vengeance, but because the best guarantee against tyranny, everywhere but especially in countries like Argentina where tyranny has often seemed acceptable to the majority, is a heightened public sense of why it is repulsive. Trials that explore and enforce the idea that torture can have no defense may encourage that sense. Allowing known torturers to remain in positions of authority, unchallenged and uncondemned, can only weaken it. (xxvii)

Nunca Mas, a text Dworkin describes as a "report from hell," with "detail almost unbearable to read," was mandated by President Raul Alfonsin, making good on an election promise to investigate the "crimes" that had been perpetrated under the military junta and those responsible for them. The commission's work culminated in the April 1985 trial of nine commanders in civilian courts, but all of the other participants in torture were given amnesty under the law of *obediencia debida*. Appointed as director of the commission was the Argentine writer Ernesto Sabato, whose literary reputation and narrative practice were thereby remobilized in a collective project, the research and writing of which contributed to a critical redefinition of the conventions of authorship no less than to the mimetic protocols and the political consequentiality of schools of realism. For Sabato, the author of the introduction to the report, the tension between reporting and judging, which anticipated the charge of vengeance versus the prevention of further human rights abuses, was written into the commission's work:

Our Commission was not set up to sit in judgement, because that is the task of the constitutionally appointed judges, but to investigate the fate of the people who disappeared during those ill-omened years of our nation's life. . . . Although it must be justice which has the final word, *we cannot remain silent* in the face of all that we have heard, read and recorded. (1–2, emphasis added)

Even in abjuring the role of judge for itself, the commission in its report and by its own example argues for an accounting; it demands public accountability: the writing of human rights.

What Dworkin referred to as "detail almost unbearable to read" is given a critical format and an immanent agenda in *Nunca Mas*, which derived from the commission's hearing of several thousand testimonies, its verification of the actual existence of hundreds of secret detention centers, and the compilation of more than fifty thousand pages of documentation in the course of its work. Divided into six chapters, the document maps the brutal transformation over seven years of the totality of Argentine demography and topography. Chapter 1, "The Repression," occupies over half the pages of the book; it elaborately, painstakingly, reconstructs through description, analysis, and testimony the massive machinery of that transformation. The following three chapters, on the victims, the judiciary during the repression, and the creation and organization of the National Commission on the Disappeared, become progressively more abbreviated. The final eight pages of the text, the last two chapters, demarcate a truncated confrontation between the doctrine behind the repression and the commission's own recommendations and conclusions, that is, between the authors of the torture and the disappearances, on the one hand, and the writers of *Nunca Mas*, on the other.

247

If for some readers the ruthless details of *Nunca Mas* pose problems of an excruciating unease incurred even through that very mediated participation in their discursive representation, the writers for their part were preliminarily concerned that "many of the events described in this book will be hard to believe" (9), the commission incurring instead an answerability—and a threatened liability—for the narrative charge sheet that they have drawn up. The disappeared of Argentina remain in a way the "living dead," unaccounted for, for the families and associates that remain, but the story of their disappearance at the hands of a state machine of terror cannot be fully assimilated within a literary-generic convention of the gothic, fantastic or "unbelievable" as their conflicted histories may appear. Rather, in presenting *Nunca Mas* to the reading public, the commission assumes the "weighty but necessary *responsibility for affirming that everything set out in this report did indeed happen*, even if some of the details of individual cases may be open to question. These questions can only be resolved conclusively by the testimony of those who took part in the events" (9, emphasis added). Although unable to right the egregious infractions of human justice committed by the military personnel, the commission, as author of this written report, must contest, indeed refute, the explanations and justifications of their perpetrators, the "doctrine behind the repression," and even the claim that the "excesses" inevitably committed were duly identified and properly brought to justice. The inherited version of "excesses" must be rewritten in order to demonstrate their place within a repression of systemic and systematic design: "The military commanders of the Process of National Reorganization reserved the term 'excess' for any offence committed by military or police personnel for their own ends, without the authority of their superiors. It was not related to the repression itself" (10).

Against the totalitarian authors of the abuses, the crimes committed against a population by a government that relied for its very authority on disappearance and its own legislated impunity—for the sake of "paralysing public protest, . . . ensuring the silence of the relatives, . . . and trying to stall investigation into the facts" (234)—the authors of the report have summoned not only a massive (if injured) surviving documentation, but the testimonies and collaboration of the survivors themselves. For example, despite their blindfolding and hooding throughout their incarceration, those survivors of the junta's secret detention centers were able, if not to identify their persecutors, then to describe in detail (enough detail to allow the creation of blueprints of the detention centers) the many sites of repression, precisely because of "the necessary sharpening of the other senses and by a whole set of patterns meticulously stored in the memory, as a means of clinging to reality and life" (58).

Nunca Mas, the commission's report, at once draws on and challenges the traditions and forms of literature and literary history. Abduction, for example, is presented as the "first act in the drama of disappearance" (10), a drama that has yet to write its final act or see its actors appear for a curtain call. In its proposed construction of authorship, however, as the assumption of authority on behalf of a population for the accounting that the military regime denied, *Nunca Mas* proposes too the reinstatement of the literary, of writing and reading—as discipline and practice—as an active, transitive, sociopolitical force. "Month after month of listening to accusations, testimonies and confessions, of examining documents, inspecting places, and doing all in our power to throw light on these terrifying occurrences, *has given us the right to assert* that a system of repression was deliberately planned to produce the events and situations which are detailed in this report" (9, emphasis added). Like the writs of habeas corpus, the demands for the body, submitted repeatedly by the mothers of the disappeared, *Nunca Mas* does not just enjoin that an individual body, or even bodies, be produced, but rather insists on the accountability of the system itself. The signification of a habeas corpus writ or of *Nunca Mas*, what they demand, is not nostalgia for a "lost presence" (in the Derridean sense), nor vengeance (of a psychoanalytic or oedipal kind), nor even the restoration of a traditional family structure; rather, it is the instantiation of another kind of writing altogether.

While the commission on the disappeared in Argentina was carrying out its officially sanctioned, public inquiry into the military junta's *pro-ceso*, the archdiocese of São Paulo in Brazil was secretly preparing its own investigation into the use of torture by Brazil's succession of military governments between 1964 and 1979. The report, *Brasil: Nunca Mais* (1985), references by its analogous title (translatable as "never again") the radical significance of its Argentine counterpart and also marks its own critical departures from that example. The textual and practical differences between the two documents are both circumstantial and theoretical, arguing the need at once to theorize historical conditions and historicize theoretical claims. Unlike the preparation of *Nunca Mas*, the work for *Nunca Mais* was carried out under the repression itself and therefore was done in secrecy. Unlike the Argentine report, which relied significantly on the testimony of the victims, the Brazilian document derived exclusively from the official records of the government's own archives. According to Joan Dassin's introduction to the English-language edition, *Torture in Brazil* (1986), the volume, a distillation of Project A, a seven-thousand-page report, represents an "analysis of the most extensive official documentation ever consulted by non-military investigators" (ix). *Torture in Brazil* combines the "report of an investigation in the field of human rights," an "examination of political repression," and an "analysis of the resistance" to that repression (3). Accordingly, it differs in structure from its Argentine counterpart: the Brazilian volume alternates between the "shocking denunciations" of torture provided by prisoners at their own trials and more "analytical passages" that provide the historical and political background to military rule in Brazil (18).

Brasil: Nunca Mais, which sold over a hundred thousand copies in its first ten weeks of publication, sought by its methodology and circumstances to force the very system of repression to speak:

> Everywhere in the world, the issue of political repression is almost always brought to public notice by the denunciations of victims or by reports written by organizations dedicated to the defense of human rights. Whether emotional or well balanced, these testimonies help reveal a hidden history. But at times they are accused of tendentiousness because they come from victims who are often politically motivated.
>
> The "Brasil: Never Again" (BNM) research project was able to resolve this problem by studying the repression carried out by the military regime through the very documents produced by the authorities performing the controversial task. (*Torture*, 4)

In *Brasil: Nunca Mais* as in *Nunca Mas*, however, a political problem remains: that of the relation between reporting human rights violations and bringing to justice the violators—whether government records or personal testimonies are invoked as sources. Just as the Mothers of the Plaza

and the authors of *Nunca Mas* were accused of seeking vengeance, of operating out of interest, so too was the Brasil: Nunca Mais project "subject
to charges that it seeks revenge, not justice" (Archdiocese of São Paulo
1986, xii). What, in other words, are the consequences—documentation
and intervention—of writing human rights?

In June 1957, after a year in hiding, Henri Alleg, a Frenchman living
in Algeria, a member of the Algerian Communist party, and the editor
250   of the banned newspaper *Alger Republicain,* was arrested by French para-
troops at the home of his friend Maurice Audin, a college professor in
Algiers. Audin, who himself had been arrested just twenty-four hours
earlier, would later "disappear," murdered by his captors, and his case
would become a rallying point for metropolitan efforts to stop torture
in France's colonies. Alleg, however, survived his torture at the El Biar
"centre de tri," and while detained in the internment camp at Lodi, Alleg
wrote and smuggled out to France his denunciation of the tortures he had
undergone. That small book, *The Question* (1958), with an introduction by
Jean-Paul Sartre, was within weeks of its publication officially banned in
France.

For four years, since 1954, France had been fighting the popular Algerian anticolonial resistance to retain its imperialist and metropolitan pre-
rogatives in North Africa and to keep Algeria "French." Another four
years would ensue before the Evian agreement, ending the war and recognizing Algerian independence, was signed, in March 1962—followed two
weeks later by a general amnesty that exonerated even the French torturers of Algerian nationalists. For the Algerians, however, and their
French supporters, like Alleg and Audin, these eight years were not
only determined by political struggle but physically, almost irretrievably,
scarred by torture. This practice, even when acknowledged by the successive French governments of the period, in the face of sporadic protest
from Algerian victims and their metropolitan defenders, was either excused as a necessary evil occasioned by the conditions of war or dismissed
as isolated "excesses" committed by inexperienced recruits.

For Alleg, torture was "the question," both a moral/political issue and
an intolerable form of questioning, whether through the use of electric
shock, beatings, drownings, cigarette burns, or the application of "truth
drugs" such as Pentothal, a question of interrogative genre of the most
dire and urgent sort that needed to be countered by a radically other, imperative discourse: "I suddenly felt proud and happy not to have given
way. I was convinced that I could still hold out if they started again, that
I would fight them to the end, that I would not help them in their job of
killing me" (102). The resistant silence that Alleg maintained against the

brutality and the machinations of his interrogators then had to be translated into a language of protest to break that other silence, the silence that complicitly condones the continued practice of torture.

Alleg, a reporter, like Ruth First, a disseminator of information, while being questioned was obliged to renounce that profession, albeit temporarily. *The Question*, written clandestinely, marks the resumption of that profession in another register, one that enlists the reader (like Sartre, who was not arrested) in its own project of political resistance. For Sartre, in the French capital, similarly committed within a profession of writing, Alleg's book was to be distinguished for having written its words in the transitive mode: "As for myself," the philosopher wrote in his introduction, "I have to read by profession, I have books published, and I have always detested those books that mercilessly involve us in a cause and yet offer no hope or solution. With the publication of *La Question*, everything is changed" (19). That solution, an answer to "the question" that in challenging the questions contests torture, is the reassertion of accountability.

Two years later, a twenty-two-year-old Algerian woman, Djamila Boupacha, arrested for allegedly planting a bomb in a university cafeteria, demanded such an accounting from her French torturers, men who had broken two of her ribs, stubbed out their cigarettes on her naked body, and deflowered her with a beer bottle. A letter from Boupacha in prison was secreted out by her brother, who had also been detained, and eventually reached the French lawyer Gisele Halimi, who agreed to take on the woman nationalist's case. In 1961, after a year and a half of litigation and media work, *Djamila Boupacha*, "the story of the torture of a young Algerian girl which shocked liberal French opinion" written by Simone de Beauvoir and Gisele Halimi, was published. It recounts the concerted, even coordinated attempts, at all levels of the government, and including the army and the judiciary, to prevent Boupacha's protests from discovering a hearing, either in the courts or in public opinion.

Djamila Boupacha, however, tells more than a story of bureaucratic obstructionism and obfuscation. It narrates as well Boupacha's political and ideological journey, from Algeria, through her acquaintance with Halimi, to France, where her case is finally transferred; the cultural instruction and initiation of her French lawyer, by way of conversations with Boupacha and her family and interviews with government officials, into the politics of resistance; and finally the collective education of at least some members of metropolitan French society through the work of the Djamila Boupacha Committee under the guidance of Simone de Beauvoir.

The book itself "remains open" even today. It was proposed by the committee when Boupacha's claim that she had been tortured was recognized by the French courts but her appeal that her violators be identified

251

and brought to justice was thwarted by that same system, in its refusal to provide photographs of the men who had been associated with her "case" at El Biar:

Simone de Beauvoir, who took the chair at this meeting, proposed that a book or a brochure should be produced, containing a complete account of the Djamila Boupacha affair. Numerous members of the Committee had already asked, on more than one occasion, that such a document should be made available: it would both form a weapon in the immediate struggle, an instrument for disseminating the truth as widely as possible, and also constitute a pledge for the future.

Simone de Beauvoir's proposal was unanimously carried: the book—this book —would be written. (170)

The three women, coauthors of the project under Djamila's name—Djamila Boupacha, the tortured Algerian militant; Gisele Halimi, the French advocate; and Simone de Beauvoir, the feminist and activist—in the narrative of their own accountability translate the protest against torture into a demand for a collective and political public accounting.

The blatant contradictions between France's tradition of "enlightenment" and its protracted use of torture in Algeria, contradictions that in a significant way animated the isolated protests of some metropolitan French against the violations of individual and political rights in North Africa, are analyzed by Rita Maran (1989) in her study of torture and the role of ideology in the French-Algerian war. In investigating the discourses of the government, the military, and the intellectuals, Maran proposes a "great contradiction . . . between France's enlightened tradition of the 'rights of man' and that most extreme of human rights violations, torture." Indeed, she goes on, and this is the problem that structures her argument, "The avowedly benevolent ideology of the civilizing mission was the mechanism by which the doctrine of the 'rights of man' was contorted in order to encourage and justify the practice of torture" (2). The human costs of this militant ideological aporia demand, argues Maran, an international human rights law, a legislation that requires, however, not only "support of that which conventional wisdom has termed the 'political will' of national governments," but also the "diligent professionalism of human rights specialists and lawyers, and pressure from concerned citizens making their voices heard through their governments and through human rights organizations" (27).

The Universal Declaration of Human Rights was adopted and proclaimed by the General Assembly of the United Nations in December 1948. Its thirty articles translated the standard literary paradigm of individual versus society and the narrative conventions of emplotment and closure by mapping an identification of the individual within a specifically international construction of rights and responsibilities. The Declaration, that is, can be read as recharting the trajectory and peripeties of the classic *bildungsroman*. Its relocation of the individual presumes, according to the preamble, that "it is essential, if man is to be compelled to have recourse, as a last resort, to rebellion against tyranny and oppression, that human rights should be protected by law." The marked discrepancies and radical disjunctures between declaration and implementation, between theory and practice, between "literature" and the "world," are demonstrated not only by the examples of France in Algeria from 1954 to 1962, **253** and of Argentina under the rule of a military junta from 1976 to 1983, but by the persistent resurgence of "recourse, as a last resort, to rebellion against tyranny and oppression."

Nearly half a century later, and despite its signing by most member governments of the United Nations, the Universal Declaration of Human Rights remains at best a vision (a conservative one at that) or in the most cynical interpretation, evidence of the absurdist inconsequentiality of the arts of writing. The political, often armed, liberation struggles that punctuate and articulate global history in this last half of the twentieth century can be read as part of the larger attempt to enforce a revolutionary implementation of that declaration. The Palestinian resistance, for example, in its demand for self-determination, insists on the application of the two paragraphs of Article 15: "Everyone has the right to a nationality" and "No one shall be arbitrarily deprived of his nationality nor denied the right to change his nationality." Djamila Boupacha's case raised the right to a "fair public hearing by an independent and impartial tribunal" (Article 10), just as the Mothers of the Plaza de Mayo demand "an effective remedy by the competent national tribunals for acts violating the fundamental rights granted [the individual] by the constitution or by law" (Article 8). Progressive immigration lawyers in the United States, in presenting to the INS—despite the United States government's calculated interest and recalcitrance—asylum cases for political refugees from El Salvador and Guatemala, for example, like the attorneys for IRA member Joe Doherty, who has been detained for over eight years in a United States prison while Britain seeks his extradition, insist on the implementation of Article 14, which asserts: "Everyone has the right to seek and to enjoy in other countries asylum from persecution." And in more than a third of the world's nations, groups, families, individuals, and organizations appeal against torture, so that "no one shall be subjected to torture or to cruel, inhuman or degrading treatment or punishment" (Article 5). The very legitimacy of these political struggles and demands is suppressed, in that the organizations themselves, their members, and associates become the vilified objects of systematic governmental repression. The very effort, "to resist tyranny and oppression," that is, the project of implementing the Universal Declaration of Human Rights, has been systematically re-rendered as an offense to be punished, through detention, imprisonment, torture, "disappearance," and extrajudicial execution, by the same governments that once signed the declaration.

Just as the "abuses" of human rights, such as torture, cannot be defined away by the governments that sponsor them as "efficient" or as the "excesses" of wayward individuals, so the struggle to implement the promises of the Universal Declaration of Human Rights is not an individual agenda, but a collective and activist assertion. Torture, argues Amnesty International (AI) in its report *Torture in the Eighties* (1984), "occurs as a result of the failure of *governments* to exercise their legal responsibilities to prevent it and to investigate and redress alleged abuses of authority by its agents" (76, emphasis in original). Like Amnesty International's annual reports and its separate government inquiries, *Torture in the Eighties* is formatted according to national governments, presented in a provocatively dispassionate alphabetical order, and sometimes sorted regionally: the "third police station" in the Ethiopian capital of Addis Ababa, cells flooded with water in Kenya, the death in detention of trade unionist Neil Aggett in South Africa; death squads in Guatemala, *picana electrica*, *pilata, cajones, feto, guardia, secadera*, and *muncielago* in Paraguay; torture in Indonesia, South Korea, and Pakistan; torture in Egypt, Iran, Iraq, and Israel.

Amnesty International, headquartered in London, was established in 1961 with a mandate to seek the release of "prisoners of conscience," to demand "fair and prompt trials" for all prisoners, and to work on behalf of all prisoners without reservation. Its local and regional chapters throughout the world write letters to the detainees themselves, collect evidence and documentation on prisoners, publicize cases, and seek to bring pressure on offending governments and regimes. Its Urgent Action network was created to enable an immediate mobilization to prevent torture in the cases of sudden arrest. The *Amnesty International Handbook* (Staunton and Fenn 1990), prepared by AI's British section, which describes in detail the history, emphases, and workings of the organization, concludes its introduction with a dramatic imperative: "Read this book and find out how to stop torture and save lives: help to free prisoners of conscience and win fair trials for all political prisoners worldwide" (4). If, as Homi Bhabha (1990) maintains, "nations, like narratives, lose their origins in the myths of time and only fully realize their horizons in the mind's eye" (1), then Amnesty International reports, by contrast, arranged as they are according to nation, are engaged in the drafting of counter national histories.

254

The "process of torture," as described in *Torture in the Eighties*, involves a systemic assault and depradation on the physical integrity of the individual and implies as well an unrelenting attack on the subject's political engagement, her or his theoretical and interventionist capabilities. Torture, according to AI, means "isolation," the sense of the absolute control of the interrogator, degradation, and ultimately "breaking down under extreme pressure and severe pain, whether the confession signed or information given is true or false" (18–20). Torture means the "censorship," the confiscation and sequestration, of the right to speak, to write—and to read. Contained, then, within AI's twelve-point program for the prevention of torture, in addition to the necessity for governments to transform their own bureaucracy, is the draft for an alternative communications network, including limits on incommunicado detention, independent investigation of reports of torture, no use of statements or confessions extracted under torture, and the prosecution of alleged torturers (249–51). This twelve-point program also proposes a new literary genre, as it were, one that includes the testimonies of political prisoners and their relatives, medical evidence, and the reports of human rights organizations, as well as a rereading of official government proclamations, claims, and signatures.

Censorship, according to William Shawcross in his introduction to Article 19's world report for 1988, "is not an issue on which many people take an absolutist position. It is this that makes freedom from censorship such a hard cause to fight." Shawcross goes on to distinguish between censorship and torture, in terms of the possibilities for mobilizing a mass struggle against them:

It is not to denigrate the work of Amnesty International to say that combating torture is a simple cause. To eradicate torture is obviously hard. But there are not many people—outside the apparatus of dictatorships—who would be seen or heard defending torture or even detention of political prisoners. On the other hand many of those who decry torture or imprisonment find it easy enough to invoke "restraint" or "the national interest" or "national security" as reasons for limiting freedom of expression and the right to know. Censorship, unlike torture, does not seem to be a black and white issue. (vii)

Nonetheless, the strategies of organized political resistance demand that both repressive practices, torture and censorship, be understood within a larger structural paradigm of coercion designed to contain political dissidence and critical insurgency. The writings of political detainees, male and female, constitute a threatening culture, a challenge to both the secrecy requirement of torture and the disciplinary sanctions that read

255

these incarcerated textual interventions out of the curriculum—thereby reinforcing the divisions that exclude the political and assimilate the academy and the prison within the repressive state apparatus. Three decades ago, Jean-Paul Sartre wrote:

> Happy are those who died without ever having had to ask themselves: "If they tear out my fingernails, will I talk?" But even happier are others, barely out of their childhood, who have not had to ask themselves that other question: "If my friends, fellow soldiers, and leaders tear out an enemy's fingernails in my presence, what will I do?" (intro. to Alleg, 15)

256

Women, writing, and political detention: the struggle against torture and the opposition to censorship are at once social and political movements, entailing new research imperatives and alternative archives, indeed countering cultural practices. When to "talk" and when to remain silent. Human rights, yes—but political status as well—for women, writing and political detainees. The silence imposed by the torturer is challenged by the demand for political resistance, raising again and again the urgent and critical relation between writing human rights and righting political wrongs.

Notes

Chapter 1. Political Detention (pp. 3–31)

1. The title of al-Fahum's book, *Wa la budda l-il-qaid in yankasiru*, is taken from a popular verse by the Tunisian poet Abu al-Qasim al-Shabi.

2. John Bender's *Imagining the Penitentiary: Fiction and Architecture of Mind in Eighteenth-Century England* (Chicago: University of Chicago Press, 1988) argues the relation between narrative closure and the development of the modern penal institution. What I would like to propose here is narrative as a way of "re-imagining the penitentiary."

3. For further discussion of this work, see Jean Franco, "Death Camp Confessions and Resistance to Violence in Latin America."

4. Muhammad Abu Nasr was gunned down in Gaza in spring 1989 by Israeli soldiers as one of the alleged kidnappers of Christopher George, the American co-director of Save the Children in the West Bank and Gaza.

5. The two available volumes of English translations of Gramsci's prison letters focus selectively on his letters to the women in his family: his wife Giulia, his sister-in-law Tatiana, and less frequently his wife and sister, and later his two sons. See Antonio Gramsci, *Letters from Prison*, ed. Lynne Lawner, and *Gramsci's Prison Letters*, ed. Hamish Henderson.

6. For an even fuller analysis of the battle of Bogside and its implications for the "technology of political control," especially the use of CS gas, see Russell Stetler, *The Battle of Bogside: The Politics of Violence in Northern Ireland* (London and Sydney: Sheed and Ward, 1970).

7. Within a year of their release, Paul Hill and Gerard Conlon had published their own prison memoirs and were active public speakers on behalf of the Birmingham Six and other republican issues. See Hill 1990 and Conlon 1990.

Chapter 2. Women and Resistance (pp. 32–68)

1. See, for example, Urdang 1979 and Davies 1983 and 1988.

2. Abou Iyad was assassinated in January 1991 at the PLO headquarters in Tunis.

3. For studies of the *testimonio*, see Beverley 1989, Yudice 1988, and the special issues on the *testimonio* of *Latin American Perspectives* 70 and 71 (Summer and Fall, 1991).

4. I wish to thank Yusuf Hassan Abdi for making available to me materials on the current situation in Kenya, from the opposition groups MWAKENYA and UMOJA in London.

5. For a study of women's war writing from Lebanon from the point of view of Western feminist theory, see Cooke 1988.

6. See, for example, the list released by the Center for Constitutional Rights in 1988 (*The Guardian*, 15 June 1988) and *Can't Jail the Spirit: Political Prisoners in the United States* (Chicago: Editorial El Coqui, n.d.).

Chapter 3. "Beyond the Pale" (pp. 78–100)

1. The SAS is an elite undercover unit of the British army, active in its colonial wars and deployed subsequently in Northern Ireland.

258

2. According to Kevin Kelley (1982), the phrase "beyond the pale" has a particular meaning in Irish history:

The Normans had overrun most of Ireland by 1250, but the Gaels fought back guerrilla-style over the next fifty years and slowly reduced the amount of territory controlled by the invader. By the early fourteenth century, Anglo-Norman writ was largely confined to a small area around Dublin, which was called the Pale. Inside this enclave, English settlers had established their first plantation in Ireland. Although the native Irish were officially excluded from the Pale, they made their influence felt within it to the same degree that the Normans had left their imprint on Gaelic regions. So pronounced was the linguistic, cultural, and political impact of the Gaels on the settlers that the colonial parliament in Dublin felt it necessary, in 1297, to take punitive measures against "degenerate Englishmen" who were adopting Irish traits.

Anglo-Norman rulers tried again to halt Gaelic encroachments by enacting the Statutes of Kilkenny in 1366. These laws forbade intermarriage between planter and Gael, required Irish people living inside the Pale to speak English at all times, and prohibited the colonizers from following the Brehon Laws, wearing native dress, talking in the Irish tongue, and adopting Gaelic names.

3. Pandora Press has published an important series of biographies of Irish political women, three of which are drawn on here: Margaret Mulvihill's (1989) study of Charlotte Despard; Margaret Ward's (1990) life of Maud Gonne; and Anne Haverty's (1988) story of Constance Markievicz.

4. Both Marion and Dolours Price were eventually released from Armagh prison, having been diagnosed as having anorexia nervosa, caused by the extensive force feeding to which they were subjected while on hunger strike in England and which interrupted the connection between eating and their metabolism. This "cause" of the disease stands in some contrast to representations, medical as well as popular, of anorexia in current United States literature on the topic. I am grateful to Felix Hull, M.D., for making much of the medical literature on the topic available to me.

5. Sinn Fein in 1980 began to seriously address these issues when it accepted at its annual Ard Fheis (meeting) the document *Women in the New Ireland*, recognizing the need to make available to women contraception, family planning, and divorce.

Chapter 4. Narrative in Prison (pp. 101–17)

1. I am grateful to Dr. Abdelwahab Elmessiri for sharing this manuscript with me.

2. *Al-Fajr*, 7 February 1988; also in *al-Afaq*, 10 March 1988. The stories were originally published in the Haifa-based *al-Ittihad*.
3. See also Harlow 1990.

Chapter 5. Sectarian versus Secular (pp. 118–38)

1. Inji Aflatun, however, the celebrated Egyptian artist and leftist intellectual, who died in 1989, did a series of paintings based on her experience in prison at that time. See the commemorative volume on Aflatun, *Inji Aflatun 1924–1989*.
2. Personal conversation on 17 July 1988 in Cairo. A similar situation was de-   259 scribed with regard to women prisoners from the 1950s and 1960s. The support of their comrades in the Communist party was strong, but later they often concealed their prison experiences from husbands who had not shared their previous political affiliations.

Chapter 6. Negotiating/Armed Struggle (pp. 139–57)

1. See also the Manifesto of Umkhonto we Sizwe issued on 16 December 1961, and reprinted in South African Communist Party 1981, 274–76, as well as Dubula 1971.
2. Recent revelations about South African "death squads" have indicated that Ruth First was indeed assassinated by orders from Pretoria. See, for example, "South African Police: Death Squad Central," *The Guardian*, 13 December 1989.
3. See Nixon 1991 for a more extended discussion of these films.

Chapter 7. *Carceles Clandestinas* (pp. 158–79)

1. For a documentary account of this action, see Tijerino 1978.
2. I am grateful to the El Rescate Human Rights Department, in Los Angeles, California, for making these statements available to me.
3. For a critical, if appreciative, reading of Enloe's book and its underestimation of the "political," see Jenny Bourne's review in *Race and Class* 32, 1 (Summer 1990): pp. 95–97.
4. Cayetano Carpio committed suicide in 1983 following the assassination that he had ordered of his colleague Comandante Ana (Melida Anaya Montes).
5. I want to thank John Beverley for pointing out this analysis to me.

Chapter 8. On Trial (pp. 180–202)

1. For biographical background on many of these prisoners, see Editorial El Coqui n.d., as well as documents and pamphlets by the tribunal, the National Lawyers Guild, and other prisoner-support organizations.
2. See *Framing the Panthers in Black and White* (1990), a video on the release of Dhoruba bin Wahad by Annie Goldson and Chris Bratton, available from Pressa, 151 First Avenue, Suite 195, New York 10003.
3. For an expanded reading of Margaret Randall's trials in United States courts, see Carolyn Warmbold, "Women of the Mosquito Press: Louise Bryant, Agnes

Smedley, Margaret Randall" (Ph.D. dissertation, University of Texas at Austin, 1990).

4. See also Mitgang 1988, Donner 1990, and Linfield 1990. There is perhaps a new literary corpus emergent here.

5. For additional selections of Ericka Huggins's poetry, see Scheffler 1989.

6. A much larger women's HSU facility in Marianna, Florida, has been prepared to receive the former Lexington inmates. Like the Marion Control Unit for male prisoners in Illinois, which has been on total lockdown—prisoners confined to their cells 23 ½ hours a day—since October 1983, the Marianna unit reproduces all the repressive features of Lexington. In the meantime, a "new and improved" version of Marion is being built in Florence, Colorado.

260

Chapter 9. The Tyranny of Home versus "Safe Houses" (pp. 205–20)

1. See, for example, such excellent studies as Americo Paredes, *"With His Pistol in His Hand": A Border Ballad and Its Hero* (Austin: University of Texas Press, 1958) and Robert Rosenbaum, *Mexicano Resistance in the Southwest* (Austin: University of Texas Press, 1981). The bibliographical and archival work being done by Clara Lomas promises to make available substantial material for writing a larger history of the signal contributions of Mexican and Mexican American women to these struggles. See, for example, Lomas's translations and introductions in *Longman's Anthology of World Literature by Women*, ed. Barbara Shollar and Marian Arkin (New York and London: Longman, 1989). See also Jean Franco, *Plotting Women: Gender and Representation in Mexico* (New York: Columbia University Press, 1989).

2. I am much indebted in these brief readings of Viramontes and Cisneros to the work of Sonia Saldivar-Hull. See "Feminism on the Border: From Gender Politics to Geo-Politics" (Ph.D. dissertation, University of Texas at Austin, 1990).

3. The United States-Mexican border has become a significant site for contemporary mainstream films as well. These should be contrasted with the critiques proposed by *El Norte*. See, for example, *Extreme Prejudice*, directed by Walter Hill (1987), and *The Border*, directed by Tony Richardson (1982). *Chulas Fronteras*, directed by Les Blank (1976), presents through the Mexican *corrido* still another version of "border culture."

4. The "necessity defense" has been similarly denied in trials of anti-nuclear protestors and students protesting CIA recruitment on college campuses. It was also refused to the UT 16, sixteen University of Texas at Austin students who were arrested following a sit-in the offices of the university president in protest at the university's investments in South Africa. They were convicted of criminal trespass and given sentences ranging from one to six months.

Chapter 10. Prison and Liberation (pp. 225–40)

1. Izat al-Ghazawi was himself arrested in May 1989, in the seventeenth month of the *intifada*, by Israeli military occupation authorities.

2. Ansar 2 was opened in 1986 in the Gaza Strip largely as a detention center for children and young people. Most notorious of all now is Ansar 3 (Ketziot), the prison camp established in the Negev Desert to hold the thousands of Palestinian prisoners arrested during the *intifada*.

3. I want to thank E. San Juan Jr., translator of this story, for providing me with background material and information on Filipino resistance struggles.

4. I am grateful to Lulu Torres-Reyes, a Filipina critic and cultural worker, for bringing the work of Mila D. Aguilar to my attention.

5. For a Bakhtinian analysis of the relation between the carnivalesque and prison writing, see Ioan Davies, *Writers in Prison* (London: Basil Blackwell, 1990), especially chapter 1.

Bibliography

Preface

Feldman, Alan. 1991. *Formations of Violence: The Narrative of the Body and Political Terror in Northern Ireland.* Chicago: University of Chicago Press.

Higgins, Rita Ann. 1992. *Philomena's Revenge.* Galway: Salmon Publishing.

Kaufman, Natalie Hevener. 1990. *Human Rights Treaties and the Senate: A History of Opposition.* Chapel Hill: University of North Carolina Press.

McAliskey, Bernadette. 1992. "Interview." By Irene Sherry. *Women in Struggle,* 1: 10–11.

Scott, James C. 1990. *Domination and the Arts of Resistance: Hidden Transcripts.* New Haven: Yale University Press.

Chapter 1. Political Detention

Aboulhejleh, Nizam. n.d. *Portrait of a Palestinian Prisoner.* Seattle, Wash.: Palestine Human Rights Committee.

Abu Libdeh, Hasan. 1982. "Wound in the Bad Time" (Jarah fi-l-zaman al-radiʾ). Jerusalem.

Abu Nasr, Muhammad. 1984. "The Two Comrades Meet" (Wa iltaqa al-rafiqan). *Filastin al-thawra* 501 (24 March): 46–47.

———. n.d. *Men . . . and Bars* (Rijal wa qudban). Nazareth: Jam ʿiya Ansar al-Sajin fi Israʾil.

Ackroyd, Carol; Margolis, Karen; Rosenhead, Jonathan; and Shallice, Tim. 1977. *The Technology of Political Control.* Harmondsworth: Penguin.

Aptheker, Bettina. 1971. "The Social Function of the Prisons in the United States." In *If They Come in the Morning: Voices of Resistance,* edited by Angela Davis. New York: The Third Press.

Benson, Mary, ed. 1976. *The Sun Will Rise.* London: International Defense and Aid Fund.

Beverley, John. 1984–85. "Writing from the Revolution: Ernesto Cardenal and Roque Dalton." *Metamorfosis* 5(2)–6(1).

Conlon, Gerard. 1990. *Proved Innocent.* London: Hamish Hamilton.

Cossali, Paul, and Robson, Clive. 1986. *Stateless in Gaza.* London: Zed Books.

Davidson, R. Theodore. 1974. *Chicano Prisoners: The Key to San Quentin.* New York: Holt, Rinehart and Winston.

Day, Susie. 1989. "Resistance Conspiracy Trial." *Z Magazine* (September): 83–89.

de Lauretis, Teresa. 1987. *Technologies of Gender.* Bloomington: Indiana University Press.

Bibliography

Diaz, Nidia. 1988. *Nunca Estuve Sola*. San Salvador: UCA Editores.

Dunne, Derek. 1988. *Out of the Maze: The True Story of the Biggest Jailbreak in Europe since the Second World War*. Dublin: Gill and Macmillan.

al-Fahum, Walid. 1984. *Birds of Neve Tertza* (Tiyur Neve Tertza). Nazareth: Maktaba al-Fahum.

———. n.d. *These Chains That We Must Break* (Wa la budda l-il-qaid in yankasiru). Akka: Maktabat-al-Jalil.

Fiori, Giuseppe. 1990. *Antonio Gramsci: Life of a Revolutionary*. Translated by Tom Nairn. London and New York: Verso.

Foucault, Michel. 1974. "'Michel Foucault on Attica: An Interview (with John Simon)." *Telos* 19 (Spring): 154–61.

———. 1979. *Discipline and Punish*. Translated by Alan Sheridan. New York: Vintage.

Franco, Jean. 1986. "Death Camp Confessions and Resistance to Violence in Latin America." *Socialism and Democracy* 2: 5–14.

Franklin, H. Bruce. 1982. *Prison Literature in America: The Victim as Criminal and Artist*. Westport, Conn.: Lawrence Hill and Co.

Gilroy, Paul. 1987. *There Ain't No Black in the Union Jack: The Cultural Politics of Race and Nation*. London: Hutchinson.

Gramsci, Antonio. 1988. *Gramsci's Prison Letters*. Translated by Hamish Hamilton. London: Zwan Publishers.

———. 1989. *Letters from Prison*. Translated and edited by Lynne Lawner. New York: Farrar Straus Giroux.

Guadalupe Martinez, Ana. 1980. *Las carceles clandestinas de El Salvador*. Sinaloa, Mexico: Universidad Autonomia de Sinaloa.

Hill, Paul. 1990. *Stolen Years*. London and New York: Doubleday.

Jenkin, Tim. 1987. *Escape from Pretoria*. London: Kliptown Books.

Kanafani, Ghassan. 1984. "The Slope." In *Palestine's Children*, translated by Barbara Harlow. London: Heinemann.

Luxemburg, Rosa. 1981. *Comrade and Lover: Rosa Luxemburg's Letters to Leo Jogiches*. Translated and edited by Elzbieta Ettinger. Cambridge: MIT Press.

McKee, Grant, and Franey, Ros. 1988. *Time Bomb: Irish Bombers, English Justice and the Guildford Four*. London: Bloomsbury.

Melossi, Dario, and Pavarini, Massimo. 1981. *The Prison and the Factory: Origins of the Penitentiary System*. Translated by Glynis Cousin. Totowa, N.J.: Barnes and Noble.

Muzaffar, Nada. 1987. "Women Defeat the Zionist Concentration Camps" (Almara'a yuqhiru mu'askarat aushfitz al-sihyuniya). *Sawt al-mara'a* 7.

Nesvisky, Matt. 1989. "The Game's Up." *Jerusalem Post*, 16 May.

Partnoy, Alicia. 1986. *The Little School: Tales of Disappearance and Survival in Argentina*. Translated by Alicia Partnoy, with Lois Athey and Sandra Braunstein. Pittsburgh: Cleis Press.

Peters, Edward. 1985. *Torture*. Oxford and New York: Basil Blackwell.

Pheto, Molefe. 1983. *And Night Fell: Memoirs of a Political Prisoner in South Africa*. London: Allison and Busby.

Rivabella, Omar. 1986. *Requiem for a Woman's Soul*. Harmondsworth: Penguin.

Rowbotham, Sheila. 1974. *Women, Resistance and Revolution*. New York: Random House.

St. John, Carmen. 1985. Foreword to *Between Struggle and Hope: The Nicaraguan Literacy Crusade*, by Valerie Miller. Boulder, Colo.: Westview Press.

Samara, Munira, and al-Dhaher, Muhammad. 1985. *Scenario of Zionist Prisons* (Sinario al-mu ʿtaqalat al-sihyuniya). Amman: Dar al-Minarat.

Sanchez, Rosaura. 1987. "Ethnicity, Ideology and Academia." *Americas Review* 15: 80–88.

Scarry, Elaine. 1985. *The Body in Pain: The Making and Unmaking of the World*. Oxford: Oxford University Press.

Spriano, Paolo. 1979. *Antonio Gramsci and the Party: The Prison Years*. Translated by John Fraser. London: Lawrence and Wishart. **265**

Subara, Dr. Ahmad. 1984. "Camp of Ghosts: Diary of a Doctor in Ansar" (Mu'askar al-ashbah: Yaumiyyat tabib fi Ansar). In *National Resistance in Southern Lebanon* (Al-Muqawama al-wataniya fi-l-junub al-lubnani). Beirut: Dar al-ʾIqraʾ.

Taʾmari, Salah. 1984. "The Untold Story of Ansar: An Eyewitness Account." *Palestine Human Rights Commitee Bulletin* 38.

Tawil, Raymonda Hawa. 1989. "A Letter to Mutawakel Taha: A Palestinian Prisoner." *The Return* (August): 4–5.

Thiongʾo, Ngugi wa. 1981. *Detained: A Writer's Prison Diary*. London: Heinemann.

Valdes, Hernan. 1975. *Diary of a Chilean Concentration Camp*. Translated by Jo Labanyi. London: Victor Gollancz.

Wazwaz, Adil. n.d. *Call . . . from Behind Bars* (Nidaʾ . . . min waraʾ al- qudban). N.p.

West, Cornel. 1988. "Marxist Theory and the Specificity of Afro-American Oppression." In *Marxism and the Interpretation of Culture*, edited by Cary Nelson and Lawrence Grossberg. Urbana and Chicago: University of Illinois Press.

Yunis, Fadl. 1983. *Cell Number 7* (Zinzana raqm 7). Amman: Dar al-Jalil.

Chapter 2. Women and Resistance

Abu Iyad (Salah Khalaf), with Eric Rouleau. 1981. *My Home, My Land: A Narrative of the Palestinian Struggle*. Translated by Linda Butler Koseoglu. New York: Times Books.

Adnan, Etel. 1982. *Sitt Marie Rose*. Translated by Georgina Kleege. Sausalito, Calif.: Post Apollo Press.

Alegria, Claribel. 1987. *They Won't Take Me Alive*. Translated by Amanda Hopkinson. London: The Women's Press.

Beverley, John. 1989. "The Margin in the Center: On *Testimonio* (Testimonial Narrative)." *Modern Fiction Studies* 35(1): 11–28.

Cabezas, Omar. 1985. *Fire from the Mountain*. Translated by Kathleen Weaver. New York: Crown Publishers.

Cooke, Miriam. 1988. *War's Other Voices: Women Writers on the Lebanese Civil War*. Cambridge: Cambridge University Press.

Dalton, Roque. 1987. *Miguel Marmol*. Translated by Kathleen Ross and Richard Schaaf. Willimantic, Conn.: Curbstone Press.

Davies, Miranda, ed. 1983, 1988. *Third World/Second Sex*. 2 vols. London: Zed Books.

Davis, Angela. 1974. *An Autobiography*. New York: Random House.

Derry Film and Video Collective. 1988. *Mother Ireland*. Videotape.

Devi, Mahasweta. 1987. "Draupadi." Translated by Gayatri Chakravorty Spivak. In *In Other Worlds: Essays in Cultural Politics*. New York: Methuen.

Devlin, Bernadette. 1970. *The Price of My Soul*. New York: Vintage Books.

Diaz, Gladys. 1983. "Roles and Contradictions of Chilean Women in the Resistance and in Exile." In *Third World/Second Sex*. See Davies.

Dietl, Gulshan. 1989. "Portrait of a Revolutionary: Leila Khalid 20 Years On." *The Middle East* (January).

Eckstein, Susan. 1989. "Power and Popular Protest in Latin America." In *Power and Protest: Latin American Social Movements*, edited by Susan Eckstein. Berkeley and Los Angeles: University of California Press.

Fanon, Frantz. 1982. *The Wretched of the Earth*. Translated by Constance Farrington. Harmondsworth: Penguin.

Farrell, Michael. 1980. *Northern Ireland: The Orange State*. London: Pluto Press.

Goldson, Annie. 1989. "Allegories of Resistance." *Afterimage* (May).

Guevara, Ernesto "Che." 1961. *Guerrilla Warfare*. New York: Monthly Review.

———. 1968. *Reminiscences of the Cuban Revolution*. Translated by Victoria Ortiz. New York: Monthly Review.

Guha, Ranajit. 1988. "The Prose of Counter-Insurgency." In *Selected Subaltern Studies*, edited by Ranajit Guha and Gayatri Spivak. New York and Oxford: Oxford University Press.

Jabbour, Hala Deeb. 1988. *A Woman of Nazareth*. Brooklyn, N.Y.: Olive Branch Press.

Kanafani, Ghassan. 1972. "The Case of Abu Hamidu and Cultural Cooperation with the Enemy." *Shu'un filastiniyya* 12: 8–18.

Kariuki, J.M. 1963. *"Mau Mau" Detainee*. Foreword by Margery Perham. London and Nairobi: Oxford University Press.

Khaled, Leila, with George Hajjar. 1973. *My People Shall Live: The Autobiography of a Revolutionary*. London: Hodder and Stoughton.

Likimani, Muthani. 1985. *Passbook Number F.47927: Women and Mau Mau in Kenya*. London: Macmillan.

Martinez, Vladimir. 1987. *Vivir signifir luchar*. San Salvador: TECOLUT.

Nana, Hamida. 1979. *Homeland in My Eyes* (Al-Watan fi-l-Aynayn). Beirut: Dar al-Adab.

Ngwenga, Jane. 1983. "Women and Liberation in Zimbabwe." In *Third World/Second Sex*. See Davies vol. 1, 1983.

Nyasha and Rose. 1983. "Four Years of Struggle in Zimbabwe." In *Third World/Second Sex*. See Davies vol. 1, 1983.

Piriz, Clara. 1988. "Marriage by Pros and Cons." In *You Can't Drown the Fire: Latin American Women Writing in Exile*, edited by Alicia Partnoy. Pittsburgh, Pa.: Cleis Press.

Sharara, Yolla Pollity. 1983. "Women and Politics in Lebanon." In *Third World/Second Sex*. See Davies vol. 1, 1983.

al-Shaykh, Hanan. 1986. *The Story of Zahra*. Translated by Peter Ford. London: Readers International and Quartet.

Sommer, Doris. 1989. " 'Not Just a Personal Story': Women's Testimonios and the Plural Self." In *Life/lines*, edited by Celeste Schenck. Ithaca, N.Y.: Cornell University Press.

Spivak, Gayatri Chakravorty. 1988. "Can the Subaltern Speak?" In *Marxism and the*

Interpretation of Culture, edited by Cary Nelson and Lawrence Grossberg. Urbana and Chicago: University of Illinois Press.

Stallybrass, Peter. 1989. "The World Turned Upside Down: Inversion, Gender and the State." Paper presented at the Pembroke Center, Brown University, March.

Tijerino, Doris, with Margaret Randall. 1978. *Inside the Nicaraguan Revolution*. Translated by Elinor Randall. Vancouver: New Star Books.

Thiong'o, Ngugi wa. 1981. *Detained: A Writer's Prison Diary*. London: Heinemann.

———. 1986. *Decolonizing the Mind: The Politics of Language in African Literature*. London: James Currey.

Turki, Fawaz. 1988. *Soul in Exile*. New York: Monthly Review Press.

Urdang, Stephanie. 1979. *Fighting Two Colonialisms: Women in Guinea Bissau*. New York: Monthly Review Press.

United Movement for Democracy in Kenya (UMOJA). 1988. *Struggle for Democracy in Kenya: Special Report on the 1988 General Elections in Kenya*. London: UMOJA.

West, Cornel. 1988. "Marxist Theory and the Specificity of Afro-American Oppression." In *Marxism and the Interpretation of Culture*. See Spivak 1988.

Yudice, George. 1988. "Marginality and the Ethics of Survival." In *Universal Abandon: The Politics of Postmodernism*, edited by Andrew Ross, 214–236. Minneapolis: University of Minnesota Press.

Yunis, Fadl. 1983. *Cell Number 7* (Zinzana raqm 7). Amman: Dar al-Jalil.

Recognition Scenes

Beyond the Walls. 1985. Directed by Uri Barbash. Film.

Dorfman, Ariel. 1984. *Widows*. Translated by Stephen Kessler. New York: Random House.

Menchu, Rigoberta. 1984. *I, Rigoberta Menchu: An Indian Woman in Guatemala*. Edited by Elizabeth Burgos-Debray, translated by Ann Wright. London: Verso.

al-Nuwwab, Muzaffar. 1988. "The Recantation." Translated by Abdul-Salaam Yousif. In *Vanguardist Cultural Practices*. See Yousif 1988.

Shohat, Ella. 1989. *Israeli Cinema: East/West and the Politics of Representation*. Austin: University of Texas Press.

Yousif, Abdul-Salaam. 1988. *Vanguardist Cultural Practices: The Formation of an Alternative Cultural Hegemony in Iraq and Chile, 1930s–1970s*. Ann Arbor: UMI.

Chapter 3. "Beyond the Pale"

Amnesty International. 1988. *Northern Ireland: Killings by Security Forces and "Supergrass" Trials*. London: Amnesty International. June.

Beresford, David. 1987. *Ten Men Dead: The Story of the 1981 Irish Hunger Strike*. London: Grafton Books.

Bernard, Margie. 1989. *Daughter of Derry: The Story of Brigid Sheils Makowski*. London: Pluto Press.

Coogan, Tim Pat. 1980. *On the Blanket: The H-Block Story*. Dublin: Ward River Press.

Curtis, Liz. 1984a. *Ireland: The Propaganda War: The British Media and the "Battle for Hearts and Minds."* London: Pluto Press.

———. 1984b. *Nothing But the Same Old Story: The Roots of Anti-Irish Racism*. London: Information on Ireland.

Bibliography

D'Arcy, Margaretta. 1981. *Tell Them Everything: A Sojourn in the Prison of Her Majesty Queen Elizabeth II at Ard Macha (Armagh)*. London: Pluto Press.

Deane, Seamus. 1985. "Civilians and Barbarians." In *Ireland's Field Day* edited by the Field Day Theatre Company. London: Hutchinson and Co.

Fairweather, Elaine; McDonough, Roisin; and McFadyean, Melanie. 1984. *Only the Rivers Run Free: Northern Ireland: The Women's War*. London: Pluto Press.

Farrell, Mairead. 1989. "Interview with Jenny McGeaver." *Spare Rib* 204 (August): 16–20.

Giolla Espaig, Aine, and Giolla Espaig, Eibhlin Nic. 1987. *Sisters in Cells*. Edited and translated by Nollaig O'Gadhra. Westport, Co. Mayo: Foilseachin Naisiunta Teoranta.

Hadden, Tom; Boyle, Kevin; and Campbell, Colm. 1988. "Emergency Law in Northern Ireland: The Context," in *Justice Under Fire*, see Jennings 1988.

Hall, Peter. 1988. "The Prevention of Terrorism Acts," in *Justice Under Fire*, see Jennings 1988.

Haverty, Anne. 1988. *Constance Markievicz: An Independent Life*. London: Pandora.

Hillyard, Paddy. 1983. "Law and Order." In *Northern Ireland: The Background to the Conflict*, edited by John Darby. Belfast: The Appletree Press; Syracuse: Syracuse University Press.

Jennings, Anthony, ed. 1988. *Justice under Fire: The Abuse of Civil Liberties in Northern Ireland*. London: Pluto Press.

Kelley, Kevin. 1982. *The Longest War: Northern Ireland and the IRA*. London: Zed Books.

Lyons, Laura. 1990. "A Feminist 'Tour' of Duty: Margaretta D'Arcy's *Tell Them Everything*." Seminar paper, University of Texas at Austin, Spring.

McAuley, Chrissie. n.d. *Women in a War Zone: Twenty Years of Resistance*. Dublin: AP/RN.

McCafferty, Nell. 1981. *The Armagh Women*. Dublin: Co-op Books.

Mac Cormaic, Eoghan. 1984. "The Price of Freedom." *Iris* 8 (August):34–42.

Markievicz, Constance. 1986. *Prison Letters*. London: Virago Press.

Mulvihill, Margaret. 1989. *Charlotte Despard: A Biography*. London: Pandora.

National Council for Civil Liberties. 1986. *Strip-Searching: An inquiry into the Strip Searching of Women Remand Prisoners at Armagh Prison between 1982 and 1985*. London: National Council for Civil Liberties.

O'Hare, Rita. n.d. "Conclusion." In *Women in a War Zone: Twenty Years of Resistance*. See McAuley n.d.

O'Malley, Padraig. 1990. *Biting at the Grave: The Irish Hunger Strikes and the Politics of Despair*. Boston: Beacon Press.

Rolston, Bill. 1989. "Mothers, Whores, Wives and Villains: Images of Women in Novels of the Northern Ireland Conflict." *Race and Class* 31 (1).

Sinn Fein, Prisoner of War Department, n.d. *Lifers*. N.p.: Sinn Fein.

Stalker, John. 1989. *The Stalker Affair*. Harmondsworth: Penguin.

Stetler, Russell. 1970. *The Battle of Bogside: The Politics of Violence in Northern Ireland*. London and Sydney: Sheed and Ward.

Strategic Policy Unit. 1987. *Breaking the Silence: Women's Imprisonment*. London: Strategic Policy Unit.

Troops Out Movement. *Strip-Searching: End It Now*. London: n.d. Pamphlet.

Ward, Margaret. 1983. *Unmanageable Revolutionaries: Women and Irish Nationalism*. London: Pluto Press.

————. 1990. *Maud Gonne: Ireland's Joan of Arc*. London: Pandora.

Williams, Maxine. 1989. *Murder on the Rock: How the British Government Got Away with Murder*. London: Larkin Publications.

Yeats, W. B. 1973. "The King's Threshold." In *The Collected Plays of W. B. Yeats*. New York: Macmillan.

Yeats, W. B, 1989. *The Collected Poems of W. B. Yeats*, edited by Richard J. Finneran. New York: Collier Books.

Chapter 4. Narrative in Prison

Abdullah, Ghassan. n.d. *Freedom of Expression . . . the Crime*. Jerusalem: Palestinian Writers Union.

al-Abnudi, Abd al-Rahman. 1988. "Death on the Sidewalk" (al-Mawt ala-l-asfalt). *Ruz al-Yusif*, 27 June–1 August.

Anderson, Perry. 1988. "Modernity and Revolution." In *Marxism and the Interpretation of Culture*, edited by Cary Nelson and Lawrence Grossberg. Urbana and Chicago: University of Illinois Press.

Darwich, Mahmoud, with Simone Bitton, Matitahu Peled, and Ouri Avneri. 1988. *Palestine mon pays: L'affaire du poeme*. Paris: Editions du Minuit.

Elmessiri, Abdelwahab. 1988. "*Intifada* or Revolution" (Intifada aw Thawra). Manuscript.

Hall, Stuart. 1988. "The Toad in the Garden: Thatcherism among the Theorists." In *Marxism and the Interpretation of Culture*. See Anderson 1988.

Hall, Stuart; Critcher, Chas; Jefferson, Tony; Clarke, John; and Roberts, Brian. 1978. *Policing the Crisis: Mugging, the State, and Law and Order*. London: Macmillan.

Hanitzotz Publishing House. 1988. *Silencing the Opposition: The Case of "Derech Hanitzotz."* Jerusalem: Hanitzotz Publishing House.

Harlow, Barbara. 1984. "Palestine or Andalusia: The Literary Response to the Israeli Invasion of Lebanon." *Race and Class* 26 (2):33–43.

————. 1990. "Constructions of the Intifada." *Polygraph* (4):35–53.

Harris, Joshua, and Wallace, Tina, with Heather Booth. 1983. *To Ride the Storm: The 1980 Bristol "Riots" and the State*. London: Heinemann.

Jameson, Fredric. 1988. "The State of the Subject III." *Critical Quarterly* 29 (4):16–25.

Kanafani, Ghassan. 1982. *Literature of Resistance in Occupied Palestine 1948–1966* (Adab al-muqawamah fi Filastin al-muhtallah). Beirut: Institute for Arab Research.

————. 1990. "Thoughts on Change and the 'Blind Language.'" Translated by Barbara Harlow and Nejd Yaziji. *ALIF* (10):132–58.

Khoury, Elias. 1988. "The Names All of Them" (Al-Asma² Kuluha). *al-Hadaf*, 31 January.

Mattelart, Armand. 1979. "Communication Ideology and Class Practice." In *Communication and Class Struggle I: Capitalism, Imperialism*, edited by Armand Mattelart and Seth Sieglaub. New York: International General.

Shahada, Edmond. 1988. *The Road to Birzeit* (al-Tariq ila Bir Zayt). Nazareth: al-Maktaba al-Haditha.

Shammas, Anton. 1988. "A Stone's Throw." *New York Review of Books*, 31 March.

Taha, al-Mutawakkil, and Amr Samha. 1988. *After Two Decades . . . and a Generation* (Ba'd 'aqdayn . . . wa jil). Jerusalem: n.p.

Tawil, Raymonda. 1983. *My Home, My Prison*. London: Zed Books.

———. 1988. *Women Prisoners in the Prison Country* (Sajinat fi-l-watan al-sajin). Akka: Dar al-Aswar.

Chapter 5. Sectarian versus Secular

Abd al-Hakim, Tahar. 1978. *Bare Feet* (al-Aqdam al-ʿariya). Beirut: n.p.

Abdalla, Ahmed. 1985. *The Student Movement and National Politics in Egypt*. London: Al-Saqi Books.

Aissa, Salah. 1987. *The Nightmare That Threatens Us* (al-Karitha alati tuhaddadna). Cairo: Madbuli.

Beinin, Joel. 1990. *Was the Red Flag Flying There?: Marxist Politics and the Arab-Israeli Conflict in Egypt and Israel, 1948–1965*. Berkeley and Los Angeles: University of California Press.

Botman, Selma. 1988. *The Rise of Egyptian Communism 1939–1970*. Syracuse: Syracuse University Press.

Cooke, Miriam. 1988. "Prisons: Egyptian Women Writers on Islam." *Religion and Literature* 20 (1).

ai-Ghazali, Zaynab. 1984. *Days of My Life* (Ayyam min hayati). Cairo: Dar al-Shuruq.

Harlow, Barbara. "Egyptian Intellectuals and the 'Normalization of Cultural Relations.'" *Cultural Critique* (4):33–59.

Kazim, Safinaz. 1986. *On Prison and Freedom* (ʿAn al-sijn wa-l-hurriya). Cairo: Al-Zahra.

Kepel, Gilles. 1985. *Muslim Extremism in Egypt: The Prophet and the Pharoah*. Translated by Jon Rothschild. Berkeley and Los Angeles: University of California Press.

Mitchell, Timothy. 1988. "The Experience of Prison in Islamicist Discourse: The Production of Zaynab al-Ghazzali's *Ayyam min Hayati*." Paper presented at conference, "Intellectuels et militants de l'Islam contemporain," Paris, 31 May–1 June.

al-Naqqash, Farida. 1985. *Prison: Two Tears . . . and a Rose* (al-Sijn: damaʾtan . . . wa warda). Cairo: Dar al-Mustaqbal al-Arabi.

———. 1988a. "Don't say, we didn't know." *Al-Ahali*, 20 July.

———. 1988b. "Prison Increased My Conviction in My Ideas: Interview with Nuha Samara." *al-Shahid* 35 (July).

Progressive Women's Union and Committee in Defense of National Culture. n.d. *Inji Aflatun 1924–1989*. Cairo: Progressive Women's Union and Committee in Defense of National Culture.

al-Saadawi, Nawal. 1982. *Twelve Women in One Cell* (Insan: ithna ʿashara imraʾa fi zinzana wahda). Cairo: Madbuli.

———. 1986. *Memoirs from the Women's Prison*. Translated by Marilyn Both. London: The Women's Press.

Said, Rifaʿat. 1986. *History of the Egyptian Communist Movement: Unity, Division, Resolution 1957–1965* (Tarikh al-haraka al-shuyuʿiyya al-misriyya: al-wahda, al-inqisam, al-hall). Cairo: Shirkat al-Aml.

Tiba, Mustafa. 1978, 1980. *Letters of a Political Prisoner to His Beloved* (Rasaʿ il sajin siyasi ila habibtihu). 2 vols. Cairo: al-Arabi.

Chapter 6. Negotiating/Armed Struggle

A Dry White Season. 1989. Directed by Euzhan Palcy. Film.

Baard, Frances, as told to Barbie Schreiner. 1986. *My Spirit Is Not Banned*. Harare: Zimbabwe Publishing House.

Benson, Mary, ed. 1976. *The Sun Will Rise: Statements from the Dock by Southern African Politial Prisoners*. London: IDAF.

Bernstein, Hilda. 1978. *For Their Triumphs and for the Tears: Women in Apartheid South Africa*. London: IDAF.

———. 1989. *The World That Was Ours: The Story of the Rivonia Trial*. London: SAWriters. **271**

Bozzoli, Belinda, and Delius, Peter. 1990. "Radical History and South African History." In *History from South Africa*, special issue of *Radical History Review* 46/47.

Brittain, Victoria, and Minty, Abdul S., eds. 1988. *Children of Resistance: Statements from the Harare Conference on Children, Repression and the Law in Apartheid South Africa*. London: Kliptown Books.

Buntman, Fran. 1988. "From Hell-Hole to a Blessing in Disguise: A Study of Politics on Robben Island." B.A. honors thesis in political science, University of Witwatersrand.

Cry Freedom, 1988. Directed by Richard Attenborough. Film.

Detainees' Parents Support Committee. 1989. *Cries of Freedom: Women in Detention in South Africa*. London: Catholic Institute for International Relations.

Dingake, Michael. 1987. *My Fight against Apartheid*. London: Kliptown Books.

Dubula, Sol. 1971. "Ten Years of Umkhonto we Sizwe." *The African Communist*, 4th quarter. Reprinted in South African Communist Party 1981.

First, Ruth. 1989. *117 Days*. New York: Monthly Review.

"Free South Africa's Children: A Symposium on Children in Detention." (1988). *Human Rights Quarterly* 10 (1).

International Defense and Aid Fund (IDAF). 1978. *Prisoners of Apartheid: A Biographical List of Political Prisoners and Banned Persons in South Africa*. London: IDAF, October.

———. 1981. *To Honour Women's Day: Profiles of Leading Women in the South African and Namibian Liberation Struggles*. London: IDAF, August.

Joseph, Helen. 1986. *Side by Side*. London: Zed Books.

Kitson, Norma. 1986. *Where Sixpence Lives*. London: Chatto and Windus.

Makhoere, Caesarina Kona. 1988. *No Child's Play: In Prison under Apartheid*. London: The Women's Press.

Malinga, Phineas. 1990. "Talking about Talks: The Politics of Negotiations." *The African Communist* (120):26–34.

Mandela, Winnie. 1985. *Part of My Soul Went with Him*. Edited by Anne Benjamin. New York: W.W. Norton.

Matthews, J., and Thomas, Gladys. 1972. *Cry Rage*. Johannesberg: Spro-Cas Publications.

Mbeki, Govan. 1964. *South Africa: The Peasants' Revolt*. Preface by Ruth First. Harmondsworth: Penguin.

Mzamane, Mbuelo. 1982. *The Children of Soweto*. Johannesberg: Raven Press.

Nixon, Rob. 1991. "Cry White Season: Apartheid, Liberalism and the American Screen." *South Atlantic Quarterly* 29, no. 4 (Summer):499–529.

Russell, Diane E. H. 1989. *Lives of Courage: Women for a New South Africa.* New York: Basic Books.

SATIS (South Africa—The Imprisoned Society). 1985. *Political Trials in South Africa: Judicial Instruments of Repression.* London: SATIS, May.

Sepamla, Sipho. 1984. *A Ride on the Whirlwind.* London: Heinemann.

————. 1981. *Third Generation.* Johannesburg: Skotaville Publishers.

Shava, Piniel Viriri. 1989. *A People's Voice: Black South African Writing in the 20th Century.* London: Zed Books.

Slovo, Gillian. 1989. *Ties of Blood.* London: Michael Joseph.

Slovo, Shawn. 1988. *A World Apart.* London: Faber & Faber.

South African Communist Party. 1981. *South African Communists Speak: Documents from the History of the South African Communist Party 1915–1980.* London: Inkululeko Publications.

Staying Strong in Detention. Johannesburg: South African Committee for Higher Education (SACHED) Trust.

Chapter 7. *Carceles Clandestinas*

Alegria, Claribel, and Flakoll, Darwin J. 1989. *Ashes of Izalco.* Translated by Darwin J. Flakoll. Willimantic, Conn.: Curbstone Press.

Anglesey, Zoe, ed. 1987. IXOK-AMAR GO: *Central American Women's Poetry for Peace.* Penobscot, Maine: Granite Press.

Anonymous. 1987. "We Cannot Be Enamored of the Moon." In IXOK-AMAR GO: *Central American Women's Poetry for Peace.* See Anglesey 1987.

Argueta, Manlio. 1987. *Cuzcatlan: Where the Southern Sea Beats.* Translated by Bill Brow. New York: Pantheon.

Arias, Arturo. 1989. "Nueva Narrativa Centroamericana." *Extramares* 1(1):57–72.

Belli, Gioconda. 1989. *La mujer habitada.* Mexico: Editorial Diana.

Bosch, Juan. 1968. "An Anti-Communist Manifesto." In *Regis Debray and the Latin American Revolution.* See Huberman and Sweezy 1968.

Bunster-Burotto, Ximena. 1985. "Surviving beyond Fear: Women and Torture in Latin America." In *Women and Change in Latin America,* edited by June Nash and Helen Safa. South Hadley, Massachusetts: Bergin and Garvey.

Bustamante, Cecilia. 1989. "The Body and Writing." *Extramares* 1(1):123–29.

Carter, Brenda et al. 1989. *A Dream Compels Us: Voices of Salvadoran Women.* Edited by New Americas Press Collective. Boston: South End Press.

Cayetano Carpio, Salvador. 1982. *Secuestro y Capucha.* Quito, Ecuador: Editorial Conajo.

Dalton, Roque. 1970. *¿Revolucion en la Revolucion? y la critica de derecha.* Havana: Casa de las Americas.

Debray, Regis. 1968. *Revolution in the Revolution?* translated by Bobbye Ortiz. Harmondsworth: Penguin.

————. 1988. "Letter to Nazim Hikmet." In *El Salvador at War: A Collage Epic,* edited by Marc Zimmerman. Minneapolis: MEP Publications.

de Ipola, Emilio. 1983. "La bemba." In *Ideologia y discurso populista.* Buenos Aires: Folios Ediciones.

Diaz, Nidia. 1988. *Nunca Estuve Sola*. San Salvador: UCA Editores.

Didion, Joan. 1983. *Salvador*. New York: Washington Square Press.

Enloe, Cynthia. 1990. *Bananas, Beaches and Bases: Making Feminist Sense of International Politics*. Berkeley and Los Angeles: University of California Press.

Forché, Carolyn. 1983. "El Salvador: An Aide-Memoire." In *In Praise of What Persists*, edited by Stephen Berg. New York: Harper and Row.

Guadalupe Martinez, Ana. 1980. *Las carceles clandestinas de El Salvador*. Sinaloa, Mexico: Universidad Autonomia de Sinaloa.

———. 1989. "Interview with Samuel Adams." *The Polemicist* 1(3) (December).

Herman, Edward, and Brodhead, Frank. 1984. *Demonstration Elections: U.S.-Staged Elections in the Dominican Republic, Vietnam and El Salvador*. Boston: South End Press.

Huberman, Leo, and Sweezy, Paul, eds. 1968. *Regis Debray and the Latin American Revolution*. New York and London: Monthly Review.

Partnoy, Alicia. 1986. *The Little School: Tales of Disappearance and Survival in Argentina*. Translated by Alicia Partnoy, with Lois Athey and Sandra Braunstein. Pittsburgh: Cleis Press.

Silva, Clea. 1968. "The Errors of the Foco Theory." In *Regis Debray and the Latin American Revolution*. See Huberman and Sweezy 1968.

Tijerino, Doris, with Margaret Randall. 1978. *Inside the Nicaraguan Revolution*. Translated by Elinor Randall. Vancouver: New Star Books.

Zimmerman, Marc, ed. 1968. *El Salvador at War: A Collage Epic*. Minneapolis: MEP Publications.

Chapter 8. On Trial

Acosta, Ivonne. 1987. *La mordaza: Puerto Rico 1948–1957*. Rio Piedras: Editorial Edil.

Amnesty International. 1988. *The High Security Unit, Lexington Federal Prison, Kentucky*. New York: Amnesty International, August.

Aptheker, Bettina. 1975. *The Morning Breaks: The Trial of Angela Davis*. New York: International Publications.

Blunk, Tim and Raymond Levasseur, eds., with the Jacobin Books Staff. 1990. *Hauling Up the Morning: Writings & Art by Political Prisoners of War in the U.S.* Trenton, N.J.: The Red Sea Press.

Boyle, Francis. 1987. *Defending Civil Resistance under International Law*. Dobbs Ferry, N.Y.: Transnational Publishers.

Brutalidad, violencia y psicologia: El caso de Alejandrina Torres. Rio Piedras: University of Puerto Rico.

Can't Jail the Spirit: Political Prisoners in the United States. (n.d.) Chicago: Editorial El Coqui.

Churchill, Ward, and Vander Wall, Jim. 1988. *Agents of Repression: The FBI's Secret Wars against the Black Panther Party and the American Indian Movement*. Boston: South End Press.

———. 1990. *The COINTELPRO Papers: Documents from the Secret Wars against Dissent in the United States*. Boston: South End Press.

Cockcroft, James. 1986. *Outlaws in the Promised Land: Mexican Immigrant Workers and America's Future*. New York: Grove Press.

Davis, Angela. 1974. *An Autobiography*. New York: Random House.

Davis, Angela, et al. 1971. *If They Come in the Morning: Voices of Resistance*. New York: The Third Press.

Deutsch, Michael E., and Richard J. Harvey. 1989. "Repression against the Independentistas." *Covert Action Information Bulletin* (31):42–46.

Donner, Frank. 1990. *Protecters of Privilege: Red Squads and Police Repression in Urban America*. Berkeley and Los Angeles: University of California Press.

Fernandez, Ronald. 1987. *Los Macheteros: The Wells Fargo Robbery and the Violent Struggle for Puerto Rican Independence*. New York: Prentice Hall.

Flynn, Elizabeth Gurley. 1986. *The Rebel Girl: An Autobiography*. New York: International Publishers.

Freed, Donald. 1973. *Agony in New Haven: The Trial of Bobby Seale, Ericka Huggins and the Black Panther Party*. New York: Simon and Schuster.

Glick, Brian. 1989. *War at Home: Covert Action Against U.S. Activists and What We Can Do About It*. Boston: South End Press.

Lichtenstein, Alexander, and Kroll, Michael. 1990. *The Fortress Economy: The Economic Role of the U.S. Prison System*. American Friends Service Committee, March.

Linfield, Michael. 1990. *Freedom under Fire: U.S. Civil Liberties in Time of War*. Boston: South End Press.

Lopez, Alfredo. 1987. *Dona Licha's Island: Modern Colonialism in Puerto Rico*. Boston: South End Press.

Marable, Manning. 1983. *How Capitalism Underdeveloped Black America*. Boston: South End Press.

Mitgang, Herbert. 1988. *Dangerous Dossiers: Exposing the Secret War against America's Greatest Authors*. New York: Ballantine Books.

New York 21. 1971. *Look for Me in the Whirlwind: The Collective Autobiography of the New York 21*. New York: Random House.

O'Melveny, Mary. 1989. "Lexington Prison High Security Unit." *Covert Action Information Bulletin* (31):49, 51–54.

Pell, Eve, ed. 1972. *Maximum Security: Letters from California's Prisons*. New York: E. P. Dutton.

Rosenberg, Susan. 1989. "Reflections on Being Buried Alive." *Covert Action Information Bulletin* (31):50.

Rosenberg, Susan with Marilyn Buck, Linda Evans, and Laura Whitelaw, eds. 1990. *Conspiracy of Voices: Poetry, Writings and Art by Women of the Resistance Conspiracy Case*. Emergency Committee to Defend the Human and Legal Rights of Political Prisoners.

Saldivar, Ramon. 1990. *Chicano Narrative: The Dialectics of Difference*. Madison: University of Wisconsin Press.

Scheffler, Judith. 1989. *Wall Tappings: An Anthology of Writings of Women Prisoners*. Boston: Northeastern University Press.

Schultz, Bud, and Schultz, Ruth. 1989. *It Did Happen Here: Recollections of Political Repression in America*. Berkeley and Los Angeles: University of California Press.

Shakur, Assata. 1987. *Assata: An Autobiography*. Westport, Conn.: Lawrence Hill and Co.

Suarez, Manuel. 1987. *Requiem on Cerro Maravilla: The Police Murders in Puerto Rico and the United States Government Coverup*. Maplewood, N.J.: Waterfront Press.

Whitehorn, Laura. 1989. "The 'Resistance Conspiracy Case,'" *Covert Action Information Bulletin* (31):47–48.

Chapter 9. The Tyranny of Home Versus "Safe Houses"

Argueta, Manlio. 1988. "Taking Over the Street." Translated by Barbara Paschke. In *Clamor of Innocence*, edited by Barbara Paschke and David Volpandesta. San Francisco: City Lights.

Bradley, Ben; Hine, Nathan P.; Vollmann, Judith; and Wasserman, Nancy, eds. 1986. *Por Amor al Pueblo: ¡Not Guilty!* Montpelier, Vt.: Front Porch Publishing.

Camarda, Renato. 1985. *Forced to Move: Salvadorean Refugees in Honduras*. San Francisco: Solidarity Publications.

Center for Constitutional Rights. 1985. *If an Agent Knocks: Federal Investigators and Your Rights*. New York: Center for Constitutional Rights.

Cisneros, Sandra. 1984. *The House on Mango Street*. Houston: Arte Publico Press.

Crittenden, Ann. 1988. *Sanctuary: A Story of American Conscience and the Law in Collision*. New York: Weidenfield and Nicolson.

Davidson, Miriam. 1988. *Convictions of the Heart: Jim Corbett and the Sanctuary Movement*. Tucson: University of Arizona Press.

Davis, Angela, et al. 1971. *If They Come in the Morning: Voices of Resistance*. New York: The Third Press.

El Norte. 1983. Directed by Gregory Navas. Film.

Flynn, Elizabeth Gurley. 1976. *The Alderson Story: My Life as a Political Prisoner*. New York: International Publishers.

Golden, Renny, and McConnell, Michael. 1986. *Sanctuary: The New Underground Railroad*. Maryknoll, N.Y.: Orbis Books.

Guadalupe Martinez, Ana. 1980. *Las carceles clandestinas de El Salvador*. Sinaloa, Mexico: Universidad Autonoma de Sinaloa.

Hiltermann, Joost. 1986. *Israel's Deportation Policy and the Occupied West Bank and Gaza*. Ramallah: al-Haq.

Hunt, Paul. 1987. *Justice? The Military Court System in the Israeli Occupied Territories*. Ramallah: al-Haq.

Juffer, Jane. 1988a. "Abuse at the Border: Women Face a Perilous Crossing." *The Progressive*, April.

————. 1988b. "Dump at the Border: U.S. Firms Make a Mexican Wasteland." *The Progressive*, October.

Lewis, Sasha G. 1979. *Slave Trade Today: American Exploitation of Illegal Aliens*. Boston: Beacon Press.

Mirande, Alfredo. 1987. *Gringo Justice*. Notre Dame, Ind.: University of Notre Dame Press.

Mitgang, Herbert. 1988. *Dangerous Dossiers: Exposing the Secret War against America's Greatest Authors*. New York: Ballantine Books.

Playfair, Emma. 1987. *Demolition and Sealing of Houses as a Punitive Measure in the Israeli Occupied West Bank*. Ramallah: al-Haq.

Saldivar-Hull, Sonia. "Helena Maria Viramontes." In *Dictionary of Literary Biography: Chicana Literature*. Forthcoming.

Sanchez, Rosaura. 1979. "The Ditch." In *Requisa Treinta y Dos: Bilingual Short Story Collection*, edited by Rosaura Sanchez. La Jolla, Calif.: Chicano Research Publications.

Shehadeh, Raja. 1985. *Occupier's Law: Israel and the West Bank*. Washington, D.C.: Institute for Palestine Studies.

275

Stout, Rex. 1965. *The Doorbell Rang*. New York: Viking.

Tomsho, Robert. 1987. *The American Sanctuary Movement*. Austin: Texas Monthly Press.

Viramontes, Helena Maria. 1985. *The Moths and Other Stories*. Houston: Arte Publico Press.

Chapter 10. Prison and Liberation

Abd al-Majid, Fayza, comp. and ed. 1982. *Night . . . and the Grand Dawn*. Beirut: Manshurat Filastin al-Muhtallah.

Aguilar, Mila D. 1987. *A Comrade Is As Precious As a Rice Seedling*. Latham, N.Y.: The Kitchen Table Women of Color Press.

Allende, Isabel. 1988. *Of Love and Shadows*. Translated by Margaret Sayers Paden. New York: Bantam Books.

Argueta, Manlio. 1980. *One Day of Life*. Translated by Bill Brow. New York: Random House.

Committee against Racism and for Democratic Rights in Iraq (CARDRI). 1986. "Ba'th Terror: Two Personal Accounts." In *Saddam's Iraq: Revolution or Reaction?* London: Zed Books.

Davies, Ioan. 1990. *Writers in Prison*. London and New York: Basil Blackwell.

Franco, Jean. 1986. "The Incorporation of Women: A Comparison of North American and Mexican Popular Narrative." In *Studies in Entertainment: Critical Approaches to Mass Culture*, edited by Tania Modleski. Bloomington: Indiana University Press.

———. 1989. *Plotting Women: Gender and Representation in Mexico*. New York: Columbia University Press.

al-Ghazawi, Izat. 1985. "The Woman Prisoner." *al-Fajr*, 13 September.

Magsilang, Angela T. 1989. "She Affirms Her Right to Self-Determination." Translated by E. San Juan Jr. *Z Magazine*, June.

Masri, Mai and Chamoun, Jean. 1986. *Zahrat al-qandul* (Wild Flowers).

Mattelart, Michele. 1986. *Women, Media and Crisis: Femininity and Disorder*. London: Comedia Publishing Group.

Pacheco, Maximo, *Lonquen*. 1980. Santiago, Chile: Editorial Aconcagua.

Pearce, Jenny. 1986. *Promised Land: Peasant Rebellion in Chalatenango El Salvador*. London: Latin American Bureau.

Rosca, Ninotchka. 1988. *State of War*. New York: W. W. Norton.

Rowbotham, Sheila. 1974. *Women, Resistance and Revolution*. New York: Random House.

San Juan, E., Jr. 1986a. *Crisis in the Philippines: The Making of a Revolution*. South Hadley, Mass.: Bergin and Garvey.

———. 1986b. "Beyond Transcendence, Toward Incantation: The Poetry of Jose Ma. Sison." In *Prison and Beyond: Selected Poems 1958–1983*. See Sison 1986.

Sison, Jose Ma. 1986. *Prison and Beyond: Selected Poems 1958–1983*. Quezon City, Philippines: Asphodel Books.

Thompson, Marilyn. 1986. *Women of El Salvador: The Price of Freedom*. Philadelphia: Institute for the Study of Human Issues.

Zankana, Haifa. 1986. "1972-8-4," *al-Ightirab al-adabi* (1):52–55.

276

Chapter 11. Writing Human Rights

Agosin, Marjorie. 1990. *The Mothers of the Plaza de Mayo.* Translated by Janice Malloy. Trenton, N.J.: Red Sea Press.

Alleg, Henri. 1958. *The Question.* Introduction by Jean-Paul Sartre. New York: George Braziller.

Amnesty International. 1984. *Torture in the Eighties.* London: Amnesty International.

———. 1990. *Report.* London: Amnesty International.

Argentine National Commission on the Disappeared. 1986. *Nunca Mas: The Report of the Argentine National Commission on the Disappeared.* New York: Farrar Straus Giroux; London: Index on Censorship.

Bhabha, Homi K. 1990. "Introduction: Narrating the Nation." In *Nation and Narration*, edited by Homi K. Bhabha. London: Routledge.

de Beauvoir, Simone, and Halimi, Gisele. 1962. *Diamila Boupacha.* Translated by Peter Green. London: Andre Deutsch and Weidenfeld and Nicolson.

Fisher, Jo. 1989. *Mothers of the Disappeared.* Boston: South End Press.

Maran, Rita. 1989. *Torture: The Role of Ideology in the French-Algerian War.* New York: Praeger.

Pomar, Jonathan. 1981. *Against Oblivion: Amnesty International's Fight for Human Rights.* London: Fontana.

Shawcross, William. 1988. "Introduction," *Article 19 World Report 1988: Information, Freedom and Censorship.* Edited by Kevin Boyle. New York: Random House.

Staunton, Marie, and Fenn, Sally, eds. 1990. *The Amnesty International Handbook.* London: Optima.

277

Index

283

UNIVERSITY PRESS OF NEW ENGLAND publishes books under its own imprint and is the publisher for Brandeis University Press, Brown University Press, University of Connecticut, Dartmouth College, Middlebury College Press, University of New Hampshire, University of Rhode Island, Tufts University, University of Vermont, and Wesleyan University Press.

Library of Congress Cataloging-in-Publication Data

Harlow, Barbara.
Barred: women, writing, and political detention / Barbara Harlow.
  p.   cm.
Includes bibliographical references (p.   ) and index.
ISBN 0-8195-5249-6 (cl). — ISBN 0-8195-6258-0 (pa)
    1. Prisoners' writings—History and criticism.   2. Prisoners as authors.   3. Literature
—Women authors—History and criticism.   4. Women prisoners in literature.   5. Po-
litical prisoners—Biography.   6. Politics and literature   7. Feminism and literature.
I. Title.
PN494.H37   1992
809'.8920692—dc20   92-53860